UNIX® Fault Management:
A Guide for System Administration

ISBN 0-13-026525-X

90000

9 780130 265258

Hewlett-Packard® Professional Books

OPERATING SYSTEMS

Fernandez	Configuring CDE: The Common Desktop Environment
Lund	Integrating UNIX® and PC Network Operating Systems
Madell	Disk and File Management Tasks on HP-UX
Poniatowski	HP-UX 11.x System Administration Handbook and Toolkit
Poniatowski	HP-UX 11.x System Administration "How To" Book, Second Edition
Poniatowski	HP NetServer Guide for Windows NT®
Poniatowski	HP-UX System Administration Handbook and Toolkit
Poniatowski	HP-UX 10.x System Administration "How To" Book
Poniatowski	Learning the HP-UX Operating System
Poniatowski	Windows NT® and HP-UX System Administrator's "How To" Book
Sauers, Weygant	HP-UX Tuning and Performance
Stone, Symons	UNIX Fault Management
Weygant	Clusters for High Availability: A Primer of HP-UX Solutions
Yawn, Stachnick, Sellars	The Legacy Continues: Using the HP 3000 with HP-UX and Windows NT

ONLINE/INTERNET

Amor	The E-business (R)evolution
Greenberg, Lakeland	A Methodology for Developing and Deploying Internet and Intranet Solutions
Greenberg, Lakeland	Building Professional Web Sites with the Right Tools
Ketkar	Working with Netscape Server on HP-UX
Lee	The ISDN Consultant

NETWORKING/COMMUNICATIONS

Blommers	Practical Planning for Network Growth
Costa	Planning and Designing High Speed Networks
Lucke	Designing and Implementing Computer Workgroups
Pipkin	Halting the Hacker: A Practical Guide to Computer Security
Thornburgh	Fibre Channel for Mass Storage

ENTERPRISE

Blommers	Architecting Enterprise Solutions with UNIX Networking
Cook	Building Enterprise Information Architectures
Sperley	Enterprise Data Warehouse, Volume 1: Planning, Building, and Implementation

PROGRAMMING

Blinn	Portable Shell Programming
Caruso	Power Programming in HP OpenView
Chew	The Java/C++ Cross-Reference Handbook
Grady	Practical Software Metrics for Project Management and Process Improvement
Grady	Successful Software Process Improvement
Lewis	The Art & Science of Smalltalk
Lichtenbelt, Crane, Naqvi	Introduction to Volume Rendering
Mellquist	SNMP++
Mikkelsen, Pherigo	Practical Software Configuration Management
Norton, DiPasquale	Thread Time: The Multithreaded Programming Guide
Ryan	Distributed Object Technology: Concepts and Applications
Simmons	Software Measurement: A Visualization Toolkit

IMAGE PROCESSING

Crane	A Simplified Approach to Image Processing
Day	The Color Scanning Handbook
Gann	Desktop Scanners: Image Quality

OTHER TITLES OF INTEREST

Kane	PA-RISC 2.0 Architecture
Loomis	Object Databases in Practice

UNIX® Fault Management:
A Guide for
System Administration

Brad Stone
Julie Symons
Hewlett-Packard Company

http://www.hp.com/go/retailbooks

Prentice Hall PTR
Upper Saddle River, New Jersey 07458
www.phptr.com

Library of Congress Cataloging-in-Publication Data

Stone, Brad, 1966–
    UNIX fault management : a guide for system adminstrators / Brad Stone, Julie Symons
        p. cm. -- (Hewlett-Packard Professional Books)
    ISBN 0-13-026525-X
    1. UNIX (Computer file) 2. Fault-tolerant computing. I. Symons, Julie, 1965– II. Title
    III. Series

    QA76.76.O63 S7594 2000
    005.4'3--dc21   99-044803

Editorial/Production Supervision: Jan H. Schwartz
Acquisitions Editor: Jill Pisoni
Editorial Assistant: Linda Ramagnano
Marketing Manager: Lisa Konzelmann
Manufacturing Manager: Maura Goldstaub
Cover Design Direction: Jerry Votta
Cover Design: Talar Agasyan
Series Interior Design: Gail Cocker-Bogusz
Manager, Hewlett-Packard Retail Book Publishing: Patricia Pekary
Editor, Hewlett-Packard Professional Books: Susan Wright

© 2000 Prentice Hall PTR
Prentice-Hall, Inc.
Upper Saddle River, New Jersey 07458

Prentice Hall books are widely used by corporations and government agencies for training, marketing, and resale. The
publisher offers discounts on this book when ordered in bulk quantities. For more information, contact:

Corporate Sales Department
Prentice Hall PTR
One Lake Street
Upper Saddle River, NJ 07458
Phone: 800-382-3419; FAX: 201-236-7141
E-mail: corpsales@prenhall.com

Product names mentioned herein are the trademarks or registered trademarks of their respective owners.

Printed in the United States of America
10 9 8 7 6 5 4 3 2 1

ISBN 0-13-026525-X

Prentice-Hall International (UK) Limited, London
Prentice-Hall of Australia Pty. Limited, Sydney
Prentice-Hall Canada Inc., Toronto
Prentice-Hall Hispanoamericana, S.A., Mexico
Prentice-Hall of India Private Limited, New Delhi
Prentice-Hall of Japan, Inc., Tokyo
Pearson Education Asia Pte. Ltd.
Editora Prentice-Hall do Brasil, Ltda., Rio de Janeiro

Contents

Chapter 5   **Monitoring the Disks**   **100**

Chapter 7 **Monitoring the Application**   **179**

Chapter 8   **Monitoring the Database**   **213**

Preface

T his book is intended for system administrators and operators who are responsible for maintaining the integrity and availability of mission-critical UNIX® systems. The book provides a description of the fault monitoring tools and techniques available for UNIX servers, including systems that are configured as high availability clusters. This book can therefore be a handy quick reference for an operator trying to troubleshoot a problem in the customer environment, by pointing out where to find key diagnostic messages and describing how to take recovery actions.

A system administrator responsible for the initial configuration and administration of UNIX systems will also find this book useful because it describes the procedures to follow to set up the appropriate levels of system monitoring. The product descriptions can also help in making purchasing decisions as the customer determines the appropriate amount of event monitoring needed in their environment.

An overview of the tasks performed by an operator is provided, with details on how events are received and processed. The remainder of the book focuses on the types of events that can be received, how they are detected, how operators receive event notifications, and how problems can be investigated and recovery performed. The goal is to introduce the necessary tools, but not to show how every possible problem can be solved.

This book provides numerous descriptions of how fault management tools and products can be used to solve a variety of problems. Many of the chapters are focused on specific computer components, such as disks or databases, to be helpful to operators with specific roles. Here is a description of the individual chapters:

Chapter 1, "Analyzing the Role of System Operators," describes the tasks performed by a system operator and the evolution of fault management.

Chapter 2, "Enumerating Possible Events," describes the various types of events that are interesting to monitor on a UNIX system.

Chapter 3, "Using Monitoring Frameworks," describes monitoring frameworks and the administrative tasks that must be done before they can be used.

Chapter 4, "Monitoring the System," describes the tools and products used to monitor the UNIX server.

Chapter 5, "Monitoring the Disks," describes the tools and products used to monitor external disk devices.

Chapter 6, "Monitoring the Network," provides an overview of the many tools available for detecting problems and events related to the use of the network.

Chapter 7, "Monitoring the Application," describes methods for monitoring the response times and availability of critical applications.

Chapter 8, "Monitoring the Database," focuses specifically on tools to detect problems and events related to database usage.

Chapter 9, "Enterprise Management," discusses the problems with trying to deal with fault management for the large-scale customer enterprise.

Chapter 10, "UNIX Futures," discusses the future plans of some of the major UNIX system vendors in the area of fault management.

Appendix A, "Standards," describes fault management standards that have emerged and how you can benefit from them.

The Glossary contains the important terms used in the book, and their definitions.

Although it is assumed that most customers concerned about fault management will implement high availability solutions, this book does not describe how to create highly available computing environments. Readers needing additional information on high availability may check Hewlett-Packard's external Web site on high availability (http://www.hp.com/go/ha) or read *Clusters for High Availability* by Peter Weygant.

In general, this book does not discuss the configuration and installation of the hardware and software components of your UNIX system. You should rely on your vendors' product manuals for this.

Many of the examples used in this book were created on HP-UX servers. Other UNIX platforms behave similarly, and we note when tools are supported only on certain UNIX platforms.

Acknowledgments

Wе would like to acknowledge a number of people who contributed to this book.

This book covers a variety of topics, and we borrowed time from a number of experts in various areas. Peter Weygant provided some guidance as to the overall structure of the book. Barb Craig, Scott Rhine, David Miller, John Payne, and Maria Fisk were helpful with their reviews of material on disk management and hardware monitoring. Mike Traynor, Pat Mahoney, and Winson Lau assisted with the chapter on network monitoring. Bob Sauers provided some performance information, and Tom Murray provided some tools that made the MIB data presentable to the reader.

Srilakshmi Sitaraman, Mike Grote, and Ninga Singireddy from Sun Microsystems gave a lot of their time and assistance in gathering information on the SyMON product.

We would like to thank Stephen Campbell at Hewlett-Packard for his descriptions of the SMART Plug-Ins products and his help in rewriting the database chapter to address many inaccuracies.

We would also like to thank Sara Robinson at BMC Software for supplying a demo copy of the BMC PATROL applications. Judy Posey at IT Masters was also very helpful in providing information and screen shots for MasterCell.

Pam Saverthal and Birgitte Ishak were also extremely helpful in processing our last-minute mailings to the publisher.

Lillian Lim from Informatica Corporation was one of the few people who was able to review many of the chapters. She also prodded us to take the book to completion.

We would like to thank Mark Orvek and the rest of Julie's project team for their patience and support.

Lastly we would like to express our gratitude to Pam Mujica and Joe Green. Without their executive sponsorship at Hewlett-Packard, this book would not have been possible.

Analyzing the Role of System Operators

System operators are responsible for maintaining the integrity and availability of the computer systems in a company's data center. An operator's responsibilities can span a wide range of tasks. Most spend the majority of their time troubleshooting and resolving problems reported by users. Other primary tasks are system health monitoring, performance monitoring, and backing up the system. Periodically, the operator is asked to perform additional tasks such as upgrading the operating system and applications, restoring files, installing patches, or performing system maintenance. It is not unusual for an operator to have more than 100 systems to maintain in the environment.

Larger organizations will have a number of system operators. On average, there is approximately one operator per ten UNIX servers. System management responsibilities may be segmented by region, by application, by problem area (performance, backup, and so forth), or by time zone. In some situations, an operator may need to pass responsibility for a problem to an operator in one of the company's data centers in another country. System, application, database, and network management may involve different people in different departments. As part of troubleshooting, an operator may ask the advice of a more experienced system administrator. Large companies may have many experts, including database administrators and network administrators, who are specialized in certain areas.

This book should be a useful tool for simplifying the operator's primary task of troubleshooting user problems. Troubleshooting involves checking the current health of the system and researching recent events and faults that may be related. The goal is to find the root cause of a problem. Many system outages are caused by operator errors made when trying to fix problems. In fact, studies by Hewlett-Packard and industry consultants such as the Gartner Group have indicated that operator error is the most common cause of unplanned downtime. The following chapters are intended to simplify the monitoring and recovery tasks.

The monitoring chapters are categorized by system component, and are self-contained, so you should be able to resolve a problem without leafing back and forth between chapters. However, because of the huge number of unique problem situations, it is impossible to list solutions to all possible problems that you may encounter. Instead, this book tries to explain a representative set of available monitoring tools, and how each can be used to solve problems. You should read the recovery sections at the end of each chapter to get an idea of general techniques for problem resolution and to get a feeling for when to apply each tool.

Trends in System Operations

With rapidly changing computer technology and the growth of the Internet, the duties of the system operator are becoming increasingly complex. New hardware platforms, new software products, and a larger number of systems and networks to manage make it difficult for system operators to rely on manual tools to do their jobs. Automation is clearly needed. For many tasks, the operator is already relying on software automation. For example, system backups used to be done with primitive commands; now there are sophisticated software packages such as Hewlett-Packard's OmniBack II and Legato's NetWorker that are commonly used to simplify and automate the task of backing up a system or set of systems.

A number of trends in the computer industry are making system monitoring much more critical. For some companies, corporate data must be available 24 hours a day, 7 days a week, and the penalty of downtime can be measured in lost revenue. In these environments, operators must not only detect current problems, but must also be able to predict when failures will occur. This book describes some of the tools that can identify trends or events that could lead to downtime.

Another industry trend is that Information Technology (IT) departments are now being measured on the percentage of time that systems are up, the performance of the systems, and how quickly operators can resolve user problems. Management software needs to indicate not only what a problem is, but also how to fix it. System management is now the largest contributor to the total cost of ownership of UNIX servers.

While customer demands on the operations staff are increasing at a rapid rate, the evolution of management tools is struggling to keep pace. Tools that once were text-based and user-initiated are now graphical and event-driven. An operator can watch multiple systems from a single, centralized console. Systems can be shown as icons with colors showing status. This gives the operator a quick overview of the state of the data center. An increasing number of problems can be detected and reported to the console.

The problem-reporting tools, however, are overwhelming the typical operator. Some help is provided by enterprise management products, which are introduced in Chapter 3, "Using Monitoring Frameworks," and then referenced throughout the rest of the book. If one component shared by many systems fails, the result can be a storm of events at the management station. In addition, a component failure can have a cascading effect as it causes other components or products to fail, too. Again, a large number of events arrive at the system or centralized console. An operator needs to be able to wade through these events to find the root causes. Chapter 9, "Enterprise Management," describes some of the emerging technologies to deal with this problem.

Before describing the fault management tools, we must first define what we mean by "fault management," which we do in the next chapter. We also give you descriptions of the types of events you need to be prepared to receive to adequately protect your UNIX servers.

Enumerating Possible Events

Fault management is a key part of system management, and it is critical to maintaining the availability of applications in your environment. This chapter defines fault management, and lists the types of faults you may detect on your servers.

Defining Fault Management

Detecting and reporting unusual or unacceptable behavior is generally referred to as *fault management* (or *event management*). A *fault* is any behavior different from specified or expected behavior, and generally is used to refer to the complete failure of a hardware component or software product.

Fault conditions can be characterized in many different ways. Faults can be caused by hardware component failures in the environment, or by the failure of software running on systems within the environment. A computer is dependent on more than the CPU and memory; for example, power supplies and fans can also fail. Loss of power in the data center, natural disasters, and the failure of air conditioning units are just a few examples of how environmental problems can cause systems to fail.

Fault isolation is something that hardware and software vendors try to achieve. This means that a fault within the software or hardware of a system should not affect the correct operation of other components in that system or other systems that the system is interacting with on the network. When fault isolation is not achieved, operators have a much more difficult time finding the root cause of problems when they occur.

An *event* is a more general term and includes faults as well as system anomalies, such as performance problems. An event includes anything that happens in the computing environment that may be of interest to someone. Events may be sent automatically, or a user (operator) may ask to be informed of events. The start of a backup, for example, may be an interesting event worth noting.

A variety of events can occur in a computer environment that are of interest to a system administrator or computer operator. Many involve failure conditions in the environment, but other important types of events also occur. In a mission-critical environment, a configuration change of any kind to the hardware or software may need to be recorded. For example, an

3

administrator may want to record when a software patch was installed on a system. This information can be used later when troubleshooting a problem on the system. In addition, the CPU utilization reaching a certain predefined threshold on a critical server may also be considered a significant event. Automated monitoring tools can detect other activities, such as an attempt to breach system security. Multiple failed "root" login attempts could be the sign of a security problem.

Events can be received in a variety of ways. Hewlett-Packard OpenView, a suite of enterprise management products, provides sophisticated event management capabilities, allowing an event message to be stored in a log, while optionally causing a graphical icon associated with the event to change color based on a status change (see Chapter 4). Recovery or troubleshooting actions can be triggered automatically, or trouble tickets can be filed so that the appropriate person can be notified of the problem and a problem history can be maintained.

Fault management includes the process of detecting, reporting, and reacting to the faults or events taking place in the computing environment. Chapter 3 describes both the types of notification methods available for reporting events and the enterprise management tools that can receive events. The rest of this chapter describes the different types of events that can be detected. Given the list of possible events, you can choose the level of monitoring that is appropriate for your environment. Subsequent chapters introduce the tools that detect the various events.

Event Categories

To effectively manage events related to a UNIX server, you first need to understand the types of events that may occur. This chapter gives examples of a wide variety of events that may occur, and provides one possible grouping of those event categories. By understanding the set of possible events that may occur, you will understand what to look for when troubleshooting a problem.

One way to categorize events is by the affected software or hardware component. These categories include: system, disk, network, application, and database events. In fact, we used this approach when determining the structure of this book. Each category of events is discussed exclusively in its respective chapter later in the book. For example, system events are described in Chapter 4.

Chapters 4 through 8 group events into the following additional categories:

- Configuration
- Faults
- Resource and performance management
- Security intrusions

The following sections describe each category, in turn, in more detail.

Environmental changes, such as power outages, are also important, but are only briefly touched upon in this book and thus are described in overview at the end of this chapter.

Configuration Events

You should know about the hardware and software configuration changes taking place on your servers. A software package installed just days before a failure may be a prime suspect. Configuration changes can be complex, and administrative tools often do not provide adequate assistance. Operator error is a common source of unplanned downtime, so it is important to keep a record of the configuration changes, as well as the time each change is made. This log can be examined later, in the event of a problem, to provide an audit trail for backing out of the changes. This can be especially important when multiple operators make changes on the same systems.

Configuration changes encompass a broad spectrum, and they may involve the application or database, operating system, or system hardware or peripherals.

Application Changes

Application changes include changing software parameters, such as the maximum number of users allowed to use a product. Restructuring a database is another example. Keeping a history of the changes made to application parameters can be difficult, and probably is done most commonly through revision comments in the configuration files themselves. Patches or bug fixes to applications are easier to track because the software includes a version number, which should be updated by the software vendor whenever new versions are released. Numerous tools are now available to track the software versions installed on your system. You should run one of these tools periodically and store the results, to maintain an appropriate change history.

Installing a new application on the server is a key event that should be recorded. You should use this application in a test environment before moving it to production. However, the application still might not behave well. You may want to use this time as a data point when looking at performance data, to see the effect of the new application.

Operating System Changes

Operating system changes are usually easier to track because they often require a system reboot before they take effect. Enterprise management products, such as HP OpenView, automatically record system reboots as events in an event log. Operating system configuration changes include changes to kernel parameters, patches, and operating system upgrades. All of these changes should be recorded.

Hardware Changes

Hardware configuration changes include the addition of a new processor or a new disk device. You may also want to remove or replace a component that is not behaving properly. Other hardware configuration changes include changing the firmware versions or patching the driver software.

Because these configuration changes often involve a system reboot, you should plan for downtime and schedule changes during a period when the systems are not being used. Planned downtime includes downtime required for scheduled maintenance, such as a software upgrade, and for configuration changes, such as adding disks, restructuring a database, or moving clients to different systems for load-balancing purposes.

The best way to update system hardware or software is to do it online. High availability cluster products, such as Hewlett-Packard's MC/ServiceGuard, support rolling hardware and OS upgrades and enable you to move applications to another system until the upgrade is complete. Although cluster products can help you automate the upgrade process, it is still beneficial to have additional online replacement capabilities, to avoid the service interruptions associated with a rolling upgrade. System vendors are now making it easier to modify hardware components without requiring a system reboot. Both Sun and Hewlett-Packard have released these capabilities for their UNIX servers, and both will be adding more capabilities in this area. Before the introduction of online replacement, you could track hardware configuration changes by monitoring system reboots and then just track the current configuration. Now you need to check for configuration changes more frequently.

The configuration change history should be stored at a central management station and should be backed up regularly. Storing it at a central site enables you to access the information even when the server has failed or is unavailable, which can be important when trying to recover from a system failure.

Faults

A *fault* broadly refers to any unexpected behavior occurring in the computing environment. A fault may report the failure of a hardware or software component, such as a database failure, or it may be a warning of a condition that could lead to a failure, such as a series of disk errors.

Faults are the most common events sent to an event management product, partly by process of elimination. Configuration changes, security intrusions, and environmental alerts are difficult to capture as events. Performance monitoring is often done in reaction to a user complaint, because it is difficult to configure the correct performance threshold conditions that should lead to events.

Faults can occur on the server itself, on a peripheral attached to the server, or on some component external to the system.

Failure of a System Hardware or Software Component

System hardware components include the CPU, memory, and I/O cards. As business servers have become more critical, hardware vendors have improved their designs to make these components more reliable. High availability solutions provide additional protection and can prevent some problems from causing a system failure.

Despite these improvements, you still need to be prepared for hardware faults. Although the reliability of each component is improving, many more components exist to manage. A company could have 100 or more servers, each with multiple processors, many disk arrays, tape libraries, and so forth. High availability systems typically include redundant components, such as mirrored disks, extra power supplies, or extra cooling fans. Failures need to be reported in a high availability environment so that a component can be fixed before a double failure occurs.

Hardware failure indications should report specific information about the failed component, such as the serial number or hardware path. This can help network support personnel locate the failed component in the server. A lower severity may be used when redundant components fail, to indicate that the problem is important but not necessarily urgent to fix. Hardware monitoring is discussed in Chapters 4 and 5.

Hardware failures used to cause the system to fail, but servers are more resilient today. Servers can now continue to run, often in a crippled state, after a hardware failure. For example, a server can detect bad memory pages and deallocate them, but this leaves less memory available for the applications. The fact that a component failure may not be obvious again points out the importance of continual monitoring of the system. Repairs can then be made during a planned downtime period.

You also need to monitor the status of the server software. The software can be divided into the following categories:

- Operating system or firmware
- System vendor applications or middleware
- Database and enterprise resource planning applications
- User applications

If the operating system fails, you will see a failure (panic) message on the server console. The server status will be shown as "DOWN" to an enterprise management product, such as HP OpenView. You need to reboot the system and look at system log files or core files to diagnose the problem.

The failure of a key software application may also be a critical event to a system operator. Typically, only one key application is configured per UNIX server, so the failure of the application is essentially equivalent to a failure of the server. If you know the processes making up the application, you can periodically check the status of the processes by using UNIX commands. Some monitoring tools can automatically notify you of the failure of an important process.

Some vendors provide high availability software to help protect your server. This software also needs to be monitored to ensure that it is working properly. Other important applications include database applications and enterprise resource planning applications. Later chapters describe some of the sophisticated monitoring products that are available for these applications. Management applications, such as a backup software application, also need to be monitored. Errors encountered during a backup should be reported, because such errors indicate that critical data is not being adequately protected.

The easiest application failure to detect is the failure of an application process. An application can also get into a process loop or deadlock situation. Although the effect is the same to the end-user, the application is unusable; this is a much more difficult situation to detect. You are unlikely to see these situations reported as external events, although you may receive some external indications, such as timeout errors, when trying to use a service. In general, to detect these types of problems, you need to measure the performance and resource usage, and compare it to baselines.

Failure of a Peripheral

In addition to the internal computer components, other important components are attached to the system. These peripheral devices include tape drives, disk devices, printers, and CD-ROM drives.

A variety of errors can affect tape drives. Tape devices should be monitored proactively, because backups normally have a small window of time to complete. Detecting failures and recovering before the backup window starts can help to ensure that the backup will succeed. You should also watch for mount requests during the backup process, to keep the backup application from being blocked for too long.

Disk errors and failures are an increasing problem, because the amount of stored informa-tion continues to grow. Many high availability environments now use RAID devices, which provide data redundancy by spreading data across an array of disks. Data can thus be reconstructed from surviving disks in the event of a disk failure. The arrays can even be repaired online. In addition to monitoring for disk failures, you may want to monitor the logical volume status, physical volume status, I/O errors, and the loss of a mirrored copy of data. Each of these types of failure conditions can be detected with monitoring software.

Various printer events can be interesting to monitor. For example, the printer can jam, fail, or be set offline. Also, the print spooler can fail and the queue can be full. Printers require vigilant monitoring because they can often get into a state in which they are not performing properly. It is important to detect problems and fix them quickly to avoid receiving user complaints.

CD-ROM drives are perhaps the least interesting of the peripheral devices to monitor. You may be interested in knowing when a drive is mounted or unmounted, but receiving only drive failure notifications is usually sufficient.

Failure or Loss of an External Service

Hardware or software failures are not the only critical events that can occur on your system. Monitoring your corporate networks is critical as well. With the movement away from main-frames to distributed client/server environments, the dependency on local area networks (LANs) and wide area networks (WANs) is increasing. If the proper precautions are not taken in designing the company data center, the loss of a single network could cause denial of service to all clients trying to access critical server machines. You also need to understand the purpose of each of your networks so that you know the consequences of a failure. For example, in a high availability environment, you have networks that are used for sending data between systems, networks dedicated for high availability status checking, and backup networks.

You can check a variety of networking faults and statistics to further analyze the status of your networks. You should watch for connectivity problems and "Node Unreachable" errors. You can also check Ethernet collision rates and use performance tools to check network bandwidth utilization.

A UNIX server is dependent on external services, such as network services. For example, a server may be active, but the Domain Name System (DNS) server for its domain may be down, preventing clients from connecting successfully. An e-mail server is another example of a machine in this category.

Similarly, hardware external to the managed system may also be important. The failure of a network router can prevent any data from getting to the managed system.

Here is a sampling of some of the important external services that you need to monitor in your environment:

- Name servers, such as DNS and Network Information Service servers
- File servers
- E-mail server
- Directory service, such as Novell Directory Service
- Boot server
- Software license server
- Web proxy server
- News server

You can set up monitoring of these services if you know the processes that make up the application. Process failures can be detected, as mentioned earlier. More proactive approaches involve actually trying to use the service to see whether it is working properly. Many other conditions are equally important, but are much more difficult to detect, such as an expired software license, which could cause you unexpectedly to be denied access to a key application.

Redundancy of these network services is a key to maintaining the availability of your server. However, this alone is not sufficient. Configuration problems and issues such as software licenses can still prevent the use of an important service.

Resource and Performance Events

In addition to looking for failure events, monitoring resource usage and performance are important. If users are unable to access critical system resources, you might as well consider the system down. The system operator needs to be notified when resource utilization reaches certain thresholds, so that measures can be taken to avert a crisis. The network, CPU, process table, filesystem, and memory are examples of critical system resources that should be monitored.

High utilization alone is not sufficient to indicate a problem. It could just indicate that you are getting optimal use of your server. You also need to determine whether system bottlenecks exist and, if so, which applications are being delayed.

This book distinguishes between resource usage and performance. Particular types of system resources have limitations. For example, you can run out of filesystem space, swap space, processes in the process table, files in the file table, system semaphores, or shared memory. You monitor resource usage so that you know when the system usage is approaching these configured limits. *Performance* describes the balance between CPU, memory, and I/O usage, and the relative usage of different applications. You want to avoid CPU, memory, and I/O bottlenecks and also ensure that high-priority applications are not blocked behind low-priority workloads. Application response time and throughput are also important to track, because those are the performance measures most visible to the users of an application.

To monitor resource usage or performance, you generally watch for threshold conditions rather than failure events. For example, to watch for CPU bottlenecks, you may enable an event to be sent whenever the CPU utilization exceeds 85 percent and the run queue has more than three processes. You may need to study a system for some time to know the appropriate threshold to monitor.

As previously shown, not all the important components are on the server. Printer queues can fill up, tapes can be full, and networks can become overloaded. An overloaded network can prevent access to the server.

Each of these events can be monitored by setting up the appropriate thresholds. Tools are available that can provide this information in real time, or give you historical information for identifying trends.

Security Intrusions

You also need to monitor suspicious activity. Threats to a data center may come internally or externally and may be the result of intentional or unintentional misuse. As an administrator, you want to ensure that system resources are available for their intended purposes.

The following events can be useful for an administrator to audit on a business system to prevent misuse of the server:

- Successful and unsuccessful login and logout events
- Granting of additional privileges to individual users
- Modifications to system configuration files or system libraries
- Administrative actions (such as user adds, host changes, and password changes)
- System-level events (such as reboots and software or hardware changes)

By monitoring failed login attempts, especially attempts to log in as superuser, you can potentially identify when someone is trying to guess a password to gain unauthorized access to the system. An intruder may modify existing configuration files to give himself or herself special privileges, so it is important to have a detailed change history for these files. After successfully logging in to the system, an intruder can reconfigure or damage system components, so you need to keep a history of system changes to be able to recover successfully later.

You can never be completely sure that your system is adequately protected, so you must monitor your system constantly and keep system backup tapes stored safely offline.

Environmental Changes

Environmental changes can also affect the availability of your servers. The following are a few examples of environmental events or changes:

- Loss of an air conditioning unit causes a sudden rise in temperature
- Natural disasters, such as fire, floods, or earthquakes, cause system downtime

- Loss of power to the data center
- Sabotage leading to damaged servers

Power outages are a major source of failure among companies who do not have emergency backup power. Data from a 1995 study by the National Power Lab indicates that at least once a day, every computer room in the U.S. experiences some problem with the building's power source, typically spikes, surges, or outages.

One solution to power problems is to use uninterruptible power supplies (UPSs). A UPS allows for graceful shutdown of the system after a loss of power. Batteries can keep systems up for a short amount of time, until diesel generators are activated. Systems can also recover transparently from failures of power supplies and fans if redundant components are used.

Many large corporations are starting to include a disaster recovery plan as part of their computer maintenance strategy. Most at least have a policy on how to recover from backup tapes after a disaster. Companies for whom downtime equates to huge sums of lost revenue are now looking at standby data centers that are ready to take over in the event of a catastrophic failure. Hewlett-Packard's MetroCluster product is one disaster recovery product available to those customers.

As shown in Figure 2-1, this book covers monitoring for events in the system, particularly those concerning the disks, network, databases, and applications. A fault or critical event in any of these areas could render mission-critical applications unusable.

Figure 2-1   Components of the application stack.

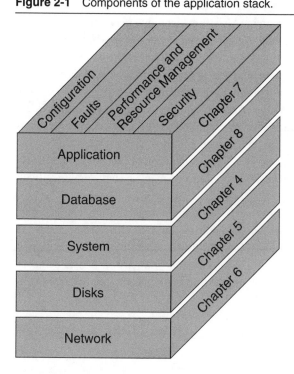

Using Monitoring Frameworks

Chapter 2 focused on the set of possible events that can occur on UNIX systems. The remaining chapters of this book describe the tools available to monitor these events, with tools for different components such as systems, disks, or networks; each discussed in a separate chapter. This chapter focuses on monitoring frameworks, which can be used to monitor many different components and systems through a common interface.

Some companies monitor systems simply by checking the size of log files every day, such as the system log file. If the file is bigger than a certain size, then something unusual has happened and the operator can investigate further by looking at the specific file contents. The problem is that this can be very labor-intensive. A lot of duplicate messages may exist, making it difficult to analyze and fix each individual problem. Also, this technique may not help to determine the root cause of the problem. Lastly, although each logged event may have a severity associated with it, prioritizing the investigation of numerous logged messages may be difficult.

Operators spend a great deal of time watching the system consoles. Small data centers might manage from a Microsoft Windows computer, with scripts executed periodically (such as daily) to check resource usage and the availability of the computer systems. System failures are detected by the loss of a window on the console, or by complaints from users. Larger data centers might manage from a workstation or server running monitoring software such as HP IT/Operations, Computer Associates' Unicenter The Next Generation (TNG), or IBM's Tivoli Management Environment. These products can show the status of many systems graphically on a single screen.

Some comprehensive monitoring products can be used to monitor multiple components, and often provide developer's kits so that you can add additional monitors. These products are referred to as *monitoring frameworks*. If a product has additional capabilities to help deploy it over many systems, it is referred to as an *enterprise management framework*. A data center is unlikely to be using more than one enterprise management framework, due to the cost, complexity, and time required to learn a second framework.

Customers are recognizing the need for management tools, and enterprise management framework providers — such as Hewlett-Packard, with its IT/Operations (IT/O), and Computer Associates, with its Unicenter TNG — are feeling pressured to provide low-cost alternatives. Both HP and CA have announced intentions to bundle low-cost versions of their software with HP-UX servers. Enterprise SyMON is a low-cost management station available on Sun systems, but because it currently lacks a developer's kit, it is not a true monitoring framework.

According to a recent *Network Computing Review* of enterprise frameworks, the products "...are as complex as the problems they are meant to solve." Monitoring frameworks can be difficult to set up and are very expensive, but the benefit is that you can monitor heterogeneous components and systems through a common interface.

This chapter describes some of the frameworks available for UNIX fault management. It identifies some of the monitoring capabilities provided or available with each framework. Hopefully, these descriptions will help you to determine which framework, if any, is best for your environment.

You may need to use multiple monitoring frameworks in your environment. Chapter 9 briefly describes how to integrate different combinations of these tools.

Distinguishing Monitoring Frameworks

We have selected a variety of frameworks to discuss in this chapter. Each has different strengths and weaknesses. Describing all the available products would be difficult, but this chapter should give you insight into the capabilities you should expect from any product that you choose to evaluate. This chapter is meant to give you a very high-level overview of features; later chapters go into more detail on product differences.

For each product, we describe its breadth of monitored components, general monitoring features and capabilities, ease of setup, approach to extensibility (developer's kits), notification flexibility, and diagnostic capability. These attributes are generally described in this opening section.

Monitored Components

Each product's breadth of coverage is described in this chapter. You should ensure that all the components that you need to monitor are available before you select a framework. Some products, such as CA's Unicenter TNG, have a smaller set of metrics available than other products, such as BMC PATROL with its set of Knowledge Modules (KMs).

Monitoring Features

This section on monitoring features describes the framework's general monitoring capabilities, making special note of any unusual capabilities, such as IT/O's event-correlation capability.

Monitor Discovery and Configuration

The first step toward actually using a monitoring framework is to determine its set of available resource monitors. The methods for doing this vary depending on the framework being used.

You can obtain resource monitors in a variety of ways. Some are freely available when you purchase a computer, while others are included with the enterprise framework. Monitors can also be sold as add-ons to the framework. Another possibility is that the monitor for a product is included with the product itself. For example, Hewlett-Packard includes Event Monitoring Service monitors with many of its networking products.

Different frameworks have different approaches to help you find the available metrics and components to monitor. With MeasureWare, you use HP's online help facility to explore the available metrics. Other tools provide a GUI to select the monitors to install or use.

After determining the available monitors, you need to choose and configure the ones that you want to use. Some monitors are configured automatically when they are installed, while others require that you manually define notification criteria and other information before they can be used.

Monitor Developer's Kits

The advantage of a framework is having all of your resources monitored through a consistent interface. However, a framework is unlikely to account for everything that might be interesting to you, especially if you have your own custom applications. In this case, you need an easy way to create a custom monitor that can be used seamlessly with the rest of the framework.

A defining characteristic of frameworks is that they provide some method to allow the customer to add a monitor, but these methods vary. Some enable you to add a monitor with scripts, while others require more programming.

Notification Methods

To make administration easier, you should have all events sent to a common location. This may be a consolidated console or system log file, for example. Monitoring multiple systems from a master console reduces the need for additional hardware dedicated to monitoring. Sending messages to a single location makes diagnosis faster and less error-prone, because operators do not need to remember the names of key log files and do not need to remember to check individual logs.

The console or log file needs to be accessible anywhere. Of course, a system log file will be inaccessible if an event led to a system outage. Within a company, a system operator may need to access logs from a remote network. Network accessibility and security may be concerns when remote access is required.

Paging is an increasingly common technique for problem notification. According to a recent System Administrators Guild (SAGE, a USENIX technical group) study, a majority of administrators now carry pagers during nonworking hours. System operators may be paged at home to diagnose problems, so access from outside the company firewall may be an issue. Paging may require software that is not provided by the framework itself. Also, a terminal interface may be needed for remote access over a modem.

Ideally, the system operator has a management tool with a graphical representation of the network and systems, and an event log file. Without a consolidated console for the managed environment, the operator is forced to log on to the system, if accessible, and troubleshoot by using local log files. Many software products write error information to the system log file, /var/adm/syslog/syslog.log.

Notification can be as simple as a color change on a system's front panel display. Notification can also be much more sophisticated, such as an ASCII message appearing on the operator's console, with the color reflecting criticality, and with actions suggested or automatically taken to try to recover from the problem.

Industry-standard notification methods include Simple Network Management Protocol (SNMP) traps, and Desktop Management Interface (DMI) notifications. SNMP traps are commonly used on UNIX operating systems, including HP-UX, for event notification. Support for DMI has only recently been added to HP-UX.

Some tools, such as the Network Node Manager (NNM), discussed in Chapters 4 and 6, rely on SNMP traps to be sent from the UNIX system to keep their network topology and maps up-to-date. They may also use SNMP to poll the systems periodically.

Many of the enterprise management frameworks provide SNMP trap handlers so that they can receive events as traps and log and display events in an event browser. Templates are needed on a management station to translate SNMP traps into an ASCII-readable format. A user can configure these templates. Some HP and third-party products provide respective OpenView templates.

Because SNMP uses an unreliable network protocol, some management frameworks provide an additional reliable mechanism. IT/O, for example, uses a proprietary Remote Procedure Call (RPC) mechanism called opcmsg. With opcmsg, you can be assured of receiving notification.

In some cases, you may not want to be notified when an event occurs, because a recovery action may have already taken place. For example, when MC/ServiceGuard software detects that a Network Interface Card (NIC) has failed, it automatically configures a standby NIC, and network traffic transparently switches to the new interface. However, even in this simple example, you probably want to be notified, to ensure that the failed NIC is fixed in a timely manner.

Events can also be sent into event correlation engines, which can do some event processing and filtering on behalf of the operator. This is described in more detail in Chapter 9.

If you have a support contract, you may want to have your customer support center notified automatically when problems occur. HP Predictive Support software has the ability to send events via modem to the HP Response Center.

You need to determine whether or not the framework you want to use has a sufficient set of notification methods available.

Diagnostic Capabilities

Another way to compare frameworks is by their diagnostic capabilities. For example, after you receive notice of a problem, how easy can you troubleshoot and resolve the problem with each of the frameworks? Some products, such as IT/O, can provide detailed instruction information along with every event.

In addition to determining what has gone wrong, you may want to take corrective actions. With some products, these actions can be predefined and automatically taken when an event arrives. In some cases, the actions are available, but need to be executed by the operator. You also need to be able to easily record the results of any actions that were taken, to help track the status of problem resolution.

IT/Operations

IT/Operations (IT/O) is an HP OpenView application that provides central operations and problem management. IT/O is a software bundle that not only includes NNM for network management, but also provides capabilities in the area of system management. With IT/O, facilities are provided that enable operators to share the management station software, and also have individual responsibilities for different sets of managed systems or types of events.

IT/O uses intelligent agents that run on each managed system to monitor and collect management information, messages, and alerts, and to send the information to a centralized console. The agents can also perform local actions without communicating with the management station. After receiving events, IT/O can initiate automatic corrective actions or prompt the operator to run predefined, operator-initiated actions. When an operator reads an individual message, guidance is given and actions may be suggested for further problem resolution or recovery.

IT/O has four main windows:

- **Node Bank:** Displays the systems managed by the operator as icons, and allows organization of the icons into node groups, which then can be viewed from the Node Group window.
- **Message Groups:** Displays logical message groups, such as Performance, Oracle, and Backup. The message groups serve as one way to organize messages in the Message Browser window.
- **Message Browser:** Shows the events that have been received by the management server, including instructions, annotations, results of automatic actions, performed actions, and acknowledgments.
- **Application Bank:** Provides access to commonly used diagnostic and administrative applications.

These four main IT/O windows are shown in Figure 3-1.

The Message Browser can filter out messages from systems that you don't care about. If you are responsible for only a specific system function, such as performance, you can configure the Message Browser to show only those messages from a specific message group.

Monitored Components

As previously described, IT/O provides assistance with multiple aspects of system monitoring, especially faults, and resource and performance management. IT/O can also help with security monitoring, with its predefined template for monitoring root login attempts.

Figure 3.1 IT/O main windows.

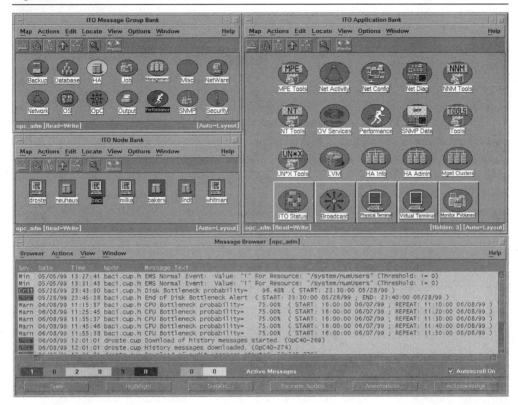

IT/O comes with predefined monitors and templates. Templates are used to configure monitors, to define message conditions, and to match patterns on received events. Templates also define Event Browser message text, severity levels, message groups, instructions, and actions. Monitors are predefined for e-mail, CPU utilization, swap utilization, and filesystem utilization, among other things. Log file templates monitor system log files for system errors, su (switch user) events, logins, logouts, and kernel messages. Templates and message conditions can be modified so that the operator gets paged under certain conditions.

Many other tools plug into IT/O to provide additional monitoring and management capabilities. IT/O has add-on modules for the managed node, called SMART Plug-Ins (SPIs). These modules provide customized knowledge of databases and applications via templates and monitors. For example, SPIs are available for SAP R/3, Baan, Oracle, and Informix. ClusterView is an HP OpenView application that provides monitoring of high availability clusters. Combined with the ability to do network and system monitoring, IT/O can provide a consistent interface for monitoring all of your components.

IT/O provides multiplatform support. The IT/O console is available on HP-UX and Sun platforms. IT/O can manage HP-UX, Sun Solaris, IBM AIX, and other platforms, including Windows NT.

Monitoring Features

Each system being monitored must have IT/O managed node software installed on it. This software includes IT/O's intelligent agents, which monitor and collect data, perform actions, and send messages to the IT/O management console.

Managed nodes are displayed in the Node Bank window. System status is reflected by the colors of the node icons in the Node Bank. Propagation rules are configurable in IT/O. For example, the color of the node icons may represent the criticality of the most serious unacknowledged event in the Message Browser.

The IT/O agent is a key to differentiating the IT/O product. The agent is considered to be intelligent and autonomous because it can take actions without requiring operator intervention. The IT/O agent performs local polling of the resources being monitored, and can filter out redundant or unnecessary events before forwarding them to the management station. This can eliminate some network traffic and help to avoid information overload for the operator. The agent can also do event correlation, which further reduces network traffic. New events can be created by consolidating data from multiple events. The IT/O correlation engine can also reach conclusions based on the absence of events.

The IT/O agent can continue monitoring and taking automated actions autonomously if it loses its connection to the management station. The agent will store events so that when the management station comes back up, no events are lost. The agent also uses a secure and reliable Remote Procedure Call (RPC) mechanism, opcmsg, to communicate with the management station.

IT/O is useful when an operator needs to manage numerous systems consistently. Templates can be modified and then downloaded to a set of systems, enabling the operator to monitor many systems identically. In other words, monitoring can be set up in a consistent way for all systems.

IT/O receives inbound events (such as SNMP traps), performs filtering, and delivers events to other processes registered for notification.

Events received by IT/O are stored in a central repository, providing a permanent history and allowing for future analysis and auditing. Events are ordered chronologically and marked by severity. The name of the system that sent the message and a timestamp are stored with each event. Additional information includes the type of the event and application sending the event. When automated actions are provided, an indication is given as to whether an action was successful. Annotations can be used to show the output from the actions.

Filtering can be used on the management station to reduce the number of events visible in the Message Browser. Filters can be based on severity, originating system, message group, or other categories.

Events in the Message Browser may be the result of an SNMP trap, log file monitoring done by an IT/O agent, or an opcmsg call made by an IT/O monitor application. Events may indicate faults, status changes, configuration changes, performance thresholds being exceeded, and so forth. Events are kept in the Message Browser until they have been acknowledged. Events can also be forwarded to other management stations or to trouble-ticketing systems.

IT/O enables you to assign roles to operators so that each can be responsible for different events, nodes, message groups, or applications.

It is important to be able to ensure that any monitoring you enable remains enabled. You don't want to lose critical events. Because the IT/O agent is responsible for obtaining the monitor data periodically, you need to ensure that the agent is always running, which you can do by using IT/O's capability of monitoring arbitrary processes. The agent can also be automatically restarted.

Monitor Discovery and Configuration

After the intelligent, autonomous agents are installed, they monitor resources according to the templates that have been assigned to the local system. IT/O comes with a set of templates that are used to define monitoring conditions, thresholds, and event messages. The templates can include configured actions, either automatic or operator-initiated. This is where you may want to configure an action such as paging.

The Message Template window shows the message templates currently configured in IT/O. Templates are grouped. For example, a template group exists for HP-UX 10.x systems.

From the Node Bank window, you can assign templates to your managed nodes or node groups. After you assign all the templates, you need to install or update the IT/O software and configuration on the managed nodes. This can be done on one or more managed nodes, so that you can quickly set up monitoring for multiple systems. With IT/O, the templates are pushed out to each managed node so that the IT/O agent can then monitor, filter information, forward messages, and perform local actions without requiring communication with the management station.

Message templates are available for receiving SNMP traps. Message conditions are defined to specify which messages are displayed in the Message Browser, the format of the displayed messages, and any actions that should be performed when an SNMP trap matches a defined message condition.

A message group can be specified in a template. When message conditions are matched, the event gets assigned to the configured message group. This can be useful when delegating operator responsibilities. When configuring operators, both node group and message group responsibilities are assigned. For example, you can assign all HA (MC/ServiceGuard) messages to the operator responsible for monitoring MC/ServiceGuard clusters.

When configuring monitoring, you can also include instructions in the template or configure actions to be performed, either automatically or manually triggered by the operator.

As shown in Figure 3-2, you can assign templates from the Message Source Templates window to nodes in the Node Bank to configure monitoring and event management.

Monitor Developer's Kit

IT/O provides default monitors for CPU utilization, disk space, and other resources. IT/O also allows users to create their own monitor scripts. The script-based monitors rely on the IT/O agent to poll them for information, but the agent can then send notifications on their behalf.

Figure 3-2   IT/O template distribution.

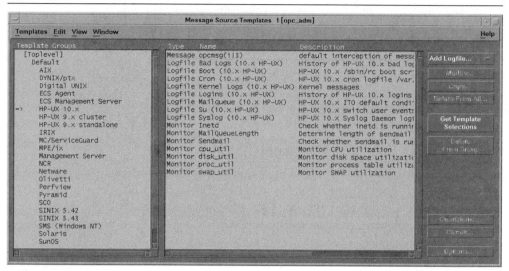

IT/O also enables you to create your own monitors and templates. For instance, you can create a template to monitor arbitrary MIB variables, such as network interface status. The IT/O agent then periodically queries the MIB object to determine whether a message should be generated. Or, you can create your own monitor program or script that is invoked periodically by the IT/O agent. These monitors or scripts can have notifications sent by the IT/O agent, or they can send IT/O notifications through the opcmon API. The monitor can then send asynchronous events, which is often more efficient than a polling mechanism. The IT/O user interface can also be used to set up monitoring of a specified log file, such as the system log file. Thus, an easy way to integrate a new monitor is to have interesting events first written to a log file.

Notification Methods

IT/O is capable of receiving events via SNMP traps. IT/O also forwards events from the IT/O agent to the management station, using opcmsg. Local agents can buffer events if the management station is temporarily unavailable.

The opcmon API can be used to forward the current value of a monitored object to the IT/O agent. The agent then checks the value against the configured threshold. If the threshold is met, the event is forwarded to the IT/O management station. Local actions, which may include logging or suppressing the message, are done before the message is forwarded. Additionally, message templates can be configured with automatic actions, such as generating an e-mail message or pager notification.

IT/O also provides a capability called "follow the sun," which enables events to be forwarded to the appropriate IT/O management station in a global environment based on the time of day. For example, if you have data centers with management stations in Japan, Europe, and

North America, each could be responsible for monitoring the company's systems for a period of eight hours each day, together providing coverage around the clock.

Diagnostic Capabilities

IT/O provides the capability to configure automatic and operator-initiated actions through templates. You can configure IT/O to take actions automatically when it receives an event matching a configured message condition. For example, when IT/O receives an MC/ServiceGuard event, the ClusterView template for that event can run an automatic action to extract additional data regarding the event from /var/adm/syslog/syslog.log and MC/ServiceGuard log files. This data is available to the operator in an annotation, available from the Message Browser.

Message templates can also include instruction text, providing more detailed information about what the operator should do upon receipt of a particular event.

IT/O provides several tools in the Application Bank that can be used to diagnose a problem, including tools to monitor local systems and remote access tools to diagnose problems. The Application Bank includes tools from HP products, other integrated products, and customer-generated tools.

Applications in the Application Bank are represented as icons. Operators select the icon representing the target system and then select the icon of the tool to run on that system. You can bring up a telnet window or, for HP-UX systems, run the System Administration Manager (SAM) on the system having problems. You can check the print status or CPU load on any UNIX system from the central management station.

The Application Bank has a two-level hierarchy, whereby similar applications are grouped together in an application group, represented as a top-level icon. Opening up an application group icon displays a window with all the Application Bank tools in that group.

IT/O has also tightly integrated performance management with fault management. You can launch GlancePlus or PerfView from within IT/O. These performance management products are described in more detail in later chapters. Data from multiple IT/O agents (such as SMART Plug-Ins) on multiple nodes can be collected, correlated, and presented in a single PerfView graph launched from the IT/O management station. These graphs can be launched in the context of an event selected in the IT/O Message Browser.

Hewlett-Packard also includes a preconfigured, single-system version of IT/O with its GlancePlus Pak 2000 product. A Java-based GUI presents diagnostic applications and an Event Browser. The product allows you to connect to information from multiple systems, as long as it is done one system at a time.

GlancePlus Pak 2000 includes the intelligent agent technology from its Enterprise version, enabling it to collect events from a variety of sources and execute automated actions. After events are received in the Event Browser, an operator can trigger some predefined recovery actions.

Additional Information

For further information, visit the HP OpenView Web site at http://www.openview.hp.com/.

Unicenter TNG

Computer Associates' Unicenter The Next Generation (TNG) is an enterprise management platform that provides graphical status monitoring. It provides system and network management for an enterprise of heterogeneous systems. Unicenter TNG provides monitoring and management for all the resources in your environment, including system resources, networks, databases, and applications.

Unicenter TNG provides a framework for an integrated management solution to manage all IT resources via a common infrastructure. The TNG framework itself includes the following components: auto discovery, object repository, Real World interface, event management, calendar management, reporting, virus detection, and desktop support. Together with vendor, third-party, and custom-built applications, Unicenter TNG provides increased management and maintenance capabilities for the enterprise.

A Common Object Repository stores the information used to create the Real World graphical views. You can browse the repository by using the Class Browser, Object Browser, or Topology Browser. Using the ObjectView, you can get details on the performance of devices, and even graph the data.

The Real World interface provides graphical views that can be organized based on business functions, geography, or any logical groupings. The views can show the topology of the enterprise in two or three dimensions. These views can be used to see the status of the systems and resources in your environment.

Unicenter TNG manages by using a distributed management approach. Distributed agents are responsible for monitoring and control. Centralized managers provide core management throughout the enterprise, including data correlation from one or more agents, workload management, and job management. The agents monitor and control based on policies provided by managers.

Monitored Components

Unicenter TNG has available agents to monitor CPU and memory, swap usage, and filesystem space. You can also monitor file sizes and modifications. Messages in log files can also be periodically checked.

The agents run on managed nodes and gather data, apply filters, and report when necessary. Some provide control or execution on behalf of the managers. The agents send notifications and can be polled. They can also collect performance data or be configured to send events and perform actions based on thresholds.

Monitoring Features

The core Unicenter TNG product contains modules for a variety of system management functions: network management, calendar management, software distribution, event management, user/security management, workload management, tape/file management, printer/spool management, and reporting. The most common management components used by Unicenter TNG customers are database, event, and performance management.

Agents are available that can do threshold monitoring and take automated or manual actions. Alarms can be sent based on metrics measured over a specified period of time. A distributed state machine for event correlation is also available.

CA Unicenter/DB Alert is a system monitor for databases and database applications. CA Unicenter/System Alert is a client/server application that provides some system and application-level monitoring. CA Unicenter/AP (Automation Point) and CA Unicenter/AHD (Advanced Help Desk) help with problem escalation, notification, and incident tracking.

Unicenter TNG is layered on top of the Unicenter suite of system management tools. It enables you to configure business views so that operators can monitor systems based on business processes, such as purchasing, inventory, or payroll, without displaying resources and systems that are not involved.

One unusual feature of Unicenter TNG is its Real World interface, a 3D view of the objects being monitored in the computing environment. Managed objects can also be shown in 2D, tree view, or text form.

Information about managed objects is stored in an object repository. Search and query tools are provided to allow management applications to extract information from the database.

Unicenter TNG's Workload Management function can be used to schedule and monitor jobs. Jobs that fail can be automatically restarted. Workload Management can also ensure that jobs do not run beyond their configured time limits.

Unicenter's Spool Management function can be used to monitor the status of the UNIX spooler daemon or a print device. It can start and stop the daemon or alter print jobs already queued to the printer.

Monitor Discovery and Configuration

Unicenter TNG provides automatic discovery of networked objects, including systems and other resources within the enterprise. Information is stored in the Common Object Repository and can be displayed topographically in the Real World interface. Discovery filters can also be used to limit discovery to a specific subnetwork or to specify which types of resources Unicenter TNG should discover. In addition to network discovery, more can be discovered if a Unicenter intelligent agent is installed on the system.

A centralized Event Console Log GUI is available in Unicenter TNG to receive events from throughout the enterprise, including any system or application message written to the system log. Users can configure additional messages from other log files to send to the Event Console. Events are shown with timestamps, the system that sent the message, the message text, and other information. Automated actions can be configured for each event. Actions can be based on pattern matching of the received messages. Messages can also be forwarded to other event managers.

For viewing agents and getting information about the agents, Unicenter TNG provides a MIB-II agent view to view MIB-II information, a node view, a Distributed State Machine (DSM) view, and an Event Browser. The DSM view tracks the status of objects across the network. It gathers information from the repository and agents, to maintain the state of objects based on configured policies. The node view displays detailed state information about the system objects that are watched by the DSM.

In conjunction with the calendar management function provided by Unicenter TNG, you can change or set event policies based on the time. For example, you may want to apply different policies during the weekend.

Computer Associates also repackages some of its monitoring and discovery features into its Unicenter TNG Framework, which it ships for free on some platforms, including HP-UX.

Monitor Developer's Kit

An Agent Factory is provided that enables software developers to integrate their own monitors with Unicenter TNG. This is similar to the EMS developer's kit, which is used to integrate new monitors into the EMS environment. A software developer's kit is also available to help other vendors integrate applications into Unicenter TNG.

Notification Methods

The management agents can detect event conditions and forward them to the management station. The events are sent as SNMP traps.

Diagnostic Capabilities

Unicenter TNG does not provide the sophisticated event correlation capabilities available from other products, such as IT/O. The Event Console can be integrated with other functions, such as problem management, which can be used to identify and escalate certain problems automatically. A trouble ticket can be generated automatically when an event arrives at the management station.

Managing events is one of the core capabilities provided by Unicenter TNG. The hub of event management is at the Unicenter TNG Event Console. Here you can configure policies to respond automatically to specific events, forward events, filter unimportant events, correlate events from several agents, and feed events into the DSM.

Unicenter TNG does not provide continuous collection of performance data, nor does it provide the sophisticated drill-down diagnostic capability found with the integration of IT/O, PerfView, and MeasureWare.

Additional Information

Additional information about Computer Associates can be found on their Web site at http://www.cai.com/unicenter/.

Event Monitoring Service

The Event Monitoring Service (EMS) is a monitoring framework for HP-UX. It provides a common interface for monitor configuration and event notification. Using the EMS developer's kit, monitors are developed in a common way. Although the framework itself is freely available, some EMS monitors are sold separately, shipped with the products they support, or bundled with the system.

EMS monitors provide help primarily with fault and resource management. Performance monitoring generally requires more sophisticated tools. Some system fault and resource monitoring capabilities are provided by the HA Monitors product and EMS Hardware Monitors. Other EMS monitors enable you to detect when you are getting low on system resources, such as file descriptors, shared memory, and system semaphores.

Monitored Components

Multiple HP products include specific EMS resource monitors, so the resources available for monitoring vary depending on the customer's installed software products. The resources available for monitoring also vary from system to system because the hardware configuration is different.

EMS Hardware Monitors are provided with the Online Diagnostics bundle, available on the HP-UX support media, also known as the HP-UX Diagnostic/IPR Media. EMS Hardware Monitors provide the ability to detect and report problems with system hardware resources, such as device errors and component failures. Monitors are available for system hardware components and various HP storage products, including system memory, SCSI disk and tape devices, AutoRAID disk arrays, high availability disk arrays and storage systems, fast/wide SCSI disk arrays, various fibre channel components, tape autoloaders, and digital linear tapes.

The HA Monitors contain several EMS monitors for monitoring filesystem space, network interface status, disk status, and MC/ServiceGuard cluster status. HA Monitors also provide monitoring for CPU load and the number of system users. The monitors include database monitoring as well.

ATM adapters and HyperFabric adapters from HP can also be monitored using EMS. An EMS monitor is included with each of these products. These resources are also integrated with MC/ServiceGuard. HA ATM, for example, first attempts to perform a local recovery in the event of a failure, but if it is unable to provide local recovery, it notifies MC/ServiceGuard to trigger a failover to an alternate node.

All the different resources that can be monitored are contained in a single EMS resource hierarchy. The portion of the hierarchy containing system hardware and kernel resources is shown in Figure 3-3. You see the entire resource hierarchy when configuring monitor requests in the EMS GUI.

Monitoring Features

EMS is designed for use in high availability environments. The user can select only the critical components to be monitored, so the resource monitor will not be delayed polling for information from non-critical components. This is different from other tools, such as IT/O, which typically gathers data from all components. The IT/O agent executes a system-wide command and then parses the output. Thus, if a noncritical component hangs, the IT/O agent could be delayed

Figure 3-3   EMS resource hierarchy.

```
/system/numUsers
/system/jobQueue1Min
/system/jobQueue5Min
/system/jobQueue15Min
/system/events/memory/<instance>
/system/status/memory/<instance>
/system/filesystem/availMb/<filesystem_name>
/system/kernel_resource/process_management/nproc
/system/kernel_resource/file_system/nflocks
/system/kernel_resource/file_system/nfile
/system/kernel_resource/misc/ncallout
/system/kernel_resource/system_v_ipc/shared_memory/shmmni
/system/kernel_resource/system_v_ipc/semaphore/semmni
/system/kernel_resource/system_v_ipc/semaphore/semmns
/system/kernel_resource/system_v_ipc/message/msgmni
/system/kernel_resource/system_v_ipc/message/msgseg
/system/kernel_resource/system_v_ipc/message/msgtql
/storage/events/disks/default/<path>
/storage/events/tape/SCSI_tape/<path>
/storage/events/disk_arrays/High_Availability/<path>
/storage/events/disk_arrays/AutoRAID/<ID>
/storage/events/disk_arrays/FW_SCSI/<path>
/storage/events/enclosures/ses_enclosure/<path>
/storage/status/disks/default/<path>
/storage/status/tape/SCSI_tape/<path>
/storage/status/disk_arrays/High_Availability/<path>
/storage/status/disk_arrays/AutoRAID/<ID>
/storage/status/disk_arrays/FW_SCSI/<path>
/storage/status/enclosures/ses_enclosure/<path>
/adapters/status/FC_adapter/<path>
/adapters/events/FC_adapter/<path>
/net/interfaces/lan/status/<interface_name>
/net/interfaces/switched/atm/<emulated_lan_name>
/net/interfaces/clic/status/<instance>
/net/subnetwork/osi/x25subnet/status/<x25_instance>
```

unnecessarily waiting for it to respond. The EMS monitor queries only the critical components by comparison.

The EMS event management libraries have been used by a number of system components on HP-UX to provide monitoring. IBM recently announced a similar set of event management routines, called Phoenix, for its AIX environments, which it hopes will be adopted by its software development partners. Sun does not provide event management libraries for Sun Solaris.

EMS is the only method for allowing a resource monitor to send events to MC/Service-Guard, which again reflects its emphasis on high availability. EMS can also send notifications via SNMP, opcmsg, TCP, UDP, and e-mail, and can write to the console, a specified text file, or another application.

EMS provides a few key functions. It is meant to provide a consistent way for a user to enable monitoring of different system components, which is done through the EMS SAM GUI, the MC/ServiceGuard SAM GUI, the Hardware Request Manager (monconfig), and a set of EMS library routines.

When configuring monitoring conditions, you have the option to request notification at every polling interval, when the value changes, or when some configured threshold has been met. The polling interval can range from 30 seconds to 1 day.

You can configure additional information to be sent along in an event, providing customization for the specific environment in which EMS is used. Also, when events occur, the resource monitor can include additional resource-specific information to aid problem diagnosis.

EMS was created with system performance in mind. An EMS resource monitor runs only if a user has asked to monitor at least one resource instance. Also, multiple resource instances can be monitored concurrently by the same monitor process. EMS APIs are provided to allow the monitor to check a resource at the appropriate time interval. Monitors that receive resource information asynchronously don't need to use these APIs and can thus operate more efficiently. This can allow for event notification to be received in microseconds, without paying the system performance penalty of frequent polling.

EMS alarms are configured separately for each client. The alarms of other products, such as MeasureWare, are system-wide. EMS can detect problems more quickly than other tools that need to wait for summary time intervals to expire. However, EMS doesn't have the concept of durations or compound conditions, which can be associated with alarms.

EMS requests are per client. A target "user" can receive customized event data, and another "user" can receive different data for the same event. EMS monitor data enables the monitor to provide customized data for an event.

To ensure that monitored resources continue to be monitored, EMS provides a "persistence client." The EMS persistence client detects when a monitor fails and automatically restarts it.

Monitor Discovery and Configuration

EMS provides a consistent GUI for the discovery and configuration of resources that can be monitored. The EMS GUI, available from SAM, can automatically discover the set of resource monitors available on a system. Resource instances can vary from system to system based on hardware and software configuration. Using EMS, you can define conditions indicating when notification events should be sent. Notifications can be sent at periodic intervals, when a component's state changes, or when a threshold condition is met. EMS also allows you to configure where events should be sent.

EMS requires monitor requests to be initiated on each local node; however, this also allows monitor requests to be customized to the local systems so that only the critical resources need to be monitored. EMS should not be considered an enterprise framework because it lacks the ability to enable monitoring across multiple systems easily.

Using the EMS GUI to configure each resource instance to be monitored may be time-consuming. The EMS Configuration GUI supports some wildcarding to make the configuration easier. Also, the EMS Hardware Monitors available with Online Diagnostics come preconfig-ured. If you are using IT/O, a tool called monvols is available to help you configure all the logi-cal or physical volumes for a selected system. The monvols tool and other tools and templates for EMS are available for free when downloading the EMS Developer's Kit from the Web at http://www.software.hp.com/products/EMS. Note, however, that monvols is available only for HP-UX 10.20.

To configure most EMS monitors, you use SAM. From its Resource Management func-tional area, you can select the Event Monitoring Service to launch the EMS GUI, and then add a new monitoring request. The initial configuration screen is shown in Figure 3-4.

MC/ServiceGuard provides one GUI, as well as command-line and configuration-file options, to configure packages to be dependent on EMS resources. In this case, event notifica-tion is sent directly from a resource monitor to MC/ServiceGuard.

The EMS configuration tools enable a user to configure a resource or set of resources to be monitored. The user chooses the type of notification desired based on applications available in the customer environment. For example, if events should be sent to an OpenView manage-ment station, the user can choose SNMP notification. SNMP can also be used to send events to other management stations, such as IBM NetView, Tivoli, or CA Unicenter TNG. If IT/O is being used, opcmsg notification is available on IT/O managed nodes. Although EMS is often used with a management platform such as HP OpenView, HP OpenView is not required. For

Figure 3-4   Initial EMS configuration screen.

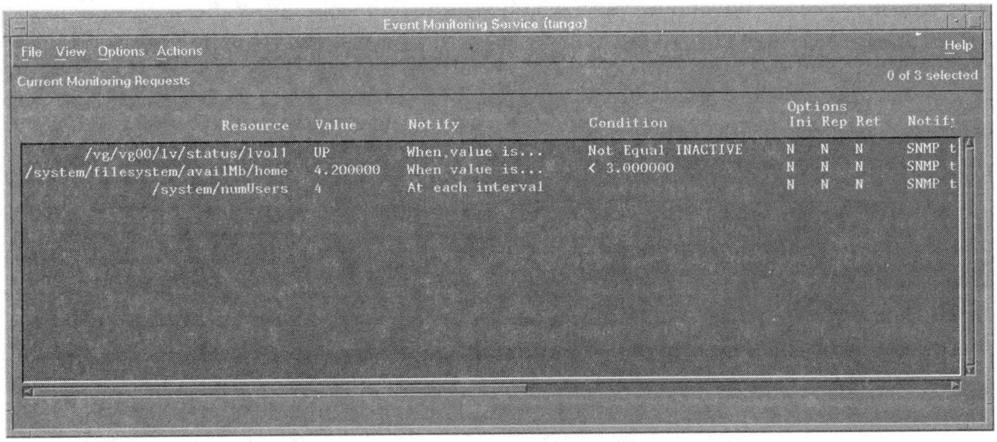

example, if a customer has written a custom fault-recovery application, event notification could be received directly by the application, using TCP or UDP.

The EMS configuration tools also enable you to browse the list of resources that can be monitored dynamically. This allows a resource monitor to monitor different resource instances on different systems, and provides a standard interface for operators to find available monitors. You can then customize the monitoring for each system. Although EMS provides more flexibility, it is also more difficult to configure, because configuration is generally done once per system.

First, the operator browses through the available resources. Then, he or she selects a resource to monitor and specifies the monitoring parameters, such as thresholds and polling intervals. After the monitor request is made, the operator is returned to the main EMS screen, where all active EMS monitor requests are displayed.

EMS hardware monitor configuration is done by using the Hardware Monitoring Request Manager, monconfig. Notification conditions can be configured in a consistent way for all the supported hardware resources on the system. As hardware is added to the system, monitoring can be enabled automatically and consistently with the way similar hardware is being monitored.

If requesting SNMP trap or opcmsg notification, additional configuration is usually required on the management station. EMS provides templates that can be used in OpenView NNM or IT/O to recognize and format traps and opcmsg notifications for viewing in their respective event browsers.

Monitor Developer's Kit

EMS provides a Developer's Kit to make it easy for customers and third parties to integrate or write their own EMS monitor programs. Customers can define their own important resources to be monitored. Using the EMS Developer's Kit also ensures that monitors will behave in a standard way.

The EMS Developer's Kit includes the necessary header files and libraries to write a custom resource monitor. Monitoring APIs are provided for the monitor to receive requests, wait during polling intervals, and send notifications. A sample monitor is also provided. The mechanism to actually check the value of a resource is resource-dependent, but APIs are provided to determine whether notification should be sent based on the value of a resource. The monitor provider does not need to write code to send different types of notification, such as SNMP traps or e-mail; this is handled by the EMS framework.

All the products in this chapter provide some mechanism to allow you to add your own resource monitors. EMS monitors are more difficult to develop because they require you to write a program instead of merely writing some scripts. EMS, however, provides more flexibility, because its monitors do not have to rely on HP-UX commands to gather data.

Information on using the EMS Developer's Kit is included with other software that is downloadable from the HP software Web site. You can find the Developer's Kit along with HP OpenView templates and other tools at http://www.software.hp.com, under the High Availability Software product category. EMS manuals are available at http://docs.hp.com/hpux/ha.

Notification Methods

EMS was designed specifically to support monitors for high availability resources. Consequently, it supports notification by using an HP-proprietary interface to MC/ServiceGuard. However, EMS can be used without MC/ServiceGuard and it supports an unusually large variety of notification options, including:

- SNMP traps
- IT/O's RPC mechanism (opcmsg)
- E-mail
- Logging to the system log file, the console, or a specific log file
- UDP or TCP messages

Notification is sent on a per-request basis, which provides additional flexibility. Several EMS events can be managed concurrently, as shown in this example:

- Client A requests Event 1 via SNMP
- Client A requests Event 2 via opcmsg
- Client B requests Event 1 via TCP
- Client B requests Event 3 via TCP
- Client C requests Event 3 via opcmsg

Notification is then sent to the specified clients when the events occur.

Diagnostic Capabilities

EMS enables the monitor to provide arbitrary data, up to 10,000 bytes, along with an event notification. This information can be unique for each event notification and it can contain vital diagnostic information. For example, a disk failure event could include the serial number of the failed disk device in its monitored data area. Additional text could describe how to fix a failed component. Monitor providers taking advantage of this capability must document how operators should interpret this information.

EMS Hardware Monitors provide detailed information about the cause of an event and give recommended actions.

Unlike other products, such as Unicenter TNG, EMS doesn't provide the ability to take automated actions in response to events. However, you can have events sent to your own customized fault-recovery application by configuring the TCP or UDP notification methods. If EMS is used with IT/O, then you can also configure templates and recovery actions into IT/O.

Additional Information

The EMS framework is freely available from HP with the Online Diagnostics on the support media and the application CD-ROMs.

For the latest information on EMS, check the HP High Availability Web site at http://www.datacentersolutions.hp.com/2_3_index.html. The EMS manuals and release notes are available at http://docs.hp.com, under High Availability.

You can learn more about the Hewlett-Packard diagnostic tools, including the EMS Hardware Monitors, on the Web at http://docs.hp.com/hpux/systems.

PLATINUM ProVision

PLATINUM technology, Inc. has a suite of products called ProVision (originally Enterprise Performance Management). The ProVision product suite collects server, database, and network performance information and has four components: DBVision, ServerVision, WireTap, and TransTracker. Data can be collected by agents running either locally on the managed system or remotely over the network. All of these components, except for TransTracker, share the same ProVision console, an NT or X Windows GUI.

ProVision has agents collecting performance data, which then is stored in a database. Configuration parameters determine when to archive, delete, and compress data. These parameters can vary for each individual metric. Utility programs are available to export and import archived data.

PLATINUM also provides solutions for software distribution and remote execution (AutoXfer), problem resolution (Apriori), security (AutoSecure), data warehousing, disaster recovery, and capacity planning.

The PLATINUM tools are accessed through an interface called PLATINUM Director, which provides monitoring through different user-configurable perspectives. Operators can use either a graphical view, showing the status of system resources or applications, or a Windows Explorer-like view, showing systems listed in a hierarchical tree format. From a Director console, administrators can first see a high-level view of events and system status, and then drill down to take actions. The Alarm window shows the status and descriptions of events, with event-specific actions available from a pull-down menu.

From the Director Explorer view, the administrator can select a system and then launch other tools, such as the job scheduler, to view the job status for a system. The AutoXfer tool can be launched to distribute software.

AutoSecure and AutoSys are certified with MC/ServiceGuard. AutoSys and Apriori have been integrated with HP OpenView. A much more complete integration has been done with Tivoli TME.

Monitored Components

DBVision is PLATINUM's product for database monitoring. DBVision gathers database statistics and supports Oracle, Sybase, Informix, and DB2. Events such as resource thresholds can be sent from different databases to a central console, where corrective actions can be taken. DBVision can detect problems such as running out of available tablespace, processes waiting for locks, and runaway processes.

ServerVision collects server performance data. Metrics include CPU utilization and swap space usage. The product can also be used to see which user is tying up system resources. ServerVision supports Sun Solaris, HP-UX, IBM AIX, NT, and other operating systems. It monitors and manages the performance of UNIX and NT servers, and provides system-wide metrics for use by other tools, such as PLATINUM's job scheduler, AutoSys. AutoSys provides dynamic load balancing and batch queue control.

WireTap shows the utilization of a network segment. The standard product categorizes network utilization by transport protocol, network protocol, application, and so forth. Optional modules can provide additional statistics for Oracle and Sybase requests, and for Web traffic.

TransTracker is a pre-deployment tool for measuring the system, database, and network usage of a transaction. Instead of requiring an application to be instrumented, TransTracker can identify transactions by collecting data from network packets.

WireTap can also be used to measure transaction response time. WireTap provides network monitoring by capturing packet-level data and categorizing it by protocol (such as HTTP or TCP). The user can identify SQL statements to look for, and can define alarm thresholds so that notification is sent when transaction response times are not being met. Web performance data for HTML requests can be provided, as well as Web server "hit" rates. Alarm information can be sent to the ProVision console or through an event adapter to the Tivoli Event Console.

PLATINUM provides a variety of database products. Solutions are available for database monitoring, database administration, and database performance bottleneck identification.

Database tools, such as Enterprise DBA and TSReorg, provide user administration, schema, and content management, as well as database reorganization. Enterprise DBA's administrative tasks can be done across different databases, with support for Oracle, Informix, and DB2 databases. Remote agents are used to perform the changes to the database. TSReorg supports both Oracle and Sybase databases. It can be used to reorganize database tables, indexes, and tablespaces. TSReorg is integrated with DBVision so that corrective actions can be automatically taken in response to an event. Tablespaces can be monitored with database reorganization triggered automatically. Tablespaces can be reorganized while the database stays online. TSReorg can also be used to view database structures graphically, showing where database fragmentation exists.

Monitoring Features

ProVision includes agents to collect performance data and a GUI to show performance graphs. ProVision can be compared to the combination of MeasureWare and PerfView, products discussed later in this book.

Performance data can be accessed via the GUI console or a character-based interface. Both real-time and historical data can be presented. The console can display performance data from multiple database instances and servers. The information can be displayed as bar graphs, time-based graphs, charts, and tabular displays. You can also create your own display with your own combination of graphics.

ProVision enables you to configure alarms using multiple thresholds and varying severities. Actions can be configured at each severity level. Actions include several notification options, such as paging, e-mail, and SNMP traps. Corrective actions can also be configured. ProVision allows multiple actions to be configured that can be scheduled to run either simultaneously or sequentially.

Monitor Discovery and Configuration

The DBVision and ServerVision instances to be monitored are defined during the installation and post-installation of ProVision. From the console, you can get summary statistics for each instance.

Some predefined alarms are provided by ProVision. You can also create your own alarms be specifying the metric and threshold condition. Alarm configuration is available from the console's Control menu. The metric name needs to be entered manually, but you can find available metrics by using the Display menu. Menus associated with the graphs list available metrics. A wildcarding capability is also available. After specifying threshold information and actions, you may need to specify additional information, such as a mail recipient or pager number.

Before configuring an alarm, you may want to see which ones have already been defined. From the console, you can see a summary of the active alarms for all monitored instances.

Monitor Developer's Kit

PLATINUM Open Enterprise Management Services (POEMS) is a framework for plugging in additional monitoring capabilities. Tools using POEMS can take advantage of common services, including PLATINUM Director, event management, and communications.

Notification Methods

Performance agents (scanners) collect data and store it in a shared memory segment, which is accessible to the archive and alarm background processes. The alarm process checks the data in the shared memory segment to determine whether alarm conditions are met.

When problems are detected, alerts can be sent to a pager, via e-mail, or to a centralized console receiving information from multiple databases or servers. Predetermined corrective actions can be taken in response to an event. These actions can be defined in customized scripts that are executed automatically.

Colors can be associated with each alarm severity when the events are shown in the Alarm window. The instance experiencing the alarm will also be highlighted within the GUI. An audible alarm is also provided at the console when the alarm arrives. Notification can be sent via e-mail or pager. Alarms can be sent to the management console or to any SNMP-capable management station using a predefined SNMP notification script.

A set of predefined corrective actions that can be used in response to alarms is provided, and you can define additional actions. Forwarding an alarm via pager or e-mail is an action that is supported. If multiple actions are provided for an alarm, they are executed in the order specified in the configuration.

A single alarm can have multiple actions associated with it. ProVision waits for a specified time and then takes the next corrective action. If the actions fix the condition, the alarm is cleared.

An alarm for a metric can have multiple thresholds associated with it. Each threshold is associated with a different severity level and can have a different troubleshooting or corrective action.

Diagnostic Capabilities

The ProVision console has the ability to drill down from graphs to get additional information. You can also launch a UNIX command from within the console. From the ProVision console, you can get troubleshooting help after an alarm is received. An online reference guide, *Advisor*, provides a summary of the problem and instructions or suggestions on how to resolve an alarm condition.

The Alarm Log, which is accessible from the console, shows an event history along with the actions that have already been taken for the alarm. *Advisor* may also suggest other graphs to display for additional information. This instruction text can be included when an alarm is forwarded via e-mail.

A variety of tools are available for database administration. DBVision integrates with PLATINUM's TSReorg product, which can be used to reorganize tablespaces or fix fragmentation problems. In addition to TSReorg, Enterprise DBA can be accessed, which provides the ability to manage users, database schemas, and database content.

Additional Information

More information about PLATINUM ProVision can be obtained at http://www.platinum.com/products/provis/index.html.

BMC PATROL

BMC Software provides monitoring capabilities through its PATROL software suite. PATROL is a system, application, and event management suite for system and database administrators. PATROL provides the basic framework for defining thresholds, sending and translating events, and performing other such tasks. PATROL consists of a console, intelligent agents, and Knowledge Modules (KMs). KMs are add-on products that contain the ability to monitor specific components.

Three types of consoles are available:

- **Operator console:** Provides the graphical display and administration of systems and applications, as shown in Figure 3-5. Manual corrective actions are performed from here
- **Developer console:** Provides the capabilities for configuration and customization of remote agents and KMs
- **Event manager console:** Adds event filtering, correlation, sorting, and escalation facilities

BMC PATROL runs on a variety of operating systems, including UNIX, NT, OS/390, and NetWare. BMC also provides additional management software for mainframe environments.

Figure 3-5   PATROL console window showing resources being monitored on system "bakers."

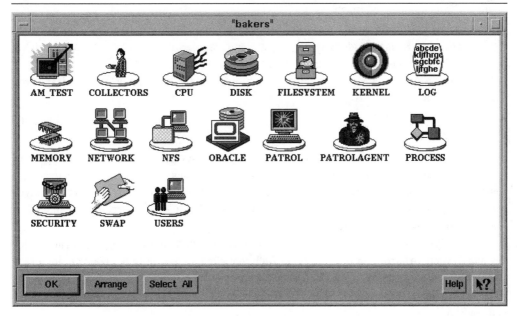

Monitored Components

Monitoring in PATROL is provided by KMs, which contain the expertise used by PATROL to know what to monitor and how to react when problems occur. KMs are used to monitor a set of parameters, which can include a description of the monitored attribute, the polling interval, the method for measuring the attribute, and a threshold for abnormal values. The KMs provide rules to detect events and perform corrective actions. Events are sent to an operator console when an error or warning condition occurs.

PATROL provides a wide variety of operating system, middleware, database, and application KMs. Different combinations of KMs can be purchased, so you can customize the solution for your own environment.

Operating system KMs are provided for UNIX, NT, and other OSs. UNIX platforms include Sun Solaris, HP-UX, and IBM AIX. Middleware KMs include Tuxedo and DCE.

Database KMs include Oracle, Sybase, Informix, DB2, Red Brick, Ingres, and others. BMC PATROL's database KMs provide more metrics than are available from the other products described in this chapter. For example, BMC PATROL provides more than 70 metrics for Oracle. About 50 metrics are monitored for Informix. Metrics include user connection information, active locks, I/O statistics, dictionary hit ratios, and CPU utilization. Server performance is also monitored. BMC formerly had a technical agreement with HP to provide the database KMs for MeasureWare. PATROL provides a strong solution for database management because it encompasses both monitoring and database administration tools.

BMC has bundled its database products into a PATROL Availability Suite for Oracle. The product bundle includes the PATROL KM for Oracle, PATROL DB-Stats for Oracle, PATROL DB-Reorg for Oracle, and the PATROL DB-Integrity products.

Application KMs include SAP R/3, Baan, and PeopleSoft. System and database KMs should also be used with these application KMs.

Details on specific KMs for system, applications, middleware, and databases are covered in separate chapters.

Monitoring Features

PATROL's operator console provides a centralized graphical display in which icons represent system components or other monitored components. Icons change color to correspond to a component's status. On the console, icons represent system components or other monitored components, and change color to correspond to the status. Detailed information can be displayed as gauges, or in graphs or text windows.

BMC PATROL has its own configuration interface and its own message browser for receiving events. Alarms can be configured such that events are sent to the console, indicated graphically, and shown in the Event Browser. Events can also be sent to the Message Browser in IT/O. Additionally, events can also be sent to other management platforms, such as Unicenter TNG or Tivoli TME, via SNMP.

PATROL can graph multiple metrics simultaneously for a single system to help with performance monitoring. If data is logged, historical graphs can also be shown.

Intelligent agents provide the ability to discover system, database, and application components in the enterprise. The agents reside on each server. On an ongoing basis, the agents look for problems. When they encounter problems, they either take preconfigured actions or send notification so that recovery can be done manually.

KMs on the monitored system provide the rules for detecting events and performing recovery actions. Events are sent to an operator console when an error or warning condition occurs. Administrators can customize the recovery actions. The PATROL agent polls for information and can adjust its sampling rate based on its performance impact. Each system has one PATROL agent, but may have many KMs.

PATROL has been certified to run in an MC/ServiceGuard environment, but inconsistency issues exist. For example, PATROL may report an SAP process failure to its operator console, while MC/ServiceGuard may have already restarted the process or moved it to another system.

Unlike MC/ServiceGuard, PATROL does not provide any failover capability. However, a limited set of automated recovery actions is available.

PATROL can show an application view in the PATROL console. IT/O provides only a node view, although ClusterView adds an application view to IT/O when used in an MC/ServiceGuard environment.

Hewlett-Packard used to rely on BMC PATROL to provide database information to its MeasureWare Agent. The database KMs were resold through a special licensing agreement. HP now uses its SMART Plug-Ins for databases to gather database information for MeasureWare.

Monitor Discovery and Configuration

You need to install the PATROL agent and KMs on each system to be monitored. Once this software is installed, you need to load (or activate) the KMs you intend to use on each system. This can be done from PATROL's operator console.

PATROL agents discover all databases, applications, and key resources when they are started. This makes it easy to start monitoring quickly. The administrator can also define additional applications and databases so that they can be discovered in the future.

Figure 3-5 shows an example of the resources being monitored by PATROL on a system called "bakers." This system has the KMs for UNIX and for Oracle loaded. You can drill down on each of these resource's classes to see the metrics being monitored, graph data, and check status.

In addition to monitoring, PATROL can automate recovery actions taken in response to error or failure conditions. The user must assign the desired recovery actions to an event. The concept of operator-initiated actions, available with IT/O, is not supported with PATROL.

PATROL can be configured to respond automatically to specific problems, and can help tune databases for optimal performance. Recovery actions can be performed locally by agents without requiring communication with the console.

Users can set thresholds. Events are sent by the PATROL Event Manager to the PATROL console. All metrics are sampled simultaneously, which can cause unnecessary system overhead for resources that are less critical or that rarely change.

Monitor Developer's Kit

BMC PATROL has an API that enables events to be sent by a non-PATROL program to the PATROL Event Manager. This is similar to IT/O, which has an API for sending RPC messages to its Event Browser. A non-PATROL program can also receive events from PATROL.

The PATROL Scripting Language (PSL), part of the PATROL Developer Console, can be used to create scripts to perform recovery actions by the PATROL agent on managed nodes. PSL can also be used to write parameters, commands, tasks, and discovery procedures for PATROL agents.

Notification Methods

PATROL Alarm Manager can be used to send notifications by pager, by e-mail, or to third-party messaging systems. Users define the resources to monitor and the notification criteria. After configuration, the alarm policies can be distributed to a predefined set of systems. The PATROL Alarm Manager keeps track of additional information, such as the number of events sent by a host, and time periods during which notifications should be sent. PATROL can also send copies of an event to multiple consoles.

The PATROL Event Translator (PET) can translate messages for various protocols. BMC provides a PET for IT/O, using the OpenView APIs, but it forwards only the event. The operator must switch to the BMC PATROL console to initiate corrective actions.

Diagnostic Capabilities

PATROL can graph multiple metrics simultaneously for a single system to help with performance monitoring. If data is logged, historical graphs can also be shown.

In addition to monitoring, PATROL can automate recovery actions taken in response to error or failure conditions. The user must assign the desired recovery actions to an event. The concept of operator-initiated actions, available with IT/O, is not supported with PATROL.

PATROL can be configured to respond automatically to specific problems, and can help tune databases for optimal performance. Recovery actions can be performed by agents without requiring communication with the console.

In addition to providing help diagnosing and recovering from problems, BMC provides PATROL DB, which includes database administrative tools such as Pathfinder, DB-Alter, DB-Reorg, DB-Change Manager, DB-Integrity, DB-Voyager, and SQL-Explorer. These tools are integrated into the PATROL framework and can be launched from the PATROL console. In contrast, IT/O provides monitoring only, relying on other software vendors to provide administrative tools.

To change UNIX kernel parameters in response to a problem, BMC uses the tool Opportune.

Additional Information

More information about BMC Software can be found on the Web at http://www.bmc.com. BMC PATROL software can be downloaded from its Web site.

BMC Software announced plans to buy BGS Systems, Inc. in early 1998. BMC intends to integrate BGS's Best/1 product for performance analysis and trending into the PATROL software suite. This includes integration of its separate agent, collection, and data store technologies. BGS provides performance management solutions for UNIX, NT, and mainframe systems. Information about BGS Systems, Inc. can be found at http://www.bmc.com.

MeasureWare

MeasureWare Agent is a Hewlett-Packard product that collects and logs resource and performance metrics. MeasureWare agents run and collect data on the individual server systems being monitored. Agents exist for many platforms and operating systems, including HP-UX, Solaris, and AIX.

MeasureWare is a monitoring framework, because MeasureWare agents collect and log performance data on several different platforms in a consistent manner. It also has two interfaces, Application Resource Measurement (ARM) and Data Source Integration (DSI), for adding additional instrumentation. A common analysis tool, such as PerfView, can be used to analyze and graph data.

The MeasureWare agents collect data, summarize it, timestamp it, log it, and send alarms when appropriate. The agents collect and report on a wide variety of system resources, performance metrics, and user-defined data. The information can then be exported to ASCII files, spreadsheets, or performance analysis programs such as PerfView. The data can be used by these programs to generate alarms to warn of potential performance problems. By using the historical data, trends can be discovered, which can help to solve resource issues before they affect system performance.

Monitored Components

MeasureWare agents collect data at three different levels: global system metrics, application metrics, and process metrics. Global and application data is summarized at five-minute intervals, whereas process data is summarized at one-minute intervals. Important applications can be defined by an administrator by listing the processes that make up the application in a configuration file.

In addition, optional modules for database and networking support are offered. MeasureWare also provides a DSI interface that enables you to pass your own data to the MeasureWare Agent.

MeasureWare has database modules for collecting database metrics for Oracle, Sybase, and Informix databases. These modules can take advantage of all the standard monitoring features of MeasureWare, such as timestamping data, logging, and forwarding alarms to HP PerfView. However, this product is similar to another HP product for database performance information, the OpenView SMART Plug-Ins for databases. SPIs also feed information into MeasureWare, providing a consistent interface with other IT/O products.

A more detailed list of metrics in each category can be found in the next few chapters on systems, disks, networks, applications, and databases. Although MeasureWare provides extensive performance and resource information, it offers limited configuration information and no data about system faults.

Monitoring Features

HP MeasureWare Agent software is installed on each managed system. The agents keep a history of a system's resource utilization, and the information can then be exported to spreadsheets or to performance analysis programs, such as HP PerfView. The data can be used by these programs to generate alarms to warn of potential performance problems. By using historical data, trends can be discovered, which can help to solve resource issues before they affect system performance.

MeasureWare allows you to define alarm conditions. You can have alarms sent based on conditions that involve a combination of metrics. For example, a CPU bottleneck alarm can be based on the CPU use and CPU run queue length.

MeasureWare agents provide alarms to PerfView for analysis, and to the IT/O management console. SNMP traps can also be sent by the MeasureWare Agent at the time threshold conditions are met. Automated actions can be taken, or the operator can choose to take a suggested action.

You can configure alarms based on a combination of multiple metrics and on duration. In this way, rules can be used to ensure that messages are sent to an operator only when a real problem occurs.

MeasureWare's extract command can be used to export data to other tools, such as spreadsheet programs.

MeasureWare Service Reporter is a Web-based metrics tool for generating reports on network performance. Network performance can be compared to service-level agreements. Reports can show the actual response times for specific applications.

MeasureWare can show application information, but an application first has to be defined. Application definitions can be used to summarize process-level data for all processes defined for an application.

With PerfView, a system administrator can analyze, alarm, forecast, and report on the MeasureWare metrics. HP OpenView IT/O can then receive event messages from the Measure-Ware Agent regarding alarm conditions. In fact, the MeasureWare Agent will detect an HP OpenView IT/O agent running on the system and automatically start sending alarms to it. Then, by clicking a database message sent to IT/O, for example, you can bring up PerfView to graph the related database and system information.

MeasureWare requires approximately 1MB of memory for data collection, and 40MB of disk space is recommended for each month of data that needs to be stored. To ensure that the MeasureWare Agent is automatically restarted after a system reboot, make sure the file /etc/rc.config.d/mwa is configured with the parameter MWA_START equal to 1.

MeasureWare is a complement to EMS and IT/O, providing performance data while EMS and IT/O focus on availability information. MeasureWare should be used when you need to see a history of resource values over time.

MeasureWare agents gather information at one- and five-minute intervals. Other tools, such as EMS, can acquire information as frequently as every second. EMS monitors can also forward important information without waiting to be polled.

The MeasureWare agents are available on HP-UX, IBM AIX, Sun Solaris, and NCR WorldMark systems.

Monitor Discovery and Configuration

When MeasureWare is activated, the data is automatically collected and analyzed at regular intervals. An administrator configures the alarm thresholds for notification.

An ASCII file contains alarm definitions. To add or modify an alarm, you need to edit this file; no GUI is available. Validation is done to ensure that the syntax is correct. On HP-UX systems, this file is located at /var/opt/perf/alarmdef. To create an alarm, you need to know the available metrics to choose from. The online help facility can show you the data that is available, with descriptions of each metric.

Applications can also be defined by an administrator by editing the parm file, located at /var/opt/perf/parm, by default. You can then monitor specific metrics for your application.

To ensure that alarms are appropriate, you can use the analyze command from within MeasureWare's utility program to test alarm conditions. analyze looks at historical data and reports when alarms would have been sent. In this way, you can determine whether you have the appropriate alarm conditions.

If you edit the parm or alarmdef file, you need to use the mwa command to instruct the MeasureWare Agent to reread the file.

You can run the perfstats utility to check the status of a MeasureWare agent.

Monitor Developer's Kit

A few different ways exist to include your own performance instrumentation along with other MeasureWare data. Through the DSI API, custom applications can send information to MeasureWare to store. MeasureWare also can timestamp and provide summaries of this data.

Additionally, the ARM APIs can be used with instrument applications so that transaction response times can be measured. This information can be passed along to MeasureWare agents for analysis. The ARM APIs are described in more detail in Chapter 7.

Notification Methods

MeasureWare agents collect information about system performance. Threshold events can be sent to PerfView, as alerts, or to IT/O, as opcmsgs. You can also configure alarms to execute a UNIX command, such as mail, to send a notification.

Alarm notification can be sent to PerfView, IT/O, or any SNMP-based management platform (such as Unicenter TNG) by using SNMP traps. Alarms can be sent to multiple destinations. MeasureWare can also be configured to execute an arbitrary UNIX command when the alarming threshold is reached. Custom applications that need to receive alarm information can be integrated in this way.

If the MeasureWare Agent detects that a system is being managed by IT/O, it automatically sends alarms to IT/O.

Diagnostic Capabilities

MeasureWare is integrated with IT/O and PerfView. A MeasureWare alarm can be received by IT/O. Drilling down on an event can launch PerfView for further analysis.

Additional Information

The list of MeasureWare metrics varies from release to release. To verify that the metric you want is available, you can check the files under /opt/perf/paperdocs/mwa/C on a system where MeasureWare is installed.

The MeasureWare Agent is available as a separate product and is also included as part of the GlancePlus Pak software bundle.

For further information, visit the HP Resource and Performance Management Web site at http://www.openview.hp.com/solutions/application/.

## Chapter 4

Monitoring the System

A computer system consists of processors, memory, and I/O devices. Users log in to the system and run business jobs or applications. Network software and interface cards connect users over the network to the computer system. This chapter focuses on monitoring the processors and memory components, as well as the user activity on the system. Disks, networks, databases, and applications are covered in separate chapters.

Identifying Important System Monitoring Categories

This chapter identifies important system resources to monitor, so that you can detect faults, avoid problems, and ultimately ensure availability. Many important system resources can be monitored for events and faults, and many system management tools are available with which to monitor them. Instead of categorizing based on specific hardware components, this chapter relates its descriptions of tools to the different ways of monitoring your system. For example, your focus as an operator may be on watching for system faults and failures, software or hardware configuration changes, system resource usage, performance management, or security. This chapter tries to show a tool's role, if any, in each of these monitoring categories.

Monitoring System Configuration Changes

This category includes monitoring for changes in hardware and software configurations that can be caused by an operating system upgrade, patches applied to the system, changes to kernel parameters, or the installation of a new software application, for example. The root cause of system problems can often be traced back to an inappropriate hardware or software configuration change. Therefore, it is important to keep accurate records of these changes, because the problem that a change causes may remain latent for a long period before it surfaces.

Adding or removing hardware devices typically requires the system to be restarted, so configuration changes can be tracked indirectly (in other words, remote monitoring tools would notice system status changes). However, software configuration changes, or the installation of a new application, are not tracked in this way, so reporting tools are needed. Also, more systems are becoming capable of adding hardware components online, so hardware configuration tracking is becoming increasingly more important.

Monitoring System Faults

After ensuring that the configuration is correct, the first thing to monitor is the overall condition of the system. Is the system up? Can you talk to it, ping it, run a command? If not, a fault may have occurred. Detecting system problems ranges from determining whether the system is up to determining whether it is behaving properly. If the system either isn't up or is up but not behaving properly, then you must determine which system component is having a problem.

This chapter addresses monitoring various components of the system for faults or events. The fault category generally covers system hardware components, including the Central Processing Unit (CPU), memory, and system buses, as well as peripherals, such as tape drives and printers. (Disks are covered in Chapter 5.) CPU and memory faults may cause system failures or degraded performance. Tape faults may result in a backup failing, a bad backup, or delays in completing a backup in a timely manner. With proactive monitoring, you can find out that a tape drive is having problems before backup is actually scheduled to begin.

Monitoring System Resource Utilization

For an application to run correctly, it may need a fixed amount of system resources. Some resources are renewable, such as the amount of CPU or I/O bandwidth an application is entitled to use during a time interval. The resource category refers to those system resources that an application acquires and then releases at its own discretion. For example, an application can allocate a segment of shared memory or launch a group of processes. Other examples included in the resource category are the number of open files or sockets, message segments, and system semaphores that an application has. The system has fixed limits for each of these resources, so monitoring their use is important. If these system tables are exhausted, the system may no longer function properly. You may want to set up alarms to notify you when the available resources in a given system table are below a certain threshold, which will give you time to react before the problem becomes critical.

Another aspect of resource utilization is studying the amount of resources that an application has used. You may not want a given workload to use more than a certain amount of CPU time or fixed amount of disk space. Some resource management tools, such as quota, can help with this.

Monitoring System Security

One way that a system's availability can be impacted is through unauthorized use. Performance and resource controls are not useful if the system is used for the wrong purposes. You need to prevent unauthorized use of system resources by using password files, network firewalls, and so forth. In addition to setting up access rights and policies, you need to monitor the system, so that you know when security has been compromised. This chapter briefly mentions some of the security tools that are available.

Monitoring System Performance

Knowing both that system resources are available and that your application is performing well is important. Eliminating bottlenecks or, even better, preventing them, allows the system to provide its intended services. Monitoring the performance of system resources can help to indicate problems with the operation of the system. Bottlenecks in one area usually impact system performance in another area. CPU, memory, and disk I/O bandwidth are the important resources to watch for performance bottlenecks. You should monitor during typical usage periods to establish baselines. Understanding what is "normal" operation helps you to identify when system resources are not behaving well. Resource management tools are available that can help you to allocate system resources among applications and users.

In this and each of the next four chapters, performance issues are contained in a separate section and described after the other tools are discussed.

One way to check for system problems is to watch the system's front panel of lights. Any change from normal (for example, color changes from green to red or a light starts flashing) could be indicative of a hardware or firmware problem. Of course, to monitor the system in this way, you need an operator to watch the front panel of the system manually. If an operator isn't always available to watch the front panel, a delay in detecting a problem may occur. Many other, more sophisticated tools are available to help you detect system problems that may occur in your system. These tools, which are covered in the following sections, range from standard UNIX commands to sophisticated add-on monitoring software suites.

Using Standard Commands and Tools

Many UNIX commands exist to check configuration, status, and resource information. These tools generally report on only a snapshot in time. You can write or use custom scripts that incorporate these or other commands and run them periodically so that you can track configuration changes or test the status of system resources over time.

The more commonly used commands are described in this section. Note that they are organized alphabetically. You may also want to check the online man pages for additional information about each command. Unless otherwise noted, the commands listed in this section are available on multiple UNIX platforms. (Tools that are specific to networking, such as netstat and nfsstat, are discussed in Chapter 6.)

In addition to these commands, you may want to check the system log file, /var/adm/syslog /syslog.log, for error messages if your system is experiencing problems. Messages written to this log file include information regarding the module experiencing the problem and the time that the event occurred, which can be very valuable when troubleshooting.

bdf and df

The bdf and df commands are commonly used to show the amount of disk and swap space used and available. bdf – i reports the number of used and free filesystem structures (inodes) in the kernel.

By default, bdf shows information for all mounted filesystems. If this information is too lengthy, you can also run the command and specify a filesystem as a command-line option. An example is shown in Listing 4-1.

ioscan

The ioscan command is used to discover and display the system hardware, usable I/O system devices, or kernel I/O system data structures. The results displayed list the default hardware path to the device, the class of hardware, and a brief description. ioscan includes information on the following hardware: processors, memory, network interface cards, and I/O devices. Listing 4-2 shows how you can check the number of processors on your system by using ioscan.

ioscan is a good tool to use to get a complete picture of your system hardware layout. It reports the status of the installed software, indicating whether the proper drivers are loaded. By storing the command output in files, you can maintain a history of the hardware configuration changes to your system.

iostat

iostat reports CPU statistics and I/O statistics for disks and terminals. For disks, it lists the device name, number of bytes transferred per second (bps), number of seeks per second (sps), and milliseconds per average seek (msps). For terminals, it shows the number of characters read and the number of characters written. For the CPU, it shows the percentages of time that the system has spent in user mode, nice mode (low-priority user processes), and system mode. Listing 4-3 shows sample output for a system with only one physical disk.

Listing 4-1   bdf output for a specific filesystem.

```
# bdf /dev/vg00/lvol3
Filesystem           kbytes     used     avail    %used Mounted on
/dev/vg00/lvol3      126976     33003    93912     26%  /
#
```

Listing 4-2   Output from ioscan for a two-processor HP-UX system.

```
# ioscan |grep processor
32          processor             Processor
34          processor             Processor
#
```

Listing 4-3 Output from the iostat command showing performance measures for disks, terminals, and CPU.

```
# iostat -t
                    tty                cpu
              tin tout         us  ni  sy  id
                0    1          1   0   2  97

   device    bps     sps     msps

   c0t5d0      0     0.0     1.0
```

You may want to use iostat to compare the activity on different disks, to see whether a load imbalance exists. It is normal for the system disk to have more activity.

ipcs

The ipcs command shows the status of active message queues, shared memory, and system semaphores. Listing 4-4 shows example output from using ipcs. You may want to consult the online manpage to see all the available options for this command.

mailstats

If your system is being used as a mail server, you may want to use mailstats to check mail statistics. The mailstats command shows the number of messages and amount of data sent or received for each mailer running on the system.

ps

The ps command is used to display information about all processes on the system. The metrics provided by ps include: Process Identifier (PID), parent PID, process start time, cumulative execution time, process state, priority, physical size (in pages), and the command with its command-line options.

ps is a quick way to get a profile of the processes on your system. It is useful for checking whether a specific application or process is running. For example, Listing 4-5 shows an easy way to display the Network File System (NFS) daemons running on your system. This listing can be used to identify runaway processes, both in CPU time and size. Numerous processes in the wait state may be an indication of a system bottleneck.

sar

sar is the System Activity Reporter. It is useful for monitoring system activity and can be used to identify memory, CPU, and kernel bottlenecks. It enables you to specify the polling interval and has

Listing 4-4 Output from ipcs showing active message queues, shared memory, and semaphores.

```
#ipcs
IPC status from /dev/kmem as of Sun Mar 14 17:47:20 1999
T     ID     KEY         MODE          OWNER     GROUP
Message Queues:
q      0 0x3c1c0330 -Rrw--w--w-     root      root
q      1 0x3e1c0330 --rw-r--r--     root      root
Shared Memory:
m      0 0x2f180002 --rw-------     root      sys
m    201 0x411c031b --rw-rw-rw-     root      sys
m    402 0x4e0c0002 --rw-rw-rw-     root      sys
m    403 0x41201219 --rw-rw-rw-     root      sys
Semaphores:
s      0 0x2f180002 --ra-ra-ra-     root      sys
s     65 0x411c031b --ra-ra-ra-     root      sys
s    130 0x4e0c0002 --ra-ra-ra-     root      sys
s    131 0x4120121a --ra-ra-ra-     root      sys
s      4 0x00446f6e --ra-r--r--     root      root
s      5 0x00446f6d --ra-r--r--     root      root
s      6 0x01090522 --ra-r--r--     root      root
s      7 0x411c1f3a --ra-ra-ra-     root      root
s      8 0x410c319a --ra-ra-ra-     root      root
#
```

Listing 4-5 Finding your NFS daemons.

```
#ps -ef |grep -E 'nfs|PPID'
    UID    PID  PPID  C  STIME    TTY      TIME COMMAND

    root    681     1  0  Dec 22   ?        0:00 /usr/sbin/nfsd 4
    root    682   681  0  Dec 22   ?        0:00 /usr/sbin/nfsd 4
    root    686   681  0  Dec 22   ?        0:00 /usr/sbin/nfsd 4
    root    688   681  0  Dec 22   ?        0:00 /usr/sbin/nfsd 4
    root 16761 16718  1 12:14:48 pts/0     0:00 grep nfs
#
```

the ability to log data to a file (in binary format). It can report on activity from many system
resources, including CPU utilization by processor, buffer cache, swapping, disks and tape, run and
swap queues, and several system tables. Refer to the online man page for the command-line options.

For CPU activity, sar shows CPU utilization by user mode, system mode, idle time waiting for I/O to complete, and idle time either on a per-processor level or averaged for all processors. Sample output is shown in Listing 4-6.

Listing 4-6 sar output showing system activity.

```
# sar 5 5

HP-UX cadbury B.10.20 A 9000/871      03/15/99

20:36:32    %usr    %sys    %wio    %idle
20:36:37      0       1       0       98
20:36:42      0       1       0       99
20:36:47      1       1       0       99
20:36:52      0       1       0       99
20:36:57      0       1       0       99

Average       0       1       0       99
#
```

By using sar -q, you can look at the average lengths of the run and swap queues, and the percentage of times the queues were occupied. This is shown in Listing 4-7. High CPU utilization and a large run queue may indicate a CPU bottleneck. A large swap queue is one sign of memory contention.

sar can be used to check the effectiveness of buffer cache use. It reports the rates of reads and writes between a disk and the buffer cache. It also reports the rates of logical reads and writes to and from the buffer cache, as well as buffer cache hit ratios.

For swapping activity, you can monitor swap-in rates, swap outs per second, and context switch rates.

sar -v reports the current size, maximum size, and number of overflows of various system tables, including the process table, inode table, and system file table.

Listing 4-7 Output from sar showing queue lengths.

```
# sar -q 5 5

HP-UX cadbury B.10.20 A 9000/871      03/15/99

20:44:03 runq-sz %runocc swpq-sz %swpocc
20:44:08    1.0      20     0.0       0
20:44:13    0.0       0     0.0       0
20:44:18    0.0       0     0.0       0
20:44:23    1.0      10     0.0       0
20:44:28    0.0       0     0.0       0

Average     1.0       6     0.0       0
#
```

swapinfo

swapinfo reports system paging or swapping activity, and memory utilization. On some implementations of UNIX, it is called swap. This command is useful for showing swap space usage and configuration. It displays for each swap type and device the kilobytes (K) available, kilobytes used, kilobytes free, and percentage used. If you have insufficient memory, you may see lots of pages being swapped or high utilization of the swap device. An example using swapinfo is shown in Listing 4-8.

For device swap areas, reserve is the number of 1K blocks reserved for filesystem use by ordinary users. For device swap areas, this value is always "-". Checking swapinfo periodically may help you to schedule additions to your swap capacity.

sysdef

The sysdef command, available on HP-UX, reports on a system's tunable kernel parameters. For each kernel parameter, this command shows the current value, value at boot time, and minimum and maximum values allowed for the parameter, as demonstrated in Listing 4-9. This command can be used both to monitor whether the system kernel is configured properly and to track whether certain kernel resource usage is at or approaching its configured limit. You can also use this command, together with ioscan, to track kernel configuration changes.

Listing 4-8 Output from the swapinfo command shows system paging activity.

```
# swapinfo
          Kb      Kb      Kb   PCT  START/       Kb
TYPE  AVAIL    USED    FREE  USED  LIMIT RESERVE  PRI NAME
dev   524288  12488  511800    2%      0       -    1 /dev /vg00/lvol2
reserve        -     246876 -246876
memory  404396 207844  196552   51% v
```

Listing 4-9 Showing current values of kernel-tunable parameters.

```
#sysdef
NAME                  VALUE    BOOT     MIN-MAX     UNITS     FLAGS
acctresume              4       -      -100-100                 -
acctsuspend             2       -      -100-100                 -
allocate_fs_swapmap     0       -         -                     -
bufpages            10714       -        0-        Pages        -
create_fastlinks        0       -         -                     -
dbc_max_pct            50       -         -                     -
dbc_min_pct             5       -         -                     -
default_disk_ir         0       -         -                     -
```

continued

Listing 4-9   (continued)

dskless_node	0	–	0-1		–
eisa_io_estimate	768	–	–		–
eqmemsize	15	–	–		–
file_pad	10	–	0-		–
fs_async	0	–	0-1		–
hpux_aes_override	0	–	–		–
maxdsiz	16384	–	256-655360	Pages	–
maxfiles	120	–	30-2048		–
maxfiles_lim	1024	–	30-2048		–
maxssiz	2048	–	256-655360	Pages	–
maxswapchunks	256	–	1-16384		–
maxtsiz	16384	–	256-655360	Pages	–
maxuprc	75	–	3-		–
maxvgs	10	–	–		–
msgmap	2555904	–	3-		–
nbuf	5772	–	0-		–
ncallout	316	–	6-		–
ncdnode	150	–	–		–
ndilbuffers	30	–	1-		–
netisr_priority	-1	–	-1-127		–
netmemmax	14356480	–	–		–
nfile	1034	–	14-		–
nflocks	200	–	2-		–
ninode	500	–	14-		–
no_lvm_disks	0	–	–		–
nproc	300	–	10-		–
npty	60	–	1-		–
nstrpty	60	–	–		–
nswapdev	10	–	1-25		–
nswapfs	10	–	1-25		–
public_shlibs	1	–	–		–
remote_nfs_swap	0	–	–		–
rtsched_numpri	32	–	–		–
sema	0	–	0-1		–
semmap	4128768	–	4-		–
shmem	0	–	0-1		–
shmmni	200	–	3-1024		–
streampipes	0	–	0-		–
swapmem_on	1	–	–		–
swchunk	2048	–	2048-16384	kBytes	–
timeslice	10	--1-2147483648		Ticks	–
unlockable_mem	2158	–	0-	Pages	–

timex

The timex command can be used to measure and report, in seconds, the elapsed time, user CPU time, and system CPU time spent executing a given command. The command to be executed is given on the timex command line. This command reports process accounting data for the command and all of its children, as well as the total system activity during execution of the command. The timex command can give you a crude idea of the impact of a command on the rest of the system.

top

The top command is useful for monitoring the system CPU and memory loads. It also lists the most active processes on the system. top output is displayed in the terminal window and is updated every five seconds, by default.

top shows CPU resource statistics, including load averages (job queues over the last 1 minute, 5 minutes, and 15 minutes), the number of processes in each state (sleeping, waiting, running, starting, zombie, stopped), the percentage of time spent in each processor state (user, nice, system, idle, interrupt, and swapper) per processor on the system, as well as the average for each processor in a multiprocessor system.

For memory utilization, top shows virtual and real memory in use, the amount of active memory, and the amount of free memory.

At the process level, top lists the top processes, based on their CPU usage. The process data displayed by top includes the PID, process size (text, data, and stack), resident size of the process (K), process state (sleeping, waiting, running, idle, zombie, or stopped), the number of CPU seconds consumed by the process, and the average CPU utilization of the process. This command can be used to identify processes that may be using large amounts of CPU or memory. Note that top can also be a quick way to check the number of processors on your system. Listing 4-10 shows the output for a four-processor system.

Listing 4-10 Output from the top command showing process activity.

```
System: gsyview1                    Fri Feb 12 13:40:24 1999
Load averages: 0.08, 0.11, 0.16
616 processes: 614 sleeping, 2 running
Cpu states:
CPU LOAD USER  NICE  SYS   IDLE  BLOCK SWAIT  INTR  SSYS
 0  0.30 0.0%  0.0%  1.3% 98.7%  0.0%  0.0%   0.0%  0.0%
 1  0.00 0.0%  0.0%  0.7% 99.3%  0.0%  0.0%   0.0%  0.0%
 2  0.01 0.0%  0.0%  0.2% 99.8%  0.0%  0.0%   0.0%  0.0%
 3  0.02 0.4%  0.0%  7.9% 91.8%  0.0%  0.0%   0.0%  0.0%
-- -- -- -- --- -- -- -- --
avg 0.08 0.0%  0.0%  2.6% 97.4%  0.0%  0.0%   0.0%  0.0%
```

```
Memory: 25754K (2356K)real, 27864K (6144K)virtual, 27838K free  Page# 1/42

CPU TTY    PID USERNAME PRI NI   SIZE   RES STATE     TIME %WCPU %CPU COMMAND
  3 pts/4 12555 jsymons 187 20 25992K  568K run       0:02  7.84 5.48 top
  0 rroot    19 root    100 20    0K    0K sleep 1449:04  1.05 1.05 netisr
  1 rroot   494 root    154 20  216K  284K sleep 1479:50  1.03 1.02 syncer
  0 rroot     3 root    128 20    0K    0K sleep  960:56  1.00 0.99 statdaemo
  0 rroot  1432 root     20 20 8120K 6956K sleep  842:38  0.61 0.61 cmcld
  3 rroot    38 root    138 20    0K    0K sleep  336:22  0.32 0.31 vx_iflush
  1 rroot     7 root    -32 20    0K    0K sleep  321:07  0.25 0.25 ttisr
  3 rroot   934 root    154 20 6100K 1436K sleep  297:15  0.22 0.22 rpcd
  1 rroot    40 root    138 20    0K    0K sleep  193:38  0.16 0.16 vx_inacti
  0 rroot 26626 root    154 20  868K  880K sleep  245:15  0.15 0.15 opcle
  2 rroot 26587 root    154 20 2580K 1348K sleep  125:22  0.07 0.07 opcmsga
  1 rroot    39 root    138 20    0K    0K sleep   88:15  0.07 0.07 vx_ifree_
  3 rroot    22 root    100 20    0K    0K sleep  159:58  0.06 0.06 netisr
  1 rroot 26586 root    154 20 8468K 1752K sleep   53:47  0.06 0.06 opcctla
```

uname

The uname command can be used to display configuration information about your system. This information includes the operating system name, machine model, and operating system version.

You may want to gather this information and store it for later use. This may be useful if you are trying to keep all of your systems on the same release of the operating system, for example.

uptime

The uptime command is probably the most commonly used command to check system resources. This command shows the current time, length of time the system has been up, number of users logged on, and the average number of jobs in the run queue for the last 1, 5, and 15 minutes.

Using uptime with the -w option shows a summary of the current activity on the system for each user. As shown in Listing 4-11, you can see the login time, CPU usage, and command activity for each user.

vmstat

The vmstat command provides good information about system resources, including virtual memory and CPU usage, and is useful for detecting whether you are low on memory or swap space.

Listing 4-11   Output from the uptime command showing paging activity.

```
uptime -w
 12:49pm  up 3 days, 2:19, 5 users, load average: 0.49, 0.56, 0.56
User     tty            login@  idle  JCPU PCPU  what
jsymons  console        12:32pm 74:17            /usr/sbin
jsymons  ttyp7          12:18pm                  uptime -w
```

For monitoring real and virtual memory, vmstat shows page faults and paging activity, including reclaimed pages and swapping rates.

For the CPU, you can see more detailed information with vmstat than that provided by iostat. vmstat shows faults, including device interrupts, system calls, and context switches. vmstat also includes the breakdown of CPU utilization by user, system, and idle time.

For processes, vmstat shows the number of processes in various states, including the following: currently in the run queue, blocked on an I/O operation, and swapped out to disk.

The statistics that you see vary depending on the command option that you specify. By specifying a time interval, you can have vmstat run continuously, so that you can see how the values vary over time. As shown in Listing 4-12, using the -s option prints paging-related activity.

who

The who command tells you who is logged in to the system, and how long each user has been connected. This command can be useful if a performance problem arises, because you can

Listing 4-12 Output from the vmstat command showing paging activity.

```
$ vmstat -s
5431 swap ins
5431 swap outs
1376 pages swapped in
426 pages swapped out
9704169 total address trans. faults taken
2159795 page ins
9236 page outs
136606 pages paged in
21451 pages paged out
2064504 reclaims from free list
2097094 total page reclaims
773 intransit blocking page faults
6040874 zero fill pages created
3925703 zero fill page faults
1457303 executable fill pages created
76804 executable fill page faults
0 swap text pages found in free list
735656 inode text pages found in free list
185 revolutions of the clock hand
105428 pages scanned for page out
16850 pages freed by the clock daemon
50286274 cpu context switches
90662460 device interrupts
2732863 traps
229976779 system calls
```

quickly determine whether an increase in the number of concurrent users has occurred. It can also be useful in checking for security intrusions, because you may notice an unexpected user.

Using System Instrumentation

Standards for network and system management, such as the Simple Network Management Protocol (SNMP) and Desktop Management Interface (DMI), were developed to help make management easier. They provide industry-standard ways to build instrumentation and interface into the instrumentation, respectively. SNMP is used to access Management Information Bases (MIBs), and DMI is used to access Management Information Formats (MIFs).

Standard MIBs and MIFs define the metrics that can be used by any vendor's instrumentation. Vendor-specific MIBs and MIFs provide vendor-specific instrumentation. This section looks at some of the system instrumentation available through each of these standards.

Many tools already exist for accessing this instrumentation. Several vendors offer browsers and monitoring capabilities that use a common interface to access instrumented objects from different hardware platforms and operating systems. For example, the common enterprise management frameworks, such as the HP Network Node Manager, include a MIB Browser tool to access MIB data. They may also include tools that can be used to monitor MIB data on remote systems from the enterprise management platform. Toolkits are available that provide an interface with which people can write their own tools to monitor or track this information. Furthermore, toolkits exist for creating your own instrumentation.

Many valuable system resources can be monitored via these standard interfaces, to detect system events or faults. Some of the resources that you may be interested in are reviewed in this section.

SNMP

A MIB is a standard way of representing information of a certain category. For example, MIB-II provides useful information about a system, such as the number of active TCP connections, system hardware and version information, and so forth. OpenView IT/Operations (IT/O), discussed later in this chapter, provides a MIB Browser. The MIB Browser tool helps you to discover which MIBs are available, and to see the information being provided by each MIB. The MIB Browser tool can check the value of anything contained in a MIB. If you find a MIB that contains some useful fields, you can use the MIB Browser to gather that data from the target system. The resulting data is displayed in the MIB Browser's output window on the screen. By browsing through available MIBs, and by querying values of selected MIB fields, you can gather specific information needed to monitor systems and troubleshoot problems.

The SNMP interface provides access to objects stored in various MIBs. MIB-II is a standard MIB that has been implemented on most UNIX systems. On HP-UX systems, the HP-UNIX MIB defines various metrics for monitoring system resources. Other vendors, such as Sun, have vendor-specific MIBs that provide similar information. Appendix A includes complete MIB definitions.

MIB-II, the "System MIB," is a standard repository for information about a computer system, and is supported on a variety of platforms, including UNIX and Windows NT. MIB-II contains information about a computer system, such as its name, system contact, and the length of time that it has been running. It also contains statistics from the key networking protocols, such as TCP, UDP, and IP. Statistics include packet transmission counts and error counts. Table 4-1 lists several variables in MIB-II that will help you to monitor system resources effectively. Both the actual MIB variable name and a description are provided for each variable.

The HP-UNIX MIB contains important information about the users, jobs, filesystems, memory, and processes of a system. The number of users logged in to the system and number of jobs running are both indications of how busy the system is. Reduced amounts of free swap space or filesystem space can serve as warnings of potential problems. The process status can be checked to see whether a particular application is still running normally on the target system. Table 4-2 contains some of the interesting metrics from the HP-UNIX MIB for monitoring system resources.

Table 4-1   Important MIB II Fields to Monitor

MIB Variable Name	*Description*
sysDescr	System description
sysObjectID	Unique identifier for the system
sysUpTime	Amount of time since the last system reboot
sysContact	System contact person
sysName	System name
sysLocation	System location
sysServices	The network services performed by this system

Table 4-2   Important HP-UNIX Variables to Monitor

MIB Variable Name	*Description*
computerSystemUsers	Current number of users on the system
computerSystemAvgJobs1	Average job queue length over the last minute
computerSystemAvgJobs5	Average job queue length over the last 5 minutes
computerSystemAvgJobs15	Average job queue length over the last 15 minutes
computerSystemMaxProc	Maximum number of processes allowed in the system
computerSystemFreeMemory	Amount of free memory
computerSystemPhysMemory	Amount of physical memory
computerSystemMaxUserMem	Maximum user memory
computerSystemSwapConfig	Amount of swap space configured
computerSystemEnabledSwap	Amount of swap enabled via swapon
computerSystemFreeSwap	Amount of free swap space
computerSystemUserCPU	Amount of CPU used by users
computerSystemSysCPU	Amount of CPU used by the system
computerSystemIdleCPU	Amount of idle CPU

DMI

System resource information can also be retrieved by using the Desktop Management Interface (DMI), which is another standard for storing and accessing management information. Management information is represented in a text file in the Management Information Format (MIF). Management information is divided into components. Each component has a Service Provider (SP) that is responsible for providing DMI information to the management applications that request it.

Several system platforms, including HP-UX, provide instrumentation for the System MIF and the Software MIF. Appendix A contains a complete listing of these MIFs.

Similar to MIB-II, the System MIF can be used to get generic system information, such as how long it has been running, and system contact information. It includes the system name, boot time, contact information, uptime, the number of users, as well as some information about the filesystem and disks.

The Software MIF provides information about the software products and product bundles installed on the system. The Software MIF can be a useful tool after a problem with a product has been discovered. By using a MIF Browser, you can examine the Software MIF to see whether the problem might be caused by a bad patch installation or a modified file. The MIF contains revision information for each product, and its creation and modification times. Version information can be checked to see whether a compatibility problem exists. Finally, the product's vendor information is provided in case product support personnel needs to be contacted.

Using Graphical Status Monitors

The graphical status monitoring tools described in this chapter are also referred to as *enterprise management frameworks*. These tools monitor multiple systems from a central location and display status information graphically.

Because you may not be able to sit at a console or watch the front panel of each system for which you are responsible, you need to be able to monitor system faults from a tool that is external (or remote) to the system. Besides, even if the console or front panel doesn't indicate any problems, network problems can make the system inaccessible to the end-user. Graphical status monitors can detect connectivity problems because they rely on network polls to gather status information.

Your server may depend on services provided by other systems. For example, network services such as the Domain Name Service (DNS), Dynamic Host Configuration Protocol (DHCP), Network File System (NFS), and e-mail are critical to the server, but are unlikely to be running on the server that you're monitoring, and consequently aren't tracked by any local monitors. This is critical information, because if the DNS is down, other systems may not be able to reach the system being monitored. Because the enterprise framework products are gathering status information about multiple systems at a central site, it is more likely that both the server and its service providers are being monitored.

Graphical status monitors provide many features that can help you to detect system faults, especially hardware or software faults. Most graphical status monitors provide hierarchical maps or visual displays that indicate status information. This saves you the time of correlating event data from logs to determine status. The graphical status monitors provide remote management capabilities, so you aren't required to have a physical console for each system. Furthermore, they can automatically discover the systems in your enterprise, so you don't have to remember system names and manually configure them. A graphical view typically can be customized by setting up filters, so that you see only those systems that you are responsible for managing.

This section describes only a couple of the available graphical status monitors. Others with similar system monitoring capabilities, such as HP's IT/O, Sun's Enterprise SyMON, or BMC PATROL, are mentioned in other parts of the book.

OpenView Network Node Manager

Network Node Manager (NNM) is a management product based on the HP OpenView platform. NNM is used primarily to view and monitor the status of network and system resources. Information is displayed graphically through a window-based display. A hierarchical set of submaps is available, enabling the customer to navigate and drill down through complex network topologies. Network and system components are represented graphically in maps as icons, which are color-coded to indicate the health of the objects represented. Events are propagated, based on severity, to higher-level submaps to indicate events, such as failures, at lower levels. Through pull-down menus available in NNM, the operator can run tools to get additional real-time status information, or remotely log in to the system and execute diagnostic commands.

One key feature of NNM is its ability to discover automatically network-addressable components, such as routers, hubs, and computer systems. Because the network discovery activity uses noticeable network resources, you may want to limit it to just the networks that you manage. This can be done by using discovery filters, a configurable option in NNM; or, alternatively, you can schedule discovery process(es) to run during off-peak hours.

After discovery is complete, the network topology information is then displayed on submaps, with colors used to indicate status. An operator can navigate through the submaps to find a particular LAN segment to monitor. In addition to viewing systems, an operator can also drill down to see system information, such as configured network interfaces. Figure 4-1 shows a segment map with icons indicating the health of each system in the segment.

NNM provides mechanisms to collect statistics and generate reports on individual network devices, including systems. NNM periodically checks the status of systems and devices by sending an ICMP echo request (ping). If no reply is received, a Node Down event is sent as an SNMP trap and logged in the Event Browser. NNM also listens to SNMP traps from SNMP supported devices. For instance, if NNM gets a Node Down trap, it changes the color of the icon representing the node that just went down.

The NNM Event Browser is a graphical display of the events that have been received from systems on the network. Events are sent to the management station as SNMP traps. The trap handler receives these traps and stores them in a database. The events can be viewed through the Event Browser, and filters can be used to prevent the operator from being flooded with noncritical information. Filters can be configured based on the sending system or event criticality, for

Figure 4-1   Network Node Manager segment submap shows the health of the systems in the segment.

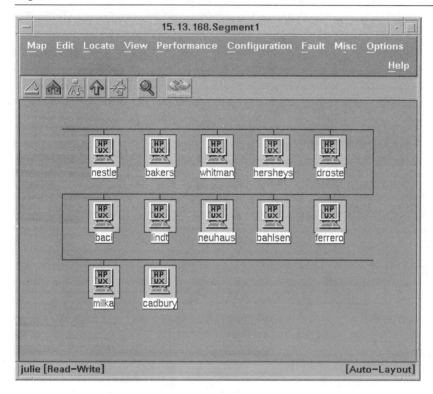

example. NNM can also process Common Management Information Protocol (CMIP) events for multivendor interoperability. You can use filtering to get history events from a particular system when troubleshooting a problem. After an event is handled, you can use the Event Browser to acknowledge the event.

By using the NNM Event Configuration utility, you can configure how specific SNMP traps should be handled, including the following:

  • Logging and display options
  • Event severity
  • Message format for display in the Event Browser
  • Automatic actions

Events can be configured to automatically display a pop-up notification, or to run a command on the management station to send e-mail, call a pager, change an icon color, or generate an audible alert.

After you recognize that a problem exists, the NNM menu interface provides many tools to troubleshoot problems or monitor the system in more detail. NNM provides a performance menu that you can use to check network activity, CPU load, and disk space, or to graph SNMP data. A configuration menu is provided so that you can check network configuration, system statistics, or the SNMP trap configuration. From the fault menu, you can try to reach the system through the network connectivity poll, a ping from the management station, or a ping initiated from another remote system. If you suspect that the route to a system is down, you can test that from the fault menu as well. A terminal window, the SAM interface (HP-UX only), and a MIB Browser are all available from the pull-down menus.

NNM also provides several utilities to help you gather and process data provided in MIBs. You can configure data collection of MIB objects and define thresholds for when to generate an event. You can build your own MIB application to collect MIB objects for graphing or generating tabular output.

As this section has described, OpenView NNM can provide help for numerous system monitoring categories. Faults can be detected and shown graphically, with failure events sent to the Message Browser. You can monitor network performance by using the performance menus. You can check some of the system resource limits by using predefined tools or the MIB Browser. NNM, however, is typically used only if you have many systems to monitor.

NNM is a building block for other HP OpenView applications. Application integration is provided through developer's kits and registration files. More than 300 applications are integrated today with HP OpenView. HP IT/O, discussed later, is one product that extends NNM's capabilities. The most commonly used partner applications are CiscoWorks, Bay Networks Optivity, 3Com Transcend, Remedy ARS, and HP NetMetrix.

OpenView NNM runs on NT and UNIX platforms. Both versions can be used to monitor UNIX systems.

ClusterView

ClusterView is a graphical monitoring tool integrated with OpenView NNM and IT/O. It provides monitoring of systems and other resources in MC/ServiceGuard environments. MC/ServiceGuard is a Hewlett-Packard high availability software product that detects system failures, network or LAN card failures, and the failure of critical applications. While MC/ServiceGuard can be configured to handle these failures automatically, it is through ClusterView that you can capture these high availability events and graphically view the health of systems that are part of MC/ServiceGuard clusters. MC/ServiceGuard is supported only on HP 9000 Series 800 systems running HP-UX 10.x or later operating systems.

MC/ServiceGuard is most commonly used in a cluster environment. Software on each system monitors the other systems. When system failures occur, MC/ServiceGuard software can detect the problem and automatically restart critical applications on an alternate node. Monitoring of failures is done automatically, but without ClusterView, you may need to use MC/ServiceGuard commands to verify that the cluster software itself is working.

MC/ServiceGuard detects numerous cluster events, such as the failure of a critical application. These events can be forwarded to a management station by using either SNMP traps or opcmsg, a proprietary communication mechanism used by IT/O. Information about an MC/ServiceGuard cluster is stored in the HP Cluster and HP MC/ServiceGuard Cluster MIBs. These Cluster MIBs are listed in Appendix A. The following is a list of the MC/ServiceGuard events that trigger SNMP traps from the MC/ServiceGuard subagent:

- MC/ServiceGuard subagent was started
- MC/ServiceGuard cluster is reforming
- MC/ServiceGuard cluster is up on this node
- MC/ServiceGuard cluster is down on this node
- MC/ServiceGuard cluster configuration has changed
- MC/ServiceGuard package is starting
- MC/ServiceGuard package is running
- MC/ServiceGuard package is halting
- MC/ServiceGuard package is down
- MC/ServiceGuard service is down
- MC/ServiceGuard package switching flags have changed
- MC/ServiceGuard relocatable IP address added
- MC/ServiceGuard relocatable IP address removed
- MC/ServiceGuard network interface local switch
- MC/ServiceGuard subnet is up
- MC/ServiceGuard subnet is unavailable
- MC/ServiceGuard node joined the cluster
- MC/ServiceGuard node has halted
- MC/ServiceGuard node has failed

MC/ServiceGuard software detects a variety of error conditions, but it does not have a sophisticated notification mechanism for customers to learn what happened. Errors often are written to the system log, which can be used to help retrace what occurred.

Whereas MC/ServiceGuard can monitor the system, network, and processes and provide automatic recovery, ClusterView provides you with event notification of these recovery events. For example, if MC/ServiceGuard detects a local LAN card failure, it can reconfigure the IP connectivity on a backup LAN card on the local system transparently. Using ClusterView, you will see an event indicating that MC/ServiceGuard has performed a local switch to a backup LAN card. The bad LAN card should be replaced, to eliminate the LAN card as a single point of failure.

ClusterView can be used to help you with diagnosis in MC/ServiceGuard environments. ClusterView is an OpenView application with custom monitoring capabilities for MC/ServiceGuard and MC/LockManager clusters. An SNMP subagent that can be used to send events to an OpenView management station is included with the MC/ServiceGuard and MC/LockManager products. These events, sent as SNMP traps, can actually be received by any management station that understands SNMP (for example, Computer Associates' Unicenter product). These events are received in OpenView's event browser.

ClusterView provides automatic discovery and real-time status and event notification via the Event Browser and graphical displays of MC/ServiceGuard clusters, systems, and packages. Templates are provided to map the cluster events to readable text. Without these templates, events are unrecognized or unmatched traps in OpenView. With these templates, the traps are formatted in the NNM Event Browser or IT/O Message Browser when ClusterView is installed.

When a system failure is detected by MC/ServiceGuard, it moves all critical resources to an alternate node. A series of SNMP traps are generated by the MC/ServiceGuard subagent as an event occurs. Figure 4-2 shows the events in the NNM Event Browser after the system "bakers" fails. MC/ServiceGuard first detects the failure and starts the two packages, ems1 and ems2, on the alternate system, lindt. The Node Down trap is generated by NNM when it detects that system "bakers" is down.

ClusterView provides additional capabilities when used with IT/O. SNMP events are sent to the Event Browser, where ClusterView provides special troubleshooting instructions and recommends actions to help resolve the problems. Some data collection activities are done automatically. For example, in response to a package failure, ClusterView automatically retrieves the system's system log file entries from the time of failure to aid in diagnosis. Common HP-UX monitoring tools, such as netstat and lanscan, are included by ClusterView in IT/O's Application Desktop, along with MC/ServiceGuard-specific tools, such as cmviewcl.

In addition to high availability clusters, ClusterView can monitor user-defined clusters. ClusterView provides a configuration tool that enables the administrator to create a cluster, and then displays that cluster on its cluster submap. The operator can then monitor all the cluster systems at a glance, because they are all in the same OpenView window. Also, the operator can launch monitoring tools, such as HP PerfView, on the cluster, avoiding the need to select each system manually when running each tool.

ClusterView can be a useful extension to the capabilities of NNM if you are managing MC/ServiceGuard clusters, MC/LockManager clusters, or groups of systems. You can view detailed

Figure 4-2   NNM Event Browser showing MC/ServiceGuard events after a system failure.

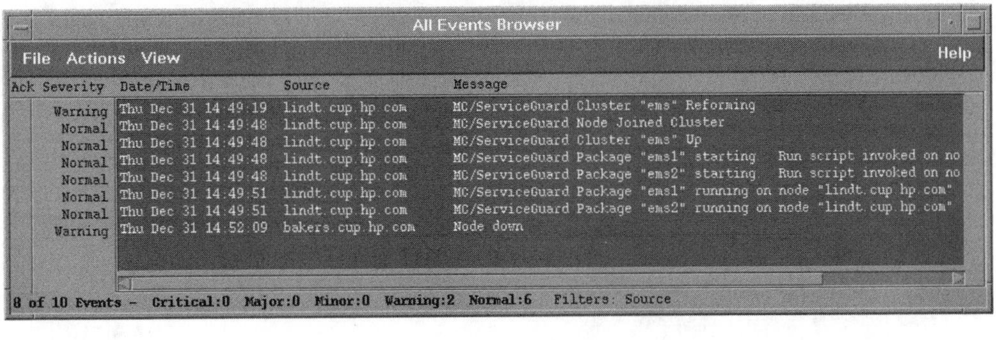

screens containing high availability configuration information about your cluster. In addition to processing faults, ClusterView provides recovery actions and troubleshooting help for these events.

ClusterView runs on HP-UX and NT systems and requires OpenView NNM or IT/O. The ClusterView software for either platform can also be used to monitor Microsoft's NT Cluster Servers, its high availability clusters. Both NT and MC/ServiceGuard clusters can be monitored concurrently from the same ClusterView software.

Unicenter TNG

Computer Associates' Unicenter TNG is an enterprise management platform that provides graphical status monitoring and provides system and network management for a heterogeneous enterprise. Unicenter TNG provides monitoring and management for all the resources in your environment, including system resources, networks, databases, and applications.

Unicenter TNG provides the framework for an integrated management solution to manage all IT resources via a common infrastructure. The TNG framework itself includes the following components: auto discovery, object repository, Real World interface, event management, calendar management, reporting, virus detection, and desktop support. Together with vendor, third-party, and custom-built applications, Unicenter TNG provides increased management and maintenance capabilities for the enterprise.

Unicenter TNG provides automatic discovery of networked objects, including systems and other resources within the enterprise. Information is stored in the Common Object Repository and can be displayed topographically in the Real World interface. Discovery filters can also be used, to limit discovery to a specific subnetwork or to specify which types of resources Unicenter TNG should discover.

A Common Object Repository stores the information used to create the Real World graphical views. You can browse the repository by using the Class Browser, Object Browser, or Topology Browser. Using ObjectView, you can get details on the performance of devices, and you can even graph the data.

The Real World interface provides graphical views that can be organized based on business functions, geographical location, or any logical groupings. The views can show the topology of the enterprise in two or three dimensions. These views can be used to see the status of the systems and resources in your environment.

Unicenter TNG provides management by using a distributed management approach. Distributed agents are responsible for monitoring and control. Centralized managers provide core management throughout the enterprise, including data correlation from one or more agents, workload management, and job management. The agents monitor and control based on policies provided by managers.

The agents run on managed nodes and gather data, apply filters, and report when necessary. Some provide control or execution on behalf of the managers. The agents send notifications, and can be polled. The agents can also collect performance data or be configured to send events and perform actions based on thresholds.

To view agents and get information about them, Unicenter TNG provides a MIB-II agent display to view MIB-II information, a node view, Distributed State Machine (DSM) view, and an Event Browser. The DSM tracks the status of objects across the network. It gathers information from the repository and agents to maintain the state of objects based on configured policies. The node view displays detailed state information about the system objects that are watched by the DSM.

Finally, managing events is one of the core capabilities provided by Unicenter TNG. The hub of event management is at the Unicenter TNG Event Console. You can configure policies to respond automatically to specific events, send SNMP traps based on events, forward events, filter out unimportant events, correlate events from several agents, or feed events into the DSM. In conjunction with the calendar management provided by Unicenter TNG, you can change or set event policies based on the time. For example, you may want to apply different policies during the weekend.

Using Event Monitoring Tools

This section covers various event monitors that are available for monitoring system resources. You can configure event monitors to generate a message when a change in status occurs or when a predefined threshold condition is met. This is different from commands, which give you status reports only when asked, and performance monitoring, which is generally studied over a long period of time. Event monitors generate a notification message soon after faults and events occur.

Event Monitoring Service

Several monitors discussed in this section are integrated into the Event Monitoring Service (EMS) framework. The EMS framework, available only on HP-UX systems, enables monitors to be provided in a consistent manner for a system. Although the EMS framework itself is freely available, some monitors are delivered with HP-UX Online Diagnostics, some are sold separately, and others are bundled with the individual products for which they provide monitoring.

EMS provides a consistent GUI for the discovery and configuration of resources that can be monitored. Using EMS, you can define conditions that indicate when notification events should be sent, which can be at periodic intervals, when a component's state changes, or when a threshold condition is met. EMS also enables you to configure where events should be sent. You can configure EMS to send events to OpenView IT/O, directly to any SNMP-capable management station, to a network application listening on a TCP or UDP port, to an e-mail address, or locally to the console, system log file, or a regular log file. Furthermore, you can configure MC/ServiceGuard to make packages dependent on these EMS resources.

EMS monitors provide help primarily with fault and resource management. Performance monitoring generally requires more sophisticated tools. Some system fault and resource monitoring capabilities are provided by the EMS HA Monitors product, discussed in the next section. Other EMS monitors allow you to detect when you are getting low on system resources, such as file descriptors, shared memory, and system semaphores.

Templates for formatting EMS SNMP traps into various enterprise management platform Event Browsers, including OpenView, CA Unicenter, and other freely available EMS tools, are available to download from the Internet at http://www.software.hp.com, under the High Availability Software product category. A developer's kit is also available so that customers and system management software providers can integrate their own EMS monitors. EMS manuals are available at http://docs.hp.com/unix/ha.

EMS High Availability Monitors

The HA Monitors product contains several EMS monitors for monitoring filesystem space, network interface status, disk status, and MC/ServiceGuard cluster status. HA Monitors also detects changes in the number of users and jobs. This product has been extended to include database monitoring capabilities as well.

Available filesystem space can be monitored for any mounted filesystem. The operational status is monitored for each configured network device. For disks, you can monitor physical volume status, logical volume status, the number of mirrored copies, and summary information.

The MC/ServiceGuard cluster monitor, included with HA Monitors, reports on cluster events, such as the failure of a cluster node, and provides monitoring that is similar to the events reported in ClusterView. The ClusterView product provides more complete monitoring of MC/ServiceGuard clusters, but it requires the purchase of HP OpenView. Here are the resources monitored by the cluster monitor:

- Cluster status
- Node status
- Package status
- Service status

Monitoring node status using EMS can be done to provide notification when MC/ServiceGuard detects problems with the system. Whereas MC/ServiceGuard's job is to detect a system failure and move the configured application package(s) to an alternate system, the EMS cluster monitor's job is to notify you of such an event.

EMS Hardware Monitors

The EMS Hardware Monitors provide the ability to detect and report problems with system hardware resources, including system memory, tape devices such as SCSI, Digital Linear Tape (DLT), and Digital Data Storage (DDS), tape libraries, and autoloaders. These monitors detect device errors, component failures, page deallocation errors, and other faults. They poll the hardware at regular intervals and most notify of hardware errors in real time. These monitors are delivered with HP-UX Online Diagnostics, which are freely available for HP-UX. The EMS Hardware Monitors provide monitoring for the following system components and Hewlett-Packard products:

- System memory
- SCSI tape devices

- DDS-2 Autoloader (A3400A)
- DDS-3 Autoloader (A3716A)
- DLT 4000 4/48 Library; HP-UX; Differential SCSI (A3544A)
- DLT 4000 2/48 Library; HP-UX; Differential SCSI (A3545A)
- DLT 4000 2/28 Library; HP-UX; Differential SCSI (A3546A)
- DLT 4000 & 7000; 2/28; Drives Differential; Robotics SE/Diff (A4850A)
- DLT 4000 & 7000; 15 slot; Deskside/Rack; Differential (A4851A)
- DLT 4000 & 7000; 4/48; Drives Differential; Robotics SE/Diff (A4855A)
- DLT 4000 & 7000; 588 slot; Drives Diff; Robotics SE (A4845A)
- DLT 4000 & 7000; 100 slot; Drives Diff; Robotics SE (A4846A)
- DLT 4000 & 7000; 30 slot; Differential (A4853A) Channel Adapters

These EMS Hardware Monitors are designed to provide consistency in the configuration interface, event detection, and message formats that provide a detailed description of a problem and a recommended recovery action.

The EMS Hardware Monitors can report low-level device errors that are encountered during an I/O session with a device. They detect and report component and Field Replaceable Unit (FRU) failures, including fan and power supply problems. Protocol errors are also detected.

For monitoring tape devices, events include problems reading or writing data, bad tapes, wrong tapes, temperature problems, tape loader errors, tape changer problems, and incorrect firmware. For monitoring system memory, the monitor checks the page deallocation table and reports an event when the table is 60, 90, or 100 percent full. This indicates that a new memory SIMM (Single In-line Memory Module) should be added to replace a failed memory chip. These threshold values are configurable.

The monitor assigns hardware events severity levels, which reflect the potential impact of an event on system operation. Table 4-3 provides a description of each severity level.

EMS Hardware Monitor configuration is done by using the Hardware Monitoring Request Manager. Notification conditions can be configured in a consistent way for all supported hardware resources on the system. As hardware is added to the system, monitoring can be enabled automatically. Figure 4-3 shows an example of using the Hardware Monitoring Request Manager to send SNMP traps of all critical and serious tape and memory events. To configure with MC/ServiceGuard, you need to use the MC/ServiceGuard configuration interface.

The EMS Hardware Monitors provide fault information only. No performance-related events are included.

When an EMS Hardware Monitor detects an event, a notification message is sent to the designated target locations. The message contains a full description, including the system on which the event occurred, the date and time when the event was detected, the hardware device on which the event occurred, a description of the problem, the probable cause, and recommended action. The event message contains detailed information, including product/device identification information, I/O log event information, raw hardware status, SCSI status, and more.

Table 4-3   Description of Hardware Event Severity

Severity	Description
Critical	An event that will or has already caused data loss, system downtime, or other loss of service. Immediate action is required to correct the problem. System operation will be impacted and normal use of the hardware should not continue until the problem is corrected. If configured with MC/ServiceGuard, the package will experience failover.
Serious	An event that may cause data loss, system downtime, or other loss of service if left uncorrected. The problem should be repaired as soon as possible. System operation and normal use of the hardware may be impacted. If configured with MC/ServiceGuard, the package will experience failover.
Major Warning	An event that could escalate to a more serious condition if not corrected. The problem should be repaired at a convenient time. System operation should not be impacted and normal use of the hardware can continue. If configured with MC/ServiceGuard, the package will not experience failover.
Minor Warning	An event that will not likely escalate to a more serious condition if left uncorrected. The problem can be repaired at a convenient time. System operation will not be interrupted and normal use of the hardware can continue. If configured with MC/ServiceGuard, the package will not experience failover.
Information	An event that occurs as part of the normal operation of the hardware. No action is required. If configured with MC/ServiceGuard, the package will not experience failover.

Most EMS Hardware Monitors are "stateless." In other words, events of the designated severity are forwarded as soon as they are detected; no aspect of history or correlation with other data is involved, except that the monitor limits repeated messages by using a repeat frequency. Determining the current status of a device is difficult, because messages are sent only when an event occurs.

To monitor for hardware device state changes, you can use a Peripheral Status Monitor (PSM), which maintains the state of monitored hardware devices and reports state changes. The PSM gathers events from the other EMS Hardware Monitors, but does not send its own notification unless a state change has occurred. By default, critical or serious events cause the PSM to change a device's status to Down.

For example, critical tape events from a tape monitor would cause the PSM to change the device's status to Down. The PSM would then send a single "Tape device status = Down" event if the administrator had requested to be notified of such an event. This may be the only message visible to the administrator. Additional disk failure messages would not be forwarded because they are not the result of a status change (in other words, the status remains Down). This reduces the number of events that need to be processed by the user. The last event received should reflect the current device status.

Figure 4-3 Configuring EMS Hardware Monitors using the Hardware Monitoring Request Manager.

```
 ─                                    hpterm                                  ·  ⌐

   =============================================================================
   ====================== Add Monitoring Request    =====================
   =============================================================================

   Start of edit configuration:

   A monitoring request consists of:
    - A list of monitors to which it applies
    - A severity range (A relational expression and a severity.  For example,
      < "MAJOR WARNING" means events with severity "INFORMATION" and
      "MINOR WARNING")
    - A notification mechanism.
   Please answer the following questions to specify a monitoring request.

   Monitors to which this configuration can apply:
     1) /storage/events/disk_arrays/AutoRAID
     2) /storage/events/disks/default
     3) /adapters/events/FC_adapter
     4) /connectivity/events/hubs/FC_hub
     5) /connectivity/events/multiplexors/FC_SCSI_mux
     6) /system/events/memory
     7) /storage/events/enclosures/ses_enclosure
     8) /storage/events/tapes/SCSI_tape
     9) /storage/events/disk_arrays/FW_SCSI
    10) /storage/events/disk_arrays/High_Availability
     Enter monitor numbers separated by commas
         {or (A)ll monitors, (Q)uit, (H)elp} [a] 6,8

   Criteria Thresholds:
     1) INFORMATION    2) MINOR WARNING    3) MAJOR WARNING
     4) SERIOUS        5) CRITICAL
     Enter selection {or (Q)uit,(H)elp} [4] 4

   Criteria Operator:
     1) <      2) <=      3) >      4) >=      5) =      6) !=
     Enter selection {or (Q)uit,(H)elp} [4] 4

   Notification Method:
     1) UDP       2) TCP       3) SNMP      4) TEXTLOG
     5) SYSLOG    6) EMAIL     7) CONSOLE   8) OPC
     Enter selection {or (Q)uit,(H)elp} [6] 3

   New entry:
         Send events generated by monitors
           /system/events/memory
           /storage/events/tapes/SCSI_tape
         with severity >= SERIOUS to SNMP

     Are you sure you want to keep these changes?
        {(Y)es,(N)o,(H)elp} [n] y █
```

Most monitors cannot automatically detect when a device has been fixed. When a problem is solved, the set_fixed command must be used manually to alert the PSM to reset the device status to Up.

When using an enterprise management tool, such as IT/O, which receives messages from multiple systems, you should use the PSM to reduce information overload. However, make sure that the stateless events are also configured to go somewhere (such as the system log file), because they provide valuable diagnostic information when a component has failed.

Monitoring hardware device status is done through the EMS Configuration GUI.

You can learn more about Hewlett-Packard's diagnostic tools on its Web site at http://docs.hp .com/hpux/systems/.

Enterprise SyMON

Sun's Enterprise SyMON is a system management platform for monitoring and managing the Sun systems in your enterprise. Enterprise SyMON provides administrators the capability to manage all of their Sun systems remotely from a common interface. Enterprise SyMON can automatically discover the Sun systems in the environment. Intelligent SyMON agents run on each system, to provide monitoring and remote management capabilities.

The console layer of Enterprise SyMON provides a visual representation of all managed objects. The console layer provides several views of the enterprise, including logical views and topological views. The Logical View window provides a hierarchical representation of the systems being managed. Indicators are used on system icons to indicate the alarm status of the system. As shown in Figure 4-4, you can see the status of the systems in the payroll domain. Badges on each system icon indicate the alarms for the node. The Domain Status Summary at the top of the window shows how many alarms are outstanding in each category. Figure 4-4 shows no down alarms, two critical alarms, one alert, one caution, and no disabled. So, Comptroller Workstation has a caution-level alarm outstanding.

When a critical event occurs, such as a hardware component failure, it is indicated in the Logical View window. As the event occurs, the failed hardware component is also highlighted in the Physical View window. You can use this photo-like view of the system to detect and isolate failed or failing components. As shown in Figure 4-5, the Physical View indicates that board 3 is disconnected, and highlights the back panel of the server to show you where the board is.

Enterprise SyMON provides event and alarm management. Alarms and actions can be configured so that events are sent via SNMP traps to the SyMON console when certain conditions or thresholds are met. Event-based actions and notifications, such as e-mail, can also be configured. Recovery actions can be associated with an event. Additional events can be defined and generated by placing rules written in the TCL scripting language in a special directory. SyMON provides features for correlating events and filtering based on priority and severity.

SyMON provides intelligent agents, which run on the systems being monitored. The agents are configured with intelligence to detect abnormal conditions, to generate alarms based on default or customized thresholds, and to perform actions automatically, based on certain predefined events.

Figure 4-4   Viewing the status of systems in the payroll domain from the SyMON console.

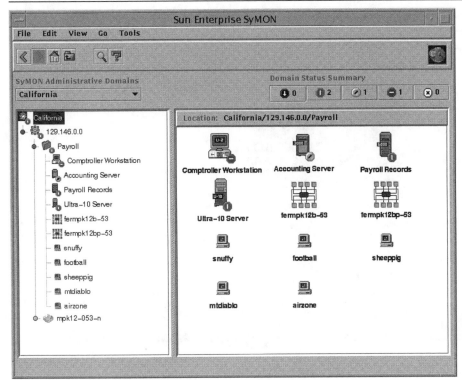

The agent architecture consists of several modules. For example, the Config-Reader module is responsible for monitoring all hardware components. The agents are extensible such that new modules can be dynamically loaded from the console without disrupting service. If you don't need certain modules, you can save resources by unloading them.

A browser window, shown in Figure 4-6, shows the different statistics that can be monitored on the left panel. The panel in the right shows current System Load Statistics. Many of the resources available to be monitored are mentioned in this section.

The Hardware Config-Reader module provides configuration management by tracking the hardware and firmware configured on the system, down to the serial number. This information is used to create logical and physical views. The SyMON agent provides hardware fault monitoring, as well as predictive failure analysis for memory and disks. The Config-Reader module monitors hardware and alerts you at the console when a problem exists. If it is a predicted memory failure, you can configure actions to do a dynamic reconfiguration to remove the bad memory. The Config-Reader reports on many hardware faults, including temperature problems and power supply status. It monitors CPU and memory board status, controllers, I/O devices, and tape devices.

Figure 4-5   Using the SyMON Physical View to identify a failed hardware component.

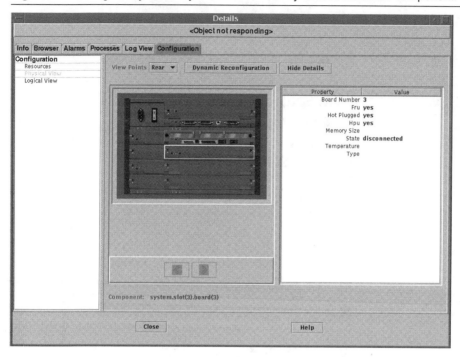

For the operating system, the agent includes modules to monitor CPU utilization, memory usage, directory size, file size and file modification time, MIB-II objects, NFS activity, inode usage, swap statistics, filesystem usage, and disk rates and service times. A file-scanning module also is available that can be used to check log files, such as the system log, for errors or specific patterns.

The Health Monitor uses rules based mostly on performance metrics to correlate the metrics to detect when alarm conditions exist. It sends an alarm when alarm conditions occur, along with suggested steps on how to improve system performance. The Health Monitor has rules to detect swap space conditions, kernel contention, CPU, disk, or memory bottlenecks, printer problems, and filesystem conditions.

SyMON agents provide active management, including active configuration management controls for dynamic reconfiguration, system domain management, and an "alternate pathing" feature for redirecting disk I/O in the event of a controller failure. With this capability, administrators can take care of repairs, such as replacing a failed memory board, without a service interruption.

Sun Enterprise Servers Models E3000 through UE10000, with Solaris 2.6 or greater, support dynamic reconfiguration. This feature enables you to replace boards online without taking down the system. You can have backup boards on standby and available for immediate use. Or, if a CPU or memory board fails, you can unconfigure and disconnect the failed board online via SyMON, agent, and you can modify templates and message conditions so that an operator is paged der certain conditions.

Many other tools plug in to IT/O to provide additional monitoring and management capa-lities. IT/O is useful when an operator needs to manage numerous systems consistently. Tem-lates can be modified and then downloaded to a set of systems, enabling multiple systems to be monitored identically. This way, monitoring can be set up in a consistent way for all systems.

IT/O has four main windows:

- **Node Bank:** Displays the systems managed by an operator as icons, and enables them to be organized into node groups.
- **Message Groups:** Displays logical message groups, such as Performance, Oracle, and backup. The message groups serve as one way to organize messages in the Message Browser window.
- **Message Browser:** Shows the events that have been received by the management server.
- **Application Desktop:** Provides access to commonly used diagnostic and administrative applications.

You can see an example of the Node Bank window in Figure 4-7. In this window, the node color reflects the color of the most critical event that has been received but not yet acknowledged.

The Message Browser can filter out messages from systems that you don't care about. If you are responsible for only a specific system function, such as performance, you can configure the Message Browser to show only those messages from a specific message group.

The IT/O Application Bank provides some other tools to monitor your system, and it also provides remote access tools to diagnose problems further. From the Application Bank, you can

Figure 4-7 IT/O Node Bank window showing node status.

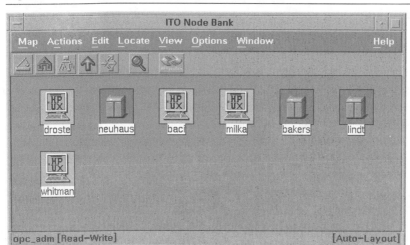

Figure 4-6 The SyMON Browser showing the various system resources

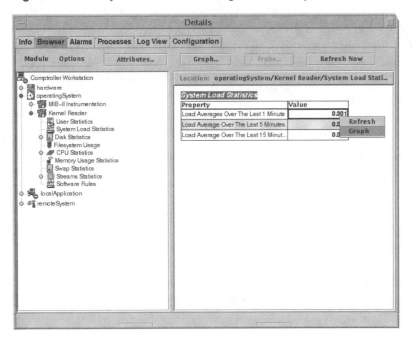

replace the board, and then connect and configure the new board, making the resource available to the system without a reboot. This feature is also available for hot-pluggable disk devices.

As previously described, SyMON can help you with configuration, fault, and resource monitoring on your system. However, SyMON is available only for monitoring Sun systems.

OpenView IT/Operations

IT/Operations (IT/O) is an OpenView application providing central operations and problem management. NNM is included as part of the IT/O product. IT/O uses intelligent agents that run on each managed system to collect management information, messages, and alerts, and send the information to a centralized console. After receiving events, IT/O can initiate automatic corrective actions. When an operator reads an individual message, guidance is given and actions may be suggested for further problem resolution or recovery.

IT/O comes with predefined monitors and templates, including monitors for e-mail, CPU utilization, and swap utilization, among other things. Using log file templates allows you to monitor system log files for system errors, switch user events, logins, logouts, and kernel messages.

IT/O enables you to define and customize your own monitors and templates so that you can monitor arbitrary MIB variables, such as the system uptime MIB variable mentioned earlier in this chapter. IT/O periodically queries the MIB object to determine whether or not a message should be generated. You can write a program or script that can be periodically invoked by an bring up a telnet window or, for HP-UX systems, run SAM on the system having problems. You can run PerfView or GlancePlus (discussed later in this chapter), check the print status, or check the CPU load on any UNIX system.

As previously described, IT/O provides assistance with multiple aspects of system monitoring, especially faults, and resource and performance management. IT/O can also help with security monitoring, with its predefined template for monitoring root login attempts.

GlancePlus Pak 2000

Hewlett-Packard also includes a preconfigured, single-system version of IT/O with its Glance-Plus Pak 2000 product. In addition to displaying performance data, the product includes a Java-based GUI that presents diagnostic applications and an Event Browser. The product enables you to connect to information from multiple systems, as long as you connect to one system at a time.

GlancePlus Pak 2000 includes the intelligent agent technology from its enterprise version, enabling it to collect events from a variety of sources and execute automated actions. After events are received in the Event Browser, an operator can trigger some predefined recovery actions.

Security Monitoring

The whole area of security is a huge subject. Entire books are dedicated to security alone. Security is usually broken down into two categories: network security and host-based security. This section focuses on host-based (or system) security, so that you can monitor and detect activities that could compromise system, application, or data availability. Host-based security intrusions usually are the most problematic. As a system administrator, you should monitor the system for activities that would prevent the system from doing what it is intended to do.

Security Overview

The level of security needed for your system depends on what you are trying to protect. Both the US government and European Information Technology Security Evaluation Criteria (ITSEC) have defined sets of security levels. The most common level is C2, which is the de facto standard for secure UNIX systems. Level B1 security, which is more secure than C2, is often required in government, military, and commercial applications. HP-UX, for example, operates in two modes of security: standard mode, which has no security, and trusted mode, which is C2-level compliant. Each level of security has different requirements.

Regardless of the level of security you are trying to provide in your environment, several categories for system security apply to all levels. The requirements in each category are more restrictive as you increase the security level. These categories are authentication, authorization, access control, data security, and physical security.

Before describing each of these categories, you need to know that implementing a host-based security plan will include defining policies for preventing intrusions and for monitoring to detect intrusions. Password policies are an example of the many policies that should be defined and enforced to try to prevent intrusions. When monitoring to detect intrusions, detection systems need to be told what to monitor.

After you implement intrusion-prevention policies, you need to put security monitoring and intrusion-detection monitors in place. You want these monitors to tell you when an intrusion was attempted, is occurring, or has occurred. The following are the system security categories that apply to all security levels, along with a description of what can be done to prevent and detect intrusions:

- **Authentication:** Usually done to verify a user's ID prior to allowing access to a system or resource. Authentication is usually accomplished with a password, which serves as proof that a user is who they claim to be. Password length and complexity restrictions, as well as password lifetime limits, are some of the devices that can be used to make getting past authentication checks more difficult for unauthorized users. More secure measures include hiding the password file, which contains encrypted passwords.
- **Authorization:** The process of granting privileges to individual users. UNIX has two main classes of users. *Root users* (or superusers) have authorization to do almost anything on a system, including administer the system, perform backups, and bypass security controls. *Regular users* have ordinary access to programs and data. Authorization can be controlled by using time-based authorization, whereby users are restricted to certain hours of the day. Fine-grained authorization allows root access to be restricted to more narrow tasks, giving users only as much power as they need to accomplish their tasks. This provides more control over system security. HP-UX has a special version of SAM, called restricted SAM, which allows restricted use by authorized users, allowing you to delegate limited authority. Monitoring for failed login attempts and super-user logins is important, to see whether anyone is gaining or attempting to gain unauthorized access to the system. IT/O is one product that provides this capability.
- **Access control policies:** Used to define which users have access to various system resources, including files, programs, and printers. Access control is generally handled through UNIX file permissions, which define read, write, and execute permissions by user, group, and everyone. Access Control Lists (ACLs) are also used to grant file access to users on a list. Or, ACLs can be used to list those users who don't have access rights to a file. You can check a file's access rights by using the ls command. You may want to monitor access rights for changes that allow other users to access these restricted files.
- **Data security:** Helps you to protect critical data. This includes backups, which can protect against accidental data loss, and data encryption, which can protect the privacy of information.
- **Physical security:** Covers the physical protection of system resources against deliberate or accidental threats. This includes ensuring against even simple threats, such as someone tripping on an exposed power cord.

Security Monitoring Tools

Auditing is a way to log security-related events on a per-user basis. It can be set up to monitor system calls, specific users, password policies, logins, superuser logins, failed login attempts, and so forth. Because auditing incurs lots of system overhead, you should try to limit it to the most critical security-related events. On HP-UX, auditing is available only in trusted mode. Auditing can be enabled on HP-UX using SAM. Although the system itself provides the library routines for auditing, data reduction and analysis tools are useful for extracting relevant information from audit logs.

Some of the common tools for looking at audit logs are:

- **OmniGuard/ITA (Axent Technologies):** Used to detect intruders and abuse. It uses data from log files and listens for SNMP traps to feed into its rules engine when detecting intruders. It can also monitor file-level accesses.
- **Stalker (Haystack Labs):** Analyzes and compares audit logs to its database, to detect system misuse, attacks, and known system vulnerabilities. It can collect and store audit logs from multiple UNIX systems at a centralized server.

MEMCO Software provides SeOS Access Control, which provides more granular root capabilities. Narrow capabilities can be granted to users to perform specific tasks. This means that you don't need to grant a user full root capabilities, which can be dangerous, just to perform system backups, for example.

You can make some simple checks to help protect your system. Check the /etc/hosts.equiv and /.rhosts files to ensure that the remote host systems listed are authorized to access the system. Also, the optional file /var/adm/inetd.sec can be used to explicitly deny or allow access to specific network services, so you should verify that this file is configured correctly.

Using Diagnostic Tools

Various support tools monitor errors and faults, configuration information, and troubleshooting for hardware components, including the CPU, system memory, and tape devices. Some of these support tools also monitor software configurations, to track changes.

Support Tool Manager

HP's Support Tool Manager (STM) provides access to a set of tools for verifying and troubleshooting HP-UX system hardware. These online diagnostic tools provide the ability to determine device status, get configuration information, and diagnose hardware problems. These tools are available by using a GUI or through commands, and have the flexibility to be invoked automatically at periodic intervals.

STM discovers the hardware devices on a system and can diagnose memory errors, Low-Priority Machine Check (LPMC) errors, I/O driver errors, Logical Volume Manager (LVM) errors, and over-temperature events. Memory errors include single-bit errors and page deallocation events.

STM includes the Automatic Configuration Mapper, shown in Figure 4-8, which gives a graphical view of your hardware configuration using color-coded icons, showing device status as well as logical relationships, such as the peripherals connected to an I/O card. Each icon on the map represents a hardware device. These icons display the device type, device identifier, device path, last active tool, and test status (from last active tool). You can launch other STM tools from this view as well.

The Information tool provides product identifier information, product description, hardware path, vendor name, firmware revision, and error log statistics, including read errors, which

Figure 4-8   STM Configuration Mapper showing the latest status of the CPU and memory.

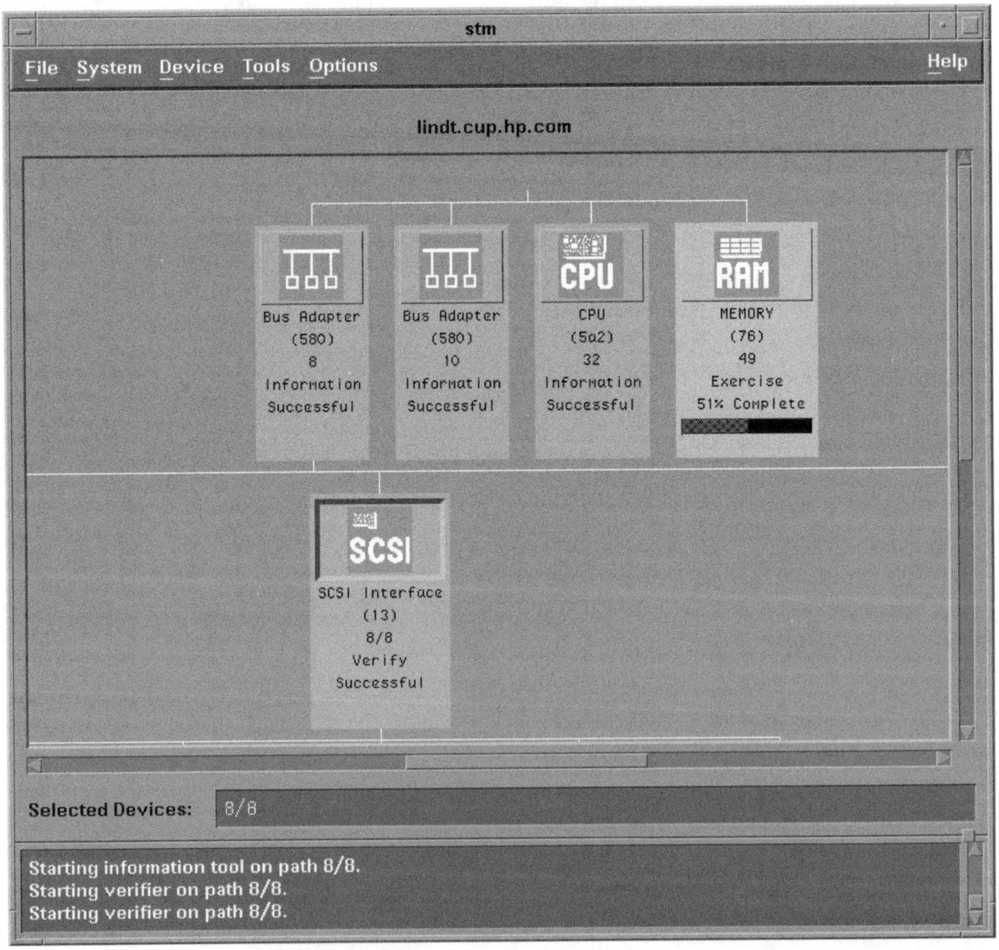

can be used to trend and anticipate problems. This tool also checks onboard log information, and can be used to track configuration changes.

Several other tools under STM perform varying levels of testing to stress a device or determine and diagnose problems:

- **Verifier tool:** Can be invoked on a particular device to verify quickly that it is connected and functioning properly.
- **Exerciser tool:** Stresses a device, to help reproduce and troubleshoot intermittent problems by stressing the hardware to the maximum point expected in a customer environment.
- **Diagnose tools:** Perform a complete test of the hardware, to help isolate failures down to the component or FRU level.
- **Expert tools:** Are sophisticated troubleshooting tools for expert users.
- **Logtool tool:** Helps you to format, filter, and extract error information from raw data contained in system logs. You can monitor recoverable errors detected by the computer, such as I/O device errors. This data can be used to troubleshoot and trend historical information, so that you can fix failures before they become critical. The errors that you see here are automatically forwarded to the EMS Hardware Monitors, which generate an event if an error is serious enough.
- **Firmware Update tools:** Provide a customer-usable way to update the firmware on hardware devices.

STM enables an operator to run a module on several devices simultaneously. In addition, the operator can start diagnostic tests running on more than one system from within the user interface.

STM provides both configuration and fault monitoring capabilities for the system. STM tools detect the same errors as the EMS Hardware Monitors, but the EMS Hardware Monitors report them in real time. After getting an EMS event, you can run STM to further diagnose a problem.

STM is used to diagnose local or remote systems. It is available on HP-UX releases 10.01 and later. STM replaces the Sherlock diagnostics. The software (product number is B4708AA) is being distributed on the HP-UX Diagnostic/IPR Media.

HP Predictive Support

HP Predictive Support detects and predicts system-related faults. When problem conditions are detected, notification is sent to the HP Response Center. This level of care is meant for customers with special support contracts with Hewlett-Packard. The Predictive Support software proactively monitors the system and automatically reports information back to the HP Response Center via modem access. Because the HP Response Center is available 24 hours a day, 7 days a week, this procedure can lead to a quick response to problems.

The Predictive Support software focuses on system event information for memory and I/O devices. Error logs are analyzed daily, with potential problems diagnosed. By proactively warning of potential problems, scheduled maintenance can replace the unplanned downtime associated with a failed component.

Predictive Support uses a set of rules on a managed node to determine when events should be sent to the HP Response Center. These conditions can be updated periodically by downloading new rules from HP. Event correlation ensures that duplicate messages are suppressed and that the Response Center is not repeatedly warned of the same root problem.

Predictive Support analyzes on-board logs, system logs, and memory logs. The software can automatically dial the HP Response Center to transmit error data and logs, or the system administrator can initiate modem transmission. Similarly, Predictive Support software updates, to include new rules for generating predictive events, can be triggered automatically or controlled by the administrator. Configuration and administration is controlled through a menu-driven interface.

System logs are scanned for I/O errors and LPMCs. Logged data is analyzed for trends associated with specific disk or tape devices, such as correctable errors. LPMC records are analyzed for internal cache errors. Memory logs are also scanned to look for error rates exceeding specified thresholds.

The Response Center determines where a failed device is located, its model number, its manufacturer, and its serial number, so that repairs can be made. This information is sent in the failure notification messages.

HP Predictive Support does not help with other areas of system monitoring, such as resource and performance management. Also, the software runs only on HP-UX systems.

HA Observatory

HA Observatory is a suite of tools used to detect and quickly diagnose system problems. The products include the Configuration Tracker, which keeps track of the server's software configuration, Network Node Manager, and HP Predictive Support. A support system and network router are also maintained at the customer site.

HA Observatory relies on HP Predictive Support to report hardware failures. In addition, configuration information collected by the Configuration Tracker is available. The Configuration Tracker generates and maintains a snapshot of the configuration so that it can detect software configuration changes.

HA Observatory uses a secure network link to HP's High Availability Support Center from a special system at the customer site. This support system, an HP 9000 Series 700 workstation, collects system configuration information from key servers and can be used to view network status and topology information. Hardware failure notifications and configuration information can be sent to HP. When permitted by the customer, HP support engineers can access the customer servers over the secure link to gather additional information.

HA Observatory is supported only on HP-UX systems and is available only to customers with BCS and CCS support contracts.

Monitoring System Peripherals

When monitoring your UNIX server, you should not forget about the system peripherals, such as disk, tape, and printer devices.

Disks

Disk devices store your corporate data, so ensuring their correct operation is critical. Disk monitoring should be included as part of any effort to monitor a system. Chapter 5 is dedicated to covering the tools for monitoring disk devices because of the importance and complexity of the subject.

Tapes

By checking for tape hardware failures periodically, problems can be found before the tape drive is needed. For example, early detection and repair can result in the evening backup application running without delays.

You should use hardware monitors, such as the EMS Hardware Monitors, to ensure that your tape drives are healthy, so that backups may occur as scheduled. As mentioned earlier, a variety of tape-related errors can be detected, such as failed I/O operations to the tape, tape loader errors, and tape changer errors.

Printers

This chapter discussed earlier how you can use MIB instrumentation to look for important system information. A Printer MIB specification typically is supported by modern network printer devices. The Printer MIB stores the status of the printer (online, offline, and so forth), as well as information about printer subcomponents, such as an empty printer tray. A tool such as IT/O can be used to enable monitoring of individual fields in the MIB, such as printer status.

Using the lpstat command, you can check the status of jobs in the print queue and verify that the print scheduler is running. Using lpstat with no options shows you information for all the printers connected to the system.

Some printer management software is also available. One example is HP JetAdmin software, which can be used to manage printers and monitor the status of jobs printing remotely. This host-based application provides real-time printer and job status information, as well as status updates, remote diagnostics and troubleshooting, an optional status log, and a remote front panel. The utilities are accessible through a graphical interface. Web JetAdmin software adds additional capabilities, such as the ability to view customized maps that show printer locations and status information from a Web browser.

Web JetAdmin 4 is an HP software application that is used to monitor all peripheral devices on the network from a Web browser. Maintenance and troubleshooting can be done on any MIB-compliant printer device, including ScanJet 5 scanners and HP SureStore CD-ROMs.

Collecting System Performance Data

Users call their IT department when they have delays in accessing data or applications. Good tools are needed to help an operator pinpoint the source of the problem. This section covers some of the interesting performance and resource-utilization metrics, and the tools available to collect data about these metrics.

A wide range of conditions may result in resource and performance problems. Running out of available memory may be caused by a failure of a memory component or by a memory leak in an application. A sudden rise in CPU utilization could be an indication of processor failure or the introduction on the system of a CPU-intensive application. Analysis is needed to determine whether resource problems can be fixed with a configuration change, hardware repair, or other techniques.

Many important system resources have configured limits. The following system resource metrics are important to monitor:

- Number of named pipes
- Number of messages and message queues
- Number of system semaphores
- Amount of shared memory
- Number of open files
- Number of processes

Earlier, this chapter discussed some of the tools that can be used to check system resource usage. The sar and sysdef commands can compare current usage to configured limits. An EMS monitor is available to detect thresholds being exceeded for the following resources:

- Callout table
- Process table
- File descriptor table
- File lock table
- Shared memory
- System semaphores
- Message queues and message segments

The performance tools discussed in this section can also detect resource usage problems.

Some system performance monitoring is available from the SAM Performance Monitors, with which an administrator can obtain information on system, disk, and virtual memory activity, for example. Text-based information is displayed in a Motif window when one of the desired metrics is selected.

Having historical information is important, to understand how the system performance has varied over time. Knowing how your system behaves under normal conditions helps when trying to troubleshoot system performance problems. Note that the performance tools themselves impact the performance of the system, so you need to find a tool with low overhead.

This section describes some common tools for measuring and monitoring system performance. Here are some of the key metrics discussed in this section:

- **Buffer cache queue length:** Refers to the number of processes blocked that are waiting for updates to the buffer cache. If this value is high, it could be an indication of a memory bottleneck.
- **Context switches:** How often processes are being swapped out of the run queue.
- **CPU utilization:** Expressed as a percentage of time spent in various execution states. Low utilization indicates that the CPU spent the majority of its time in the idle state.
- **CPU run queue length:** The average number of processes in the run state waiting to be scheduled.
- **Memory utilization:** Usually expressed as a ratio of the amount of memory in use versus the total memory available.
- **Paging:** Refers to the transfer of data between virtual memory (disks) and physical memory.
- **Swapping:** Refers to the transfer of data between physical memory and a special virtual memory area reserved for swapping.

Performance tools, such as BMC PATROL and MeasureWare, don't always provide the same set of metrics on all platforms. For simplicity, this section focuses on the Sun Solaris and HP-UX platforms only. Also, these products are continually being enhanced, so the actual metrics available for use in your environment may not precisely match the information presented in this section.

MeasureWare

HP MeasureWare Agent is a Hewlett-Packard product that collects and logs resource and performance metrics. MeasureWare agents run and collect data on the individual server systems being monitored. agents exist for many platforms and operating systems, including HP-UX, Solaris, and AIX.

The MeasureWare agents collect data, summarize it, timestamp it, log it, and send alarms when appropriate. The agents collect and report on a wide variety of system resources, performance metrics, and user-defined data. The information can then be exported to spreadsheets or to performance analysis programs, such as PerfView. The data can be used by these programs to generate alarms to warn of potential performance problems. By using historical data, trends can be discovered. This can help address resource issues before they affect system performance.

MeasureWare agents collect data at three different levels: global system metrics, application, and process metrics. Global and application data is summarized at five-minute intervals, whereas process data is summarized at one-minute intervals. Important applications can be defined by an administrator by listing the processes that make up an application in a configuration file.

Table 4-4 Categories of MeasureWare Agent Information

Category	Metric Type
System	CPU, disk, networking, memory, process queue depths, user/process information, and summary information
Application	CPU, disk, memory, process count, average process wait states, and summary information
Process	CPU, disk, memory, average process wait states, overall process lifetime, and summary information
Transaction	Transaction count, average response time, distribution of response time metrics, and aborted transactions

The basic categories of MeasureWare data are listed in Table 4-4. Also included are optional modules for database and networking support. MeasureWare agents also collect data provided through the DSI interface.

The following lists the global system metrics that are available from MeasureWare on HP-UX and Sun Solaris. Additional metrics provided by MeasureWare are covered in other chapters.

- CPU use during interval
- Number and rate of physical disk inputs/outputs
- Maximum percent full of all disk file sets
- System CPU use during interval
- User CPU use during interval
- CPU use at nice priorities
- CPU idle time during interval
- Rate of system procedure calls during interval
- Main memory use
- Swap space use on disk
- Number and rate of memory page faults during interval
- Number of process swaps during interval
- Percentage of virtual memory currently in active use
- Number of processes in run queue during interval
- Number of processes waiting for a disk during interval
- Number of processes waiting for memory during interval
- Number of processes currently in sleep state during interval
- Number of processes waiting for other reasons during interval
- Number of user sessions during interval
- Number of processes alive during interval
- Number of processes active during interval
- Number of processes started during interval

- Number of processes completed during interval
- Average runtime of completing process during interval
- Operating system version
- Number of processors in the system
- Number of disk devices and their device IDs
- Main memory size
- Swapping space allocated
- Disk I/O information (see Chapter 5)
- Networking statistics (see Chapter 6)

Note that, in addition to performance metrics, MeasureWare provides useful configuration information, such as number of processors and the number of disk devices.

The following additional global system metrics are available on HP-UX:

- CPU use at real-time priorities
- CPU use for context switching during interval
- CPU use for interrupt handling during interval
- Number of processes waiting for interprocess communications during interval
- Number of processes waiting on network transfers during interval
- Number and rate of terminal transactions during interval
- Average terminal transaction "think" time
- Average terminal transaction first response time
- Average terminal response to prompt time
- Distribution of transaction first response times
- Distribution of transaction response to prompt times

You can have alarms sent based on conditions that involve a combination of metrics. For example, a CPU bottleneck alarm can be based on the CPU use and CPU run queue length.

MeasureWare agents provide these alarms to PerfView for analysis, and to the IT/O management console. SNMP traps can also be sent at the time a threshold condition is met. Automated actions can be taken, or the operator can choose to take a suggested action.

MeasureWare's extract command can be used to export data to other tools, such as spreadsheet programs. Additionally, Application Resource Measurement (ARM) APIs (described in detail in Chapter 7) can be used to instrument applications so that response times can be measured. The application response time information can be passed along to MeasureWare agents for analysis.

Although MeasureWare provides extensive performance and resource information, it provides limited configuration information and no data about system faults. For further information, visit the HP Resource and Performance Management Web site at http://www.openview.hp.com /solutions/application/.

GlancePlus

GlancePlus is a real-time, graphical performance monitoring tool from Hewlett-Packard. It is used to monitor the performance and system resource utilization of a single system. Both Motif-based and character-based interfaces are available. The product can be used on HP-UX, Sun Solaris, and many other operating systems.

GlancePlus collects information similar to the information collected by MeasureWare, and samples data more frequently than MeasureWare. GlancePlus can be used to graphically view the following:

- Current CPU, memory, swap, and disk activity and utilization (see Figure 4-9)
- Application and process information
- Transaction information, if the MeasureWare Agent is installed and active
- Alarm information, color-coded to reflect severity
- CPU utilization, with per-processor information available for multiprocessor systems
- Memory utilization, split among cache, user, and system memory
- Disk utilization, with the I/O paths of the top disk users indicated
- I/O activity, by filesystem or logical volume

GlancePlus is also capable of setting and receiving performance-related alarms. Customizable rules determine when a system performance problem should be sent as an alarm. The rules are managed by the GlancePlus Adviser. The Adviser menu gives you the option to Edit

Figure 4-9   The GlancePlus main screen showing system utilization.

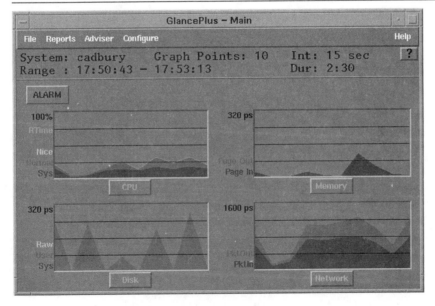

Listing 4-13   Defining alarms in GlancePlus.

```
alarm CPU_Bottleneck > 50 for 2 minutes
  start
    if CPU_Bottleneck > 90 then
      red alert "CPU Bottleneck probability= ", CPU_Bottleneck, "%"
    else
      yellow alert "CPU Bottleneck probability= ", CPU_Bottleneck, "%"
  repeat every 10 minutes
    if CPU_Bottleneck > 90 then
      red alert "CPU Bottleneck probability= ", CPU_Bottleneck, "%"
    else
      yellow alert "CPU Bottleneck probability= ", CPU_Bottleneck, "%"
  end
    reset alert "End of CPU Bottleneck Alert"
```

Adviser Syntax. When you select this option, all the alarm conditions are shown, and you can then modify them.

Alarms result in onscreen notification, with the color representing the criticality of the alarm. An alarm can also trigger a command or script to be executed automatically. Instead of sending an alarm, GlancePlus can print messages or notify you by executing a UNIX command, such as mailx, using its EXEC feature.

To configure events, you need to edit a configuration file. The GlancePlus Adviser syntax file (/var/opt/perf/adviser.syntax) contains symptom and alarm configuration. Additional syntax files can also be used. A condition for an alarm to be sent can be based on rules involving different symptoms. Listing 4-13 shows an example of how you can set up an alarm for CPU bottlenecks that is based on CPU utilization and the size of the run queue.

You can also execute scripts in command mode. To execute a script, type:

```
glance -adviser_only --syntax <script file name>
```

In this example, a yellow alert is sent to the GlancePlus Alarm screen if a CPU bottleneck is suspected. As a bottleneck becomes more likely, the alarm changes to red. You can define the threshold for when the alarm should be sent. The symptoms are re-evaluated at every time interval.

Here is a sampling of some of the useful system metrics that can be monitored with GlancePlus:

- CPU utilization
- CPU run queue length
- Number of processors
- Filesystem buffer cache queue length
- Disk utilization and queue length
- Physical memory capacity

- Amount of physical memory available
- Memory page fault rate
- Total swap space
- Amount of swap space available
- Filesystem I/O rates
- Amount of buffer cache available
- Available shared memory
- Available file table entries
- Available process table entries
- Most active processes
- Wait states
- System table resources
- Open file information

More than 600 metrics are accessible from GlancePlus. Some of these metrics are discussed in other chapters. The complete list of metrics can be found by using the online help facility. This information can also be found in the directory /opt/perf/paperdocs/gp/C.

GlancePlus allows filters to be used to reduce the amount of information shown. For example, you can set up a filter in the Process view to show only the more active system processes.

GlancePlus can also show short-term historical information. When selected, the alarm buttons, visible on the main GlancePlus screen, show a history of alarms that have occurred.

GlancePlus also shows Process Resource Manager behavior, if PRM is installed, and allows the PRM process group entitlements to be changed.

For further information, visit the HP Resource and Performance Management Web site at http://www.openview.hp.com/solutions/application/.

PerfView

PerfView is a graphical performance analysis tool from Hewlett-Packard. It is used to graphically display performance and system resource utilization for one system or multiple systems simultaneously, so that comparisons can be made. A variety of performance graphs can be displayed. The graphs are based on data collected over a period of time, unlike the real-time graphs of GlancePlus. This tool runs on HP-UX or NT systems and works with data collected by MeasureWare agents.

PerfView has the following three main components:

- **PerfView Monitor:** Provides the ability to receive alarms. A textual description of an alarm can be displayed. Alarms can be filtered by severity, type, or source system. Also, after an alarm is received, the alarm can be selected to display a graph of related metrics. An operator can monitor trends leading to failures and then take proactive actions to avoid problems. Graphs can be used for comparison between systems and to show a history of resource consumption. An internal database is maintained that keeps a history of alarm notification messages.

- **PerfView Analyzer:** Provides resource and performance analyses for disks and other resources. System metrics can be shown at three different levels: process, application (configured by the user as a set of processes), and global system information. It relies on data received from MeasureWare agents on managed nodes. Data can be analyzed from up to eight systems concurrently. All MeasureWare data sources are supported. PerfView Analyzer is required by both PerfView Monitor and PerfView Planner.

- **PerfView Planner:** Provides forecasting capability. Graphs can be extrapolated into the future. A variety of graphs (such as linear, exponential, s-curve, and smoothed) can be shown for forecasted data.

PerfView can be used to monitor critical system resources. Figure 4-10 shows the Perf-View Analyzer graphing memory utilization and paging rates. Other predefined graphs exist for history, CPU, memory, and queue information. For example, the history graph shows CPU, active processes, disk utilization, memory pageout rates, and swapout rates.

Figure 4-10   PerfView graph showing memory utilization and paging rates.

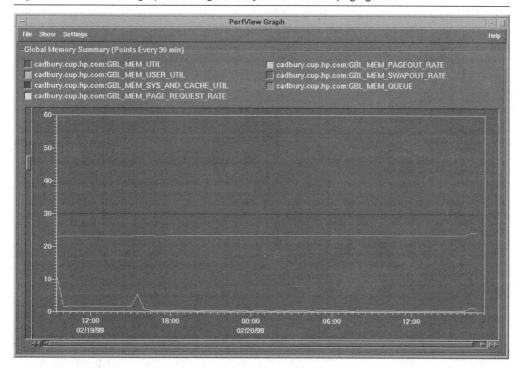

The PerfView Analyzer graph shown in Figure 4-11 compares the performance of two systems simultaneously. Up to eight systems can be compared in one graph. Comparing system utilization can be useful when determining where to deploy new applications, or when adding new users.

PerfView's ability to show history and trend information can be helpful in diagnosing system problems. Graphing performance information can help you to understand whether a persistent problem exists or if an anomaly is simply a momentary spike of activity.

To diagnose a problem further, PerfView Monitor can allow users to change time intervals, to try to find the specific time a problem occurred. The graph is redrawn showing the new time period.

PerfView is integrated with several other monitoring tools. You can launch GlancePlus from within PerfView by accessing the Tools menu. PerfView can be launched from the IT/O Applications Bank as well. When troubleshooting an event in the IT/O Message Browser window, you can launch PerfView to see a related performance graph.

PerfView Monitor is not used with IT/O. Instead, the IT/O Message Browser is used. When an alarm is received in IT/O, the operator can click the alarm and a related PerfView graph can be shown.

PerfView can show information collected from multiple systems in a single performance graph. The PerfView and ClusterView products have also been integrated to enable the operator

Figure 4-11   PerfView graph comparing two systems.

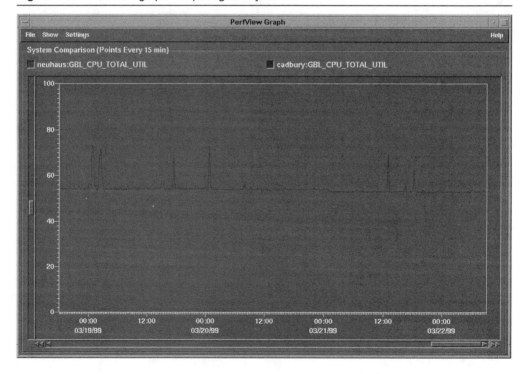

to select a cluster symbol on an HP OpenView submap and launch the PerfView application. This quickly shows a performance comparison between all systems in the cluster.

For further information, visit the HP Resource and Performance Management Web site at http://www.openview.hp.com/solutions/application/.

BMC PATROL for UNIX

BMC Software provides monitoring capabilities through its PATROL software suite. PATROL is a system, application, and event management suite for system and database administrators. PATROL provides the basic framework for defining thresholds, sending and translating events, and so forth. Optional products, called Knowledge Modules (KMs), are capable of monitoring specific components. For example, BMC PATROL includes KMs for UNIX, SAP R/3, Oracle, Informix, and other applications. In fact, more than 40 KMs are available from BMC for use with PATROL.

With the PATROL KM for UNIX, managed components include the CPU, memory, users, kernel, processes, printers, security, and filesystems. These components are discovered automatically and represented on the PATROL console with status icons. System utilization can be shown as graphs, to capture trends, and data can either be displayed in real time or saved in log files.

Like other graphical monitoring tools, PATROL provides an Event Manager window, which can show received events. Figure 4-12 highlights disk and NFS events received at the console.

For memory and swap resources, PATROL can show total real memory available, total virtual memory available, a list of swap devices, the number of processes swapped, and swap space utilization.

Figure 4-12   PATROL Event Manager showing disk and NFS events.

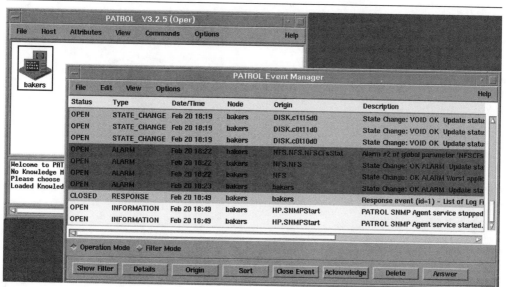

For the CPU, PATROL can show bottlenecks and utilization information, along with a variety of statistics, such as CPU idle time, run queue length, and swap queue length. Information about the operating system itself is also maintained, such as the name, version, and creation date.

PATROL can display the total number of processes, the number of zombie processes, and heavy CPU users. Through the PATROL console, you can perform administrative tasks, such as reprioritizing processes.

PATROL also can display the total number of users and sessions, and can check security by monitoring the number of failed user and privileged logins. You can check the printer queue to see how many jobs are in the queue and to determine the state of the printer.

PATROL can monitor the filesystem and can automatically determine the effectiveness of the buffer cache. Regular reports can be generated to check disk usage per user, to create a list of the largest files, or to list files that have not been accessed in a long time. Corrective actions, such as removing core files, can also be configured.

In addition to the system metrics monitored by PATROL, the KM for UNIX includes a set of tools to provide additional system monitoring, including tools to monitor CPU usage, paging activity, I/O caching, swap activity, and system log files, tools to check filesystem and kernel file resources, and tools to monitor printer queues.

The following list shows some of the parameters available for monitoring from the PATROL KM for UNIX:

- CPUCpuUtil
- CPUIdleTime
- CPUInt
- CPULoad
- CPUProcsWaiting
- CPUProcSwch
- CPURunQSize
- CPUSysTime
- CPUUserTime
- KERSysCall
- MEMActiveVirPage
- MEMFreeMem
- MEMPageAnticipated
- MEMPageFreed
- MEMPageIn
- MEMPageOut
- MEMPageScanned
- PRNQlength
- PROCAvgUsrProc

- PROCCpuHogs
- PROCNoZombies
- PROCNumProcs
- PROCProcWait
- PROCUserProcs
- SWPSwapFreeSpace
- SWPSwapIn
- SWPSwapOut
- SWPSwapSize
- SWPSwapUsedPercent
- USRNoSession
- USRNoUser

The BMC PATROL KM for UNIX is supported on Bull, DG AViiON, DEC Alpha, DEC Ultra, Hewlett-Packard, NCR, Olivetti, OSF/1, Pyramid, RS/6000, SCO, Sequent, SGI, Sun Solaris, SunOS, Unisys, and UNIXWare systems.

Candle

The Candle Corporation provides software for mainframes and distributed systems. The Availability Command Center is a suite of integrated performance monitors and availability management solutions. The Candle Command Center for Distributed Systems is used to manage the performance and availability of computer systems and applications. Command Center solutions are available for UNIX, NT, IBM AIX, and MVS platforms. The Command Center for Distributed Systems can monitor many systems from a single console.

Candle's management agents provide detailed performance and availability metrics. The OMEGAMON Monitoring Agent for UNIX provides system information standardized across multiple UNIX platforms (IBM AIX, HP-UX, Sun Solaris, and SunOS). Available metrics include OS and CPU performance, process status, and disk performance. Disk performance is expressed as kilobytes per second, percent busy, and transfers per second. Disk performance and other tools can be launched from the Command Center console.

The Command Center provides some predefined threshold conditions for sending alerts. You also can change these conditions. If you decide to change the threshold conditions, they are automatically redistributed to the appropriate systems. Different alarm severity levels can be used.

The Command Center's event correlation engine and Visual Policy Editor can be used to create rules that automatically recognize the symptoms of problems and develop automated responses.

Candle has performed additional testing of the Command Center with MC/ServiceGuard to ensure that its Command Center for Distributed Systems product runs in that environment. More information about Candle Corporation's products can be found on the Web at http://www.candle.com.

Using System Performance Data

This section provides a brief introduction on how you can use performance monitoring tools to avoid, identify, and address system performance problems. An extensive tutorial on system performance is beyond the scope of this book.

A *bottleneck* in one system resource can render other system resources unusable. You need to ensure that all system components have sufficient capacity to operate at their optimal level. You can use performance data to avoid bottlenecks, by detecting trends to establish appropriate resource entitlements for each application, and to help eliminate problems when they occur.

This section does not discuss how to troubleshoot network performance issues, which is covered in Chapter 6.

Note that performance monitoring itself can create problems in your environment. Sending regular performance data from each system to a central location could result in hundreds of megabytes per day of network traffic and data storage for medium-sized companies. You should make sure that all the data you are collecting is going to be used. Instead of sending all data, you should send only the unusual or exceptional information. However, enough data should be sent to be able to identify trends for capacity planning. You should store a fixed amount of detailed performance data locally on each system so that you can troubleshoot problems when they appear.

Avoiding Performance Issues

The first step that you can take toward avoiding performance problems is to establish baselines for your environment. Collect performance data when your system is performing well, for long enough to get a valid representation of your system's workload, so that you have something to contrast with a poorly performing system.

Next, you should see whether the CPU, memory, and I/O resources are well-balanced. You should also do capacity planning, to ensure that your system has sufficient headroom to support any additional users and applications that you may be expecting. If excess capacity is not available, you should develop a plan for addressing future growth.

Another area to check is the allocation of system resources. Use the sar and sysdef commands, for example, to see whether any resources are at their configured limits. Check the available swap space and entries in the file and process tables to see whether these are sized appropriately. Use EMS to set up early warnings as the usage of other system resources increases. Because changing these limits often requires that you restart the system, early detection can allow you to plan for the time when the system will be unavailable.

Another way to protect system resources is to use the Process Resource Manager (PRM), a resource management tool used to balance system resources among PRM groups. PRM groups are configured by the administrator and consist of a set of HP-UX users or applications. PRM is then used to give each PRM group a certain percentage of the CPU, real memory, or disk I/O bandwidth available on the system. PRM ensures that each PRM group gets a minimum percentage of the system's resources, even during heavy loads.

PRM can be used in conjunction with HP GlancePlus to adjust system configuration. For example, if an administrator detects unwanted system load for a PRM group, GlancePlus can be used to lower that group's entitlement dynamically.

Normally, if one PRM group doesn't need its system resources, PRM allocates them to other groups that may need them. However, PRM can also help with capacity planning, by allowing resource maximums to be specified. Thus, if an administrator knows that a system will soon have 25 percent more users, the administrator can allocate a maximum of 80 percent of system resources to simulate the upcoming load.

Although PRM can ensure that users get a certain percentage of CPU resources, it can't prevent all system performance problems. For example, an application sending large network packets but using very little CPU resources can starve a more critical application, because network bandwidth is not controlled by PRM.

PRM can also be used to adjust workload dynamically in a high availability environment. For example, if three MC/ServiceGuard packages are each running with similar PRM entitlements, and one package fails to another system, this can be automatically detected, and a new PRM configuration can be applied, giving the two remaining packages higher entitlements.

Despite these efforts, you still are likely to have some performance problems to investigate. The next sections describe how to use the data collected by the various performance monitoring tools to address performance issues.

Detecting CPU Contention

UNIX commands, such as top and uptime, and performance monitoring tools, such as Glance-Plus, provide CPU utilization information. CPU utilization and run queue length can be used together to determine whether a CPU bottleneck exists. High CPU utilization alone may not be indicative of a problem; batch jobs may be consuming the CPU remaining from interactive users. However, if interactive users are getting poor response times, that indicates a problem, such as a system bottleneck.

If the run queue is greater than one, the likelihood that a CPU bottleneck exists increases as the CPU utilization gets closer to 100 percent. Make sure that the high utilization and large run queue are sustained for a period of time.

If a CPU bottleneck is identified, recovery may depend on the applications and processes consuming large amounts of CPU. This can be determined by using performance monitoring tools such as GlancePlus. Applications spending the majority of their time in system code may need to be changed. In some cases, an application can be recompiled, optimized, or restructured to improve its performance. If batch processing is causing a problem, a job scheduler can be used to route jobs to less utilized systems. Less important applications, such as batch processes, can also be reconfigured to run at a lower priority by using nice. An application may need to be aborted or moved to another system if it continually thrashes with other applications. Tools such as PRM can be enabled or reconfigured to handle resource allocation among applications or users. PRM can keep applications within configured CPU limits.

Checking System Resource Usage

This chapter has described a variety of tools to monitor system resource usage. System table utilization can be checked by using tools such as GlancePlus. Using EMS monitors to set up thresholds is another useful approach.

The number of processes allowed and the number of concurrent open files allowed are two parameters that should be checked and that can be reconfigured using SAM.

Many actions to correct this type of problem require restarting the system, but if the problem is due to a runaway application, you may be able to detect the problem before other applications are affected. You can abort the application before system resources are depleted.

Detecting Memory and Swap Contention

To check for a real memory bottleneck on the network server, you can first check the amount of free memory. It should not drop below 5 percent of the total available. If the system cannot keep up with the demands for memory, it will start paging and swapping. Excessive paging and swapping, viewed from GlancePlus, may be a sign of a memory bottleneck. Two other signs that may indicate a memory bottleneck are a high percentage of processes blocked on virtual memory and large disk queues on swap devices.

To lower the swap rate, you may want to configure a higher percentage of available disk space for swapping. Increasing the capacity of the system by adding more memory or disk space may also eliminate the bottleneck. PRM can be used to ensure that the most important applications get a sufficient percentage of the memory.

If the amount of memory being used seems unusually high, you can use performance tools to determine which processes are using the most memory. A program may need to be redesigned to use memory more efficiently. A program may also need to be examined for memory leaks.

Detecting Disk and File System Bottlenecks

System, application, and disk information should be studied together to resolve disk performance issues. MeasureWare provides a lot of information about an application's disk utilization, which may need to be correlated with system data.

To avoid disk bottlenecks, you need to balance I/O across filesystems, disk spindles, and disk controllers to reduce uneven queuing and delays. Performance monitoring tools such as GlancePlus can be used to find the process with the highest I/O rate, and also the busiest physical disk. Checking the I/O rate only is insufficient, because a slower device has a higher utilization than a faster disk with the same I/O rate. If a single disk has greater than 50-percent utilization for an extended period of time, it may be an indication of an I/O bottleneck. The percentage should be compared with that of other disks, to see whether a severe load imbalance exists. However, a high utilization is not sufficient to identify a problem. The disk may still be capable of handling more I/O. A continually long disk queue length is also needed to indicate a problem. Heavily used disks are likely to have large disk queue lengths as well.

Both BMC PATROL and MeasureWare collect read cache hit ratio information. Determining how many logical reads are satisfied by the system's buffer cache is an indication of whether the cache size was configured correctly. Because increasing the cache size negatively affects the system memory available for other purposes, the appropriate cache hit ratio depends on the type of workload being run on the system. For I/O-intensive applications, you may want to configure your system such that this ratio is as high as 90 or 95 percent. Similarly, you may want to ensure that your write cache hit ratio is at least 75 percent. If your hit rates are too low, the system buffer cache may be too small.

After you determine that the system buffer cache is too small, you can increase its size on HP-UX by using SAM. Select the Configurable Parameters option from the Kernel Configuration functional area. The appropriate parameter to modify depends on whether a static or dynamic buffer cache is being used, which can also be checked on this screen. Fixed-size buffer caches are most effective if the environment and workload are static. Dynamic buffer caches fluctuate in size based on the demands for I/O or virtual memory, and are useful when workloads vary. If the nbuf and bufpages system parameters are set to 0, a dynamic buffer cache is in use. When using a dynamic buffer cache on systems with greater than 1GB of real memory, you should lower the maximum size below 50 percent, because caches greater than 500MB actually cause performance degradations.

Detecting disk contention is discussed in Chapter 5. If no problem seems to exist with the CPU, memory, or disk, other possibilities include networking or system table utilization. Checking network utilization is discussed in Chapter 6.

Avoiding System Problems

To avoid system problems related to misconfigurations, you need to have appropriate product documentation and business policies in place. The administrators making the changes should have access to caveats and a history log of past changes. Changes should be logged and a revision control system should be used so that you can quickly revert an old configuration.

System components will fail, but you can reduce consequential problems by investing in high availability or resiliency products and features. In the 1997 D. H. Brown survey of high availability providers, Hewlett-Packard was rated above average in its ability to detect and recover from failures. HP-UX provides dynamic memory resiliency, dynamic processor resiliency, and dynamically loadable kernel modules. Single-bit CPU cache errors can be corrected automatically. Memory Error–Correcting Code (ECC) and checksums reduce memory problems, but don't eliminate the need to monitor the memory subsystem. HP supports error thresholds for memory and disks, and its Memory Page Deallocation feature enables dynamic memory deselection for failing memory locations.

As vendors improve the resiliency of their operating systems, CPU failures become less likely to cause a system to fail. In some cases, if diagnostic tools detect a problem with a CPU, the processor can be deallocated while the operating system continues to run. For example, this can be done if the rate of corrected single-bit CPU cache errors exceeds a predefined threshold. The processor can also be deallocated if a problem is found in the self-test during boot.

For companies with HP support contracts, HP Predictive Support can be used to detect trends that might lead to system problems. An engineer can then be sent to the customer site to make repairs before a problem becomes serious.

You also must back up your data regularly to prepare for any problems. The backups should be tested regularly to ensure that they are working properly.

You should also try to avoid performance and resource management problems by closely monitoring how your system is being used. Techniques for accomplishing this are described in the previous section.

Recovering from System Problems

When a server fails and can't be immediately repaired, high availability cluster software (such as MC/ServiceGuard) can be used to reduce the downtime associated with the situation and to keep services available. MC/ServiceGuard detects the failure of an application and automatically restarts the application on another system. This automatic detection and recovery can save you downtime. MC/ServiceGuard can detect a failure and restart an application on another system in under one minute.

However, even with the kernel's capability to mask certain failures and high availability software's capability to move applications to redundant servers, ultimately you still need to repair the failed components. For hardware problems, Support Tool Manager can provide fast diagnosis on HP-UX systems. SyMON can be used for Solaris environments.

You may need to find a software or firmware patch to fix your problem. For HP-UX, you can obtain patch information from the HP Web site by following links to support information. Customized patch bundles are available for customers with HP software support agreements. For Sun Solaris, you can access patch information over the Web through a service called Sun-Solve Online.

Recovering from a security violation by a malicious intruder may be more difficult. The system administrator may need to revert to system backup tapes from a known good system state.

Comparing System Monitoring Tools

This section provides a brief summary and comparison of the tools discussed in this chapter. The summary is organized by the key focus areas of system monitoring: configuration, faults, and resource and performance management.

Limited tools are available for monitoring configuration changes. The burden is largely on you to run tools such as iostat and STM to gather configuration data, and then to store that data in your own defined areas for comparison purposes later. The DMI Software MIF contains some software configuration information, but DMI management tools are not yet available. The Configuration Tracker is one tool that is available for monitoring software configuration changes.

ClusterView can track changes made to high availability cluster configurations. More tools are needed that can track changes to hardware and software configuration information. This will be more important as it becomes easier to add or remove components while a system stays active.

System component failures can be reported through EMS for HP-UX, and SyMON for Sun Solaris systems. These products, with their automatic failure notifications, are preferred to using tools manually to probe the state of hardware components. Hardware monitors and monitor developer's kits are available for both products. Both can send notifications by using a variety of methods, including SNMP, but EMS has tighter integration with NNM and IT/O. SyMON provides integrated recovery actions with its product. Note that detecting failures of the system requires a remote monitoring tool, such as NNM.

If you don't have access to a performance management product, some low-budget performance monitoring can be done with UNIX commands, principally iostat, vmstat, top, uptime, sar, and swapinfo.

GlancePlus provides performance monitoring in real time for a large number of metrics on a single system. SyMON, by contrast, has very little performance data. For historical performance data, sampled over a longer time period, you should use a tool such as MeasureWare or BMC PATROL. If you want the tool to be integrated with a performance management product, then you may want to use MeasureWare, which provides tight integration with PerfView. Both products can report information via SNMP.

Some amount of resource monitoring can be done with performance monitoring tools or EMS. Additional resource usage data is available from ipcs, sysdef, and the HP-UNIX MIB.

Case Study: Recovering from Memory Faults

In this case study, the system administrator, Bill Landis, is responsible for maintaining system availability 24 hours a day, 7 days a week for the Silicon Valley Hospital's billing system. Based on past experience, he wants a system for which system components, such as CPU and memory, can be replaced without the need to bring down the system. Bill has a Sun Enterprise 10000 server, which has dynamic reconfiguration capabilities. To take advantage of Sun's dynamic reconfiguration, Bill is configuring his system memory so that it can be taken offline and replaced in the event of a board failure.

Verifying Configuration

The system's real memory is divided into memory banks, which become ineligible for dynamic reconfiguration when they contain kernel pages. With Sun's dynamic reconfiguration features, you can configure kernel pages to use certain memory banks. Once configured, you use the Dynamic Reconfiguration screen (shown in Figure 4-13) in SyMON to verify that these banks aren't "permanent" and are available to be unconfigured.

As Figure 4-13 indicates, the memory board in slot 2 is configured, but it isn't assigned to a permanent memory bank. As a result, Bill can use this screen in SyMON to take the memory

Figure 4-13   Using SyMON dynamic reconfiguration to replace a failed memory board.

Board Logical ID	Board Type	Information	Busy	Connection	Configuration
ac0:bank0	memory	slot0 1Gb base 0x0 permanent	n	connected	configured
ac0:bank1	memory	slot0 empty	n	empty	unconfigured
ac4:bank0	memory	slot2 empty	n	empty	unconfigured
ac4:bank1	memory	slot2 1Gb base 0x180000000	n	connected	unconfigured
sysctrl0:slot0	cpu/mem	non-detachable	n	connected	configured
sysctrl0:slot1	dual-sbus	non-detachable	n	connected	configured
sysctrl0:slot2	cpu/mem	disabled at boot	n	connected	configured
sysctrl0:slot3	unknown		n	empty	unconfigured
sysctrl0:slot4	sbus-upa	no ffb installed	n	connected	configured
sysctrl0:slot5	unknown		n	empty	unconfigured

Dynamic Reconfiguration
sqa-4000 [192.9.205.9]

System Boards

Configure
UnConfigure
Connect
Disconnect
Test Memory...

Details

Condition=ok
When=[Mar 18 11:26]
Board Physical ID= /devices/central@1f,0/fhc@0,f8800000/clock-board@0,900000:slot2
Command Status= NULL

Close

offline. In contrast, slot 0 is associated with a permanent memory bank and can't be disconnected while the system is running.

Setting Up Monitoring and Reconfiguration

From the Enterprise SyMON console, Bill loads the Config-Reader and Dynamic Reconfiguration modules to ensure that he will be notified of hardware faults, so that he can handle the faults
without having to take the system down. The Config-Reader module is located under Hardware
and the Dynamic Reconfiguration module is located under local applications (shown in Figure
4-7, earlier in this chapter).

Memory Board Failure Occurs

When a critical memory fault occurs, the icon for the system on the SyMON console indicates
the alarm. Bill looks at the Alarm window to see more details about the event. He notices that a
memory board has failed. Using the Logical View, like the one shown in Figure 4-14, he locates
the failed memory board. Using the Physical View, like the one shown earlier in Figure 4-5, he
locates the exact location of the physical board in the system.

Fixing the Failure and Restoring Service

Bill accesses the Dynamic Reconfiguration screen from the SyMON console. First, he selects
the failed memory slot and clicks the Disconnect button to unconfigure and disconnect the
board. Next, he replaces the failed board and then connects the board by clicking the Connect
button; he leaves it temporarily unconfigured, however, while he performs a memory test using

Figure 4-14 Using the SyMON Logical View to locate a failed memory board.

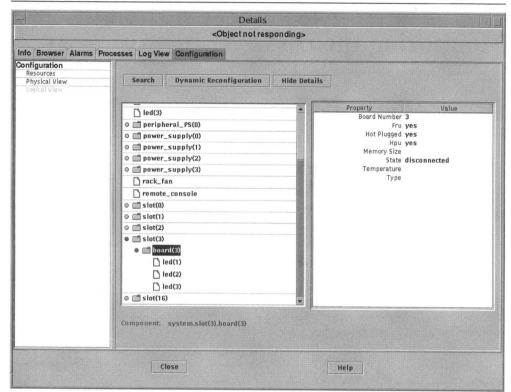

the Test Memory button, to ensure that the new board is functional. Finally, Bill clicks the Configure button to make these memory resources available to the system.

Bill was able to handle a failed memory board in this environment with very little impact to the system. Sun's dynamic reconfiguration capabilities, available from SyMON, provide a powerful feature that allows failed memory, CPU, and I/O resources to be fixed without having to bring down the system.

Monitoring the Disks

$\mathbf{D}$isk technologies provide some level of protection against failure. To reduce or eliminate system downtime due to disk failures, technologies such as Redundant Array of Inexpensive Disks (RAID) or mirroring must be used to provide data redundancy. RAID technology uses parity data to ensure that recovery is possible in the event of a disk failure. Mirroring allows multiple copies of data to be maintained. Three-way mirroring, in particular, provides added data protection during backups, because mirroring continues on the disks that are not being backed up.

With data redundancy, data is protected if an initial failure occurs, but the initial failure may result in a loss of redundancy, or a single point of failure (SPOF). Thus, a subsequent failure may result in loss of data. So, even though these technologies protect against single failures, notification of such failures is critical to reduce the risk of downtime. Fixing a failure and restoring data redundancy before the next failure occurs is key to maintaining availability. Data redundancy and fault monitoring do not replace the need for a regular backup strategy.

Although RAID and mirroring may protect against a single hardware failure, many other potential events exist that may affect the availability of data on the disk and increase the risk of downtime. The key to eliminating the risk of failure and downtime is to monitor your critical disk resources. You must know which resources to monitor and what tools are available to do that monitoring. This chapter addresses monitoring of disk resources, from the hardware device level up to filesystem resources. It does not cover backup, recovery, or tape storage devices.

Identifying Important Disk Monitoring Categories

As already mentioned, redundancy is the best way to protect against initial failures. The key to high availability is to always maintain redundancy so that a disk fault does not adversely affect system and data availability. Sometimes, however, this isn't enough. If the resources aren't performing normally, availability can be affected by degraded performance, too.

Regardless of whether you have your disks configured for high availability, monitoring can help protect against failures. Although redundancy helps to provide protection from an initial hardware failure, monitoring needs to be done to protect not only against a second failure, but also against other failures that may affect availability.

The events and measures that you can use to maintain availability are broken down into several categories of system monitoring:

- **Disk configuration:** Includes monitoring for the addition or removal of disk resources, as well as ensuring that the proper software and firmware versions are installed. Tracking configuration changes can help when you are troubleshooting problems later. Ensuring that a device is using the correct version of firmware can also eliminate problems.
- **Fault management:** Includes monitoring any kind of errors or events that may occur on the hardware, the physical disk devices. This category covers device errors, such as media errors, read errors, seek-time errors, and bad blocks, as well as component failures, such as FRU failures, controller failures, RAID failures, fan failures, and more.
- **Resource management:** Includes monitoring the resources that provide storage space on disks. Filesystem space, mount points, logical volumes, mirrored copies, and physical volume links are all important disk resources to monitor. At the filesystem level, you must ensure that sufficient filesystem space is available for applications to run successfully. All filesystems must be mounted and available to their users. Filesystems are often configured using *logical volumes*. When data is mirrored, it is the logical volumes that are mirrored. Monitoring data mirrors can be critical to maintaining redundancy and increasing availability. Physical volumes and the links to those volumes are considered disk resources.
- **Performance management:** Includes monitoring disk performance metrics, such as disk read and write throughput rates. Swap rates are also important, because they can be used to identify resource contention, which can affect availability. Disk performance resources can be monitored to ensure that I/O traffic is balanced across the available disk resources.

The following sections list various tools that you can use to monitor the disk resources listed in the preceding categories. These tools include basic commands, system instrumentation available through standard interfaces, event monitors, diagnostic tools, and performance monitors.

Using Standard Commands and Tools

Many UNIX commands exist to check configuration, status, and resource information. These tools generally report on only a snapshot in time. You can periodically track configuration changes or test the status of disk devices or resources by writing and using custom scripts that include these (and other) commands.

bdf and df

The bdf and df commands can be used not only to see the mounted filesystem configuration, but also to report filesystem usage and capacity information. You can use this command to do the following:

• Monitor filesystem space, to avoid filesystem capacity limits
• Check that the necessary filesystems are mounted
• View the relationship between the filesystem mount points and associated logical volumes

Listing 5-1 shows the output of bdf.

diskinfo

The diskinfo command can be used to get device information for CS/80, Subset/80, and Hewlett-Packard Small Computer Standard Interface (SCSI) disk devices. Using this command, an operator can check disk access. In this way, the disk is pinged to see whether it is okay. You can use diskinfo to get device status and configuration information. Listing 5-2 shows some sample output.

fsck

The fsck command performs filesystem consistency checks and interactive repair. If it finds inconsistencies, it provides a mechanism to repair the inconsistencies in the filesystem. You should run this tool if you suspect a corrupt filesystem, or just run it periodically for preventative maintenance.

Using fsck with the –m option checks whether the filesystems have any errors that need to be corrected. If they do not, it reports that the filesystems are already mounted, as shown in Listing 5-3.

Using fsck with the –n option generates a more detailed report. Blocks, pathnames, and reference counts are checked. Listing 5-4 shows a portion of an fsck report containing information on multiple filesystems. Note that it shows an error with /dev/vg00/rlvol5.

Listing 5-1   Output from the bdf command for monitoring filesystem space.

```
Filesystem         kbytes    used    avail %used Mounted on
/dev/vg00/lvol3    102400   18723   78457   19% /
/dev/vg00/lvol1     47829    6438   36608   15% /stand
/dev/vg00/lvol8    155648   51011   98168   34% /var
/dev/vg00/lvol7    307200  228550   73747   76% /usr
/dev/vg00/lvol6     49152    1214   45007    3% /tmp
/dev/vg00/lvol5    102400   84310   16981   83% /opt
/dev/vg00/lvol4    921600  446758  445205   50% /home
```

Listing 5-2   Output from the diskinfo command.

```
# diskinfo /dev/rdsk/c0t5d0
SCSI describe of /dev/rdsk/c0t5d0:
            vendor: SEAGATE
        product id: ST34572WC
              type: direct access
              size: 4194157 Kbytes
   bytes per sector: 512
```

Listing 5-3 Output from fsck showing that the filesystems are mounted.

```
# fsck -m
fsck: sanity check, /dev/vg00/lvol3 is already mounted
fsck: sanity check, /dev/vg00/lvol1 is already mounted
fsck: sanity check, /dev/vg00/lvol4 is already mounted
fsck: sanity check, /dev/vg00/lvol5 is already mounted
fsck: sanity check, /dev/vg00/lvol6 is already mounted
fsck: sanity check, /dev/vg00/lvol7 is already mounted
fsck: sanity check, /dev/vg00/lvol8 is already mounted
#
```

Listing 5-4 Output from fsck showing a filesystem problem.

```
** /dev/vg00/rlvol4 (NO WRITE)
** Last Mounted on /home
** groups
1479 files, 0 icont, 68427 used, 31242 free (338 frags, 3863 blocks)
** /dev/vg00/rlvol5 (NO WRITE)
** Last Mounted on /opt
** Phase 1 - Check Blocks and Sizes
** Phase 2 - Check Pathnames
** Phase 3 - Check Connectivity
UNREF DIR  I=28054
 OWNER=root MODE=40777
SIZE=0 MTIME=Dec  2 14:03 1998
** Phase 4 - Check Reference Counts
UNREF DIR I=28054
 OWNER=root MODE=40777
SIZE=0 MTIME=Dec  2 14:03 1998
CLEAR?  no
** Phase 5 - Check Cyl groups
9033 files, 0 icont, 439919 used, 58726 free (1830 frags, 7112 blocks)
** /dev/vg00/rlvol6 (NO Phase 1 - Check Blocks and Sizes
** Phase 2 - Check Pathnames
** Phase 3 - Check Connectivity
** Phase 4 - Check Reference Counts
** Phase 5 - Check Cyl WRITE)
** Last Mounted on /tmp
** Phase 1 - Check Blocks and Sizes
** Phase 2 - Check Pathnames
** Phase 3 - Check Connectivity
** Phase 4 - Check Reference Counts
** Phase 5 - Check Cyl groups
269 files, 0 icont, 23451 used, 7146 free (98 frags, 881 blocks)
```

After getting a report indicating a problem, you may want to run fsck interactively to fix
the problem. This is shown in Listing 5-5.

Listing 5-5   Output from fsck showing a filesystem repair.

```
# fsck
fsck: /dev/vg00/lvol3: root file system
continue (y/n)? n
fsck: /dev/vg00/rlvol1: mounted file system
continue (y/n)? n
fsck: /dev/vg00/rlvol4: mounted file system
continue (y/n)? n
fsck: /dev/vg00/rlvol5: mounted file system
continue (y/n)? y
** /dev/vg00/rlvol5
** Last Mounted on /opt
** Phase 1 - Check Blocks and Sizes
** Phase 2 - Check Pathnames
** Phase 3 - Check Connectivity
UNREF DIR  I=28054
 OWNER=root MODE=40777
SIZE=0 MTIME=Dec  2 14:03 1998
** Phase 4 - Check Reference Counts
UNREF DIR I=28054
 OWNER=root MODE=40777
SIZE=0 MTIME=Dec  2 14:03 1998
CLEAR? y

FREE INODE COUNT WRONG IN SUPERBLK
FIX? y

** Phase 5 - Check Cyl groups
SUMMARY INFORMATION (INODE FREE) BAD
BAD CYLINDER GROUPS
FIX? y

** Phase 6 - Salvage Cylinder Groups
9032 files, 0 icont, 439919 used, 58726 free (1830 frags, 7112 blocks)
***** MARKING FILE SYSTEM CLEAN *****

***** FILE SYSTEM WAS MODIFIED *****
fsck: /dev/vg00/rlvol6: mounted file system
continue (y/n)? n
fsck: /dev/vg00/rlvol7: mounted file system
continue (y/n)? n
fsck: /dev/vg00/rlvol8: mounted file system
continue (y/n)? n
#
```

ioscan

The ioscan command is useful for viewing the hardware configuration of a system. For disk resources, this includes the interface cards as well as the I/O devices. The command displays the hardware path to the hardware module, the class of the hardware module, and a brief description. This is good for tracking the system's disk configuration.

Listing 5-6 shows the output from the ioscan command; the –f option generates a full listing.

lvdisplay

The lvdisplay command can be used to get information for disk resource management. It displays Logical Volume Manager (LVM) logical volume configuration information and the logical volume status. Information about mirrored copies is included if you are using MirrorDisk/UX. Listing 5-7 shows the logical volume status and mirrored copies, among other information, in the output from lvdisplay.

Listing 5-6 Output from the ioscan command showing information about hardware devices configured on a system.

```
# ioscan -f
Class       I  H/W Path  Driver  S/W State  H/W Type   Description
==================================================================================
bc          0            root    CLAIMED    BUS_NEXUS
bc          1  8         ccio    CLAIMED    BUS_NEXUS  I/O Adapter
bc          2  8/0       bc      CLAIMED    BUS_NEXUS  Bus Converter
tty         0  8/0/0     mux2    CLAIMED    INTERFACE  MUX
ext_bus     0  8/4       c720    CLAIMED    INTERFACE  GSC add-on F/W SCSI
target      0  8/4.5     tgt     CLAIMED    DEVICE
disk        0  8/4.5.0   sdisk   CLAIMED    DEVICE     SEAGATE ST34572WC
target      1  8/4.6     tgt     CLAIMED    DEVICE
ctl         4  8/4.6.0   sctl    CLAIMED    DEVICE     Initiator
target      2  8/4.12    tgt     CLAIMED    DEVICE
disk        2  8/4.12.0  sdisk   CLAIMED    DEVICE     SEAGATE ST32272WC
target      3  8/4.13    tgt     CLAIMED    DEVICE
disk        3  8/4.13.0  sdisk   CLAIMED    DEVICE     SEAGATE ST32272WC
target      4  8/4.14    tgt     CLAIMED    DEVICE
disk        4  8/4.14.0  sdisk   CLAIMED    DEVICE     SEAGATE ST32272WC
target      5  8/4.15    tgt     CLAIMED    DEVICE
disk        5  8/4.15.0  sdisk   CLAIMED    DEVICE     SEAGATE ST32272WC
```

Listing 5-7   Output from the lvdisplay command showing logical volume information

```
# lvdisplay /dev/vg00/lvol1
-- Logical volumes --
LV Name                        /dev/vg00/lvol1
VG Name                        /dev/vg00
LV Permission                  read/write
LV Status                      available/syncd
Mirror copies                  0
Consistency Recovery           MWC
Schedule                       parallel
LV Size (Mbytes)               48
Current LE                     12
Allocated PE                   12
Stripes                        0
Stripe Size (Kbytes)           0
Bad block                      off
Allocation contiguous          strict/contiguous/
```

Information about the individual fields being displayed can be found in the online man page for the command.

pvdisplay

The pvdisplay command provides status and configuration information for disk resource management, specifically for physical volumes within LVM volume groups. For each physical volume, you can display the logical volumes that have extents allocated on the physical volume, and the usage of all the physical extents. Listing 5-8 shows the output from pvdisplay.

Listing 5-8   Output from the pvdisplay command showing information about physical volumes within LVM volume groups.

```
# pvdisplay  /dev/dsk/c0t5d0
-- Physical volumes --
PV Name                        /dev/dsk/c0t5d0
VG Name                        /dev/vg00
PV Status                      available
Allocatable                    yes
VGDA                           2
Cur LV                         8
PE Size (Mbytes)               4
Total PE                       1023
Free PE                        607
Allocated PE                   416
Stale PE                       0
IO Timeout (Seconds)           default
```

vgdisplay

The vgdisplay command is used to get information about LVM volume groups configured on the system. This command can be used to get disk resource status and configuration information. You can get configuration information about each logical volume, physical volume, and physical volume group for each volume group that is active on the system. You can get the status of volume groups, logical volumes, and physical volumes as shown in Listing 5-9. Some of the information available from lvdisplay and pvdisplay is also provided by this command. For example, using the verbose option, you not only get the volume group status, but also the status of all the logical volumes within the volume group.

You can use lvdisplay or pvdisplay to obtain more detailed information about logical or physical volumes, respectively.

Using System Instrumentation

Standards for network and system management, such as the Simple Network Management Protocol (SNMP) and the Desktop Management Interface (DMI), have been developed to help make

Listing 5-9 Output from the vgdisplay command showing information about a volume group.

```
# vgdisplay -v /dev/vg00
-- Volume groups --
VG Name                    /dev/vg00
VG Write Access            read/write
VG Status                  available
Max LV                     255
Cur LV                     8
Open LV                    8
Max PV                     16
Cur PV                     1
Act PV                     1
Max PE per PV              2000
VGDA                       2
PE Size (Mbytes)           4
Total PE                   1023
Alloc PE                   416
Free PE                    607
Total PVG                  0

   -- Logical volumes --
   LV Name                 /dev/vg00/lvol1
   LV Status               available/syncd
   LV Size (Mbytes)        48
   Current LE              12
   Allocated PE            12
```

management easier. These standards provide an industry-standard way to build instrumentation, and an industry-standard way to interface into the instrumentation. SNMP is used to access Management Information Bases (MIBs), and DMI is used to access Management Information Formats (MIFs).

Standard MIBs and MIFs define the metrics that can be provided by any vendor. The information provided is generally referred to as *instrumentation*. Private MIBs and MIFs provide vendor-specific instrumentation. This section looks at some of the disk instrumentation available through each of these standards.

Many tools already exist for accessing instrumentation. Several vendors offer browsers and monitoring capabilities that use a common interface to access instrumented objects from different hardware platforms and operating systems. For example, each of the common enterprise management frameworks, including HP OpenView Network Node Manager, HP OpenView IT/Operations, and CA Unicenter TNG, provide a MIB Browser tool to access MIB data. An example is shown in Figure 5-1. Toolkits exist to provide an interface so that developers can write their own tools to monitor or track this information. Toolkits also exist for doing custom instrumentation.

Both standards provide disk-type information and more information is being instrumented as time goes on.

Simple Network Management Protocol

A MIB is a standard way of representing information of a certain category. For example, MIB-II provides useful information about a system, such as the number of active TCP connections, system

Figure 5-1   Using the MIB Browser in OpenView IT/O to access disk-related information.

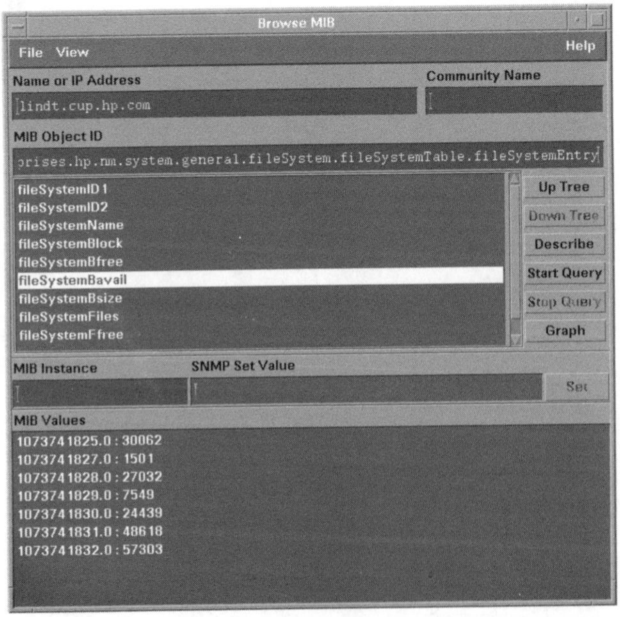

hardware and version information, and so forth. OpenView IT/O, discussed later in this chapter, provides a MIB Browser that helps you to discover which MIBs are available and to see the information being provided by each MIB. The MIB Browser tool can check the value of anything contained in a MIB. If you find a MIB that contains some useful fields, you can use the MIB Browser to gather that data from the target system. The resulting data is displayed in the MIB Browser's output window. By browsing through available MIBs, and by querying values of selected MIB fields, you can gather specific information needed to monitor systems and troubleshoot problems.

The SNMP interface provides access to objects stored in various MIBs. On HP-UX systems, the HP-UNIX MIB defines various metrics for monitoring disk resources, such as filesystem usage. Other vendors, such as Sun, have vendor-specific MIBs that provide similar information. Complete MIB definitions are listed in Appendix A, "Using Standards."

Objects in the File System Table of the HP-UNIX MIB can be monitored to detect when filesystem usage reaches a certain threshold, so that you can avoid filesystem faults, such as running out of space. Here is a list of the objects available for each entry in the File System Table:

- `fileSystemName`
- `fileSystemBlocks`
- `fileSystemBfree` (free blocks)
- `fileSystemBavail` (free blocks available to non–superusers)
- `fileSystemBsize`
- `fileSystemFiles`
- `fileSystemFfree`
- `fileSystemDir`

Note that a table entry exists for each mounted filesystem.

Desktop Management Interface

DMI instrumentation is provided for the HP-UX MIF, also known as the System MIF. For monitoring disks, DMI instrumentation is provided for disk hardware devices, as well as for configuration, status, and events. Filesystem resource information is also available in the System MIF. The DMI-instrumented, disk-related metrics are listed next. The complete System MIF and Software MIF definitions are in Appendix A.

The Host Storage Table contains information about logical storage areas. It is good for monitoring disk usage and allocation failure events. It contains the following fields:

- `Type`
- `Description`
- `Allocation Units`
- `Size`

- Used
- Storage Allocation Failures

The Host Devices Table contains information about the hardware devices on a system. It is good for monitoring hardware configuration and faults. It contains the following fields:

- Device Type
- Description
- Device ID
- Device Status (Running, Warning, Down, Testing, Reserved, Unknown)
- Device Errors

Events can also be generated for the status change of a device, initialization failure, and configuration errors for devices in the Host Devices Table. The events contain an assigned severity such as Information, OK, or Critical.

The Host Disk Storage Table contains storage information for devices in the Host Devices Table. It contains the following fields:

- Access (Read-only, Read/Write)
- Media Type (for example, Hard Disk, Floppy Disk, and so on)
- Removable
- Capacity (in kilobytes)
  The File System Table contains the following fields:
- FSMountPoint
- RemoteFSMount
- FSAccess
- FSBootable
- FSLastFullBackupDate
- FSLastPartialBackupDate

Many vendors are developing more DMI instrumentation for disk resources, as well as device-specific information.

Using Event Monitoring Tools

Event monitoring involves generating notification messages as soon as faults and other interesting conditions are detected. This is unlike UNIX commands, which report status information only when asked. You can configure event monitors to generate an event when a change in status occurs or when a predefined threshold condition has been met. Some event monitors generate events when faults or errors occur at the disk device level.

Several monitors discussed in this section are integrated into the Event Monitoring Service (EMS) framework. The EMS framework, available only on HP-UX systems, enables monitors to be provided in a consistent manner for a system. Whereas the EMS framework itself is freely available, the monitors are usually available as separate products or are bundled with the individual products for which they provide monitoring.

EMS provides a consistent graphical user interface (GUI) for the discovery and configuration of resources that can be monitored. EMS monitors can be configured to send events to OpenView IT/O. In addition, EMS events can be sent directly to any SNMP-capable management station, to a network application listening on a TCP or UDP port, to an e-mail address, or locally, to the console, system log file, or user log file. MC/ServiceGuard can allow packages to be dependent on these EMS resources, as well.

HA Monitors is a software package of EMS monitors. It includes monitors for filesystem space, user and job information, network interface status, MC/ServiceGuard cluster status, and disk volume status.

Event Monitoring Service Disk Volume Monitor

The EMS Disk Volume Monitor (DVM) is included in the HA Monitors product. It can be used to monitor disk resources that are configured using LVM, including copies of mirrored logical volumes.

The EMS DVM can be used in conjunction with MirrorDisk/UX. Using MirrorDisk/UX is completely transparent to an application. However, this can sometimes be a problem. A disk could fail and a mirror could take over, but the operator wouldn't know about the failure, so the failed disk wouldn't get repaired. Eventually, another failure would occur, with no backup for the data. The EMS DVM provides help for this situation.

The EMS DVM is responsible for monitoring a variety of attributes:

- Physical volume summary
- Physical volume and physical volume link status
- Logical volume summary
- Logical volume status
- Logical volume copies

These attributes (or resources) are structured into a resource hierarchy. Figure 5-2 shows the EMS DVM's resource hierarchy. The resource instances, such as the volume group names or logical volume names, vary from system to system, based on the configuration. The EMS DVM requires monitor requests to be initiated on each local node; however, this also allows monitor requests to be customized to the local systems, so that only the critical disk resources need to be monitored.

The physical volume summary provides a summary status of all physical volumes in a volume group. In determining the summary status, the EMS DVM notes which physical volumes are not up, and their associated physical volume group. The possible values for the physical volume summary status are shown in Table 5-1.

Figure 5-2   EMS DVM resource hierarchy.

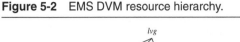
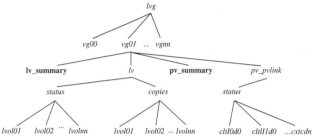

   The physical volume status and physical volume link status are checked when the EMS DVM attempts to communicate with a device over a particular physical path. The volume group does not have to be active. Valid values are UP, DOWN, and BUSY. If you have configured redundant links to your physical volumes, and the primary link fails, the LVM switches transparently to an alternative path to the device. This results in a SPOF. If you are monitoring the physical volume link status, you will be notified and can take action to restore redundancy by re-establishing an alternative path.

   The logical volume summary summarizes the LVM status values of all logical volumes in the volume group. The possible values for the logical volume summary status are shown in Table 5-2.

   The logical volume status reports the LVM subsystem's status for the selected logical volume. Inactive logical volumes have an INACTIVE status. Active logical volumes have either an UP or DOWN status, depending on whether at least one copy of all the data is available.

   The EMS DVM uses logical volume copies to report the number of copies of data available within the logical volume. In this way, the failure of a mirror can be detected. The value returned by the monitor is the number of complete copies of the data that are available. In the screen shown in Figure 5-3, the DVM is being configured to monitor mirrored copies of all logi-

Table 5-1   DVM Status Values for Physical Volume Summary

Status	Physical Volume Summary Interpretation
UP	All physical volumes in this volume group are up
PVG_UP	At least one PVG exists for which all physical volumes are up
SUSPECT	Some PVs are not up; cannot conclude if all data is available
DOWN	Some data is not available

Table 5-2   DVM Status Values for Logical Volume Summary

Status	Logical Volume Summary Interpretation
UP	Active and all logical volumes are up
DOWN	Active and at least one logical volume is down
INACTIVE	Inactive; if /etc/lvmtab changes, status moves to this from INACTIVE_DOWN
INACTIVE_DOWN	Inactive, and the last time the volume group was activated, the status was down

Figure 5-3   Configuring the EMS DVM to monitor mirrored copies.

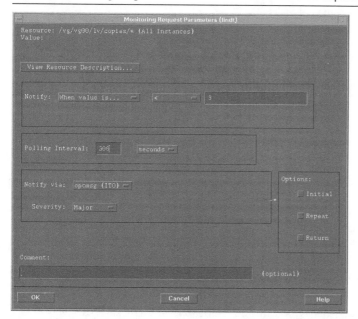

cal volumes (**All Instances**) in the vg00 volume group. Notification is specified to be sent to IT/O (via a proprietary method called opcmsg) when the number of copies drops below three.

On high-end HP-UX systems, numerous volume groups and logical volumes may be configured. Using the EMS Configuration GUI to configure each to be monitored may be time-consuming. The EMS Configuration GUI supports some wildcarding capabilities to make configuration easier. Also, an IT/O tool called monvols helps in configuring all the logical or physical volumes for a selected system. The monvols tool and other tools and templates for EMS are available for free on the Web at http://www.software.hp.com. Note, however, that monvols is available only for HP-UX 10.20.

EMS Hardware Monitors

EMS Hardware Monitors provide the ability to detect and report problems with system hardware resources, such as disk components. EMS Hardware Monitors help you to monitor for faults, such as device errors and component failures. They not only poll the hardware at regular intervals, but they also notify you of hardware errors in real time. EMS Hardware Monitors are delivered with HP-UX Online Diagnostics, which is freely available for HP-UX. EMS Hardware Monitors provide monitoring for the following Hewlett-Packard products:

- AutoRAID disk arrays
- High availability disk arrays
- High availability Storage Systems

- Fast/Wide SCSI disk arrays
- Standalone SCSI and fibre channel disks
- Fibre channel SCSI multiplexors
- Fibre channel adapters
- Fibre channel arbitrated loop hubs

These EMS Hardware Monitors are designed to provide a commonality in the configuration interface, event detection, and message formats, which include a detailed message describing the problem and how to fix it.

The EMS Hardware Monitors can report low-level device errors encountered during an I/O with a device. They detect and report component and FRU failures, including fan and power supply problems. Protocol errors are also detected.

Hardware monitoring is critical for maintaining a system's high availability. For example, when using an AutoRAID disk array, two controllers may be used for high availability. The AutoRAID Monitor reports events that could indicate the failure of a controller. These events could result in a loss of hardware redundancy. Other events indicate a potential loss of data redundancy, such as the failure of a disk component or the failure to recover data redundancy after a component failure. Many events may indicate a SPOF and the loss of high availability. Notification of these events is critical so that the failure can be fixed to eliminate the risk of downtime.

Hardware events are assigned a severity level by the monitor. These severity levels reflect the potential impact of the event on system operation. Table 5-3 provides a description of each severity level.

Table 5-3   Description of Hardware Event Severity

Severity	Description
Critical	An event that will or has already caused data loss, system downtime, or other loss of service. Immediate action is required to correct the problem. System operation will be affected and normal use of the hardware should not continue until the problem is corrected. If configured with MC/ServiceGuard, the package will experience failover.
Serious	An event that may cause data loss, system downtime, or other loss of service if left uncorrected. The problem should be repaired as soon as possible. System operation and normal use of the hardware may be affected. If configured with MC/ServiceGuard, the package will experience failover.
Major Warning	An event that could escalate to a more serious condition if not corrected. The problem should be repaired at a convenient time. System operation should not be affected, and normal use of the hardware can continue. If configured with MC/ServiceGuard, the package will not experience failover.
Minor Warning	An event that will not likely escalate to a more serious condition if left uncorrected. The problem can be repaired at a convenient time. System operation will not be interrupted, and normal use of the hardware can continue. If configured with MC/ServiceGuard, the package will not experience failover.
Information	An event that occurs as part of the normal operation of the hardware. No action is required. If configured with MC/ServiceGuard, the package will not experience failover.

EMS Hardware Monitor configuration is done using the Hardware Monitoring Request Manager. Notification conditions can be configured in a consistent way for all of the supported hardware resources on a system. As hardware is added to the system, monitoring can be enabled automatically. Figure 5-4 shows an example of using the Hardware Monitoring Request Manager to send e-mail notification of all critical and serious hardware events. To configure with MC/ServiceGuard, you need to use the MC/ServiceGuard configuration interface.

When an EMS Hardware Monitor detects an event, a notification message is sent to the designated target locations. The message contains a full description, including the system on which the event occurred, the date and time when the event was detected, the hardware device on which the event occurred, a description of the problem, the probable cause, and a recommended action. Figure 5-5 shows the detailed message for a media failure event on a SCSI disk. Although not shown, the message contains more detailed information, including product/device identification information, I/O log event information, raw hardware status, SCSI status, and more.

Figure 5-4   Using the Hardware Monitoring Request Manager to configure hardware monitoring.

```
=================================================================
=============== Monitoring Request Manager Main Menu ===============
=================================================================
Select:
   (S)how monitoring requests configured via monconfig
   (C)heck detailed monitoring status
   (L)ist descriptions of available monitors
   (A)dd a monitoring request
   (D)elete a monitoring request
   (M)odify an existing monitoring request
   (E)nable Monitoring
   (K)ill (disable) monitoring

   (Q)uit
   Enter selection: [s] s
=================================================================
=================== Current Monitoring Requests ===================
=================================================================

EVENT MONITORING IS CURRENTLY ENABLED.


NOTE: Predictive's monitor requests are not managed by this application,
and are displayed only by the "C" command.
Refer to Predictive's release notes (/opt/pred/bin/Rel_NOTES.PRED)
for further details.


The current monitor configuration is:
  1) Send events generated by all monitors
     with severity >= INFORMATION to TEXTLOG /var/opt/resmon/log/event.log
  2) Send events generated by monitors
        /storage/events/disk_arrays/AutoRAID
        /storage/events/disks/default
        /adapters/events/FC_adapter
        /connectivity/events/hubs/FC_hub
        /connectivity/events/multiplexors/FC_SCSI_mux
        /storage/events/enclosures/ses_enclosure
        /storage/events/tapes/SCSI_tape
        /storage/events/disk_arrays/FW_SCSI
        /storage/events/disk_arrays/High_Availability
     with severity >= SERIOUS to EMAIL julie@company.com
Standard input: END
```

Figure 5-5   Media failure event reported by an EMS Hardware Monitor.

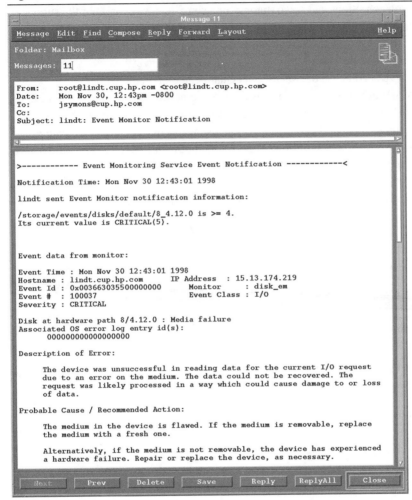

Most EMS Hardware Monitors are "stateless." In other words, events of a designated severity are forwarded as soon as they are detected; no aspect of history or correlation with other data is provided, except that the monitor limits repeated messages by using a repeat frequency. Therefore, determining the current status of a device is difficult, because messages are sent only when an event occurs.

To monitor for hardware device state changes, you can use the Peripheral Status Monitor (PSM), which maintains the state of monitored hardware devices and reports state changes. The PSM gathers events from other EMS Hardware Monitors, but does not send its own notification unless a state change has occurred. By default, critical or serious events cause the PSM to change a device's status to DOWN.

For example, critical disk events from a disk EMS Hardware Monitor cause the PSM to change the device's status to **DOWN**. The PSM then sends a single "disk device status = down" event, if a user had requested that event. This may be the only message visible to the user. Additional disk failure messages would not be forwarded, because they did not result in a status change (in other words, the status remained **DOWN**). This reduces the number of events that need to be processed by the user. The last event received should reflect the current device status.

Most of the Hardware Monitors can't automatically detect when a device has been fixed. When a problem is solved, the set_fixed command must be used to alert the PSM manually to set the device status back to **UP**.

When using an enterprise management tool such as IT/O, which receives messages from multiple systems, you should use the PSM to reduce information overload. However, make sure that stateless events are also configured to go somewhere (such as the system log file), because they provide valuable diagnostic information when a component has failed.

You can learn more about the Hewlett-Packard diagnostic tools on its Web site at http://docs.hp.com/hpux/systems/.

HARAYMON and ARRAYMOND

The High Availability Disk Array Monitor (HARAYMON), available on HP-UX 9.*x*, notifies the system console of all failures of disk array FRUs in high availability disk array products. AutoRAID disk arrays have a similar monitor, called ARRAYMOND. Failures are reported to the system console and to a user-identified list of e-mail addresses (configured in an ASCII file). Each error message can optionally include the location of the array(s) connected to the host system, the event history of the array(s) connected to the host system, and the system administrator's phone number or mail stop.

Listings 5-10 and 5-11 show some messages displayed by HARAYMON for various error conditions. HARAYMON can detect disk failures, fan unit failures, controller module failures, power supply unit failures, and battery backup unit failures.

Listing 5-10 shows a disk module failure. Note that in addition to a timestamp and the failure type being displayed, the array and slot number (within the array) containing the failed device are also reported. The array containing the failed disk module is 48.0.1, and the slot number containing the failed disk is B2.

Listing 5-10   Output from HARAYMON showing disk module failure.

```
================================
Mon Nov 23 10:58:50 PST 1998
High Availability Array Monitor
================================
Drive Failure
Product ID HP A3232A_RAID_5
Physical Device 48.0.1
Disk Position: B2
```

Listing 5-11 shows a fan unit module failure. Specific product information is shown so that the proper component can be replaced.

Listing 5-11   Output from HARAYMON showing a fan unit module failure.

```
================================
Mon Nov 23 11:32:44 PST 1998
High Availability Array Monitor
================================
Fan Unit Failure
Product ID HP A3232A_RAID_5
Physical Device 48.0.1
Fan Number B
```

HARAYMON and ARRAYMOND have been rendered obsolete on newer HP-UX systems (Release 10.20 or greater) by the EMS Hardware Monitors. You may want to disable the HARAYMON and ARRAYMOND daemons if you are using the EMS Hardware Monitors.

OpenView IT/Operations

IT/Operations (IT/O) is an OpenView application that provides central operations and problem management. NNM is included as part of the IT/O product. IT/O uses intelligent agents that run on each managed system to collect management information, messages, and alerts, and to send the information to a centralized console. After receiving events, IT/O can initiate automatic corrective actions. When an operator reads an individual message, guidance is given and actions may be suggested for further problem resolution or recovery.

IT/O has the following four main windows:

- **Node Bank:** Displays iconographically the systems managed by an operator, and allows for them to be organized into node groups.
- **Message Groups:** Displays logical message groups, such as performance, Oracle, or backup. The message groups serve as one way to organize messages in the Message Browser window.
- **Message Browser:** Shows the events that have been received by the management server.
- **Application Desktop:** Provides access to commonly used diagnostic and administrative applications.

IT/O comes with predefined monitors and templates. For monitoring disk resources, it has a monitor for the root filesystem for Hewlett-Packard, Sun, and other platforms. The predefined message template defines the message condition so that when the root filesystem usage exceeds 90 percent, a warning is sent to the IT/O Message Browser. The message condition defining this criterion is shown in Figure 5-6.

Figure 5-6   IT/O message condition template for monitoring root filesystem usage.

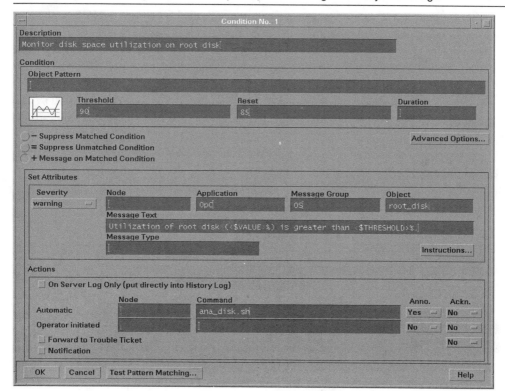

IT/O enables you to define and customize your own monitors and templates. The monitor for the root filesystem can be modified for other critical filesystems. Or, you can define your own monitors and templates to monitor MIB variables, such as the filesystem MIB variables mentioned earlier in this chapter. IT/O periodically queries the MIB object to determine whether a message should be generated. You can write a program or script that is periodically invoked by an IT/O agent. Templates and message conditions can be modified so that the operator is paged under certain conditions.

Many other tools plug in to IT/O to provide additional monitoring and management capabilities. One key example is the monvols EMS utility mentioned earlier in this chapter. This utility integrates into the IT/O Application Bank. It enables monitoring of all physical or logical volumes for all volume groups on a particular system.

IT/O is useful when an operator needs to manage numerous systems consistently. The disk monitoring template can be modified and then downloaded to a set of systems. In this way, multiple systems can be monitored identically.

Enterprise SyMON

Sun Microsystems has an enterprise management product called Enterprise SyMON, a management solution that includes monitoring tools for Sun platforms. It can be thought of as a scaled-down version of IT/O. SyMON provides an event browser and a detailed display of systems and hardware. A graphical view of the physical system layout can be shown. SyMON can be used to monitor the health of disk resources and to isolate hardware and software faults. It analyzes health information to predict potential disk hardware failures. For diagnostics, SyMON can launch the SunVTS diagnostic system or view the system log. Performance monitoring capabilities are also provided.

SyMON can be configured to send SNMP traps for events. Only hardware events are included, such as disk, memory, or tape failures. However, additional events can be generated by placing various rules written in the Tool Command Language (TCL) scripting language in a special directory. Recovery actions can be associated with an event.

Using Diagnostic Tools

Various support tools provide monitoring of errors and faults, configuration information, and troubleshooting for hardware components, including disks.

Support Tool Manager

HP Support Tool Manager (STM) is a set of tools for HP-UX systems that is used for verifying and troubleshooting system hardware. These tools provide the ability to determine device status, get configuration information, and diagnose hardware problems. These tools are available using a GUI or through commands, and have the flexibility to be invoked automatically at periodic intervals.

STM includes the Automatic Configuration Mapper, which provides a graphical view of your hardware configuration using color-coded icons that show device status, as well as logical relationships, such as the peripherals connected to an I/O card. Each icon on the map represents a hardware device. These icons display the device type, device identifier, device path, last active tool, and test status (from the last active tool). From this view, you can launch the other STM tools. Figure 5-7 shows the Automatic Configuration Mapper, which is the main screen of STM.

The Information tool provides product identity information, product description, hardware path, vendor name, firmware revision, and error log statistics, including read errors, which can be used to trend and anticipate problems. This tool can also be used to track configuration changes.

Several other tools under STM perform varying levels of testing to stress a device or determine and diagnose problems:

- **Verifier:** Can be invoked on a particular device to verify quickly that the device is connected and functioning properly
- **Exerciser:** Stresses a device to help troubleshoot intermittent problems

Figure 5-7   STM Automatic Configuration Mapper shows disk hardware devices.

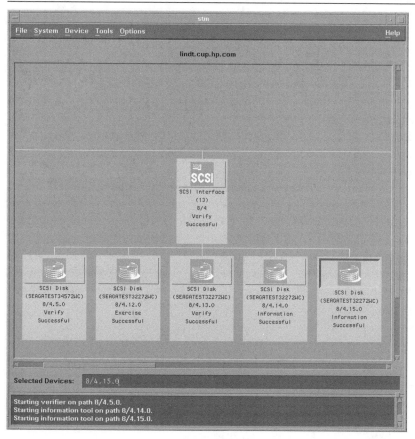

- **Diagnose:** Helps to isolate failures down to the FRU level, so that you can determine whether the selected FRU is failing

Note that the Information, Verifier, and Exerciser tools are free, but the Diagnose tool may require the purchase of a special license.

The Logtool Utility in STM helps you to format, filter, and extract error information from raw data contained in system logs. The raw data collected by the Logtool includes many of the recoverable errors generated by the operating system, including bus errors, memory errors, and low-priority machine checks. You can use this data to troubleshoot and look for trends in historical information, so that you can fix failures before they become critical.

You should use STM in conjunction with the EMS Hardware Event Monitors, because after you receive an EMS event regarding your system hardware, you can run some of the diagnostic tools under STM to diagnose the problem further.

HP Predictive Support

HP Predictive Support is a high level of support from the Hewlett-Packard customer support team. It provides fault monitoring, trending, and HP Response Center notifications. Predictive Support includes monitoring of system hardware devices for faults.

With Predictive Support, you can have Hewlett-Packard proactively monitor your HP-UX systems for you. Predictive Support provides detection of potential problems in your system before the system's availability is noticeably affected. Predictive Support includes both software for hardware monitoring and a link to the HP Response Center. Predictive Support monitors detect failures and predict potential problems. Predictive Support then informs the HP Response Center via e-mail or modem (if allowed) to take any necessary action to prevent unscheduled downtime at the customer.

Predictive Support monitors determine potential problems by analyzing patterns in logged errors pertaining to disk drives, such as bad blocks and recoverable I/O errors. Errors are periodically extracted from system log files and other logs. Based on the rule sets, a notification may be sent to the Response Center, which could result in a service call by an HP support engineer to replace a device having sporadic errors before it actually fails.

Predictive Support now uses EMS to receive alerts for fibre channel disk devices. EMS Hardware Monitors are used to send alerts as errors and faults are detected. These events are logged and correlated by the Predictive Support monitors.

Collecting Disk Performance Data

This section describes some common tools for measuring and monitoring disk performance. The following are some key terms that you need to know for this section:

- **Block I/O:** The reads and writes that are held in the buffer cache (*buffered*) and then transferred in fixed-size blocks.
- **File I/O:** The I/O access to a physical disk, which does not include virtual memory. It includes filesystem I/O, system I/O, raw I/O, and block I/O.
- **Logical I/O:** The read or write system call made by an application to the filesystem. The call results in physical I/O if the data is not in the buffer cache.
- **Physical I/O:** Data transferred from memory to disk, or vice versa. Physical I/O includes both file I/O and virtual memory I/O.
- **Raw I/O:** Unbuffered I/O between a user application and the physical disk that bypasses the filesystem's buffer cache (also known as *character mode*).
- **Virtual memory I/O:** The reads and writes from the disk for memory-mapped files and for paging out pages from a swap area.

Performance tools, such as BMC PATROL and HP MeasureWare Agent, do not always provide the same set of metrics on all platforms. For simplicity, this section focuses only on the Sun Solaris and HP-UX platforms. Also, these products are continually being enhanced, so the actual metrics available for use in your environment may not precisely match the information presented in this section.

MeasureWare

HP MeasureWare Agent is a Hewlett-Packard product that collects and logs resource and performance metrics. MeasureWare agents are installed on the individual server systems to be monitored. MeasureWare agents exist for many platforms and operating systems.

MeasureWare agents collect data at the global, application, and process levels. Many of the system metrics are described in Chapter 4, "Monitoring the System." This section lists the additional global metrics that are used to monitor disk devices.

The following is a list of system-wide disk-related metrics available on HP-UX and Sun Solaris:

- Number of disk drives configured on system
- Average utilization of busiest disk during interval
- Number and rate of physical disk reads during interval
- Number and rate of physical disk writes during interval
- Number and rate of physical disk transfers during interval
- Number and rate of disk reads by filesystem during interval
- Number and rate of disk writes for memory management during interval
- Percentage of logical reads satisfied by memory cache
- Number and rate of filesystem reads, per disk drive, during interval
- Number and rate of filesystem writes, per disk drive, during interval
- Disk utilization, per disk drive, during interval

These additional system-wide disk-related metrics are available on HP-UX:

- Number and rate of logical disk I/Os during interval
- Number and rate of logical disk reads during interval
- Number and rate of logical disk writes during interval
- Number and rate of logical disk transfer reads
- Number and rate of logical disk transfer writes
- Number and rate of disk writes by filesystem during interval
- Number and rate of disk reads for memory management during interval
- Number and rate of disk reads for system during interval
- Number and rate of disk writes for system during interval
- Number and rate of raw reads during interval
- Number and rate of raw writes during interval
- Number and rate of logical disk reads, per disk drive, during interval
- Number and rate of logical disk writes, per disk drive, during interval

• Number and rate of raw reads, per disk drive, during interval
• Number and rate of raw writes, per disk drive, during interval
• Number and rate of memory manager transfers, per disk drive, during interval
• Number and rate of system transfers, per disk drive, during interval
• Average number of requests in queue, per disk drive

MeasureWare can also provide information on swap space utilization and the "fullest filesystem," which is the filesystem with the highest percentage of disk space in use.

GlancePlus

GlancePlus is a real-time, graphical performance monitoring tool. It is used to monitor the performance and system resource utilization of a single system. Both Motif-based and character-based interfaces are available. The product can be used on HP-UX, Sun Solaris, and many other operating systems.

GlancePlus can be used to view and graph a system's current CPU, memory, swap, and disk activity. GlancePlus has screens dedicated to each of these main resources.

GlancePlus can display a variety of data useful for disk monitoring:

• Disk utilization and queue length per disk device
• Disk I/O rates by filesystem
• Disk I/O rates per process
• Number of configured disks
• Physical reads and writes per disk and per filesystem
• Reads and writes per logical volume
• Number of configured LVM volume groups
• Filesystem capacity and utilization
• Swap space capacity and utilization
• System table resources

The specific list of available metrics can be found when running GlancePlus, through its online help facility.

GlancePlus is also capable of setting and receiving performance-related alarms. Customizable rules determine when a system performance problem should be sent as an alarm. The rules are managed by the GlancePlus Adviser. An Adviser menu option allows you to Edit Adviser Syntax. When you select this option, all of the alarm conditions are shown and can be modified, as demonstrated in Figure 5-8.

Notice in Figure 5-8 how the swap-related alarms are integrated into the same definition file along with network-related alarms. When alarms occur, they can be reflected directly in the GlancePlus interface.

Figure 5-8   Using GlancePlus to configure alarms for monitoring swap space utilization.

```
                        GlancePlus – Edit Adviser Syntax
 File   Syntax   Reset   Window                                          Help
 REPLACE MODE                                                             ?
 alarm Network_Bottleneck > 50 for 2 minutes
   start
     if Network_Bottleneck > 90 then
       red alert "Network Bottleneck probability= ", Network_Bottleneck, "%"
     else
       yellow alert "Network Bottleneck probability= ", Network_Bottleneck, "%"
   repeat every 10 minutes
     if Network_Bottleneck > 90 then
       red alert "Network Bottleneck probability= ", Network_Bottleneck, "%"
     else
       yellow alert "Network Bottleneck probability= ", Network_Bottleneck, "%"
   end
     reset alert "End of Network Bottleneck Alert"


 # The following alarm assumes that on a good network, very few errors occur:
 alarm GBL_NET_ERROR_1_MIN_RATE > 10
   start
     yellow alert "Network error rate is greater than ten per minute"
   end
     reset alert "End of non-zero network error rate condition"


 # The following are system table alarms.  If gpm overhead is a concern, and
 # you think you will not have system table shortage problems, you may wish
 # to delete these alarms.

 # Global swap space utilization alarm:
 alarm GBL_SWAP_SPACE_UTIL > 95
   start
     red alert "Global swap space is nearly full"
   end
     reset alert "End of global swap space full condition"
```

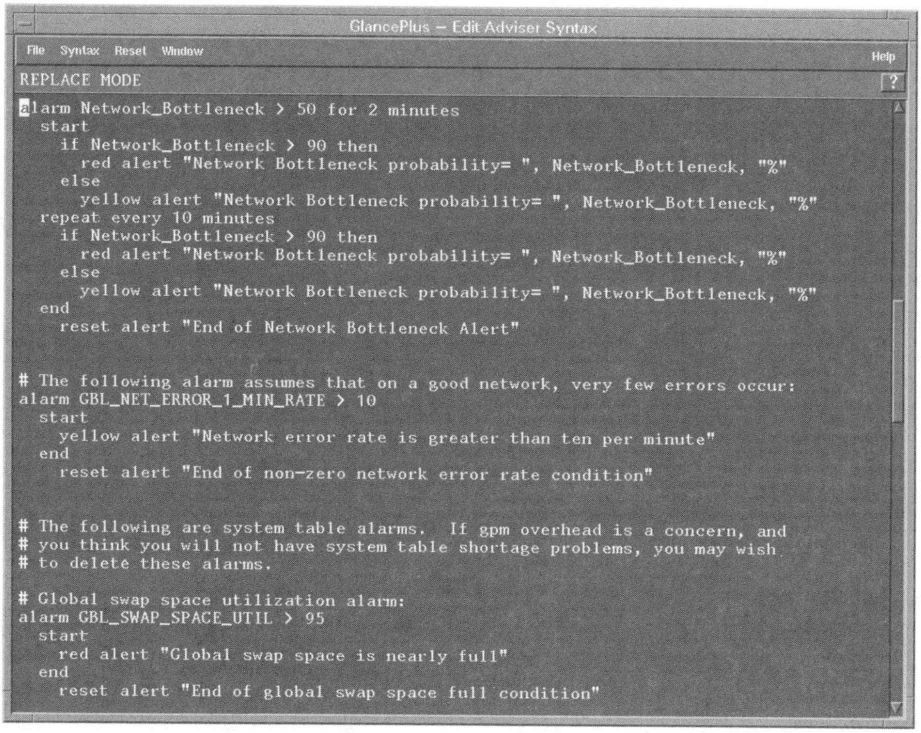

GlancePlus can be launched from the command line, or you can start it from the Performance Monitors functional area in SAM (on HP-UX).

PerfView

PerfView is a graphical performance monitoring tool that is used to monitor the performance and system resource utilization for multiple systems in your environment. A variety of performance graphs can be displayed. The graphs are based on data collected over a period of time, unlike the real-time graphs of GlancePlus. PerfView can show graphs from multiple systems simultaneously, so that comparisons can be made.

PerfView is integrated with other monitoring tools. For example, you can launch Glance-Plus from within PerfView by accessing the Tools menu. And, PerfView can be launched from the IT/O Applications Bank. When troubleshooting an event in the IT/O Message Browser window, you can launch PerfView to see a related performance graph.

PerfView relies on MeasureWare data, so it can display performance information only for systems that support the MeasureWare Agent. Refer to the previous section on MeasureWare to see a list of the disk metrics available.

PerfView has three main components:

- **PerfView Monitor:** Provides the ability to receive alarms. A textual description of an alarm can be displayed. Alarms can be filtered by severity, type, or source system. Also, after an alarm is received, the alarm can be selected, to display a graph of related metrics. An operator can monitor trends leading to failures, and can then take proactive actions to avoid problems. Graphs can be used for comparison between systems and to show a history of resource consumption. An internal database is maintained that keeps a history of alarm notification messages.
- **PerfView Analyzer:** Provides resource and performance analysis for disks and other resources. System metrics can be shown at three different levels: process, application (configured by the user as a set of processes), and global system information. It relies on data received from MeasureWare agents on managed nodes. Data can be analyzed from up to eight systems concurrently. All MeasureWare data sources are supported. PerfView Analyzer is required by both PerfView Monitor and PerfView Planner.
- **PerfView Planner:** Provides forecasting capability. Graphs can be extrapolated into the future. A variety of graphs (such as linear, exponential, s-curve, and smoothed) can be shown for forecasted data.

PerfView's ability to show history and trend information can be helpful in diagnosing disk problems. Graphing performance information can help you to understand whether a persistent problem exists or is an anomaly (simply a momentary spike of activity). Figure 5-9 shows a PerfView graph illustrating an application's I/O performance over time. Additional system performance metrics are also included in the graph.

To diagnose a problem further, PerfView Monitor allows the user to change time intervals, to try to find the specific time that a problem occurred. The graph is redrawn showing the new time period.

BMC PATROL

BMC provides monitoring capabilities through its PATROL software suite. PATROL provides the basic framework for defining thresholds, sending and translating events, and so forth. Optional products called Knowledge Modules (KMs) contain the ability to monitor specific components. For example, BMC PATROL includes KMs for UNIX, SAP R/3, Oracle, Informix, and other applications. In fact, more than 40 KMs are available from BMC for use with PATROL.

BMC provides a tool with its UNIX KM to provide information about disks and disk usage. The following disk and filesystem metrics are available on HP-UX and Sun Solaris:

- Number and rate of system data transfers, per disk drive, during interval
- Average service time, per disk drive
- Average disk seek time, per disk drive
- Percentage of time the drive is busy fulfilling a transfer request

Figure 5-9   PerfView can show the history of an application's I/O access rate.

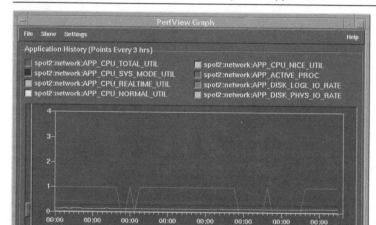

- Average time spent waiting in queue, per disk drive
- Rate of physical disk reads, per disk drive
- Rate of raw reads, per disk drive
- Rate of logical disk reads, per disk drive
- Percentage of logical reads in the buffer cache
- Rate of physical disk writes, per disk drive
- Number of logical writes to system buffer
- Percentage of logical blocks written to buffer cache
- Average number of requests in queue, per disk drive
- Percentage of time that CPU spends waiting for I/O operations

BMC can also monitor the percentage of swap space in use, and the amount of filesystem space in use, per filesystem.

The disk monitoring capabilities of BMC PATROL are similar to those of MeasureWare. Some minimal configuration information is provided, but its primary value is in tracking resource and performance information. Indirectly, BMC PATROL can provide some fault information as well. For example, if disk utilization suddenly drops to zero on a particular disk drive, it may be an indication that the disk has failed. Of course, it could also be an indication that an application has terminated and is no longer using the disk.

Using Disk Performance Data

To address disk performance problems, you first need to collect the appropriate data. MeasureWare and BMC PATROL are two examples of tools that collect the necessary performance metrics. This section provides a brief overview of how to interpret the data to determine whether a disk performance problem exists.

This chapter shows only those metrics related directly to disks. However, you should also study system and application-related performance information, because disk information alone may not be sufficient to solve a problem. MeasureWare provides a lot of information about an application's disk utilization that may need to be correlated with system data. For example, the root cause of a disk performance problem may be an I/O-intensive application that is not supposed to be running during production hours. Looking at application and system data in conjunction with disk data can help to find the culprit.

All performance monitoring tools can provide system CPU utilization information. If an application's response time is low, and the system's CPU utilization is less than 95 percent, this may be an indication that a disk bottleneck exists. Other important metrics are disk utilization, disk queue lengths, and the time the system spends waiting for I/O to complete.

To avoid disk bottlenecks, you need to balance I/O across filesystems, disk spindles, and disk controllers to reduce uneven queuing and delays. Performance monitoring tools, such as Glance-Plus, can be used to find the process with the highest I/O rate, and also the busiest physical disk. Checking only the I/O rate is insufficient, because a slower device will have a higher utilization than a faster disk with the same I/O rate. If a single disk has greater than 50-percent utilization for an extended period of time, this may be an indication of an I/O bottleneck. The percentage should be compared with that of other disks to see whether a severe load imbalance exists. However, high utilization is not sufficient to identify a problem. The disk may still be capable of handling more I/O. A continually long disk queue length must be present to indicate a problem. Heavily used disks are also likely to have long disk queue lengths.

Both BMC PATROL and MeasureWare collect read cache hit ratio information. Determining how many logical reads are satisfied by the system's buffer cache is an indication of whether the cache size was configured correctly. Because increasing the cache size negatively affects the system memory available for other purposes, the appropriate cache hit ratio depends on the type of workload being run on the system. For I/O-intensive applications, you may want to configure your system such that this ratio is as high as about 90 or 95 percent. Similarly, you may want to ensure that your write cache hit ratio is at least 75 percent. If your hit rates are too low, the system buffer cache may be too small.

After you determine that the system buffer cache is too small, you can increase its size on HP-UX by using SAM. Select Configurable Parameters from the Kernel Configuration functional area. The appropriate parameter to modify depends on whether a static or dynamic buffer cache is being used, but this can be checked on this screen as well. *Fixed-size buffer caches* are most effective if the environment and workload are static. *Dynamic buffer caches* fluctuate in size based on demands for I/O or virtual memory, and are useful when workloads vary. If the nbuf and bufpages system parameters are set to zero, then a dynamic buffer cache is in use. When using a dynamic buffer cache on systems with greater than 1GB of real memory, you should lower the maximum size below 50 percent, because caches greater than 500MB actually cause performance degradations.

The Process Resource Manager (PRM) can be used to control system CPU, real memory, and I/O bandwidth allocations between users and applications. Users or applications are assigned to PRM groups, and each group is configured with the desired system resource entitlement. This can help to provide application isolation, by preventing one application from affecting the performance of another application. CPU controls alone are often sufficient, but sometimes, an I/O-intensive application may be using very little CPU. Other applications that need to use the same I/O interface may be starved. If multiple applications are sharing access to a volume group, PRM can be used to allocate an appropriate minimum entitlement of disk bandwidth to each. PRM can throttle disk throughput for PRM groups by ordering logical I/O requests, so that requests for lower-priority processes are delayed, allowing requests from higher-priority processes to get through. Resource capping isn't available for I/O bandwidth, so an application can use all of the available bandwidth if no other applications need it.

PRM controls disk bandwidth only for disks under LVM. Determining the best entitlements to configure may be difficult and may require some experimentation. Before enabling a disk bandwidth configuration in PRM, you can collect data on the current usage of different PRM groups. This can be done by first configuring the CPU entitlements in PRM with no disk records specified. The prmconfig and prmmonitor commands can then be used to collect current usage statistics for a specified volume group. PRM is available only on HP-UX.

If GlancePlus is available, PRM behavior can be shown on the GlancePlus screens. For example, the actual I/O bandwidth used by each PRM group can be shown. Also, GlancePlus can be used to change PRM resource group entitlements.

These are just a few examples of how disk information can be used to address performance problems.

Avoiding Disk Problems

The previous section discussed how to use performance data to fix disk performance problems. Proper configuration can help you to avoid performance problems. Commands such as newfs and tunefs can be used for the High-Performance File System (HFS) to set block size and reduce the number of inodes.

The best way to avoid disk faults is to configure for redundancy and monitor critical disk resources proactively. Products exist at the hardware level that provide both data redundancy and redundant hardware components. Monitoring for hardware faults provides failure notification of redundant components. Although these faults may not cause data to be unavailable, the problems should be fixed immediately. Otherwise, a subsequent failure could cause a loss of data or availability.

Tools such as HP Predictive Support help to indicate when disks are likely to fail. You can also monitor hardware device events, so that you can replace a disk during nonproduction hours (planned downtime), instead of waiting for it to fail. Similarly, use the EMS DVM to detect the loss of a mirror, and then replace the disk before another drive fails.

At the resource level, you need to ensure that the filesystems are accessible. Monitoring the configuration and resource status can help to ensure that the filesystems are up and accessible to those who require them. Monitoring filesystem usage is critical. If a filesystem fills up, applications may have failures. By using tools such as Online JFS, you can increase filesystem capacity online, without affecting availability. By using three-way mirroring, you can perform backups on one mirror, while still maintaining data redundancy.

You should monitor free space on all disk drives to see whether you are nearing configured limits. The EMS File System Monitor can be used for this purpose. Archive files that have not been used for a long time, and remove them from the system. You can use commands such as du to view the usage for each directory and locate large files.

The availability of tools may depend on the filesystem being used. A journalled filesystem can track updates to a file, so that if the file is damaged, it can then be recovered. Online JFS is an optional product that can be used in conjunction with a journalled filesystem. Online JFS can create large file extents to avoid fragmentation, perform online filesystem resizing when a filesystem nears its configured limit, and provide data on fragmentation that is occurring. Online JFS has a defragmentation capability as well. Directories and extents can be reorganized by using the fsadm command.

Recovering from Disk Problems

If you are unable to avoid a disk problem, a variety of tools can help you recover, depending on the problem you are facing. Recovering from system misconfigurations, load imbalances, and disk failures is discussed in this section.

Many tools and techniques are available to help correct a disk load imbalance after it is discovered. Frequently accessed files and swap areas can be spread over different filesystems, spindles, and disk controllers. Disk striping and LVM can be used to spread access across multiple disks. LVM stripe sizes are defined when logical volumes are created. You need to understand I/O access patterns so that you can set the appropriate stripe sizes. More disks may need to be added so that the load can be spread out effectively.

You may want to dedicate disks to a single application to avoid contention problems. A more drastic solution to a performance problem may be to move an application and its data to another system, on which it may have more exclusive access to system resources, including CPU and memory. In some cases, you may be able to study and redesign an application to make fewer disk I/Os.

As long as you have been making regular system backups, you should be able to recover without a loss of data.

Comparing Disk Monitoring Products

The best way to keep track of your disk configuration is to use the UNIX commands provided with the operating system, such as ioscan and vgdisplay. The information tools in STM can provide additional configuration information, such as the firmware revision and serial numbers. You may want to save all of this output for comparison purposes later. Then, if a disk problem occurs, the configuration history can help to track when a change was made. The System Administration Manager presents a textual summary of the disk configuration for HP-UX systems. On Sun Solaris systems, Enterprise SyMON can be used to graphically display the physical system layout.

If configuration information needs to be collected from a variety of systems, querying the system MIB by using a MIB Browser may be more efficient, especially for multiplatform environments, because you will need to remember only one tool to get the information.

Disk failures can be detected initially by using EMS DVM, or the EMS Hardware Monitors for the appropriate hardware device. EMS DVM is unique in that it can also be used to detect the loss of a disk mirror. After a problem is reported, you may use STM for further diagnosis. These products are available only on HP-UX. Enterprise SyMON provides some basic hardware diagnostics for Sun Solaris environments, including the ability to send events for disk failures.

To avoid the need to monitor and repair disk devices, you may want to establish a support contract with Hewlett-Packard. In that case, disk problems are reported directly to the Hewlett-Packard Response Center, and based on trending information collected by HP Predictive, a support engineer may be sent to replace the disk before a failure actually occurs.

MeasureWare and BMC PATROL have comparable disk monitoring functionality, and both primarily provide disk performance metrics. The choice of tool is likely to depend on the other activities that you are doing. For example, PerfView receives its information only from MeasureWare agents. BMC PATROL and MeasureWare can both send information to IT/O. BMC PATROL's UNIX KM, which provides disk metrics, can be used with a wide variety of other KMs. Both tools collect a large amount of data, so you may want to analyze how each performs in your environment before you select one.

Case Study: Configuring and Monitoring for Mirrored Disks

At Silicon Valley Hospital, Nancy Jergens is responsible for maintaining patient records on the hospital's records computer system. To provide extra data protection and high availability, she has decided to use MirrorDisk/UX to mirror the /patient filesystem containing the patient records.

Nancy sets up two-way mirroring on the logical volume containing the patient records. The logical volume lvol_patients is mounted at /patient.

Verifying Configuration

After Nancy configures the mirroring, she verifies the configuration by using the lvdisplay command. As shown in Listing 5-12, Nancy verifies that the logical volume, lvol_patients, is available and mirrored with one copy.

Setting Up Monitoring

Nancy knows that if one of her mirrored copies fails, her patient data will be protected, because she has another copy. But, she wants to be told when she has only one copy left. Unless she monitors for this, she won't be told when a mirrored copy fails.

Listing 5-12 Using lvdisplay to verify mirroring status and copies.

```
# lvdisplay /dev/vg_hospital/lvol_patients
-- Logical volumes --
LV Name                        /dev/vg_hospital/lvol_patients
VG Name                        /dev/vg_hospital
LV Permission                  read/write
LV Status                      available/syncd
Mirror copies                  1
Consistency Recovery           MWC
Schedule                       parallel
LV Size (Mbytes)               100
Current LE                     25
Allocated PE                   50
Stripes                        0
Stripe Size (Kbytes)           0
Bad block                      on
Allocation                     strict
```

Using the EMS Configuration GUI, Nancy configures EMS DVM to monitor the mirrored copies of the logical volume containing the patient records. As shown in Figure 5-10, she sets up

Figure 5-10 Using EMS to monitor mirrored copies.

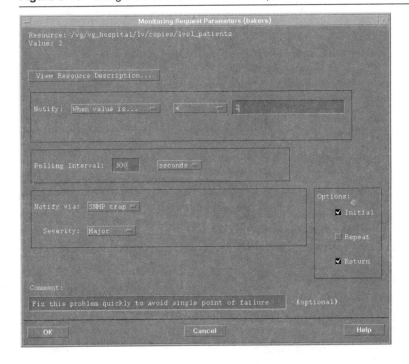

Figure 5-11   IT/O Message Browser shows an EMS event indicating a mirrored disk failure.

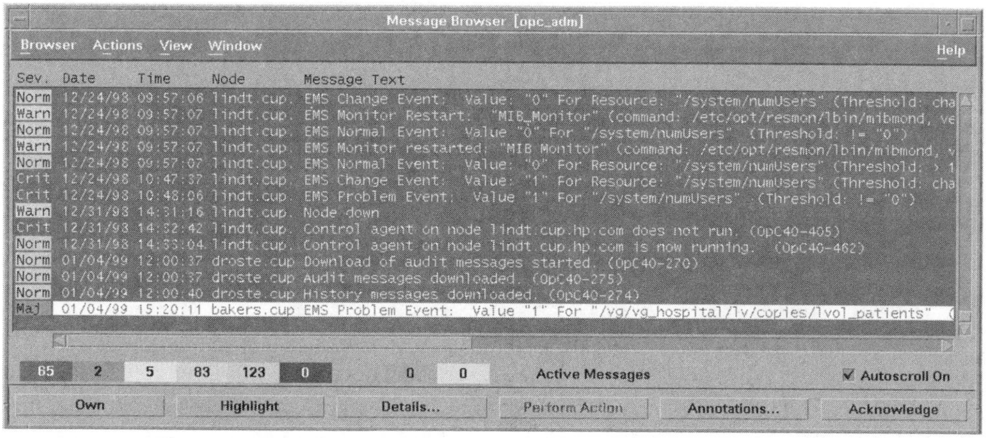

the monitoring request so that she will be notified via SNMP at her OpenView IT/O management station when the number of mirrored copies of the lvol_patients logical volume drops below
two. Nancy configures the notification event to have Major severity.

You may notice that lvdisplay shows 1 as the number of mirror copies, but EMS shows the
current number of copies as 2. EMS DVM looks at the total number of copies. lvdisplay reports
the number of mirrored copies.

Mirror Fails

Something happens on one of the disks that keeps the data mirrored. MirrorDisk/UX can no
longer mirror the data. The data is no longer protected from failure. Fortunately, Nancy is monitoring for this, and an event is sent to the IT/O Message Browser. As shown in Figure 5-11, a
major (Maj) severity EMS event is displayed in the Message Browser.

Restoring Mirrors

After running the diagnostic tools in STM, Nancy identifies the failed component. After swapping in a new drive, she synchronizes the copies so that each copy of the data is identical.

Verifying Configuration

Now that Nancy has fixed the failed disk, she uses the lvdisplay command to verify that the logical volume is once again available and that she has a mirrored copy of the data.

Nancy continues to monitor the copies by using EMS DVM, knowing that she will be notified if the mirror fails again.

Monitoring the Network

With the introduction of client/server computing, and the more recent explosion of Internet usage, the importance of maintaining your corporate networks has increased dramatically. A discussion of network management could easily fill an entire book, so this chapter instead addresses only the monitoring aspects of network management, specifically showing you how to study network performance and detect and recover from network component failures.

Identifying Important Network Components to Monitor

In addition to monitoring a system and its components, it is critical to monitor the networks connecting the system to the end-users. Without connectivity to end-users and adequate performance, the service provided by a system is useless. This chapter shows how to monitor all aspects of your networked environment.

Networking is a broad category and it can be broken down into a variety of components. These network components are shown in Figure 6-1. The client in this picture is the end-user connecting to the corporate network from the user's desktop computer, and the server is the UNIX computer system, providing access to the corporate databases, performing network services such as Network File System (NFS), and so on. Note that the failure of any of these components can affect service availability, so it is important to provide high levels of redundancy throughout the corporate backbone. Network problems can be due to an application, defects in the network protocol software in the operating system, hardware problems with the LAN card or cabling, etc.

To isolate a network problem, you need monitoring tools. The tool discussions in this chapter are organized by network component, such as routers and network interfaces, so that you can more easily see the specific monitoring tools available for each component. Some tools with a variety of capabilities are discussed in multiple sections of this chapter. Tools are available that show you the status of a network graphically, and that detect faults as well as configuration, resource, and performance problems. The most common problems are performance-related, and include both temporary and sustained performance overloads.

This chapter focuses primarily on TCP/IP networks, because the TCP/IP protocol suite is driving most Internet use.

Using Graphical Network Status Monitors

As mentioned earlier, networking involves numerous different components, such as routers, hubs, bridges, and the system's Network Interface Cards (NICs) and operating system. You will see in this chapter that tools are available to address each of these components individually. Before introducing each of these tools, this section shows how some network management products can reduce the complexity of monitoring your corporate networks. The products discussed in this section, referred to as *graphical network status monitors*, reduce complexity by providing summary information about the devices at a central location. You don't need to log in remotely to each network device, and you can see status at a glance.

Popular network management products include Hewlett-Packard's Network Node Manager, Computer Associates' Unicenter TNG, Sun's Net Manager, IBM's NetView, and HP's Net-Metrix. These products offer various unique capabilities, such as the ability to discover automatically all the network devices in your computing environment and display the real-time status of each graphically on network topology maps. A sample of these products is provided in this section. Sun Enterprise SyMON is also discussed in this section, because it is a low-cost alternative to the other products. NetMetrix is discussed later in the chapter, along with other performance tools, because of its primary emphasis on network performance.

Network Node Manager

Network Node Manager (NNM) is a management product based on the HP OpenView platform. It is used primarily to view and monitor the status of network and system resources. Information is displayed graphically in a windows-based display. A hierarchical set of windows, or submaps, are available to enable users to navigate through the network topologies.

From the initial network view, you can drill down to the submap that shows the systems on a specific network segment, as shown in Figure 6-1. Specific statuses of systems are depicted by using different colors for the system icons. The ability to group systems by their network segment can help to isolate a problem to a specific network.

As with other network management products, NNM can automatically discover and monitor the status of network-addressable components, such as routers, hubs, and computer systems, via management protocols such as the Simple Network Management Protocol (SNMP). Any IP-addressable device that is accessible from the management system can be displayed. The network topology information is then displayed on submaps, as shown in Figure 6-1. In larger computing environments, you may want to reduce the network overhead of the discovery process by using *discovery filters*, which enable you to specify the subnetworks that you want to

Figure 6-1   NNM displays network segments.

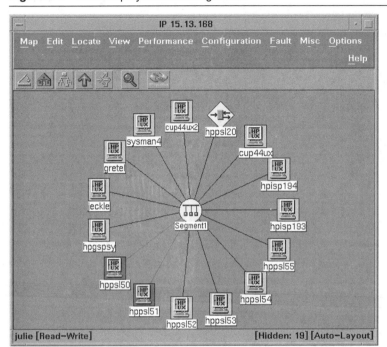

be explored. This can also help to limit the scope of the systems managed from a single management station in your organization.

An operator can navigate through the submaps to find a particular LAN segment containing important systems to monitor. In addition to viewing the overall status of a network device,
an operator can drill down to see system information, such as configured network interfaces. A
system's standby network interfaces — those without a configured IP address — can also be
shown. The icons can help you distinguish between configured and standby interfaces, as shown
in Figure 6-2. Icons without an "IP" symbol are standby interfaces.

NNM includes a graphical Event Browser, which displays the events received from systems on the network. Events are sent to the management station as SNMP traps. The trap daemon receives these traps and stores them in a database to maintain an event history. The events
can be viewed through the Event Browser, and filters can be used to prevent the operator from
being flooded with noncritical information. Filters can be based on several attributes, including
the sending system, criticality of the event, or the time. NNM can also process Common Management Information Protocol (CMIP) events for multivendor interoperability.

NNM periodically polls network devices to verify that they are working. If no reply is
received, a Node Down event is sent as an SNMP trap and logged in NNM Event Browser. This
results in a color change of the graphical icon in NNM that represents the device. NNM's reliance

Figure 6-2   NNM displays a system's network interface status.

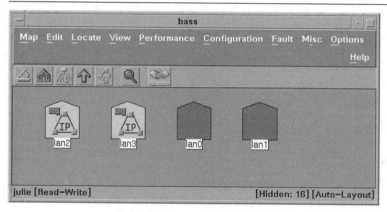

on network connectivity to determine status information can create problems if not all networks are globally accessible. If the management station doesn't have a route to a private subnetwork, the subnetwork will appear to be down when examined from the management station.

Pull-down menus enable the operator to run tools to get additional real-time information. These tools can be used to check a system's network configuration, including addresses, the routing table, ARP cache entries, and system services. The Fault menu includes tools to test a system's network connectivity, ping the system from the management station, remote ping between two remote systems, and locate the SNMP route to the system. Some of these tools are explained in more detail later in the chapter. Finally, NNM tools are available to collect, set thresholds for, and display the MIB data via SNMP. NNM also provides an xnmgraph utility, which enables the user to input any historical data that was collected and see it in graph form.

For additional diagnostic information, you can remotely log in from NNM to the system and execute diagnostic commands. The NNM toolbar provides this feature via telnet, and also provides the capability to launch System Administration Manager (SAM) on the remote system.

OpenView's MIB Browser tool also provides diagnostic capability. A Management Information Base (MIB) is a standard way of representing information of a certain category. For example, the MIB-II provides useful information about a system, such as the number of active TCP connections, details about system hardware, and version information. By using the MIB Browser, you can discover which MIBs are available and see the information being provided by each MIB. The MIB Browser tool can check the value of anything contained in a MIB on the remote system. When you find a MIB that contains some useful fields, you can use this tool or other MIB tools to gather that data from the target system. The MIB data is displayed in the MIB Browser's output window on the screen. By browsing through available MIBs and querying values of selected MIB fields, you can gather specific information needed to monitor systems and troubleshoot problems. Figure 6-3 illustrates how you can use the MIB Browser to check the status of the NICs on a given system.

Figure 6-3 NNM's MIB Browser.

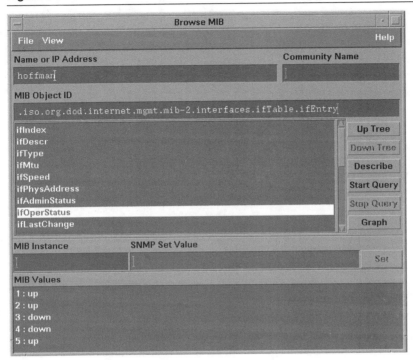

A more detailed description of MIBs, as well as definitions of some of the important MIBs for UNIX servers, are provided in Appendix A.

NNM software can run on UNIX and NT management stations and is a building block for other HP OpenView applications. Application integration is provided through developer's kits and registration files. Many applications are integrated today with HP OpenView, with the most commonly used partner applications being CiscoWorks, Bay Networks Optivity, 3Com Transcend, Remedy ARS, and HP NetMetrix.

IT/Operations

Hewlett-Packard has a product called OpenView IT/Operations (IT/O), a software bundle that not only includes NNM for network management, but also extends its capabilities to provide more in the area of system management. IT/O provides facilities that enable operators to share the management station software, but retain responsibilities for different sets of managed systems.

IT/O includes an Application Bank that allows HP products or customer-generated tools to be iconified and available for use by the operator. Operators select the target system, and then select the tool to run on that system. A two-level hierarchy of tools may be defined. Examples of available tools include GlancePlus and PerfView. These tools can then be used to monitor performance on an arbitrary target system from the central management station.

The IT/O Application Bank includes three application groups with networking tools: Net Activity, Net Config, and Net Diag. Each of these groups has several tools. The Net Activity group, shown in Figure 6-4, has tools to monitor network activity, including interface traffic, Ethernet errors, Ethernet traffic, SNMP traffic, SNMP operations, SNMP errors, interface statistics, SNMP authorization failures, and TCP connections. The Net Config and Net Diag groups provide many of the same tools provided in NNM pull-down menus mentioned earlier in this section.

Unicenter TNG

Computer Associates' Unicenter TNG product is comparable to HP's IT/O product. It discovers IP-addressable components and can display them as icons on maps. The maps can reflect the network topology. An Event Browser is also included and can be used to keep a history of SNMP events received from the monitored systems. This Event Browser is shown in Figure 6-5.

Computer system status is reflected on the map with different colors. Like NNM, Unicenter TNG also has difficulty showing the status of private networks correctly.

Computer Associates (CA) repackages some of its monitoring and discovery features into its Unicenter TNG Framework, which it ships for free on some platforms, such as HP-UX. Additionally, CA has done some special integration with HP's Event Monitoring Service (EMS) product (discussed later in this chapter), so that the status of monitored resources on the system can be shown graphically.

Enterprise SyMON

Sun Enterprise SyMON is a low-end product for network monitoring. It is able to discover computer systems that are reachable from the management station, and can group systems into

Figure 6-4 Networking tools available from the IT Application Bank.

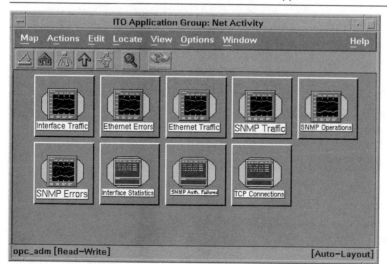

Figure 6-5   Unicenter TNG Event Browser.

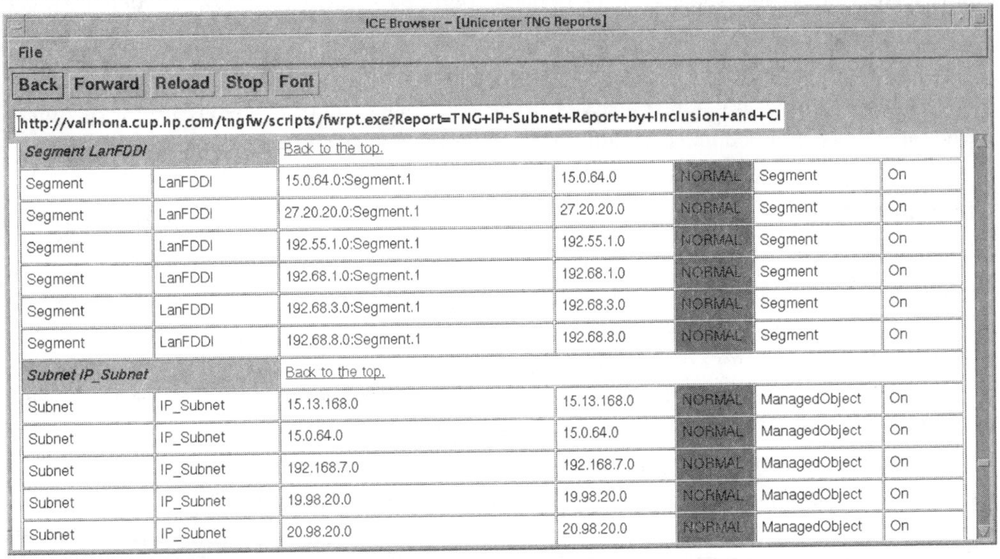

ICE Browser – [Unicenter TNG Reports]						
File						
Back **Forward** **Reload** **Stop** **Font**						
http://valrhona.cup.hp.com/tngfw/scripts/fwrpt.exe?Report=TNG+IP+Subnet+Report+by+Inclusion+and+Cl						
Segment LanFDDI		Back to the top.				
Segment	LanFDDI	15.0.64.0:Segment.1	15.0.64.0	NORMAL	Segment	On
Segment	LanFDDI	27.20.20.0:Segment.1	27.20.20.0	NORMAL	Segment	On
Segment	LanFDDI	192.55.1.0:Segment.1	192.55.1.0	NORMAL	Segment	On
Segment	LanFDDI	192.68.1.0:Segment.1	192.68.1.0	NORMAL	Segment	On
Segment	LanFDDI	192.68.3.0:Segment.1	192.68.3.0	NORMAL	Segment	On
Segment	LanFDDI	192.68.8.0:Segment.1	192.68.8.0	NORMAL	Segment	On
Subnet IP_Subnet		Back to the top.				
Subnet	IP_Subnet	15.13.168.0	15.13.168.0	NORMAL	ManagedObject	On
Subnet	IP_Subnet	15.0.64.0	15.0.64.0	NORMAL	ManagedObject	On
Subnet	IP_Subnet	192.168.7.0	192.168.7.0	NORMAL	ManagedObject	On
Subnet	IP_Subnet	19.98.20.0	19.98.20.0	NORMAL	ManagedObject	On
Subnet	IP_Subnet	20.98.20.0	20.98.20.0	NORMAL	ManagedObject	On

"domains" for easier administration. Figure 6-6 shows how this discovery is configured. SyMON provides system status based on the criticality of events received from a system. SyMON can also be used to generate performance graphs.

Sun Enterprise SyMON can be used to report network alarms through its graphical display. Events can be generated by configuring rules in the Tool Command Language (TCL) scripting language. SyMON provides an intelligent agent on the managed node that has access to a large set of system data, including the MIB-II. Rules can be configured for the network portion of the MIB-II to send alarms when the interface card's status changes, for example.

SyMON also includes diagnostic capabilities. In response to an event, you can drill down to a physical view of the system that includes a photo view of the failed component, based on preloaded GIF files for each system model.

The intelligent agent on the managed system can support additional modules being loaded. For example, a module exists that can report events for the NFS. The user can choose which additional modules to load.

SyMON is only available for monitoring Sun systems.

Monitoring Network Interface Card and Cable Failures

The Mean Time Between Failures (MTBF) for a single Network Interface Card (NIC) can be many years. However, in a large computing environment, you are still likely to experience LAN card failures. This section shows how you can monitor LAN card failures, verify that physical cables are set up properly, and discover related problems, such as a link disconnection. You can also see how to identify the type of network link being used.

Figure 6-6   Configuring discovery in SyMON.

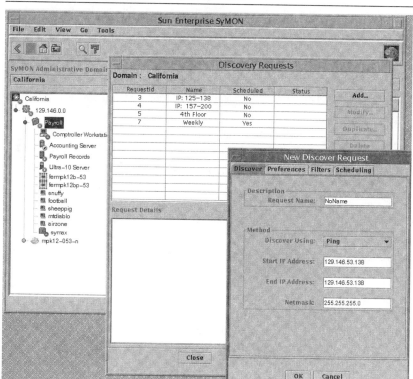

This section refers to monitoring the networking components that correspond roughly to the physical and data link layers of the Open Systems Interconnection (OSI) model. This section also shows how to obtain a LAN's status and statistics, the LAN station addresses used by each UNIX server, and information on LAN packet errors. This section concludes with some of the monitoring tools that are specific to certain network links, such as X.25, Asynchronous Transfer Mode (ATM), and Fiber Distributed Data Interface (FDDI).

Using SNMP Instrumentation

As mentioned earlier in this chapter, important monitoring information can be stored in standard MIBs, and can then be queried by using a MIB Browser. The MIB Browsers are publicly available and are also included with the NNM, IT/O, and other network management products. The MIB data can also be obtained by using a custom SNMP application, but you need to know the Object Identifiers (OIDs) of the fields you are interested in querying, which are provided in the MIB specifications. Standard MIB documents are provided as Requests For Comments (RFCs) from the Internet Engineering Task Force (IETF), and are available on the Web at http://www.ietf.org.

The MIB-II (defined in RFCs 1213 and 1214) contains numerous useful fields for monitoring network links. Information about each network interface is available, including its current status. You can compare the total number of input packets to the number of input packets received in error. Similar fields are available for output packets. Together, these fields can be an indication of how well a network is behaving.

You may also want to check the number of inbound packets that were discarded despite being received without error. If packets are being discarded, this could indicate a lack of system memory reserved for network buffers.

Each network interface has both an administration status and an operation status defined in the MIB-II. Administration status is up, down, or testing. It refers to the desired state of the interface. Operation status is also up, down, or testing, and it corresponds to the current operational state of the interface.

Network statistics are accumulated from the time the system was booted, or since the last manual reset of the statistics. Because this usually is a long period of time, a single MIB query is unlikely to be useful. You will probably want to set up ongoing monitoring and calculate the change in value over time to get an idea of network traffic over a NIC and the current error rate. Output errors are likely to indicate a problem getting to the link from the local system.

Using Standard Commands and Tools

Each UNIX operating system includes a variety of commands that can be helpful in determining the status of a network interface. The more commonly used HP-UX commands are described in this section. You may want to check the online man pages for additional information about each command.

In addition to these commands, you may also want to check the system log file, /var/adm/syslog/syslog.log, for LAN-related error messages if your system is experiencing network problems.

ioscan

The ioscan command is used to provide information about all the I/O paths on a system. It can show the hardware paths to your LAN cards and help you to distinguish between a built-in LAN card and additional LAN cards. You can also see the specific type of LAN card being used. ioscan shows errors if the hardware or software has not been properly installed. Errors may be due to the wrong network driver being installed, meaning that you would need to rebuild the kernel with the correct driver. Listing 6-1 shows an HP-UX system with one built-in LAN card and three EISA cards.

Listing 6-1 The ioscan command with grep, which shows only network information.

```
chacha#ioscan |grep lan
8/16/6              lan              Built-in LAN
8/20/5/1              lan            EISA card HWP1990
8/20/5/7              lan            EISA card HWP1990
8/20/5/8              lan            EISA card HWP1990
chacha#
```

lanscan

The lanscan command shows the hardware path to each LAN device, the station address, link status, network management ID, and link technology being used (for example, Ethernet or FDDI). The *station address* is the unique identifier for a LAN card and is also referred to as a physical address or Media Access Control (MAC) address. You can compare the information from lanscan, as shown in Listing 6-2, to that provided by ioscan, shown in Listing 6-1. With this additional information, you can uniquely identify your LAN card so that you can configure it for the appropriate corporate network. Also, if you are using an analyzer to look at network packets on a LAN, lanscan will help you to map the station address in the packet to a network interface on a system.

Note that an interface has both a hardware state and a network interface state. The hardware state corresponds to the configured state of the device, and the network interface state corresponds to the current operational state. In the example in Listing 6-2, lan1 has been configured UP, but is not operating properly.

lanadmin

The lanadmin command can be used to display or change the station address, Maximum Transmission Unit (MTU), or speed setting of each configured network interface. It can also be used to display or reset the MIB-II network interface statistics. The statistics include the interface name, administrative status, operational status, number of error packets, and other information. For Ethernet links, lanadmin also displays statistics from RFC 1284 (Ethernet-like interface information), which can indicate the number of collisions happening on the link.

Some overlap exists with other commands. For example, the station address is also available from lanscan, and the MTU can also be obtained from netstat (discussed later).

lanadmin can be used to reinitialize a LAN card. For example, if networking fails during system startup, you may be able to enable networking by using lanadmin to reset the LAN card, and then use ifconfig (described later) to bring the card up with the proper IP address.

Numerous statistics are available from lanadmin, as shown by using the lanadmin menu-driven interface in Listing 6-3. Note that to use the lanadmin command, you need to specify the network management ID number of the LAN card, which can be obtained from the lanscan command.

Listing 6-2 Output from lanscan command showing the list of LAN cards.

```
# lanscan
Hardware Station      Crd Hardware Net-Interface  NM MAC   HP DLPI Mjr
Path     Address      In# State    NameUnit State ID Type  Support Num
8/16/6   0x080009C3FA7D 0  UP       lan0      UP    4  ETHER Yes     52
8/20/5/1 0x080009ACC83C 1  UP       lan1      DOWN  5  ETHER Yes     176
8/20/5/7 0x080009ACD860 2  DOWN     lan2      DOWN  6  ETHER Yes     176
8/20/5/8 0x080009ACF11E 3  DOWN     lan3      DOWN  7  ETHER Yes     176
#
```

Listing 6-3   Output from lanadmin execution.

```
cancan#lanadmin
          LOCAL AREA NETWORK ONLINE ADMINISTRATION, Version 1.0
                     Sun, Oct 4,1998  16:49:08
               Copyright 1994 Hewlett-Packard Company.
                     All rights are reserved.
Test Selection mode.
          lan      = LAN Interface Administration
          menu     = Display this menu
          quit     = Terminate the Administration
          terse    = Do not display command menu
          verbose  = Display command menu
Enter command: lan
LAN Interface test mode. LAN Interface Net Mgmt ID = 4
          clear    = Clear statistics registers
          display  = Display LAN Intf status and statistics registers
          end      = End LAN Interface Admin, return to Test Selection
          menu     = Display this menu
          nmid     = Network Management ID of the LAN Interface
          quit     = Terminate the Administration, return to shell
          reset    = Reset LAN Interface to execute its selftest
Enter command: display
                     LAN INTERFACE STATUS DISPLAY
                     Sun, Oct 4,1998  16:49:12
Network Management ID              = 4
Description                        = lan0 Hewlett-Packard LAN Interface Hw Rev 0
Type (value)                       = ethernet-csmacd(6)
MTU Size                           = 1500
Speed                              = 10000000
Station Address                    = 0x80009e72436
Administration Status (value)      = up(1)
Operation Status (value)           = up(1)
Last Change                        = 14829
Inbound Octets                     = 30754920
Inbound Unicast Packets            = 0
Inbound Non-Unicast Packets        = 0
Inbound Discards                   = 0
Inbound Errors                     = 0
Inbound Unknown Protocols          = 0
Outbound Octets                    = 46132380
Outbound Unicast Packets           = 202335
Outbound Non-Unicast Packets       = 0
Outbound Discards                  = 5
Outbound Errors                    = 0
Outbound Queue Length              = 0
Specific                           = 655367
```

```
Press <Return> to continue
Ethernet-like Statistics Group
Index                           = 4
Alignment Errors                = 0
FCS Errors                      = 0
Single Collision Frames         = 0
Multiple Collision Frames       = 0
Deferred Transmissions          = 0
Late Collisions                 = 0
Excessive Collisions            = 0
Internal MAC Transmit Errors    = 0
Carrier Sense Errors            = 67445
Frames Too Long                 = 0
Internal MAC Receive Errors     = 0
LAN Interface test mode. LAN Interface Net Mgmt ID = 4
        clear     = Clear statistics registers
        display   = Display LAN Intf status and statistics registers
        end       = End LAN Interface Admin, return to Test Selection
        menu      = Display this menu
        nmid      = Network Management ID of the LAN Interface
        quit      = Terminate the Administration, return to shell
        reset     = Reset LAN Interface to execute its selftest
Enter command: quit
cancan#
```

Note that the lanadmin command has made the landiag command, available on earlier HP-UX releases, obsolete. Also note that you should not use the lanadmin command with an Asynchronous Transfer Mode (ATM) adapter. ATM provides other commands for use with ATM adapters. These are listed later in this chapter.

linkloop

The linkloop command is used to verify LAN connectivity. A local network management ID and a local or remote station address is specified, and the connectivity is then checked by sending test packets. In the example shown in Listing 6-4, connectivity is checked between lan2 (with a network management ID of 6) and a network interface on a remote system.

Because linkloop tests only the physical and data link layers, the remote station must be on the same network segment. The test packets are not routable using IP addresses; you must specify the station address of the destination system instead.

If you are unsure of the station address of a remote host, one command you can use is arp, which shows the current Address Resolution Protocol (ARP) cache entries. ARP provides the mapping between an IP address and a station address. The arp command also shows the host name associated with each IP address. This command is helpful only if connectivity has previously been established or a static ARP entry is being used. You may need to run lanscan on the remote system to determine its station address. The arp command is discussed in more detail later in this chapter.

Listing 6-4   Output showing lanscan and linkloop, which are used to test connectivity.

```
cancan#lanscan
Hardware Station        Crd Hardware Net-Interface   NM  MAC      HP DLPI Mjr
Path     Address        In# State    NameUnit State  ID  Type     Support Num
8/16/6   0x080009E72436 0   UP       lan0     DOWN   4   ETHER    Yes     52
8/20/5/1 0x0800096BBED4 1   UP       lan1     DOWN   5   ETHER    Yes     176
8/20/5/7 0x0800096BEE5A 2   UP       lan2     UP     6   ETHER    Yes     176
8/20/5/8 0x0800096BBEDE 3   DOWN     lan3     DOWN   7   ETHER    Yes     176
cancan#
cancan#linkloop -i 6 0x0800094A1861
Link connectivity to LAN station: 0x0800094A1861
--OK
cancan#
```

Using Additional Products to Monitor Network Links

The standard commands shipped with the UNIX operating system provide substantial capabilities for monitoring your network links. However, you can also buy products that extend these capabilities. A few examples are given in this section.

EMS HA Monitors

The Event Monitoring Service (EMS) is a free software package for HP-UX systems to monitor system hardware components. EMS provides libraries so that additional hardware and software monitors can be added. Hewlett-Packard provides the HA Monitors product, which can be used to detect LAN interface status changes. HA Monitors discovers all the network interfaces. Monitoring can be enabled for one or all network interfaces. This status information is similar to that provided by the MIB-II or lanscan, but EMS allows for information to be communicated automatically through a variety of notification methods. For example, EMS can send an e-mail message, log an event to the system log or an arbitrary text file, or report a problem to MC/ServiceGuard, HP's high availability cluster software. Events can also be reported via TCP, User Datagram Protocol (UDP), SNMP, opcmsg (a proprietary communication protocol used by IT/O), or e-mail, as long as it does not require the use of a failed NIC.

To configure EMS network monitoring, you use SAM. From the Resource Management functional area, you select the Event Monitoring Service and then select the action to add a new monitoring request. Resources are grouped into categories, and by selecting /net, you can see the interfaces available to be monitored. You can choose an interface to be monitored, or select all of them, and then enter the monitoring parameters. A portion of the EMS configuration is shown in Figure 6-7.

ATM and HyperFabric adapters can also be monitored by using EMS. An EMS monitor is included with each of these products.

Figure 6-7 Configuring network status monitoring in EMS.

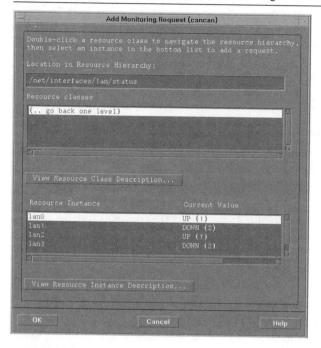

MC/ServiceGuard

MC/ServiceGuard is a high availability software product that detects system failures, network or LAN card failures, and the failures of critical applications. MC/ServiceGuard can be configured to handle these failures automatically. For example, a failed critical application can be restarted. The failure of a LAN card can result in the automatic configuration of a backup LAN card to take over the network load.

MC/ServiceGuard is much more than a monitoring product, because it also provides transparent application restart when failures are detected. If you are responsible for monitoring a network, and MC/ServiceGuard is being used in your environment, then you should become familiar with how the MC/ServiceGuard product uses the network.

Although MC/ServiceGuard can be used for a single system to provide transparent LAN failover, it is more commonly used in a cluster environment. In this case, if a system failure occurs, an application can be restarted on another system. This capability requires MC/ServiceGuard to be sending packets over the network, to ensure that its cluster members are still alive. You may want to have a dedicated network for this high availability communication, to ensure that high network utilization doesn't cause an unnecessary migration of your application. MC/ServiceGuard monitors subnetworks and can send an SNMP trap when a subnetwork goes up or down. If you are using an SNMP-based management application, this can be a quick way to learn that you are having network problems.

MC/ServiceGuard takes advantage of the ability to have multiple IP addresses bound to a single network interface card. This allows an application to be migrated to another system without the clients needing to learn a new address; the IP address moves with the application. MC/ServiceGuard distinguishes between a "stationary" IP address, which is associated with one computer system, and "floating" IP addresses, which are associated with applications and are migrated with them to other systems.

MC/ServiceGuard sends SNMP traps when its IP addresses are added or removed from the system. To see whether these floating IP addresses are being used on your system, you can use netstat_in, which shows all of your configured IP addresses. The ifconfig command shows only the stationary IP address for a specified network interface. These commands are discussed in more detail later in the chapter.

Note that MC/ServiceGuard is supported only on HP 9000 Series 800 systems running HP-UX 10.*x* or later operating systems. However, other system vendors provide similar high availability networking products.

MeasureWare

MeasureWare is a software product that collects system performance information. Collected data can be used by performance tools such as HP PerfView.

MeasureWare monitors numerous metrics on HP-UX, Sun Solaris, and other platforms. Although the information is collected primarily for performance reasons, it can also be helpful in inferring the status of network components. For example, if the rate of inbound LAN packets suddenly dropped to zero on a busy network interface, it might signal a link problem. After you detect a potential problem, you should use other tools to diagnose where the problem might be happening.

MeasureWare is discussed in more detail in "Collecting Network Performance Data," later in this chapter.

Using Link-Specific Commands

You should be able to diagnose the health of Ethernet and Token Ring links by using only the tools already described. Additional commands are available for other network links, such as FDDI, X.25, and ATM. The remaining portion of this section describes some of the link-specific commands that are available to help with fault diagnosis and troubleshooting.

Using FDDI Status Commands

Fiber Distributed Data Interface (FDDI) is a high-speed LAN technology that is capable of data transfer rates of 100 megabits per second. FDDI supports dual fiber-optic rings, which provide a level of redundancy. Systems can connect to an FDDI network through an FDDI device called a *concentrator,* which can provide some fault tolerance by ensuring that the network won't be impacted by a failed system. NICs with dual-attach capability can directly connect into separate concentrators, for additional protection.

You can check whether your system is using FDDI by executing the lanscan command. The link type is shown for each LAN card. In addition to lanscan, other common commands can be used with FDDI links, such as ioscan, linkloop, and lanadmin.

You can execute fddiinit with the device file of your FDDI adapter, to initialize the adapter and connect the system to the network. If this command fails, the cables may not be connected properly, the card may not be operational, or the concentrator may not be up.

If the adapter is initialized successfully, you can get additional information about the card by using fddistat, which also requires the device file (for example, /dev/lan1). If the card is set up properly, the output should indicate that the ring is operational and that the line state of the station connection is WRAP_S.

An additional command, fddinet, can be used to display connection information about the local ring, a specified remote node, or all nodes connected to the same FDDI ring.

X.25 Status Commands

X.25 is a packet-switching network standardized by CCITT. x25stat can be used to detect problems with an X.25 link. It provides the status of the X.25 device and card, configuration information, and virtual circuit statistics. Executing x25stat −f −d /devicefile shows you the number of errors on the X.25 link. If the link state is not listed as NORMAL, then a problem exists.

Statistical information shown through x25stat includes the current number of virtual circuits configured and the bytes transferred over each subnetwork. x25stat can also show statistics for a specific virtual circuit, such as the number of data packets sent or received.

If IP is not working over X.25, you can check that your network address has been configured correctly and see the mapping between IP and X.25 addresses by using x25stat −a. You may need to reinitialize X.25 using x25init.

The x25check and x25server commands are used together to test the X.25 network. x25server is a background process that waits for call requests from x25check. x25check sends packets to a remote system running x25server, and the packets are echoed back. This can be used to test your X.25 link to the network or the X.25 switch. If successful, x25check also shows the time spent setting up the virtual circuit.

ATM Status Commands

Asynchronous Transfer Mode (ATM) is a high-speed network technology. Some network commands, such as lanscan and netstat, are generic and can be used with ATM links. netstat −i, for example, shows the statistics for ATM network interfaces. However, some ATM-specific status commands are also available, and are described next.

To get information about an ATM adapter, its MAC address, and associated virtual circuits, you can use the atmmgr command. The command requires a card instance number to be specified. Additional information can also be shown, depending on the command options specified. For example, atmmgr 0 show −p shows the status, statistics, and MAC address.

To do an external loopback test, you can use the atmloop command. You must first use atmstop to stop the ATM adapter, and then replace the cable with a loopback hood. After the test,

Listing 6-5 Output from atmmgr showing AAL5 statistics.

```
cancan: atmmgr 0 show -a

AAL5 statistics

CRC-32 errors in received SDUs       : 0
SDUs lost due to reassembly timeout  : 0
SDUs too big                         : 0
```

you can issue an atmstop again and then use atminit to initialize the adapter after removing the hood. The atminit command can be used to reset or initialize an adapter, but all Switched Virtual Circuits (SVCs) will be lost.

To get information about ATM network interfaces and ARP cache entries, use the elstat and elarp commands, respectively. These commands require a network interface name to be specified, such as el101.

To check ATM Adaptation Layer (AAL) interface statistics, use a card instance number of 0, as shown in Listing 6-5.

If the AAL5 interface is working correctly, the number of errors should be low.

Additional ATM commands include atmcheck and atmserver, which can be used to check ATM hardware and end-to-end connectivity, and atminit_net, which resets or initializes a specific network interface on an ATM adapter. This does not stop the ATM adapter, so activity on other network interfaces is not impacted.

HA ATM

HA ATM is a product from Hewlett-Packard that protects ATM links in the event of a failure. HA ATM is integrated with EMS and MC/ServiceGuard. Local recovery is aided through its EMS integration, and remote recovery involves both EMS and MC/ServiceGuard.

The HP ATM adapter enables you to run one Classical IP (CIP) interface and up to 32 Emulated LAN (ELAN) interfaces simultaneously. High availability is provided only for ATM with LAN emulation.

HA ATM protects against a single failure in the ATM network. It detects local ATM ELAN interface failures and can perform local recovery by switching to another local ELAN interface. HA ATM can detect and recover locally from problems with the core ATM software, or with the ATM adapter, link, or ATM switch. EMS events can be sent when a failure is detected. MC/ServiceGuard is notified via EMS when HA ATM is unable to provide local recovery.

MC/ServiceGuard remote recovery is used when a system failure occurs or the system loses all of its adapters, switches, or cables. To process a remote failover, MC/ServiceGuard moves all ATM applications defined as packages to the remote system, and configures any package IP addresses on the remote system's ELAN interface on an ATM adapter.

Monitoring Networking and Transport Protocols

Networking problems can be difficult to diagnose, because networking involves a variety of hardware and software components. The previous section focused on the physical cable and

LAN card. This section shows tools for checking the behavior of the networking protocols, primarily those in the TCP/IP protocol suite.

This section describes monitoring for the network and transport layers of the OSI seven-layer networking model. These layers include the protocols for data transmission, routing, sequencing, and flow control. In a LAN environment, error detection and recovery are the responsibility of the transport layer. A variety of key resources need to be monitored at these layers, such as the IP addresses being used by each client and server, the number of active connections to a server, and error statistics for each protocol.

Using SNMP Instrumentation

The MIB-II was discussed earlier because of its ability to report status information for each network interface. The MIB-II also contains information for some key networking protocols, such as IP, ICMP (Internet Control Message Protocol), TCP, ARP, and UDP.

If you have access to a MIB Browser, then you may want to browse this MIB to see the interesting statistics that you can access. For example, for IP, you can check the amount of data being sent or discarded, and the amount being received, and get an idea of the fragmentation, reassembly, or delivery errors that are occurring. For ICMP, you can determine the number of times a destination was unreachable. For TCP, you can look at the number of connection attempts and see the current connections. For UDP, you can see the number of open sockets.

This section is brief, because very similar information is provided by the netstat command, which is discussed in detail later in this section. Unless you are monitoring the MIB variables of multiple systems through a network management product, you probably want to use the netstat command.

Using Standard Commands and Tools

Common UNIX commands for obtaining network and transport protocol information are included in this section.

ping

The ping command uses ICMP echo to test connectivity to a remote node and record round-trip times and routes for network packets. The percentage of packets lost is also shown. Because ICMP uses IP for its data transmission, ping not only tests the link itself, but it also tests for correct network protocol behavior. Transport protocols such as TCP and UDP are not involved in a ping. Listing 6-6 shows an example of the ping command. Note that ping can be used with an IP address or system name. If used with a name, ping can determine whether the name resolution service is working properly.

If the ICMP sequence numbers are not in numerical order, a hardware problem may be present. If no response is made to a ping, a variety of problems are possible. If other systems can be pinged, especially systems with the same route, then the remote system might have failed. If no system can be pinged, it could be a sign that the local system is not connected to the network.

Listing 6-6 Output from ping command.

```
cancan#ping chacha
PING chacha.cup.hp.com: 64 byte packets
64 bytes from 15.13.173.94: icmp_seq=0. time=0. ms
64 bytes from 15.13.173.94: icmp_seq=1. time=0. ms
64 bytes from 15.13.173.94: icmp_seq=2. time=1. ms
64 bytes from 15.13.173.94: icmp_seq=3. time=0. ms
----chacha.cup.hp.com PING Statistics----
4 packets transmitted, 4 packets received, 0% packet loss
round-trip (ms)  min/avg/max = 0/0/1
cancan#
```

The ping command may fail for other reasons, such as the failure of an intermediate system or a misconfigured routing table.

One downside of the ping command is that one end of the communication must be the system you are logged into. The communication problem may be between two other systems. With NNM's Remote Ping tool, you can specify an arbitrary pair of systems to ping each other.

ifconfig

The ifconfig command is used to configure network interfaces and it can be used to determine whether IP has been set up correctly. The output, shown in Listing 6-7, provides information such as the IP address associated with the interface and the subnet mask.

The operational state is included in the output.

Listing 6-7 Output from ifconfig command.

```
cancan#ifconfig lan2
lan2: flags=863<UP,BROADCAST,NOTRAILERS,RUNNING,MULTICAST>
        inet 15.13.173.93 netmask fffff800 broadcast 15.13.175.255
cancan#
```

arp

The Address Resolution Protocol (ARP) is used when a sending system knows the IP address of the destination, but not the station address. An ARP request is broadcast on the network, asking the destination or intermediate router to respond with its station address. Recently used IP-address-to-station-address mappings are stored in an ARP cache.

The arp command can be used to display the current entries in the ARP cache. This can be a useful tool if you think that two systems may be using the same IP address. You can check the MAC address on the remote system and compare it to the value in the local system's ARP cache. You may also want to use a LAN analyzer to see whether multiple ARP replies are being received by the local system. Note that in the arp output in Listing 6-8, one station address (0:60:3E:81:E:A0) appears multiple times. This system is a router supporting multiple network interfaces.

Listing 6-8   Output from arp command showing remote station addresses.

```
# arp -a
hpovsg.cup.hp.com (15.13.169.163) at 8:0:9:78:2d:eb ether
cup44ux.cup.hp.com (15.27.217.36) at 0:60:3e:81:e:a0 ether
hpssc16.cup.hp.com (15.13.169.233) at 8:0:9:4a:18:61 ether
hphamc1.cup.hp.com (15.13.174.176) at 8:0:9:84:71:94 ether
hphamc2.cup.hp.com (15.13.174.177) at 8:0:9:84:21:e8 ether
c3p0.cup.hp.com (15.13.171.249) at 8:0:9:e3:92:69 ether
wayne.cup.hp.com (15.13.171.185) at 8:0:9:87:bb:6d ether
chewy.cup.hp.com (15.13.172.249) at 0:60:b0:59:ae:14 ether
perseus.cup.hp.com (15.61.200.218) at 0:60:3e:81:e:a0 ether
hpssc02.cup.hp.com (15.13.169.219) at 8:0:9:82:2d:e8 ether
clue.cup.hp.com (15.13.168.123) at 8:0:9:92:e9:7f ether
cup44ux.cup.hp.com (15.13.168.124) at 8:0:9:5a:f9:e5 ether
chacha.cup.hp.com (15.13.173.94) at 8:0:9:c3:fa:7d ether
#
```

Another way to find out which computer system is associated with a given station address is to use NNM, which has a Locate menu option. By specifying the station address using this menu option, NNM searches its object database to find the corresponding system.

The arp command can also be used to add or delete entries from the ARP cache. This is useful if you want to use ping to diagnose IP and ARP failures.

netstat

The netstat command can be used to show information about network interfaces and protocols. Statistics can be shown for the TCP, UDP, IP, ICMP, ARP, and other protocols. netstat can be used to show all active TCP connections and their current TCP state. With netstat, you can display all the IP addresses currently configured on the system. For example, you can determine the total number of TCP connections requested and accepted. Information can be displayed on the network traffic sent on a configured network interface and its configured IP addresses. Internal data structures, such as socket structures and routing tables, can also be shown.

Listing 6-9 shows how netstat can be used to get statistics about network interfaces. These statistics are also available from the lanadmin command, but lanadmin doesn't provide IP address information. During periods of normal operation, the error rates shown here should be very low (much less than 1 percent). Note that, in this example, MC/ServiceGuard is being used on the system, and multiple IP addresses are bound to the same network interface.

On HP-UX, use netstat –in to make sure that two network interfaces are not using the same network address (or subnetwork address), because this is not supported on HP-UX.

With netstat, you can see protocol statistics for each of the key networking protocols. Listings 6-10 through 6-13 show sample output for IP, ICMP, TCP, and UDP, respectively.

ICMP provides numerous useful error statistics. Destination unreachable errors can be caused by many things, including an unknown destination name, routing problem, or bad hardware.

Listing 6-9   Output from netstat showing configured IP addresses.

```
bass:/>netstat -in
Name    Mtu  Network      Address        Ipkts Ierrs    Opkts Oerrs  Coll
lo0     4136 127.0.0.0    127.0.0.1    4693211     0  4693219     0     0
lan3    1500 15.13.168.0  15.13.168.61 30925479    0  7106611     0     0
lan2    1500 192.5.1.0    192.5.1.61     873225    15 1555027   382 20374
lan2:1  1500 192.5.1.0    192.5.1.3           16     0       0     0     0
lan2:2  1500 192.5.1.0    192.5.1.9           16     0       0     0     0
lan2:3  1500 192.5.1.0    192.5.1.7           16     0       0     0     0
lan2:4  1500 192.5.1.0    192.5.1.5           16     0       0     0     0
lan2:5  1500 192.5.1.0    192.5.1.19          16     0       0     0     0
lan2:6  1500 192.5.1.0    192.5.1.15          16     0       0     0     0
lan2:7  1500 192.5.1.0    192.5.1.13          16     0       0     0     0
lan2:8  1500 192.5.1.0    192.5.1.17          16     0       0     0     0
lan2:9  1500 192.5.1.0    192.5.1.29          16     0       0     0     0
lan1*   1500 none         none                 0     0       0     0     0
bass:/>
```

Listing 6-10   Using netstat to show IP statistics.

```
# netstat -p ip
ip:
        112231915 total packets received
        0 bad header checksums
        0 with size smaller than minimum
        0 with data size < data length
        0 with header length < data size
        0 with data length < header length
        0 illegal ip source address
        178 ip version unsupported
        193 fragments received
        0 fragments dropped (dup or out of space)
        1 fragment dropped after timeout
        0 packets forwarded
        2382091 packets not forwardable
        0 redirects sent
```

Listing 6-11   Using netstat to show ICMP statistics.

```
# netstat -p icmp
icmp:
        7368 calls to generate an ICMP error message
        0 errors not generated because old message was ICMP
        0 errors not generated 'cuz old message was broadcast
        Output histogram:
                echo reply: 215963
                destination unreachable: 7368
```

```
64 messages with bad code fields
21 messages < minimum length
0 messages with a bad checksum
0 messages with bad length
Input histogram:
        echo reply: 12231
        destination unreachable: 182468
        source quench: 35
        routing redirect: 108
        echo: 215963
        time exceeded: 18
        address mask request: 124
215963 responses sent
```

A source quench is a request to a system to reduce its transmission rate because of congestion. Routing redirect messages are used to request that a system use an alternate route to a destination network.

Listing 6-12 Using netstat to show TCP statistics.

```
#netstat -p tcp
tcp:
        275906 packets sent
                7346 data packets (948597 bytes)
                0 data packets (0 bytes) retransmitted
                12967 ack-only packets (1627 delayed)
                0 URG only packets
                22 window probe packets
                1 window update packet
                255570 control packets
        523932 packets received
                14736 acks (for 912101 bytes)
                3299 duplicate acks
                0 acks for unsent data
                12785 packets (854136 bytes) received in-sequence
                3 completely duplicate packets (0 bytes)
                0 packets with some dup. data (0 bytes duped)
                2837 out-of-order packets (0 bytes)
                2 packets (0 bytes) of data after window
                0 window probes
                55 window update packets
                0 packets received after close
                0 discarded for bad checksums
                0 discarded for bad header offset fields
                0 discarded because packet too short
```

Continued

Listing 6-12   Using netstat to show TCP statistics. (Continued)

```
249910 connection requests
2842 connection accepts
5677 connections established (including accepts)
255585 connections closed (including 14 drops)
247075 embryonic connections dropped
15772 segments updated rtt (of 265683 attempts)
0 retransmit timeouts
        0 connections dropped by rexmit timeout
0 persist timeouts
0 keepalive timeouts
        0 keepalive probes sent
        0 connections dropped by keepalive
```

You can monitor TCP statistics over time to see whether new connections are being established, for example.

netstat –a can be used to show the state of TCP connections and UDP sockets. You can determine, for example, whether a connection is fully established or the server is still waiting for a connect request from a client. The output will show the name of the network service if it is registered in /etc/services.

The netstat command can also be used to show the amount of memory in use and dedicated to network packets. If insufficient memory is available for IP fragmentation reassembly on the destination or intermediate systems, network performance can be affected. Data will need to be retransmitted. You can check the number of fragments being dropped by using netstat –sp ip. The ndd command can be used to display and change the ip_reass_mem_limit value.

nettl

nettl is HP-UX's host-based facility for tracing network packets leaving and coming into the system. Tracing is available for links such as IEEE802.3 and FDDI, as well as upper-level protocols such as TCP/IP and the OSI transport layer. nettl also logs information about network events.

To use nettl, you first need to start the tracing facility. You then need to start a specific trace, using nettl –tn. You can list the specific networking subsystems that you want included in the trace, such as the network or transport layer.

Listing 6-13   Using netstat to show UDP statistics.

```
# netstat -p udp
udp:
        0 incomplete headers
        0 bad data length fields
        0 bad checksums
        2217 socket overflows
        0 data discards
```

A trace file is specified when starting a trace. Depending on the size of the output, nettl creates two trace files. A suffix of .TRC0 is appended to the most recent trace file, and the older file will have a .TRC1 extension. Listing 6-14 shows how to start and stop a trace of the ICMP traffic sent for a ping request.

After the trace data is collected, you can format the output by using netfmt. The formatted data can also be written to a file. Listing 6-15 shows a portion of the formatted file that resulted from the preceding trace.

Because of its impact on system performance, you should use nettl only when you can't diagnose a problem through other tools or when the system has significant excess capacity.

Listing 6-14   ICMP/ping trace example.

```
# nettl -start
# nettl -tn pduin pduout -e ns_ls_icmp -f pingtrc
# ping hoffman
PING hpssc16.cup.hp.com: 64 byte packets
64 bytes from 15.13.169.233: icmp_seq=0. time=2. ms
64 bytes from 15.13.169.233: icmp_seq=1. time=2. ms
64 bytes from 15.13.169.233: icmp_seq=2. time=2. ms

----hpssc16.cup.hp.com PING Statistics----
3 packets transmitted, 3 packets received, 0% packet loss
round-trip (ms)  min/avg/max = 2/2/2
# nettl -tf -e all
# netfmt -Nnl -f pingtrc.TRC0 > pingfmt
# nettl -stop
```

Listing 6-15   ICMP/ping formatted trace output.

```
^^^^^^^^^^^^^^^^^^^^^^^^^^^^^^ARPA/9000 NETWORKING^^^^^^^^^^^^^^^^^^^^^^^^^^@#%
   Timestamp              : Tue Jan 26 PST 1999 10:41:05.634676
   Process ID             : [ICS]            Subsystem      : NS_LS_ICMP
   User ID ( UID )        : -1               Trace Kind     : PDU IN TRACE
   Device ID              : -1               Path ID        : -1
   Connection ID          : 0
   Location               : 00123
~~~~~~~~~~~~~~~~~~~~~~~~~~~~~~~~~~~~~~~~~~~~~~~~~~~~~~~~~~~~~~~~~~~~~~~~~~~~~~~
--------------------------- ICMP Header ---------------------------------
type: ECHOREPLY          chksum: 0xffe3        id: 10715        seq: 1
code: none
--------------------------- User Data ---------------------------------
   0: 36 ae 0c 41 00 09 a8 44 08 09 0a 0b 0c 0d 0e 0f   6..A...D........
  16: 10 11 12 13 14 15 16 17 18 19 1a 1b 1c 1d 1e 1f   ................
  32: 20 21 22 23 24 25 26 27 28 29 2a 2b 2c 2d 2e 2f   !"#$%&'()*+,-./
  48: 30 31 32 33 34 35 36 37 -- -- -- -- -- -- -- --   01234567........
```

Monitoring Network Services

A variety of applications can be accessed over the Internet or via corporate intranets. For instance, a client application may use the network to access an application on the server system. The application running on the server system is referred to as a *network service*.

The availability and response time of the network service is what the user cares about. This section discusses tools for monitoring the network service. Some of the more common network services are discussed, such as the Domain Name System (DNS), Network Information Service (NIS), and Network File System (NFS). Other applications are discussed in Chapter 7.

Many network services are started by a daemon process in response to a client request. The daemon process is called inetd. You can use ps to see whether this daemon is running. If it is not running, you should try to restart it by executing /usr/sbin/inetd as superuser. You can use netstat −a to list the network applications currently running on a system. The TCP or UDP socket ports associated with each service are listed in the file /etc/services. If a service is not running, you may want to check this file to see whether the service is configured. The service should also be listed in the file /etc/inetd.conf. The inetd daemon writes errors and informative messages to /var/adm/syslog/syslog.log when new services are started or stopped.

There are other important network services that are up all the time (or should be). These services include NFS and HTTP. The rest of this section lists monitoring tools specific to each network service.

Monitoring DHCP/BOOTP Servers

The Bootstrap Protocol (BOOTP) allows systems to obtain their network configuration information, such as their IP address, from a remote server system. The BOOTP service bootpd may use the Trivial File Transfer Protocol (TFTP) to transfer data back to the client. Make sure that both are configured as Internet services in /etc/services and /etc/inetd.conf.

When receiving a BOOTP request, a service checks whether it has information for the client in its database. If it does, it replies with the information; otherwise, it may forward the request to another system. You may need an analyzer to ensure the key parameters set by the client in the BOOTP request are correct.

Client information is put in the file /etc/bootptab. If BOOTP is working correctly in general, but not for a specific system, you should check this file to ensure the configuration information is correct. You may want to issue a test from the server by using bootquery, which can be used to send test BOOTP requests to the BOOTP server. In this way, you can verify that the service is starting in response to a query. By specifying the client address in the query, and by enabling replies to this client to be broadcast — a configuration option in /etc/bootptab — you can see the actual reply sent by this BOOTP server.

Dynamic Host Configuration Protocol (DHCP) is a superset of BOOTP. Both bootpd and DHCP can write some error messages to the system log file. If you are troubleshooting a problem, make sure that bootpd is started with the −d 2 command option, to enable informative log messages to be written to the system log file.

DHCP allows for clients to obtain their IP address from a pool of available addresses. The /etc/bootptab file is used for BOOTP clients and for DHCP clients with fixed IP addresses. Clients belonging to a pool are configured in /etc/dhcptab.

On HP-UX, dhcptools can be used to trace DHCP packets or to examine the internal state of the DHCP daemon. This can be used, for example, to find configuration problems. The operator can determine whether IP addresses are available to be given out to clients, and the total number of IP addresses available. dhcptools also has an option to allow for packet tracing of DHCP requests and replies.

Note that monitoring the server status is difficult, because DHCP can shut itself down when it has nothing to do.

Monitoring DNS/NIS Name Servers

Domain Name System (DNS) and Network Information Service (NIS) are two services for providing name resolution. NIS has additional capabilities, such as maintaining consistent configuration information across multiple systems.

An easy way to check these services is to make a query to the server application. In addition to checking the service availability, you can get a snapshot of the response time. Note that in this and other examples, the monitoring of the service is being done from the client system.

The configuration file /etc/resolv.conf contains the IP addresses of name servers being used by the local system. An example is shown in Listing 6-16. You may want to ping the servers listed in this file if you are having trouble with name resolution.

Name Service Switch

The Name Service Switch enables you to specify which name service should be used for name resolution and other queries. You may want to check the /etc/nsswitch.conf file to see how name resolution is being done on your system. The nsquery command can be used to test the behavior of the Name Service Switch.

nslookup

nslookup can be used to determine whether a name server is aware of a particular host name. Listing 6-17 shows a name server successfully resolving the system name to an IP address.

Monitoring FTP

File Transfer Protocol (FTP) is used for transferring files efficiently between systems. An easy way to check whether FTP is working is to use ftp to transfer an arbitrary file. Along with an indication

Listing 6-16   Checking name servers in /etc/resolv.conf.

```
# more /etc/resolv.conf
domain cup.hp.com
nameserver 15.27.217.36 # cup44ux
nameserver 15.13.168.63 # hpperf1
```

Listing 6-17   Using nslookup to get a system's IP address.

```
# nslookup gsyview1
Name Server:  cup44ux.cup.hp.com
Address:   15.27.217.36

Name:    gsyview1.cup.hp.com
Address:   15.13.174.132
```

of the success of the request, ftp tells you the transfer rate. While connected, you can check the status of the remote FTP session by using the status FTP command, as shown in Listing 6-18.

ftp denies access to the local user accounts listed in /etc/ftpusers, so be sure to check this file if ftp is not working for certain users.

Monitoring NFS

The Network File System is meant to give users a transparent view of remote filesystems, and to make those remote filesystems appear to be attached locally. NFS can be a useful tool to share filesystems to save disk space and make management easier. All NFS clients share the single copy of the file that is stored on the NFS server. The downside of the transparency is that a client may not be aware of the network traffic they are causing by reading a simple file. Also, the client may not know that others are simultaneously accessing the files.

Numerous things can go wrong with NFS. Processes can die or hang. The key processes for NFS are nfsd, automount, lockd, statd, and portmap. The status of these processes can be checked with the ps command.

NFS requests are processed by NFS server daemons (nfsd). These daemons read requests from a single UDP socket. The number of daemons is adjustable, with the optimal number dependent on system load and NFS activity. If you do not have enough daemons running, then the kernel may drop some NFS requests when they arrive, to avoid overflowing the storage area

Listing 6-18   Output from FTP status command showing status of remote machine.

```
ftp> status
Connected to hpssc16.cup.hp.com.
No proxy connection.
Mode: stream; Type: binary; Form: non-print; Structure: file
Verbose: on; Bell: off; Prompting: on; Globbing: on
Store unique: off; Receive unique: off
Case: off; CR stripping: on
Ntrans: off
Nmap: off
Hash mark printing: off; Use of PORT cmds: on
ftp>
```

reserved for these packets. You can detect this problem by checking the number of UDP socket overflows using netstat –s. Increasing the number of daemons should reduce socket overflows and increase NFS performance. However, no tools exist to help you determine how many daemons to add. An excess of NFS daemons may be identified through an increasing load average on the server. Also, because the number of overflows is a system-wide statistic, the problem may be due to another UDP application. You may want to use netstat to show the current UDP activity, before you assume that any problems are due to NFS.

If you are responsible for monitoring NFS, you should also check the status of exported filesystems, and disks to see whether they are full or unavailable. NFS statistics should be checked to see whether NFS timeouts have been reported. MeasureWare collects statistics on the number and rate of NFS requests during a time interval. BMC PATROL provides a tool with its UNIX KM to monitor NFS activities and Remote Procedure Calls (RPCs).

nfsstat

The nfsstat output can give you an idea of the type of NFS workload occurring in your environment. This can be useful if you want to establish benchmarks to measure your typical server load.

nfsstat can report information for an NFS client, an NFS server, or both. The example in Listing 6-19 shows the statistics for an NFS client.

The bad transaction identifier (XID) metric indicates the number of times replies are received without a request outstanding. This could be an indication that client requests are timing out too quickly and being resent. If the client has many bad XID packets and timeouts, you should increase the timeout value by using the mount utility.

A large number of symbolic link resolutions on the server may indicate that the client has configured inappropriate names as mount points.

Listing 6-19 Output showing a client's NFS statistics.

```
# nfsstat -c

Client rpc:
calls      badcalls   retrans    badxid     timeout    wait       newcred
200        0          0          0          0          0          0

Client nfs:
calls      badcalls   nclget     nclsleep
200        0          200        0
null       getattr    setattr    root       lookup     readlink   read
0   0%     133 66%    0   0%     0   0%     0   0%     0   0%     0   0%
wrcache    write      create     remove     rename     link       symlink
0   0%     0   0%     0   0%     0   0%     0   0%     0   0%     0   0%
mkdir      rmdir      readdir    statfs
0   0%     0   0%     0   0%     67 33%
#
```

NetMetrix for NFS

NetMetrix provides an extension for monitoring the NFS service. Monitors are used to capture the network traffic, after which NFS service performance can be calculated. Graphs can show information such as the load, response time, number of retransmissions, and number of errors.

HA NFS

An HA NFS toolkit is available as an add-on to the MC/ServiceGuard product. NFS server failures can be detected and reported to MC/ServiceGuard, with NFS service restarted on another node. NFS locks are not maintained during the failover.

Monitoring Remote Connectivity

rlogin and telnet provide remote login capability so that clients can access the UNIX systems. For rlogin, the application started by inetd is called rlogind, and for telnet, the daemon is telnetd. The who command can show you the users that are logged into a system. Use ps –ef lgrep rlogind to see how many users are remotely connected, and for how long they have been connected.

Monitoring Web Servers

Monitoring Internet services is a new phenomenon, and tools to monitor Web servers are just beginning to emerge. Netscape's SuiteSpot server software is being bundled with HP OpenView technology for Internet monitoring and fault management for high-end, enterprise-level HP-UX users.

The HP OpenView Internet Service Manager provides tools to manage Web resource utilization and performance. Monitoring is done from an IT/O management station. Management is provided for the following UNIX-based Internet services: Netscape Enterprise Server, Netscape Fastrack Server, Netscape News, Netscape Proxy Server, Netscape Mail, NCSA Web Server, and Apache Web Server. Internet Service Manager can also identify broken HTML links.

CompuWare also has some tools, such as EcoScope and Single View, which can be used to monitor Web servers. Network traffic can be analyzed at the protocol level to capture HTTP packets. Single View can then report on the traffic load, with specialized Internet utilization reports for Web (HTTP), secure Web (HTTPS), and other protocols.

Monitoring Network Hosts

On a shared network medium, monitoring only the client and server systems is insufficient. Other network devices may be critical for network connectivity. Name servers were previously discussed; if the name service is unavailable, your application may be unable to connect to the server, because it can't determine the server's IP address. The router responsible for transferring your packets to the server's LAN segment may also be down.

In addition to network faults, performance problems could occur. Congestion on a shared LAN can prevent your data from being transmitted. Performance monitoring tools are discussed in the next section.

Other network devices, or hosts, may also be interesting to monitor, such as a network printer. This section discusses how you can ensure the correct operation of these additional network hosts.

Network Node Manager

As described earlier in this chapter, graphical network status monitors, such as Network Node Manager, can discover any IP-addressable device accessible from the management station, including routers, switches, hubs, and network printers. If you are trying to isolate a network problem, you may want to examine the entire path between the client and server. NNM is one tool that can help you do this. By drilling down from the global network submap, you can examine individual network segments.

Figure 6-8 shows the devices on one LAN segment. The devices include NT and HP-UX computers, as well as routers and printers. Colors indicate the status of each device, and are based on NNM's ability to poll the system and get a response.

Resolving a connectivity problem may involve navigating through multiple network segments. You may have multiple routers in your environment, in which case you need to know the routes that your packets should be taking. This requires that you understand your system's routing tables.

netstat

Knowing the network topology is important for resolving communication problems. If hosts can communicate successfully on each side of a gateway or repeater, but not to systems on the other side, this most likely indicates a problem with the forwarding device.

Figure 6-8   NNM topology.

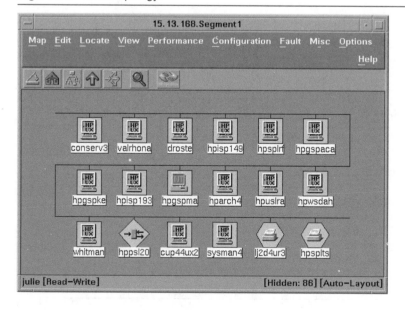

The netstat –rn command can be used to show your current configuration of routes from the local system to remote networks, as shown in Listing 6-20. If you are experiencing long delays in packet transmission to remote networks, you may want to examine the routing algorithms being used on the network. Many networks use routing algorithms that minimize the number of hops that a packet must take, because that improves both the delay and amount of network bandwidth used, which in turn can boost network throughput.

The netstat –rs command can show statistics related to the system's use of remote routes, as shown in Listing 6-21. If a bad route is indicated, you should check whether your router is behaving properly.

If connectivity between two systems is a problem, check whether or not each system can reach other networks. The routing table may not have the right route to all the LANs. You may want to compare this configuration to the routing tables of a working system. If the routing information is wrong, you can use the route command to add and delete routing table entries.

Interconnect & Router Manager

Routers and bridges are the network devices that connect your LAN segments together. It is critical that these devices continue to work. You can use some of the same tools to monitor a router

Listing 6-20   Output from netstat showing routing information.

```
cancan#netstat -rn
Routing tables
Destination     Gateway         Flags   Refs      Use   Interface   Pmtu
15.13.173.93    127.0.0.1       UH         1    27985   lo0         4608
127.0.0.1       127.0.0.1       UH         0   494200   lo0         4608
192.7.27.93     127.0.0.1       UH         0        0   lo0         4608
default         15.13.173.93    U          1   415198   lan2        1500
15.13.168.0     15.13.173.93    U          3    82816   lan2        1500
192.7.27        192.7.27.93     U          0        0   lan0        1500
cancan#
```

Listing 6-21   Output from netstat –rs showing routing statistics.

```
# netstat -rs
routing:
        108 bad routing redirects
        0 dynamically created routes
        0 new gateways due to redirects
        1 destination found unreachable
        0 uses of a wildcard route
        0 routes marked doubtful
        0 routes cleared of being doubtful
        0 redirects deleted
#
```

that you use to monitor your UNIX server. The router's status can be seen at a glance from tools such as NNM. Note that your UNIX server can also be configured to function as an IP forwarder.

Routers provide some of the same instrumentation as other computer systems. For example, the MIB-II is supported by all the major routers. If your router is behaving strangely and going up and down, you could check this behavior by monitoring the amount of time since the last reboot. This information is stored in the MIB sysUpTime field of the MIB-II.

Hewlett-Packard provides management software specifically for monitoring routers, bridges, and hubs. The HP Interconnect & Router Manager uses SNMP to monitor the status of AdvanceStack hubs, AdvanceStack bridges, and AdvanceStack routers. This product is integrated with NNM.

Other vendors also provide management solutions for their network devices. For example, many switches now provide Web interfaces to monitor device status and obtain statistics.

Collecting Network Performance Data

This section describes some of the tools available for collecting network performance information. Some overlap exists between network performance management and system performance management. For example, a network application may have a low network transmission rate because it isn't getting sufficient CPU time to send its data. Consequently, overlap also exists between the tools used for system and network performance management.

Using RMON and RMON-II Instrumentation

RMON I and RMON II (defined in RFCs 1757 and 2021, respectively) together form a standard for network performance management. Monitors, or probes, are placed on specific LAN segments and then collect data on those segments. Packet statistics and performance history can be stored. An RMON management application can collect data from remote RMON probes and present it at a central site. Alarms can also be triggered based on specified conditions and sent to the management station.

The RMON definition consists of the following optional sections, or groups:

- Statistics
- History
- Alarm
- Hosts
- HostsTopN
- Matrix
- Filter
- Capture
- Event

The statistics section provides information on the amount of data being sent on a particular Ethernet interface, including the number of broadcasts, errors, and collisions. You can also see the distribution of packets of different sizes.

The history group allows statistics to be sampled at a specified polling interval and summed over time. The RMON statistics are Ethernet-centric, but extensions to support Token Ring are defined in RFC 1513.

The alarm and event groups are used to report when configured thresholds are met. Statistics are periodically checked to see whether a threshold has been met. After an event is sent, no additional events are sent until the opposite threshold has been met.

RMON probes can discover new systems, or hosts, by watching the source and destination station addresses in packets passing on the LAN segment. The hosts group stores each address seen on the interface. A variety of important statistics are kept about each system, such as the number of packets sent and received, the number of error packets sent, and the number of broadcasts sent. This can be invaluable information for catching a misbehaving system that is dominating the network bandwidth on a LAN segment.

The hostsTopN group keeps track of the top systems on the segment for a specific statistic, such as packets received, error packets sent, or broadcast packets sent. The number of systems in the list is configurable.

The matrix group can be used to determine traffic problems. Statistics are kept on the network conversations between two addresses. Information collected includes the number of packets sent in either direction, and the number of error packets sent.

The filter and capture groups work together to capture packets sent on a segment. A management station can then download the packets.

RMON focuses on the data link and network layers of the network stack. RMON-II extends the specification to include the transport, session, presentation, and application layer protocols. Additional groups provided by RMON-II include:

- Protocol Directory
- Protocol Distribution
- Address Mapping
- Network Layer Host
- Network Layer Matrix
- Application Layer Host
- Application Layer Matrix

The Protocol Directory lists all the protocols that the monitor supports. A monitor can add more protocols, but the extensibility is limited.

The Protocol Distribution group shows per-protocol statistics for the amount of data and number of packets being sent on a LAN segment. From this information, you can calculate the bandwidth utilization per protocol and, hopefully, isolate a troublesome application.

The Address Mappings group is used to map a network address to the station address to which it is bound. The Network Layer Host group then shows the amount of traffic for each network address. The Network Layer Matrix group shows network traffic statistics between pairs of network addresses. You can also see the top traffic producers.

The Application Layer Host shows network traffic statistics for a particular network address, broken down by protocol. Similarly, the Application Layer Matrix shows network traffic statistics for traffic between a pair of network addresses.

As previously mentioned, both Ethernet and Token Ring use the RMON standard. Other standards are being considered for other link types. For example, to account for the switching technology in ATM, a new specification called AMON has been proposed by Hewlett-Packard. Other vendors have additional proposals for supporting ATM.

NetMetrix Site Manager

As mentioned earlier, NetMetrix Site Manager can be used to monitor the status and utilization of your network devices. Some of the different errors reported were discussed earlier. Utilization reports can also be generated, such as the top users on a network segment, and the devices sending the most packets.

NetMetrix also includes a MIB Browser so that you can query the MIB values of a selected network device.

MeasureWare

The MeasureWare Agent is a Hewlett-Packard product that collects and logs resource and performance metrics. MeasureWare agents run and collect data on the individual server systems being monitored. Agents exist for many platforms and operating systems, including HP-UX, Solaris, and AIX.

The MeasureWare Agent collects data, summarize it, timestamp it, log it, and send alarms when appropriate. The agents collect and report on a wide variety of system resources, performance metrics, and user-defined data. The information can then be exported to spreadsheets or to performance analysis programs, such as PerfView. The data can be used by these programs to generate alarms to warn of potential performance problems. By using historical data, trends can be discovered. This can help to solve resource issues before they affect system performance.

MeasureWare agents collect data at three different levels: global system metrics, application metrics, and process metrics. Global and application data is summarized at five-minute intervals, whereas process data is summarized at one-minute intervals. Important applications can be defined by an administrator by listing the processes that make up the application in a configuration file.

The basic categories of MeasureWare data are system, application, process, and transaction. Optional modules exist for database and networking support, too. MeasureWare agents also collect data provided through the Data Source Integration (DSI) interface. For instance, data from NetMetrix is provided by the Network Response Facility (NRF) via DSI integration.

The following network metrics are available from MeasureWare. Additional metrics provided by MeasureWare are covered in other chapters.

- Number of configured LAN interfaces
- Number and rate of NFS requests during interval
- Rate of LAN errors
- Rate of LAN collisions
- Number and rate of inbound LAN packets, per LAN interface, during interval
- Number and rate of outbound LAN packets, per LAN interface, during interval
- Number and rate of LAN errors, per LAN interface, during interval
- Number and rate of LAN collisions, per LAN interface, during interval

MeasureWare agents provide data and alarms to PerfView for analysis, and also to the IT/O management console. SNMP traps can be sent at the time that a threshold condition is met. Automated actions can be taken, or the operator can choose to take a suggested action.

MeasureWare's extract command can be used to export data to other tools, such as spreadsheet programs.

Application Resource Measurement (ARM) APIs can be used to instrument applications so that response times can be measured. The application response time information can be passed along to MeasureWare agents for analysis. The ARM APIs are described in more detail in Chapter 7.

GlancePlus

GlancePlus is a real-time, graphical, performance monitoring tool from Hewlett-Packard. It is used to monitor the performance and system resource utilization of a single system. Both Motif-based and character-based interfaces are available. The product can be used on HP-UX, Sun Solaris, and many other operating systems.

GlancePlus collects information similar to that collected by MeasureWare, and samples data more frequently than MeasureWare. GlancePlus can be used to graphically view current system and network resource activity and utilization. It can also show application and process information. Transaction information can be shown if the MeasureWare Agent is installed and active. In addition to system metrics, GlancePlus can show alarm information, color-coded to reflect severity.

GlancePlus is also capable of setting and receiving performance-related alarms. Customizable rules determine when a system performance problem should be sent as an alarm. The rules are managed by the GlancePlus Adviser. The Adviser menu includes the Edit Adviser Syntax option, which you can select to view and optionally modify all alarm conditions.

Alarms result in onscreen notification, with color representing the criticality of an alarm. An alarm can also trigger a command or script to be executed automatically. Instead of sending an alarm, GlancePlus can print messages, or notify you by executing a UNIX command, such as mailx, by using its EXEC feature.

To configure events, you need to edit a configuration file. The GlancePlus Adviser syntax file (/var/opt/perf/adviser.syntax) contains the symptom and alarm configuration. Additional syntax files can also be used. A condition for an alarm to be sent can be based on rules involving different symptoms.

You can also execute scripts in command mode. To execute a script, type:

```
glance -adviser_only -syntax <script file name>
```

GlancePlus can be used to show general network performance characteristics for a system. For example, GlancePlus can show the rate of incoming network packets, and the percentage of all packets that were errors or Ethernet collisions. This can be shown either globally or for each network interface. An example of a GlancePlus networking graph is shown in Figure 6-9. You can see packet transmission rates and error rates in this graph.

GlancePlus can also be used to focus on a specific network problem area, such as a network interface. Also, focusing on a specific network interface can enable the operator to ignore non-critical network components, such as the interface to a subnetwork under development.

For NFS, GlancePlus keeps track of performance statistics, such as the number of read operations per second, number of write operations per second, and number of I/O operations per second for all clients or servers communicating with the server.

More than 600 metrics are accessible from GlancePlus. Some of these metrics are discussed in other chapters. The complete list of metrics can be found by using the online help facility. This information can also be found in the directory /opt/perf/paperdocs/gp/C.

GlancePlus enables you to use filters to reduce the amount of information shown. For example, you can set up a filter in the process view to show only the more active system

Figure 6-9   GlancePlus view of network performance.

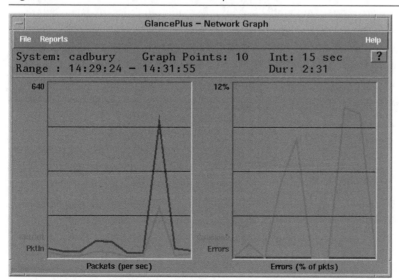

processes. GlancePlus can also show short-term historical information. When selected, the alarm buttons, visible on the main GlancePlus screen, show a history of alarms that have occurred.

GlancePlus will also show the Process Resource Manager's (PRM) behavior, if PRM is installed, and allows you to change PRM process group entitlements. PRM is a Hewlett-Packard product for dividing a system's CPU, memory, or I/O bandwidth resources among users or applications.

PerfView

PerfView is a graphical performance analysis tool from Hewlett-Packard that is used to graphically display performance and system resource utilization for one system or multiple systems simultaneously, so that comparisons can be made. A variety of performance graphs can be displayed. The graphs are based on data collected over a period of time, unlike the real-time graphs of GlancePlus. This tool runs on HP-UX or NT systems and works with data collected by MeasureWare agents.

PerfView has the following three main components:

- **PerfView Monitor:** Provides the ability to receive alarms. A textual description of an alarm can be displayed. Alarms can be filtered by severity, type, or source system. Also, after an alarm is received, the alarm can be selected, to display a graph of related metrics. An operator can monitor trends leading to failures, and then take proactive actions to avoid problems. Graphs can be used for comparison between systems and to show a history of resource consumption. An internal database is maintained that keeps a history of alarm notification messages.
- **PerfView Analyzer:** Provides resource and performance analyses for system resources. System metrics can be shown at three different levels: process, application (configured by the user as a set of processes), and global system information. It relies on data received from MeasureWare agents on managed nodes. Data can be analyzed from up to eight systems concurrently. All MeasureWare data sources are supported. PerfView Analyzer is required by both PerfView Monitor and PerfView Planner.
- **PerfView Planner:** Provides forecasting capability. Graphs can be extrapolated into the future. A variety of graphs (such as linear, exponential, s-curve, and smoothed) can be shown for forecasted data.

PerfView's ability to show history and trend information can be helpful in diagnosing system problems. Graphing performance information can help you to understand whether a persistent problem exists or an anomaly is simply a momentary spike of activity. An example of a PerfView graph of network performance statistics in shown in Figure 6-10. Each network statistic is listed at the top of the graph and is color-coded.

To diagnose a problem further, PerfView Monitor can allow users to change time intervals, to try to find the specific time a problem occurred. The graph is redrawn showing the new time period.

Figure 6-10   PerfView graph of network performance.

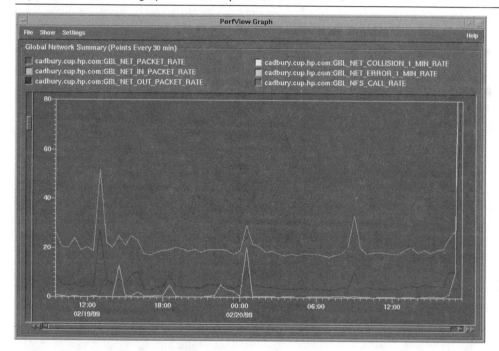

PerfView is integrated with several other monitoring tools. You can launch GlancePlus from within PerfView by accessing the Tools menu. PerfView can also be launched from the IT/O Applications Bank. When troubleshooting an event in the IT/O Message Browser window, you can launch PerfView to see a related performance graph.

PerfView Monitor is not used with IT/O. Instead, the IT/O Message Browser is used. When an alarm is received in IT/O, the operator can click the alarm, and a related PerfView graph can be shown.

In a single performance graph, PerfView can show information collected from multiple systems. The PerfView and ClusterView products have also been integrated to enable the operator to select a cluster symbol on an HP OpenView submap and launch the PerfView application, to quickly show a performance comparison between the cluster systems.

Additional information about MeasureWare, GlancePlus, and PerfView can be found at the HP Resource and Performance Management Web site at http://www.openview.hp.com/solutions/application/.

BMC PATROL for UNIX

BMC PATROL does not provide a separate networking Knowledge Module (KM). Instead, the BMC System KM includes monitors for network metrics. The System KM can identify network overloads. From the console, it can show TCP/IP-related processes and list NIS accounts and groups. The alerts can be sent via SNMP to other management stations by using Patrolink.

Network General Sniffer Pro

A LAN analyzer can show you the type of traffic being transferred on your network. Identifying the protocols being used can give some indication of the types of applications running in the environment. With this information, you can determine whether protocol filtering is needed. An analyzer may be the only reliable way to detect an improperly terminated LAN cable. Network General's Sniffer Pro product views, captures, and analyzes network traffic without affecting server performance or introducing network traffic.

However, many vendors are now providing analyzers as pure software solutions. Sniffer Pro is a software solution that can run on your management station and collect data on different LAN segments. An example network performance graph is shown in Figure 6-11.

Figure 6-11   Sniffer Pro summary of LAN statistics.

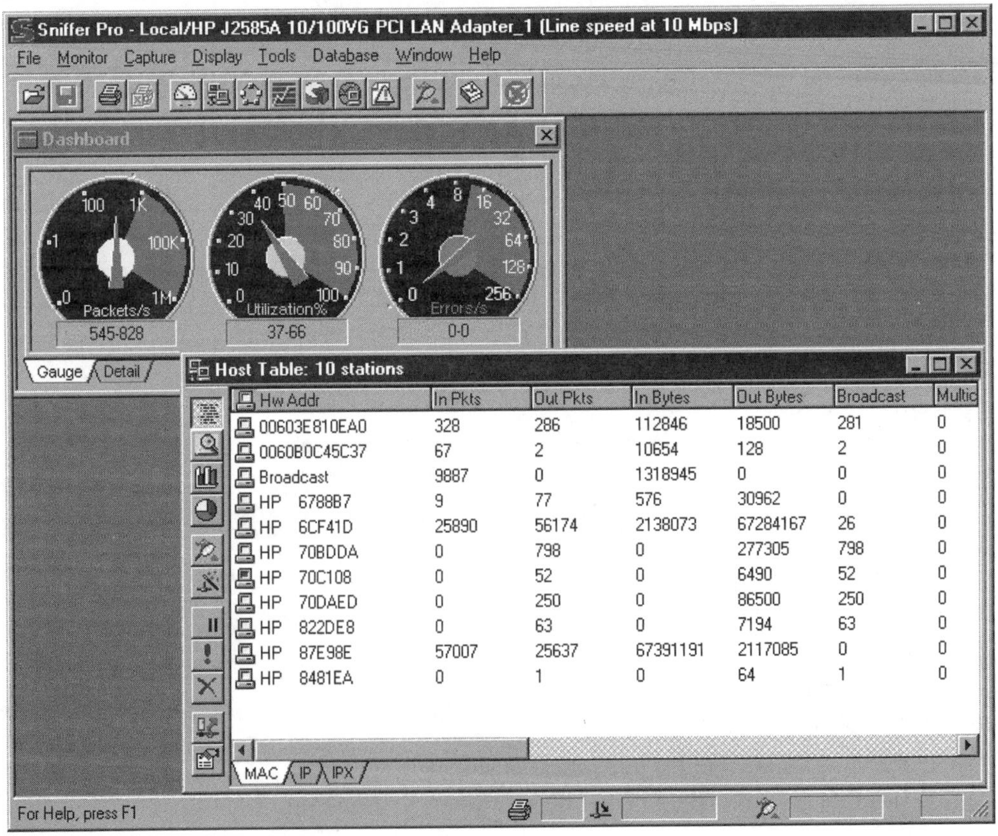

Using Network Performance Data

This section provides a brief introduction on how you can use the network performance monitoring tools to detect and address network performance problems. Various types of network performance problems are possible. Potential problems could be an overloaded server, a congested network, or a faulty network masquerading as an overloaded network. You can use the performance tools to avoid these problems, if possible, or at least to correct them quickly when they occur.

Avoiding Performance Issues

To avoid network performance issues, key networks should be monitored regularly to look for trends. You should first use tools such as PerfView and NetMetrix to collect baseline data from when the computing environment is behaving normally. You may want to put some NFS commands into scripts to create your own benchmarks. Be sure that your mixture of NFS commands reflects the typical usage for your environment. In addition to benchmarking utilization rates, you should determine what collision rates are typical by using lanadmin or MeasureWare. Data should be collected over a period of time to get an accurate view of the network load. As loads increase, you should be prepared to segregate network traffic, add more LAN cards, or restrict the number of new applications being used on the network.

Network performance problems can be caused by an increase in the number of users or the introduction of a new application into the production environment. By proactively collecting performance information, you can identify when a jump in usage occurred and you may be able to trace it to a new application or a user's inappropriate use of the network. Network analyzers and tools such as NetMetrix can be used to identify the applications and users dominating network traffic. A new network application initially should be deployed in a test environment so that its network load can be characterized. If its network usage is unexpectedly high, it can be redesigned before deployment into the production environment, or the production environment can be modified to support the new workload.

Detecting Overloaded Network Servers

If the server performing a network service, such as NFS, is overloaded, it won't be able to handle network traffic effectively. The problem could be a CPU, memory, or disk I/O bottleneck, or an inability of the server's NIC to handle the load.

To check for a CPU bottleneck on the network server, check the CPU utilization and run queue length. GlancePlus/UX can provide this information. CPU utilization greater than 95 percent and a high processor run queue length may indicate a CPU bottleneck. One option is to increase the capacity of the server by adding more processors, but this is not always possible. Also, it may not be sufficient to fix the problem, if the service is single-threaded.

To check for a real memory bottleneck on the network server, you can first check the amount of free memory. It should not drop below 5 percent of the total available. If the system can't keep up with the demands for memory, it will start paging and swapping. Excessive paging and swapping, viewed from GlancePlus, may be a sign of a memory bottleneck. Increasing the capacity of the system by adding more memory may eliminate the bottleneck.

You can check for an I/O imbalance on the network server by using tools such as iostat. High activity on the system disk is normal, but delays among nonsystem disks should be roughly the same. You may want to move files around to balance the disk load if an imbalance exists. You may also want to check your system's buffer cache hit ratio to see whether your buffer cache size is too small. Tools such as MeasureWare and BMC PATROL can provide information about your system buffer cache. If all of your disks are more than 75-percent utilized, then you are diskbound and may need faster or additional disks.

Detecting Network Congestion

For Ethernet links, you can use the collision rate to determine whether or not a performance problem is due to congestion. lanadmin can be used to calculate the collision rate. You can calculate the rate by dividing the number of collisions by the number of outbound packets. A collision rate consistently greater than 5 to 10 percent indicates a congested network. You can also calculate the average collision rate for a network by totaling the number of output packets of all systems on the network and then dividing by the total number of collisions. If this average collision rate is greater than 10 percent, it is another sign that you need to take some action.

Network utilization averaging more than 35 to 40 percent of capacity on a shared medium is another sign of network congestion. If the utilization rate persists, it is likely to lead to collisions on the network.

As mentioned, lanadmin can be used to identify network congestion. Compare the current collision rate to the rate that you benchmarked during normal operation. Specifying netstat –a shows statistics for each open connection, including the send queue, which indicates the number of packets waiting to be sent. This should be 0 for most connections. If it is a large number, it could be an indication of network congestion. You should check this over a period of time to see whether the problem persists.

If you determine that a network is congested, and the network is being used appropriately, then you may need to partition the network into subnetworks and use gateways to isolate independent streams of data. (Techniques for identifying the appropriate location for a LAN bridge or gateway is beyond the scope of this book.) If configured properly, this can reduce the collisions on shared media and thus improve network performance. You should take advantage of any planned downtime to reconfigure networks, add additional LAN cards, or move applications to other systems on different networks.

Information about NFS usage can be shown by using nfsstat. Specifying nfsstat –c shows the client's NFS statistics. If the number of bad XID packets is approximately equal to the number of retransmissions, then one of the client's NFS servers is having trouble keeping up with the workload and is forcing the client to resend requests. Check each of the NFS servers to see whether any have system resource bottlenecks, as discussed earlier in this section. The disk is the most common resource bottleneck for an NFS server. If the nfsstat output shows that only the number of retransmissions is high, then the network is congested or faulty.

Avoiding Network Problems

According to a 1998 survey by the MERIT Project, sponsored by Computer Associates, networking was identified as the area most in need of management automation to reduce outages. Network downtime can be prevented by watching for trends in performance that could lead to overloads, and by providing redundancy, so that single network component failures are not noticed by users.

Network outages are often due to network bandwidth problems. By using tools such as NetMetrix and PerfView, increases in network usage can be identified and addressed before they become problems. Users can reduce network bandwidth requirements by using tools such as compress on files before transferring them over the network. The previous section discusses ways to avoid network performance problems.

You can't keep a networking component from failing, but you can set up your system so that users are not impacted by the failure. To prevent the downtime associated with a NIC failure, high availability software and redundant LANs can be used. MC/ServiceGuard can detect failed LAN cards and automatically configure a backup LAN card to take over the work. MC/ServiceGuard also supports the ability to automatically move TCP/IP addresses on Ethernet, FDDI, Token Ring, 100VG, and ATM LANs. High availability networking products that provide additional protection are available from HP, such as HA NFS and HA ATM.

You may also want to use MC/ServiceGuard to protect your network application. It can detect application failures and restart the application locally or move it to another system if the problem is persistent.

You should take advantage of the support for redundancy in various network services. The Domain Name Service, for example, enables you to configure primary and secondary servers. Name resolution can also be set up to rely on a configuration file or an alternate name service if the DNS server is unavailable. By setting up this redundancy, you can avoid the connectivity problems that would result from a failed name server.

High availability software was mentioned as a way to mask network failures. However, a fault needs to be detected and corrected before any additional failures cause unplanned downtime. EMS can be used to report the failure of a NIC. Use any planned downtime as an opportunity to replace the LAN card.

Recovering from Network Problems

This section discusses how to diagnose and then correct network problems. Networking is a broad area, spanning geographical distances and a variety of software and hardware components. Faults may be due to a NIC, transceiver, connector, cable, or other network device. Network communication problems may be due to a software configuration problem or misbehaving network software. You need to use a combination of the tools discussed throughout this chapter to isolate the problem.

Problems related to performance were discussed earlier, in the section "Using Network Performance Data." Distinguishing between performance problems and network faults is often difficult. For example, a failed network device stops responding to packets, which may lead to a flood of retransmissions. A variety of network faults can be detected by using network performance tools. netstat and nfsstat are examples of commands that can be used for both performance monitoring and fault diagnosis.

An early step in troubleshooting should be to try to identify what is unique about the problem. For example, if only one user is experiencing a problem, then something could be wrong with that user's configuration or access rights. If the problem involves only a specific network service, you may want to check whether the service has recently been updated. Similarly, if a communication problem involves a specific computer system, you should check whether that system has recently had a software or hardware configuration change.

The following sections provide some troubleshooting steps that can help you to locate a network problem.

Isolating the Fault

If a user is unable to use a network service, the first thing that you probably should do is use ping to see whether you can reach the user's system and the network server. ping is an easy command to remember and can isolate the problem to the appropriate part of the networking stack. ping tests the physical, data link, and network layers of the networking stack. If ping succeeds, then you should check the transport layer or higher layers for the problem. If this fails, then you have isolated the problem to the network or lower layers.

Depending on the network topology in your computing environment, a possible scenario is that you can access the user's system and network server from your management station, but the user can't access the network server directly. If the user's topology is different from your own, you may need to ping from the user's system, or use the remote ping capability of NNM. If the ping behavior differs, it may indicate a routing problem.

If a ping failure occurs, you should verify the name resolution before continuing. You can use nslookup to see whether the name resolves to the correct IP address. Another option is to use ping and specify the IP address instead of the system name. You may try pinging from different subnetworks to eliminate some of the network components as the source of the problem. You can also check the ARP cache to see whether the IP address is being resolved to the correct MAC address.

Network and Lower Layers

If you suspect a problem with the lower network protocol layers, you should first verify the network configuration by using ioscan, lanscan, and ifconfig. The lanscan command should display the status of all the LAN cards shown through ioscan. ifconfig shows you whether the IP address has been properly bound to the network interface and whether the subnet masks are set correctly.

If these commands do not return the correct information, then a link or software configuration error may exist. You should check the system log file for link-level errors.

You may be able to confirm a LAN card error by checking the LEDs on the card itself. Usually, green is good and red or yellow is bad. Check the appropriate hardware user manual for the detailed interpretation of these LEDs.

You can test the data link layers of the source and destination systems by using linkloop. If this command fails, the link layer would seem to be the problem and you should check the LAN cables, transceivers, and other network hardware. lanadmin can show you LAN statistics, to see whether excessive packet errors or collisions are occurring. If the linkloop test succeeds, you should next check the network configuration, using netstat –in.

If network problems started when a new system was added to the LAN, the new system may be using a duplicate IP address. You can use netstat –in on each system on the LAN to see whether duplicates are present.

If you suspect that packets are being routed inappropriately, you can use traceroute to identify the route UDP packets are taking from the source system to the destination. The command shows the route and time taken between gateways. This can help you to determine whether a router has failed or a routing table is configured incorrectly.

If netstat shows bad checksums under the IP, ICMP, TCP, or UDP protocols, it is an indication that packets are getting corrupted, possibly on their way through a gateway. If the server is attached to multiple gateways, you may need to send test packets through each gateway to isolate the culprit. Just check the number of bad checksums after sending the packets through each gateway to determine which one is faulty. You then need to repair the faulty gateway device.

The number of input and output errors reported by netstat should be very low, unless a power failure recently occurred. If netstat reports an increasing number of input errors, it could be an indication of corrupt packets being received from another system on the network, or a damaged LAN cable. Try to isolate the source of the remote packets to identify the culprit. If you see an increasing number of output errors, then your system's NIC could be bad.

When a network cable problem is suspected, a LAN analyzer can be used to isolate the problem. The analyzer is attached to the problematic network and can determine the distance to the failed component. A cable may be improperly terminated, or a network segment may need to be replaced.

Transport and Higher Layers

If the network and link layers seem to be working properly, you should next check the transport layer to the destination system by using a network application such as telnet or FTP. The netstat command can be used on the server to see which network applications are currently running. If a desired service has failed, it may need to be restarted. You may want to look in /var/adm/syslog/syslog.log for potential causes of the failure. netstat can also show useful protocol statistics.

If connectivity to the network server seems okay, but a service is not responding, performance problems may exist with the server or services, or the service may have failed. You may be running the wrong version of the service. Compare the version of the service on a working system with that on a system where the service is failing. To check the version of a service such as FTP, type what ftpd.

A service may exist on the system, but it may not be running because of security reasons. If a service is not being started, check whether the optional file /var/adm/inetd.sec is being used. This file can be used to deny or allow access to each network service. If the user is authorized, make sure that this file is not configured to deny access. Some services have their own specific security files. For example, FTP denies access to local accounts listed in /etc/ftpusers.

Monitoring the Application

Earlier chapters focused on the systems, networks, and disks that connect the end-users to the application. This chapter describes the tools available to an operator to monitor the application. Although the name would suggest that a system operator is responsible primarily for monitoring the operation of the system, in fact, the business application is what is most important. It doesn't matter that the system is up if the application itself is unavailable. Maintaining application availability means maintaining the availability and performance of all components that the application depends on, including databases, networks, storage, and the system itself.

Important Application Components to Monitor

Applications can be monitored from several different perspectives. This chapter divides application monitoring into configuration management, fault management, and resource and performance management.

An application can fail for many reasons. Software logic problems, hardware faults, limit conditions (such as running out of memory or overflowing a counter), and race conditions (such as forgetting to request a semaphore) can all cause an application to fail. In some of these cases, an operator can determine what happened by other system events (such as available memory dropping below a threshold). However, having monitors watching specific applications is often useful. Customized application monitors may be able to identify hundreds of different causes of application problems, saving you from some of the effort involved in troubleshooting a failure. Continual monitoring during business hours is needed to ensure the service is available. "By far, application software failures account for the greatest portion of downtime," according to a 1996 Gartner Group study.

Configuration management includes both ensuring that the application was configured initially without errors and monitoring any changes that are made to the configuration files. This change history can be used to detect and recover from any inappropriate configuration changes.

In addition to monitoring whether or not the application is running, monitoring its performance is also important. If an application is hung or performing poorly, the end-user considers the service to be unavailable. Checking system performance can be a useful gauge as to how well the application is performing. A Unix environment often has only one important application per system. However, more specific tools are needed to diagnose and recover from application problems.

For important applications, it may be useful to monitor the resources that the application needs, even if the application is not running. For example, tapes should be checked periodically so that tape hardware failures are detected before the backup application starts running. This helps to ensure that the backup completes within the desired time window.

Another reason to monitor the application is to determine its resource usage over time. This can be used to bill back clients for their use of a service. You may want to check the number of resources in use by the application for several reasons. The application may be nearing configuration limits or taking an inappropriate share of system resources.

A trend in companies' IT/O departments is to implement "service-level agreements." Instead of merely maintaining the availability of key systems and the networking backbone, IT/O departments are now measured based on their ability to provide specific levels of availability and response times for their end-users. The focus is on the service provided by the application. When measuring performance or availability in a computing environment, measuring in terms of the end-user service or application is most important.

Identifying Application Types

Different types of applications require different levels of monitoring. Some of the tools described in this chapter are primarily used for certain types of applications.

Here are some types of important applications:

- MC/ServiceGuard packages
- Database applications
- Enterprise Resource Planning (ERP) applications
- System Service applications
- Management applications

Some applications are critical to a company's business. A failure may result in significant lost revenue for the company. You may want to protect these applications with high availability software. HP's MC/ServiceGuard is a high availability software product that detects system failures, network or LAN card failures, and the failures of critical applications. MC/ServiceGuard can be configured to handle these failures automatically. For example, a failed critical application can be restarted. The failure of a LAN card can result in the automatic configuration of a backup LAN card to take over the network load. MC/ServiceGuard configures mission-critical applications into "packages" by using the System Administration Manager (SAM). These packages are then monitored and controlled by MC/ServiceGuard.

Database applications are important to monitor because they reference critical business data. Oracle, Sybase, and Informix are the most common database management system vendors. Database servers are discussed in Chapter 8.

ERP software applications are used to integrate the data in different parts of a corporation, such as manufacturing, payroll, human resources, and accounting. By sharing information efficiently with different parts of the organization, a corporation can detect and respond more quickly to changing business conditions. ERP is now a $1 billion software business. Common ERP applications include SAP R/3, Baan, and PeopleSoft.

Some overlap exists between these categories. For example, a database application may be configured as an MC/ServiceGuard package, and some Oracle applications are used as part of ERP solutions. This chapter distinguishes between tools that can be used for any application and tools that are customized for specific ERP applications.

Some applications are shipped with the operating system to perform essential services. Many of these applications, such as sendmail, NFS, telnet, and rlogin, are covered in the system and networking chapters, and thus are not discussed here.

Although this chapter focuses on ERP and general application monitoring, you should remember that management applications also require careful attention. Without monitoring the management applications, such as the system monitors, how do you know the system is still being monitored? Backup applications are another example. What if the backup fails every night, but no one notices? Some commercial products are available to help ensure that your backups were successful. Many system applications, such as OmniBack and OpenSpool, are shipped with IT/Operations (IT/O) templates and filters. OmniBack provides sophisticated monitoring, and can be monitored by any SNMP-based product, in addition to IT/O. During backup job execution, network-wide consolidated notification is provided.

Using Standard Commands and Tools

This section describes standard commands and system instrumentation that can be used for monitoring any application. Some Unix commands are available that can help you to determine the status of your application. Commands to report the overall status of your system are described in Chapter 4.

In addition to these commands, you may want to check the system log file, /var/adm/syslog/syslog.log, for error messages if your system is experiencing problems. Messages written to this log file include information on the module experiencing the problem and the time the event occurred, which can be very valuable when troubleshooting.

ps

The ps command can be used to show the processes running on the system. This can be a quick way to determine whether an application is running — if its process names are known.

On larger systems with many active processes, you may want to restrict ps output by using the various options. ps –p restricts the listing to a specific process list, and ps –u shows only those processes with a matching user ID.

A process name may not be unique on the system, so you may need to look at additional information, such as the user ID. The ps command can provide the following information:

- User ID of process owner
- Process Identifier (PID)
- PID of parent process
- Start time of process
- Controlling terminal for process
- Cumulative execution time for process
- Command name and arguments

top

The top command is useful for monitoring process information, as well as system CPU and memory loads. top output is displayed in the terminal window and is updated every five seconds, by default.

top shows CPU resource statistics, including load averages (job queues over the last 1, 5, and 15 minutes), number of processes in each state (sleeping, waiting, running, starting, zombie, and stopped), percentage of time spent in each processor state (user, nice, system, idle, interrupt, and swapper) per processor on the system, as well as the average for each processor in a multi-processor system.

At the process level, top lists the most active processes on the system, based on their CPU usage. The process data displayed by top includes the PID, process size (text, data, and stack), resident size of the process (in K), process state (sleeping, waiting, running, idle, zombie, or stopped), number of CPU seconds consumed by the process, and the average CPU utilization of the process. top can be used to identify processes that may be using large amounts of CPU or memory.

Listing 7-1 shows an example of the output you see when running top. Note that system and process information are displayed on the same screen, so that you can quickly get an overview of what is happening.

vmstat

The vmstat command supplies good information about system resources, including virtual memory and CPU usage. vmstat is useful for detecting when you are low on memory or swap space. CPU utilization is shown by user, system, and idle time.

For processes, vmstat shows the number of processes in various states. These states include: currently in the run queue, blocked on an I/O operation, and swapped out to disk. This can help to give you an idea of whether or not a process is functioning properly.

Listing 7-1   top output showing most active processes.

```
System: hpgsslha                                    Sat Apr 24 10:27:04 1999
Load averages: 0.15, 0.08, 0.04
174 processes: 172 sleeping, 1 running, 1 zombie
Cpu states:
 LOAD    USER   NICE    SYS    IDLE  BLOCK   SWAIT    INTR   SSYS
 0.15    0.2%   0.0%    1.2%  98.6%   0.0%    0.0%    0.0%    0.0%


Memory: 55028K (8924K) real, 56188K (15136K) virtual, 60528K free   Page# 1/13

 TTY    PID USERNAME PRI NI    SIZE    RES STATE    TIME %WCPU   %CPU COMMAND
   ?   1729 root      20 20   6676K  5488K sleep  871:04  1.12   1.12 cmcld
   ?      3 root     128 20     0K     0K sleep  555:03  0.68   0.68 statdaemon
  p2  10779 bstone   178 20    580K   316K run      0:00  0.77   0.51 top
   ?      7 root     -32 20     0K     0K sleep  231:40  0.30   0.30 ttisr
   ?    262 root     154 20    280K    24K sleep  169:33  0.23   0.23 syncer
   ?   1439 root     154 20     80K    84K sleep   51:43  0.06   0.06 instl_bootd
   ?   1718 root     168 20     64K   128K sleep   20:55  0.05   0.05 spserver
   ?   1424 root     154 20    104K   120K sleep   14:05  0.05   0.05 inetd
   ?   1455 root     154 20    304K   184K sleep   29:29  0.05   0.05 nmbd
   ?   1641 root     154 20   5100K  1224K sleep   40:50  0.05   0.04 swagentd
   ?   1347 root     127 20    104K    76K sleep   30:50  0.03   0.03 netfmt
   ?   1662 root     154 20     80K   128K sleep   12:00  0.03   0.03 hpnpd
   ?  15563 jimg     154 20    460K   140K sleep    6:59  0.03   0.03 xload
   ?   2005 root     154 20   2760K    68K sleep   23:51  0.02   0.02 ns-admin
```

The statistics that you see will vary depending on the command option specified. By specifying a time interval, you can have vmstat run continuously so that you can see how values vary over time.

Using System Instrumentation

Standards for network and system management, such as Simple Network Management Protocol (SNMP) and Desktop Management Interface (DMI), have been developed to help make management easier. They provide industry-standard ways to build instrumentation and to interface into the instrumentation. SNMP is used to access Management Information Bases (MIBs), and DMI is used to access Management Information Formats (MIFs).

Standard MIBs and MIFs define the metrics that can be instrumented by any vendor. Vendor-specific MIBs and MIFs provide vendor-specific instrumentation. This section looks at some of the system instrumentation available through each of these standards, which can be used to obtain information about your application.

Many tools already exist for accessing this instrumentation. Several vendors offer browsers and monitoring capabilities that use a common interface for accessing instrumented objects from different hardware platforms and operating systems. For example, the common enterprise management frameworks, such as HP Network Node Manager (NNM), include a MIB Browser tool to access MIB data. They may also include tools that can be used to monitor MIB data on remote systems from the enterprise management platform. Toolkits also exist that provide an interface in which users can write their own tools to monitor or track this information. Other toolkits enable users to create their own instrumentation.

SNMP

A MIB is a standard way of representing information of a certain category. For example, MIB-II provides useful information about a system, such as the number of active TCP connections, system hardware and version information, and so forth. OpenView IT/O, discussed later in this chapter, provides a MIB Browser that helps you to discover which MIBs are available and to see the information being provided by each MIB. With the MIB Browser tool, you can check the value of anything contained in a MIB. If you find a MIB that contains some useful fields, you can use the MIB Browser to gather that data from the target system. The resulting data is displayed onscreen in the MIB Browser's output window. By browsing through available MIBs and querying values of selected MIB fields, you can gather specific information needed to monitor systems and troubleshoot problems.

The SNMP interface provides access to objects stored in various MIBs. MIB-II is a standard MIB that has been implemented on most Unix systems. On HP-UX systems, the HP-UNIX MIB defines various metrics for monitoring system resources. Other vendors, such as Sun, have vendor-specific MIBs that provide similar information. You can find complete MIB definitions in Appendix A.

The HP-UNIX MIB contains information about each of the processes running on the system. Useful information includes the PID, CPU utilization, priority, and resident set size. If numerous processes are active on a system, searching through the process table in the MIB may be difficult. If you want to find information only for a specific process, you may prefer to write a small program that uses the pstat interface, covered later in this section, which provides the same information as the MIB process table, as well as additional fields. However, the MIB is a useful source for collecting data about multiple processes, especially if you do not want to write your own application.

If you are using MC/ServiceGuard to protect your application, then you may also want to use the HP MC/ServiceGuard MIB, which contains information about each configured MC/ServiceGuard application, or package. Information about a package includes the name, description, current status, system on which it is currently running, processes making up the package, and alternate nodes for the package. Note that the MIB does not show any EMS resource dependencies for a package. You have to use the MC/ServiceGuard command cmviewcl –v to obtain this additional information.

The Network Services MIB and Relational Database Management System MIB are used for database applications. From these MIBs, you can learn the database version, database status, length of time the application has been running, and number of current users. Some resource and performance information is also available.

DMI

System resource information can also be retrieved by using DMI, which is another standard for storing and accessing management information. Management information is represented in a text file in the MIF. It is divided into components, each of which has a Service Provider (SP) that is responsible for providing DMI information to the management applications that request it.

Several system platforms, including HP-UX, provide instrumentation for the System MIF and Software MIF. Appendix A contains a complete listing of these MIFs.

Similar to MIB-II, the System MIF can be used to get generic system information (such as how long it has been running) and system contact information. It includes the system name, boot time, contact information, uptime, number of users, and some information about the filesystem and disks.

The Software MIF provides information about the software products and product bundles installed on a system, and can be a useful tool after the discovery of a problem with an application. By using a MIF Browser, you can examine the Software MIF to see whether a problem might have been caused by a bad patch or modified file. The MIF contains revision information, including creation and modification times, for each product. Version information can be checked to see whether a compatibility problem exists. Finally, the product's vendor information is provided, in case you need to contact the product's support personnel.

Vendors such as Hewlett-Packard are working to provide enterprise-wide repositories of software configuration information. Tools are needed to compare application versions on different systems and update systems to the same revision level.

pstat

Occasionally, you may want to write your own application program to get access to information about specific processes. This interface is referred to as pstat. Your program can generate output for only the interesting processes, which can be much easier than wading through top or ps output looking for important information.

Listings 7-2 and 7-3, respectively, show a program that obtains pstat statistics and the output from running the program. The program displays information for the process(es) matching the names that you enter. The pstat interface can also show overall system information, as demonstrated in Listing 7-2.

For the example in Listing 7-3, the concern is that an application named memhog is using too much memory, so the program is being used to check memhog's memory usage at various times, and to track the overall system load. This can be more convenient than running other tools, such as top or GlancePlus, and sifting through the output.

Listing 7-2 Program code using pstat.

```
/* pstat example */
#include <stdio.h>
#include <stdlib.h>
#include <sys/time.h>
#include <sys/types.h>
#include <sys/socket.h>
#include <netinet/in.h>
#include <sys/errno.h>
#include <sys/pstat.h>

convert_status (status,stat)
char *status;
long stat;
{
    switch (stat) {
    case 1: strcpy (status,"sleeping");
            break;
    case 2: strcpy (status,"running");
            break;
    case 3: strcpy (status,"stopped");
            break;
    case 4: strcpy (status,"dead (zombie)");
            break;
    case 5: strcpy (status,"other");
            break;
    case 6: strcpy (status,"idle");
            break;
    }
}

main()
{
    struct pst_status pst;
    struct pst_dynamic dyn;
    struct pst_static mystatic;
    struct timeval temp;
    struct timezone dummy;
    char target[80];
    char status[14];
    int indx = 0;
    int duration;
    long prm_id;
    unsigned long now;
    gettimeofday(&temp,&dummy);
    printf ("Enter process name:");
```

```
    scanf ("%s",target);
    now = temp.tv_sec;
    while ( pstat_getproc(pst,sizeof (struct pst_status),
                          1,indx) > 0) {
        if (strcmp(target,pst.pst_ucomm)==0) {
            duration = now - pst.pst_start;
            convert_status(status,pst.pst_stat);
            printf ("PID %8d  Status: %s\n",pst.pst_pid,status);
            printf ("Started %d seconds ago\n",duration);

            printf ("Real pages(DATA %d  TEXT %d  STACK %d)\n",
                    pst.pst_dsize,pst.pst_tsize,pst.pst_ssize);
            printf ("RSS %d   MAX RSS(hwm) %d\n",
                    pst.pst_rssize,pst.pst_maxrss);
            printf ("Number of swaps: %d\n",pst.pst_nswap);
        }
        indx = pst.pst_idx+1;
    } /* end while loop */

    printf ("Overall System Info:\n");
    pstat_getstatic(mystatic,sizeof(struct pst_static),
                    0,0);
    pstat_getdynamic(dyn,sizeof(struct pst_dynamic),
                     0,indx);
    printf ("Run queue len(1- %lf,",dyn.psd_avg_1_min);
    printf ("5- %lf,",dyn.psd_avg_5_min);
    printf ("15- %lf)\n",dyn.psd_avg_15_min);
    printf ("Physical Memory: %d\n",mystatic.physical_memory);
    printf ("Active Real Memory: %d  Free pages: %d bytes\n",
            dyn.psd_arm,dyn.psd_free*mystatic.page_size);
}
```

Listing 7-3 Program output showing pstat information.

```
# ./pstatex
Enter process name:memhog
PID    24549  Status: running
Started 247 seconds ago
Real pages(DATA 1955  TEXT 3  STACK 3)
RSS 1979   MAX RSS(hwm) 1979
Number of swaps: 0
Overall System Info:
Run queue len(1- 0.000000,5- 0.000000,15- 0.000000)
Physical Memory: 393216
Active Real Memory: 0  Free pages: 0 bytes
#
```

The example in Listing 7-3 shows only memory information, but a variety of additional metrics are also available. Here is a summary of the information available for each process:

- User ID, PID, effective user ID, real and effective group ID, and parent PID
- Number of real pages used for data, text, or stack
- Number of real pages used for shared memory, memory mapped files, and so forth
- Number of virtual pages used for data, text, stack, shared memory, and so forth
- Priority and nice value
- Terminal device ID
- Process group and PRM group ID
- Address of process in memory
- User and system time spent executing
- Time process started
- Process status and status flags
- Processor last used by process
- Command line and executable base name for process
- CPU time used
- Current and high-water mark of resident set size
- Number of swaps, page faults, and page reclaims
- Number of signals or socket messages received
- Number of socket messages sent
- Scheduling policy of process
- Session ID
- File ID of process' root directory, current directory, and executable
- Highest file descriptor currently opened
- Number of characters read and written

More information about the process and system metrics available from this interface can be found in the system include file, /usr/include/sys/pstat.h.

Fault Detection Tools

This section describes products that can be used to detect application failures. Additional tools for monitoring application performance are discussed later in the chapter.

IT/Operations

IT/Operations (IT/O) is a sophisticated management product for system operators. Systems in the enterprise can be displayed on maps onscreen, with colors representing their current status. An Application Bank is included for default and customized tools that can be launched from a particular system. Events can be sent from systems throughout the enterprise, and configured recovery actions can then be taken.

IT/O can also be used to monitor specified components on a managed system. Some pre-defined monitors are provided, one of which has the ability to monitor specific processes. An event is sent to the IT/O console if a process fails. A recovery action can be configured to restart the application.

Although IT/O can detect an application failure and restart the application, it does not have sufficient high availability capabilities to move an application to another system or ensure that only one copy is running. More extensive high availability capabilities are provided by MC/ServiceGuard, which is discussed next.

MC/ServiceGuard

MC/ServiceGuard is a high availability product from Hewlett-Packard that is used to protect your critical applications and servers. MC/ServiceGuard is most commonly used in a multisystem (cluster) environment. The MC/ServiceGuard software on each system monitors the other systems in the cluster. MC/ServiceGuard can detect the failure of systems, networks, and applications. For example, MC/ServiceGuard can recover transparently from a LAN failure.

After deciding which applications need to be protected, you configure them as packages by using MC/ServiceGuard commands or the graphical interface accessible from SAM. Numerous attributes of the application need to be defined, such as the following:

- Name of application
- Scripts used to start and stop application
- Processes or services that make up application
- Subnetworks used by application
- Alternate systems on which application can run
- Additional resource dependencies

MC/ServiceGuard then monitors these services and dependencies. If a failure occurs, the package is either restarted locally or moved and restarted on another system. Similarly, when a system failure occurs, MC/ServiceGuard software can detect the problem and automatically restart critical applications on an alternate node.

MC/ServiceGuard software detects a variety of error conditions, but does not have a sophisticated notification mechanism for you to learn what happened. Errors are often written to the system log file, which helps retrace what happened.

Because MC/ServiceGuard can automatically move applications to other systems, it may be difficult for you to know the current status of your application. MC/ServiceGuard commands, such as cmviewcl, can tell you the current state of a cluster and its packages. The HP MC/ServiceGuard MIB also contains this information. However, a package can be moved for a variety of reasons, and MC/ServiceGuard doesn't tell you the reason. You may want to check the system log file (/var/adm/syslog/syslog.log) on each cluster system for its specific MC/ServiceGuard activity. An example of the events logged to the system log file during a package failover is shown in Listing 7-4. In the example, cake is the system name, and cmcld is part of the MC/ServiceGuard product. The package failed because a service on which it depended failed.

Not all applications work well in an MC/ServiceGuard environment. For example, applications that use the gethostname() system call may not work properly after the application is moved to another node. MC/ServiceGuard provides a list of application guidelines that should be followed. About 100 applications have been specifically tested with MC/ServiceGuard, either by an HP organization or by the application's company. These applications include many of the key applications described in this book, such as BMC PATROL, Unicenter TNG, PeopleSoft, SAP R/3, and Baan Triton. In addition to certifying applications, MC/ServiceGuard provides optional application toolkits for specific applications, such as HA NFS and HA DCE.

Note that MC/ServiceGuard is supported only on HP 9000 Series 800 systems running HP-UX 10.x or later operating systems.

ClusterView

You can use the ClusterView product to help with diagnoses in high availability environments. ClusterView is an OpenView application with custom monitoring capabilities for MC/Service-Guard and MC/LockManager clusters. ClusterView requires NNM or IT/O.

ClusterView relies on a high availability SNMP subagent, which is included with the MC/ServiceGuard and MC/LockManager products. It can be used to send events to an Open-View management station. These SNMP traps can actually be received by any management station that understands SNMP (such as Computer Associates' Unicenter product). These events are received in NNM's Event Browser. If the subagent is running on an IT/O-managed system, it automatically detects the IT/O software and sends events by using the proprietary IT/O Remote Procedure Call (RPC) mechanism, which is more reliable than SNMP traps.

ClusterView can be used to graphically show application status. Color is used to represent status, and a line is used to link an application to the system on which it is running. Because applications can be moved manually or automatically, this link is important for finding an application's current location. ClusterView does not show any resource or performance problems that may exist for an application. Other tools must be used to provide that capability.

Figure 7-1 shows how ClusterView displays the application packages configured in an MC/ServiceGuard cluster. Lines connect the packages to the systems on which they are running.

Listing 7-4 syslog output showing a package failover.

```
Apr 23 15:17:48 cake cmcld[983]: Service PKG*4172 terminated due to an exit(0).
Apr 23 15:17:48 cake cmcld[983]: Halted package ems1 on node cake.
Apr 23 15:17:48 cake cmcld[983]: Package ems1 cannot run on this node because
switching has been disabled for this node.
Apr 23 15:17:54 cake cmcld[983]: (tart) Started package ems1 on node tart.
```

Figure 7-1   ClusterView showing application packages.

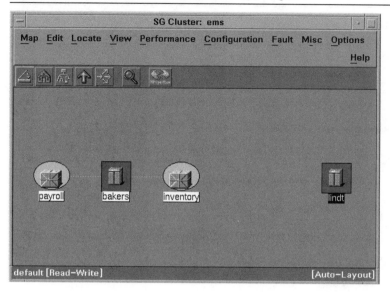

ClusterView provides additional capabilities when used with IT/O. The SNMP events are sent to the Event Browser, where ClusterView provides special troubleshooting instructions and recommends actions to help resolve the problems. Some data collection activities are done automatically. For example, in response to a package failure, ClusterView automatically retrieves the system's system log file entries from the time of failure to aid in diagnosis. Common HP-UX monitoring tools, such as netstat and lanscan, are included by ClusterView in IT/O's Application Bank, along with MC/ServiceGuard-specific tools, such as cmviewcl.

For each cluster, node, or package that is shown on an OpenView submap, the operator can view an additional detail screen. The detail information is obtained by querying the HP MC/ServiceGuard MIB on the cluster. An example package detail screen is shown in Figure 7-2. The package details can tell you alternate systems on which the package is configured to run.

In addition to high availability clusters, ClusterView can monitor user-defined clusters. ClusterView provides a configuration tool that enables administrators to create a cluster, which ClusterView will then display on a cluster submap. For example, you may want to group all of your systems running Informix into an Informix cluster. The operator can then monitor all the clustered systems at a glance, because they are all in the same OpenView submap. Also, the operator can launch monitoring tools such as HP PerfView on the cluster, avoiding the need to select each system manually when running each tool.

ClusterView runs on HP-UX and Windows NT systems. The ClusterView software for either platform can also be used to monitor Microsoft's NT Cluster Servers, its high availability clusters. Both NT and MC/ServiceGuard clusters can be monitored concurrently from the same ClusterView software.

Figure 7-2   Output from ClusterView package detail screen.

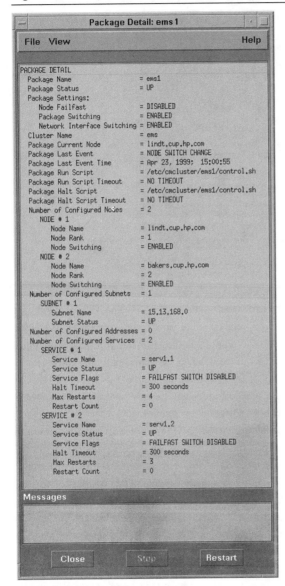

Event Monitoring Service

As mentioned earlier, MC/ServiceGuard can monitor and migrate application packages. However, its application monitoring is limited to determining whether an application is running or has failed. MC/ServiceGuard relies on the Event Monitoring Service (EMS) to monitor additional components that are important to the application. The application package may be dependent on a resource, such as a disk volume. Any package dependencies are specified when the package is initially configured. When the package is started by MC/ServiceGuard, EMS begins continual monitoring of each resource.

EMS can report resource problems to MC/ServiceGuard so that an application can be restarted. EMS can also report important events to a log file or management station. This can aid in troubleshooting, because the operator can receive information about the specific component that failed (instead of simply learning that an application was restarted, with no explanatory text).

A variety of events can be reported by EMS. Several networking links have customized monitors. A database monitor is available to monitor Oracle server status. The disk monitor can report logical and physical volume status information. All EMS monitors can be used with or without the MC/ServiceGuard product.

EMS also provides a software developer's kit that enables you to write your own monitor and use it along with other monitors. In this way, you can provide custom monitoring for your own homegrown application.

EMS is available only for HP-UX platforms.

EcoSNAP

Compuware's EcoSNAP (formerly called Fault-XPERT) is another tool for detecting application failures. EcoSNAP is used to detect and troubleshoot application failures, both in production and during product development. Similar to MC/ServiceGuard, no application changes are required for EcoSNAP to be able to monitor and detect failures. Faults are reported to a console, and additional details that can aid in diagnosis can be provided along with a fault notification.

EcoSNAP can also be configured to take certain actions when an application fails. In general, applications are started by the EcoSNAP starter program. If an application is already running, monitoring can be started by executing a special EcoSNAP command.

EcoSNAP consists of four modules:

- **Fault Agent:** Detects application faults. It is activated when a Unix signal or CICS abnormal end call (abend) is issued. After key information is captured by the Agent, control is returned to the OS. Information captured includes the application name, fault type and program offset, system information (such as the server name), and CICS for AIX and HP-UX transaction information.
- **Fault Messenger:** Sends notification when a fault occurs. The failure event is sent to a configured console and system log file. It can also be sent via page or e-mail.
- **Fault Manager:** Provides a visual display of the faults that have occurred. The program name, fault code, program offset, server name, user ID, and date and time of the fault are all displayed. The display lists all faults that have occurred, and history information can be used to identify trends.
- **Fault Analyzer:** Can be used after viewing a fault in the Fault Manager display to drill down for additional diagnostic details. Additional information available includes a program

stack trace from the time of the failure, the OS name and version, the shared libraries used, a list of accessed files, filesystem information, the state of program variables at the time of the failure, and the failing source statement for C and C++ programs. The computer screen from the time of the fault can be displayed. Fault Analyzer can provide a list of possible causes of a problem as well.

By providing fault information, such as stack traces, EcoSNAP can help in diagnosing problems with an application. Multiple applications can be monitored simultaneously.

EcoSNAP works by detecting Unix signals that cause an application to fail. These signals are then trapped, and program diagnostic information is captured before the application actually terminates. This information is later made available through a GUI that enables the user to drill down on an individual fault. The following set of Unix signals and abnormal termination errors can be detected by EcoSNAP:

- Signal or exception error
- Deadlock timeout condition
- Operation failed during RPC
- Unable to synchronize
- Communications operation failure
- Invalid command
- Unable to initialize application server
- Illegal instruction
- Bus error
- Segmentation violation
- Write on pipe error
- Floating-point exception
- Software termination signal
- Quit (generated from terminal)
- Hangup (generated from terminal)

EcoSNAP runs on Sun Solaris, HP-UX, IBM AIX, and other platforms. More information about EcoSNAP can be obtained from Compuware Corporation's Web site at http://www .compuware.com.

Monitoring Tools for ERP Applications

ERP applications are used for supply-chain management within an organization. The top ERP applications are SAP R/3, Baan, PeopleSoft, and Oracle applications. This section describes the monitoring tools that have been customized for ERP applications, emphasizing SAP R/3, because it is the leader in this market.

Some ERP application vendors provide a monitoring capability, such as SAP's Computing Center Management System (CCMS) management tool and the EarlyWatch program, which periodically check SAP performance. However, other vendors provide more complete monitoring capabilities. This section focuses on Envive Corporation's monitoring capabilities for SAP, and three monitoring vendors, BMC Corporation, Hewlett-Packard, and Compuware Corporation, who provide customized monitoring products for multiple applications. Emphasis is placed on HP-UX solutions, because HP 9000s are the leading Unix platform for ERP applications from PeopleSoft, Baan, SAP, and many other key applications.

As with other ERP applications, the availability of SAP R/3 depends not only on the application, but also on the underlying database, network, and OS. SAP R/3 is a multi-tiered application with an application server, print servers, and a database server. Properly monitoring SAP R/3 requires the monitoring of all of these components. Products such as SMART Plug-Ins and BMC PATROL are advantageous because of the breadth of monitors that they have available.

Envive

Envive provides several tools for monitoring SAP R/3:

- **Inspector for R/3:** Manages SAP R/3 performance and availability, provides root-cause analysis and predictive analysis, and recommends recovery actions. The product analyzes 40 to 50 different categories of performance problems and collects and stores its information in a database on a dedicated NT server.
- **Service-Level Manager for R/3:** Reports global SAP R/3 usage, performance, and availability information. Reports can be generated comparing actual service levels to service-level agreements that have been defined. Predefined reports are available that can be scheduled to be generated at regular intervals. Response time, transaction rate, and total bytes transferred are examples of the types of statistics that can be included on these reports.
- **StopWatch:** Provides end-user response time information for SAP R/3. For every SAP R/3 transaction, StopWatch collects the total round-trip response time, which includes network time, SAP R/3 time, and client idle time. Reports are provided by user, transaction, or network segment. StopWatch is installed on the same LAN segment as the SAP R/3 application server so that it can capture LAN traffic and correlate logical transaction statistics.

Envive claims to be able to detect 1500 different SAP R/3 symptoms, including deadlocks and a hung application. The applications have been certified with HP's MC/ServiceGuard.

SMART Plug-Ins

IT/O's ability to detect availability problems for an application or server was discussed earlier in the chapter. IT/O is meant to provide a consistent interface for managing systems, applications, and networks. The goal of HP's SMART Plug-Ins (SPIs) is to extend the monitoring capabilities of IT/O by providing preconfigured monitors for applications and databases. SMART Plug-Ins solutions are meant to be used with IT/O with minimal or no configuration. Corrective actions are also predefined for many SPI events. Tools such as BMC PATROL have similar capabilities, but are not as tightly integrated with IT/O.

IT/O can make it easy to deploy monitors on multiple systems. Monitoring templates are distributed from a central IT/O management station. The monitors can also be integrated with MeasureWare and PerfView, so that you can correlate performance data with system and database performance data.

SMART Plug-Ins are available for both SAP R/3 and Baan ERP applications. The SAP SPI can monitor the following conditions:

- Errors in log and trace files
- Status of the processes in R/3 instance
- Dialog task frequency, response time, and wait time
- Update task frequency, response time, and wait time
- Batch task frequency, response time, and wait time
- Spool task frequency, response time, and wait time

The SAP SPI can also send batch job alerts for jobs that were aborted, ran longer than expected, or failed to start. It can also send the following CCMS alerts:

- ABAP/4 (the programming language for SAP R/3) database events
- R/3 instance buffer problems
- Tracing information
- Enqueue server messages
- R/3 general messages
- Rolling and paging activities
- Internal R/3 database events
- Configuration status information
- Detailed information for system log file messages

The SAP R/3 SPI is tightly integrated with the SAP CCMS administrative tool. CCMS can be launched in response to a reported problem. Other management tools can also be launched from the IT/O console. The SAP server is supported on both HP-UX and Windows NT systems. The product can be used with the HP OpenView Manager for SAP R/3, which can generate reports on application servers and database uptime.

SPIs for Baan IV can monitor the status of Baan applications. Along with monitoring the status of each Baan instance, SPIs for Baan IV can monitor log files, license usage, and shared memory usage. Corrective actions can be taken in response to alerts, such as restarting a Baan instance or printer daemon. Reports can be generated on the Baan service's availability or license usage. The Baan managed node must be an HP-UX server. Baan has specially certified this SPI as a product that is well-integrated with the Baan application.

In addition to the ERP applications, plug-ins are available for Oracle, Informix, and NT Internet server. Hewlett-Packard plans to increase the number of SPIs available.

BMC PATROL Knowledge Modules

BMC Software provides monitoring capabilities through its PATROL software suite. PATROL is a system, application, and event management suite for system and database administrators. PATROL provides the basic framework for defining thresholds, sending and translating events, and so forth. Optional products called Knowledge Modules (KMs) contain the capability to monitor specific components. For example, BMC PATROL includes KMs for Unix, SAP R/3, Oracle, Informix, PeopleSoft, and other applications. In fact, more than 40 KMs are available from BMC for use with PATROL.

PATROL consists of a console, intelligent agents, and KMs. The console provides a centralized graphical display in which icons represent system components or other monitored components. Icons change color to correspond to status. The PATROL console also provides an event browser, where you can filter, correlate, sort, and escalate events. Alarms can be configured so that events are sent to the console, indicated graphically, and shown in the event browser.

Intelligent agents provide the ability to discover the system, database, and application components in the enterprise. The agents reside on each server. On an ongoing basis, the agents look for problems, and when they locate one, they either take preconfigured actions or send notification so that recovery can be done manually.

The KMs contain the expertise used by PATROL to know what to monitor and how to react when problems occur. KMs are used to monitor a set of "parameters," which can include a description of the monitored attribute, the polling interval, the method for measuring the attribute, and a threshold for abnormal values. The KMs provide rules to detect events and perform corrective actions. Events are sent to an operator console when an error or warning condition occurs.

BMC provides tools in its Unix KM that can help in monitoring applications. For example, the ACTIVEPROCESS tool monitors active processes. The PROCESS tool displays statistics on active and zombie processes. The USER tool monitors user sessions and user processes. Each of these tools appears with a special icon in the PATROL GUI. In addition to its generic application-monitoring capability, BMC provides specialized KMs for the key ERP applications. Application KMs include SAP R/3, Baan, and PeopleSoft.

PATROL's SAP KM replaces the monitoring aspect of SAP's CCMS management tool. The KM displays CCMS ABAP alerts, buffer alerts, dispatcher queue alerts, enqueue alerts, operating system alerts, and other CCMS alert messages.

Monitoring the R/3 system and application servers is important for SAP. The gateway service is also important. The System, Database, and SAP R/3 Application KMs should be used together to monitor the SAP application, because each KM monitors important metrics. After configuration, BMC discovers the R/3 instances and allows the operator to view an SAP instance and its associated databases and systems. BMC has worked closely with SAP AG to get access to additional SAP R/3 information through a set of ABAP functions. BMC PATROL also provides administrative actions for SAP R/3.

With the SAP R/3 KM installed, the PATROL console displays custom icons for each R/3 system, R/3 instances, CCMS alerts information, printing saplpd processes, R/3 users, tablespaces, and performance information. Database and system icons are also provided.

SAP failures are often due to running out of free space. The System KM can check the filesystem space and available memory. The System KM also supplies important performance metrics, such as network I/O and disk I/O rates.

The key SAP R/3 attributes being monitored include the following:

- Status of the R/3 instance
- Historical trend of user activity for an R/3 instance
- Number of active batch processes
- Number of active dialog processes
- Number of active update processes
- Number of active spool processes
- Number of active enqueue processes
- Users currently logged in to the R/3 instance
- Printer status and queue length
- Buffer performance information
- R/3 buffer storage utilization
- Work-process frequency, response times, and average wait times
- System log information
- Dispatcher queue size
- Transaction times
- Enqueue errors

SAP R/3 is built on an RDBMS, so it's also important to monitor the database. The key database metrics provided are:

- Tablespace free space
- Segments allocated to target database tablespace
- Free space deficit
- Archive log free space
- Cache hit ratio
- Dictionary cache hit ratio
- Open cursors
- Transaction rate
- Processes used

- Active transactions
- Block change rate

The available database metrics, such as transaction rates and cache hit ratios, are described in detail in Chapter 8, as is system information, such as filesystem capacity, CPU utilization, and memory paging information. Important system metrics are described in Chapter 4.

PATROL presents various application "views" to help you monitor each R/3 function. For example, a printer view shows all the printers for a target R/3 system. Status is indicated with icons that are different colors. The first view shows all the target R/3 systems that have been discovered. From this view, you can determine the type of database being used and the number of users currently accessing the R/3 system. Other views exist for printers, memory, CPU, swap, database information, R/3 instance and user information, CCMS alerts, and performance. In each view, you can click icons to obtain additional information.

BMC has been certified to run in an MC/ServiceGuard environment, but issues of inconsistency have arisen. For example, PATROL may report an SAP process failure to its BMC Console, while MC/ServiceGuard may have already restarted the process or moved it to another system.

The PATROL KM for SAP R/3 is supported on Sun Solaris, IBM AIX, and HP-UX, among other platforms.

EcoSYSTEMS

Compuware Corporation provides the EcoSYSTEMS suite of management tools, which includes EcoTOOLS for system and network management, EcoSCOPE for monitoring application performance, and EcoSNAP for managing application failures. The products are supported on both NT and Unix platforms, with HP-UX, IBM AIX, SunOS, and Sun Solaris among the supported Unix platforms.

EcoSCOPE can automatically discover which of hundreds of predefined applications are running on the network, and the user can add application definitions to the EcoSCOPE database. EcoSCOPE can then monitor the number of users accessing an application, the application's response time, byte counts for each application, and the traffic load per application.

A key feature of EcoSCOPE is its ability to monitor application response times. No application changes are needed to get the response time information. EcoSCOPE provides application- or session-level response times, including Oracle transaction information. The response times for individual verbs in an Oracle or Sybase SQL statement can be monitored, to help diagnose long database response times. Minimum, maximum, standard deviation, and mean response time information can be displayed.

Compuware's EcoSCOPE can analyze application traffic at the protocol level. You can see network traffic by application and by protocol. You can recognize multicast and broadcast packets and determine the application sending them. The traffic loads between two nodes can be displayed per application.

EcoTOOLS is used for network and system management. It monitors resource utilization and system availability, and provides both historic and real-time analyses. Alerts can be sent via console messages, pages, or e-mail. Corrective actions are provided, such as restarting a server, re-establishing network connections, or restarting a key application or database. EcoTOOLS can also provide a history of the events leading up to a failure.

EcoTOOLS centrally collects data from the software agents that reside on each server. Support is provided for more than 600 agents. Alarms can be viewed from the master console. Events and data are stored in centralized or distributed repositories. From the central console, the user can also view hardware and software inventory. A GUI enables users to choose new resources to monitor and set thresholds.

Monitoring information is provided at the application, database, network, and OS levels. The system information being monitored includes CPU utilization, disk utilization, and memory usage (such as available swap space). EcoTOOLS can identify the top memory consumers, run-away processes, or shortages in key system resources, such as process table entries, semaphores, and inode entries. Hung printers or peripheral devices can also be detected. System security is provided by verifying that user passwords are installed, checking for unauthorized attempts to access resources, and checking for modifications to system files and directories.

EcoTOOLS provides specific monitoring analysis for the following:

- SAP R/3
- PeopleSoft
- Oracle applications

SAP R/3 services are monitored for their memory performance, CPU performance, and availability. In an HP-UX Oracle environment, additional monitoring is available. EcoTOOLS can monitor the number of SAP users, the application response time and throughput, the buffer usage and configuration status, server workload, and CCMS alerts.

For PeopleSoft, EcoTOOLS can monitor the health of the database. Orphan processes that are created when PeopleSoft application users shut down their systems can be detected and killed. EcoTOOLS can also monitor the dispatch queues of Tuxedo, which is commonly used with PeopleSoft.

The available Oracle tablespace can be monitored. Also, when near limits, additional space can be added. EcoTOOLS monitors the Oracle alert log and concurrent request logs by looking for user-specified strings and sending alerts when they are found. Key Oracle background processes are monitored as well. Performance information, such as the number of pending jobs and long-running jobs, can be monitored for the Oracle Concurrent Manager.

Reports can be generated on resource utilization, traffic load, and response time. Users can also define their own reports. Reports on resource usage patterns, for example, can be used for capacity planning. Service-level agreements can be implemented by allowing application and database performance requirements to be defined, and then they can be monitored to ensure that the requirements are met. Exception reports can also be generated.

EcoTOOLS has done specific integration work with the Tivoli and CA Unicenter management frameworks. The EcoTOOLS Plus Module for Tivoli TME 10 forwards events to the Tivoli Enterprise Console. Tivoli templates and filters are incorporated, which make it easier to run the EcoTOOLS GUI and distribute agent software from the Tivoli Enterprise Console. Similar integration has been done for CA Unicenter.

Resource and Performance Monitoring Tools

This section describes tools for monitoring your application's overall performance and system resource utilization. It does not cover other areas, such as system call optimization for the application or code profiling.

Collecting application performance metrics is difficult, because defining the components making up the application is difficult. Some processes may be utility programs used by multiple applications. Even when the processes are known and are unique to an application, a performance tool may have difficulty mapping the use of shared resources, such as network buffers, to specific processes.

Different products have different ways of defining applications. For example, Measure-Ware and PRM (Process Resource Manager) each have a different way of configuring applications. These methods are described briefly later in the chapter. PLATINUM's ServerVision also can monitor a group of processes as one application based on a user configuration. You must realize that you may need to reconcile the differences between the products' unique definitions to analyze application performance data properly.

Application Resource Measurement

Because measuring the performance of an application is difficult, Hewlett-Packard and Tivoli Systems jointly developed an open set of APIs for measuring application response time. This standard set of APIs is called Application Resource Measurement (ARM). If applications are modified to use the new APIs at key points, end-users can then measure and control end-to-end performance of those applications. API calls are made in the application to mark the beginning and end of a transaction. A Software Developer's Kit (SDK) is freely available for ARM from either Tivoli or Hewlett-Packard to make this process easier. Only a few ARM APIs exist and they are listed in Table 7-1.

Table 7-1 ARM APIs

Name	Function
arm_init	Initialize the ARM environment for the application
arm_getid	Name each transaction class used in the application
arm_start	Mark the start of execution of a transaction instance
arm_update	Update information about a transaction instance
arm_stop	Mark the end of a transaction
arm_end	Clean up the application's memory used by ARM

Baan has announced that the next release of its ERP application will be instrumented using the ARM API, which will make collecting application performance data for Baan more straightforward.

MeasureWare

The MeasureWare Agent is a Hewlett-Packard product that collects and logs resource and performance metrics. MeasureWare agents run and collect data on the individual server systems being monitored. Agents exist for many platforms and OSs, including HP-UX, Solaris, and AIX.

The MeasureWare Agent collects data, summarize it, timestamp it, log it, and send alarms when appropriate. The agents collect and report on a wide variety of system resources, performance metrics, and user-defined data. The information can then be exported to spreadsheets or to performance analysis programs, such as PerfView. The data can be used by these programs to generate alarms warning of potential performance problems. By using historical data, trends can be discovered, which can help to address resource issues before they affect system performance.

The MeasureWare agents collect data at three different levels: global system metrics, application, and process metrics. Global and application data is summarized at five-minute intervals, whereas process data is summarized at one-minute intervals. Process information is recorded only at interesting time periods, such as when the process starts, terminates, or exceeds a defined threshold for CPU or disk utilization.

The basic categories of MeasureWare data are listed in Table 7-2. Optional modules for database and networking support also are available. The Data Source Integration (DSI) capability is used to integrate your own data with other data collected by the MeasureWare Agent.

Transaction data is available for applications that are using the ARM API, described earlier. Separate log files are created for each of these categories, as well as a file for individual device data. However, only system and process data is logged by default. Many of the system metrics collected by MeasureWare are described in Chapter 4. This section describes the additional metrics that are available for applications and processes.

Table 7-2   Categories of MeasureWare Agent Information

Category	Metric Type
System	CPU, disk, networking, memory, process queue depth, user/process information, and summary information
Application	CPU, disk, memory, process count, average process wait state, and summary information
Process	CPU, disk, memory, average process wait state, overall process lifetime, and summary information
Transaction	Transaction count, average response time, distribution of response time metrics, and aborted transactions

Although MeasureWare provides extensive performance and resource information, it provides limited configuration information and no data about system faults. It may be beneficial to use MeasureWare with a fault monitoring tool, such as EMS.

For MeasureWare to aggregate process-level data into an application, the application has to be defined first. The administrator associates an application name with a group of processes. To define a new application, edit the file /var/opt/perf/parm. In this example, metrics are logged for an application called ORACLE, which will be an aggregation of process metrics collected for all processes whose names begin with ora:

```
application = ORACLE
file=ora*
```

Note that wildcards can be used, which can be handy if all the individual processes are not known in advance, or many processes exist. Additional configuration options enable you to associate processes with an application, based on the process priority or the user or group name. Note that a process can belong to only one application, and MeasureWare finds the first match for the process, so be sure to list your most important applications first in the configuration file.

If you want to receive messages when the MeasureWare data being logged hits certain thresholds, you can specify these alarm conditions in the /var/opt/perf/alarmdef configuration file. Additional alarm definition files can also be used. Alarm conditions are checked at the time the data is logged. The alarms can be sent to PerfView, IT/O, or any SNMP-capable management station. The target configuration information is specified in the alarm generator database (agdb).

Actions can be performed on the local system in response to an alarm. The local action is one way to provide your own notification method in response to an alarm. For example, you can execute a Unix command to send the administrator a message. Note that if alarms are being sent to an IT/O agent, MeasureWare, by default, won't take any local actions, under the assumption that IT/O will be configured to take the local actions instead of MeasureWare.

You can have alarms sent based on conditions that involve a combination of metrics. For example, a CPU bottleneck alarm can be based on the CPU use and CPU run queue length. Durations can be specified along with an alarm condition. The condition must be true for the specified time before an alarm is sent. An alarm severity can also be specified.

If you want MeasureWare alarms to be sent to PerfView, you need to configure this through the PerfView interface. The MeasureWare tool agsysdb is used to add a new trap destination system for SNMP alerts.

The example in Listing 7-5 shows an alarm definition to send alerts when the finance_app application exceeds a limit on its CPU utilization. First, a warning alert is sent. If the problem persists, a critical alert is sent. Depending on how the alarm generator has been configured, the alarm goes to the PerfView Alarms window, the IT/O Message Browser, or an SNMP-based management station. Note that the application must also be defined in the parm file.

MeasureWare includes a program called utility that can do a variety of tasks. The analyze command in the utility program is used to analyze the data in a log file against alarm definitions

Listing 7-5   MeasureWare alarm definition for an application's CPU utilization.

```
ALARM finance_app:app_cpu_total_util > 30 FOR 5 MINUTES
START
{
    WARNING ALERT "Your app is busy."
    EXEC "echo 'finance app is very busy'|mailx root"
}
REPEAT EVERY 15 MINUTES
    CRITICAL ALERT "finance app continues to be busy."
END
    RESET ALERT "finance app no longer busy."
```

in an alarm definitions configuration file. You can then decide whether the alarm definitions will generate too many or too few alarms. You can see what messages would have been printed and what programs would have been executed. An alarm summary report shows a count of the number of alarms and the amount of time each alarm would have been active.

MeasureWare's extract command in the utility program can be used to export data to other tools, such as spreadsheet programs. The extract command makes raw log files usable by Perf-View as well.

The following application-level metrics are available on HP-UX and Sun Solaris:

- CPU use during interval
- Number and rate of physical disk transfers during interval
- Average number of processes in application
- Average number of active processes in application
- Number of application processes that completed during interval
- Runtime of completing application processes
- Average process priority in application
- Standard deviation of process priorities
- CPU use for user processes during interval
- CPU use for system processing
- Main memory use
- Swap space use on disk

These additional application-level metrics are available on HP-UX:

- Number and rate of I/O transfers to all devices
- Number of terminal transactions during interval
- Average terminal first-response time
- Average terminal response-to-prompt time
- Number of user-defined transactions during interval

- Average user transaction response time
- Time processes waited for CPU
- Time processes waited for disk I/O
- Time processes waited for memory
- Time processes waited for software impedes
- Time processes waited for terminal input
- Time processes waited for LAN I/O
- Time processes waited for other I/O
- Time processes directed to wait
- CPU use at nice priorities
- CPU use at real-time priorities
- Number and rate of logical disk reads during interval
- Number and rate of logical disk writes during interval
- Number and rate of physical disk reads during interval
- Number and rate of physical disk writes during interval
- Number and rate of memory manager reads/writes during interval
- Number and rate of system reads/writes during interval
- Number and rate of raw reads/writes during interval
- Number and rate of filesystem reads/writes during interval
- Sum of process' private and shared memory, in kilobytes

MeasureWare Agents also collect data for individual processes. These process-level metrics are available on HP-UX and Sun Solaris:

- PID
- Application number
- Program name
- Login user name
- Login device name or number
- Parent and group identification numbers
- Execution priority/scheduling queue
- Last reason for stopping execution
- CPU use during interval
- Number and rate of physical disk transfers during interval
- Total time process ran
- CPU use for system processing
- CPU use for user processing
- Number and rate of logical disk reads during interval
- Number and rate of logical disk writes during interval
- Memory-resident set size

- Size of test+data+stack memory
- Number of page faults to memory
- Number of page faults to disk
- Number and rate of logical disk transfers during process lifetime
- Total number of terminal transactions
- Average terminal first-response time overall
- Average terminal response-to-prompt time overall
- Total number of user transactions
- Average user response-to-prompt time overall

These additional process-level metrics are available on HP-UX:

- Total I/O transfer rate and count of all devices during interval
- CPU use at nice priority
- CPU use at real-time priority
- CPU use for context switching
- CPU use for interrupt handling
- Number and rate of filesystem reads during interval
- Number and rate of filesystem writes during interval
- Number and rate of memory management transfers during interval
- Number and rate of system transfers during interval
- Number of terminal transactions during interval
- Average terminal first-response time
- Average terminal response-to-prompt time
- Number of user-defined transactions during interval
- Average user transaction think time
- Average user transaction response time
- Time process directed to wait
- Time process waited for disk
- Time process waited for terminal input
- Time process waited for software impedes
- Time process waited for virtual memory
- Time process waited for LAN transfers
- Time process waited for diskless workstations
- Time process waited for network filesystem
- Time process waited for interprocess communications
- Time process waited for system
- Time process waited for other I/Os
- Time process waited for other reasons

The data collected through ARM can be integrated with other MeasureWare data. The MeasureWare Transaction Tracker technology is used to provide metrics for an application using ARM. The following metrics are available on both HP-UX and Sun Solaris:

- Transaction name
- Transaction count
- Transaction average response time
- Distribution of response-time metrics
- Number of aborted transactions
- Response times of aborted transactions

The utility program includes the ability to generate reports on log files. System-wide changes can be found in this way, such as the addition of a new disk device. Reports can also be generated that provide summaries of each application's CPU and disk utilization.

To verify that MeasureWare is working correctly, you can use the perfstat –t command, which shows you recent status and error information.

GlancePlus

GlancePlus is a real-time, graphical, performance monitoring tool from Hewlett-Packard. It is used to monitor the performance and system resource utilization of a single system. Both Motif-based and character-based interfaces are available. The product can be used on HP-UX, Sun Solaris, and many other operating systems.

GlancePlus collects information similar to MeasureWare, but samples data more frequently. GlancePlus can be used to graphically view current CPU, memory, swap, and disk activity and utilization at the system level. It can also show application and process information. Transaction information can be shown if the MeasureWare Agent is installed and active.

For monitoring applications, the application must be defined. To define an important application, use the configuration file located at /var/opt/perf/parm, which is also used by the Measure-Ware and PerfView products.

GlancePlus is also capable of setting and receiving performance-related alarms. Customizable rules determine when a system performance problem should be sent as an alarm. The rules are managed by the GlancePlus Adviser. When you select the Edit Adviser Syntax option from the Adviser menu, all the alarm conditions are shown, which you can then modify. The Glance-Plus Adviser syntax file (/var/opt/perf/adviser.syntax) contains the symptom and alarm configuration. Additional syntax files can also be used. A condition for an alarm to be sent can be based on rules involving different symptoms.

Alarms result in onscreen notification, with color representing the criticality of the alarm. An alarm can also trigger a command or script to be executed automatically. Instead of sending an alarm, GlancePlus can print messages or notify you by executing a Unix command, such as mailx, by using its EXEC feature.

Listing 7-6 shows an alarm for the ora_app application. If you know how many processes should be active, GlancePlus can be used to monitor their health. The APP_ALIVE_PROC metric measures the number of processes in this group that were alive during the time interval. The metric could include fractions for processes that terminated during the interval. An alarm could then be sent if APP_ALIVE_PROC is below the expected value for that application, as shown in Listing 7-6.

You can also execute the scripts in command mode by typing:

```
glance -adviser_only -syntax <script file name>
```

In this example, a yellow alert will be sent to the GlancePlus alarm screen if the number of processes for ora_app drops below five. The symptoms are re-evaluated every time interval.

GlancePlus allows filters to be used to reduce the amount of information shown. For example, you can set up a filter in the process view to show only the more active system processes. GlancePlus can also show short-term historical information. When selected, the alarm buttons, visible on the main GlancePlus screen, show a history of alarms that have occurred.

If Process Resource Manager (PRM) is being used, GlancePlus shows how well PRM application groups are staying within their resource entitlements. From GlancePlus, you can also change PRM process group entitlements.

Here are some specific application metrics available from GlancePlus:

- CPU utilization (user and system) per application
- I/O utilization per application
- Virtual memory utilization per application
- CPU utilization per process
- Disk utilization per process
- Memory utilization per process
- Number of open files per process

If the MeasureWare Agent is also being used, transaction-level information is available. Transactions must be defined by the application using the ARM API. The following are some of the available metrics:

- Transaction average response time
- Distribution of transaction response times

Listing 7-6 Defining alarms in GlancePlus.

```
alarm ora_app:app_alive_proc < 5
start
  yellow alert "Oracle app died"
end
  reset alert "end of Oracle alert"
```

- Number of aborted transactions
- Response time of aborted transactions

Figure 7-3 shows how transaction information can be shown together with a service-level objective. The administrator wants to achieve transaction response times under five seconds. The graph shows the number and distribution of transactions that are meeting or exceeding the objective.

More than 600 metrics are accessible from GlancePlus. Some of these metrics are discussed in other chapters. The complete list of metrics can be found by using the online help facility. This information can also be found in the directory /opt/perf/paperdocs/gp/C. For further information, visit the HP Application and System Management Web site at http://www.openview.hp.com/solutions/application/.

PerfView

PerfView is a graphical performance analysis tool from Hewlett-Packard. It is used to graphically display performance and system resource utilization for one system or for multiple systems simultaneously, so that comparisons can be made. A variety of performance graphs can be displayed. The graphs are based on data collected over a period of time, unlike the real-time graphs of GlancePlus. This tool runs on HP-UX or NT systems and works with data collected by MeasureWare agents.

Figure 7-3   GlancePlus shows transaction data.

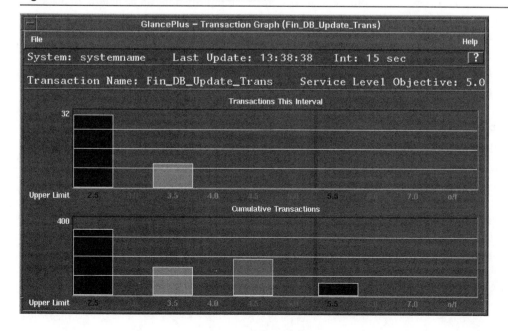

PerfView has three main components:

- **PerfView Monitor:** Provides the ability to receive alarms. A textual description of an alarm can be displayed. Alarms can be filtered by severity, type, or source system. Also, after an alarm is received, the alarm can be selected, which displays a graph of related metrics. An operator can monitor trends leading to failures, and can then take proactive actions to avoid problems. Graphs can be used for comparison between systems and to show a history of resource consumption. An internal database is maintained that keeps a history of alarm notification messages.
- **PerfView Analyzer:** Provides resource and performance analysis for disks and other resources. System metrics can be shown at three different levels: process, application (configured by the user as a set of processes), and global system information. It relies on data received from MeasureWare agents on the managed nodes. Data can be analyzed from up to eight systems concurrently. All MeasureWare data sources are supported. PerfView Analyzer is required by both PerfView Monitor and PerfView Planner.
- **PerfView Planner:** Provides forecasting capability. Graphs can be extrapolated into the future. A variety of graphs (such as linear, exponential, s-curve, and smoothed) can be shown for forecasted data.

In addition to graphing and analyzing system resources, process and application resources can be graphed and analyzed using PerfView. PerfView can use the application definitions created by MeasureWare. PerfView can then be used to show a history of a specified application's utilization. PerfView's ability to show history and trend information can be helpful in diagnosing system problems. Graphing performance information can help you to understand whether a persistent problem exists or an anomaly is simply a momentary spike of activity.

To diagnose a problem further, PerfView Monitor can allow the user to change time intervals, to try to find the specific time a problem occurred. The graph is redrawn showing the new time period.

Process Resource Manager

The Process Resource Manager is a resource management tool from Hewlett-Packard that is used to balance system resources among PRM groups. PRM groups are configured by the administrator and consist of a set of HP-UX users or applications. PRM is then used to give each PRM group a certain percentage of the CPU, real memory, or disk I/O bandwidth available on the system. PRM ensures that each PRM group gets a minimum percentage of the system's resources, even during heavy loads. PRM can also ensure that a group does not get more than a configured percentage of the CPU.

PRM can be used in conjunction with HP GlancePlus to adjust the system configuration. For example, if an administrator detects unwanted system load for a PRM group, GlancePlus can be used to lower that group's entitlement dynamically.

The PRM configuration file is /etc/prmconf. In this file, you specify the PRM groups and their desired resource entitlements. Both HP-UX users and applications can belong to PRM groups. An application is referenced by its executable path name. In cases in which alternate process names are specified when a process is started, these alternate process names can also be configured. Wildcards can be used if the exact alternate process name is not known in advance. In this way, PRM provides more granular control over Oracle applications, because the Oracle database server has one executable, but spawns processes for each database instance, with the instance name embedded in the process name.

Normally, if one PRM group does not need its system resources, PRM allocates those resources to other groups that may need them. However, PRM can also help with capacity planning by allowing resource maximums to be specified. Thus, if an administrator knows that 25 percent more users will soon be on the system, the administrator can allocate a maximum of 80 percent of system resources to simulate the upcoming load.

PRM can also be used to dynamically adjust the workload in a high availability environment. For example, if three MC/ServiceGuard packages are each running with similar PRM entitlements, and one package fails to another system, this can be automatically detected and a new PRM configuration can be applied that gives the two remaining packages higher entitlements.

To check the actual resource usage of each PRM group, use the prmmonitor command. GlancePlus can also show this information graphically.

Controlling Application Performance

If a system performance problem exists, a performance monitoring tool, such as GlancePlus, can be used to find the main application or processes using the system resources. The problem may be due to a hung application that is holding key semaphores, a poorly structured application making unnecessary system calls or leaking memory, etc. A temporary solution may involve stopping and restarting the application. Longer-term solutions may involve restructuring the application, recompiling, or optimizing the program.

If a performance problem is due to multiple applications competing for system resources, you may want to use a product such as PRM to control resource allocation. PRM can ensure that critical applications get the appropriate resource entitlements. You may need to study the resource usage of competing applications on the system before you create the optimal PRM configuration.

Recovering from Application Problems

Some application problems can be caused by accidental or inappropriate changes to application configuration files. EMS provides the capability to monitor these configuration files, and can report events whenever a change occurs. The text of the file can be included along with the event, which then can be used to provide a history of configuration changes so that an incorrect change can quickly be undone.

When a server has failed and can't be immediately repaired, high availability cluster software, such as MC/ServiceGuard, can be used to reduce the downtime associated with the failure and keep services available. MC/ServiceGuard can detect the failure of an application and automatically restart the application on another system in under one minute. Some preconfigured solutions already exist for some important applications, such as BEA Tuxedo, CICS, and NFS.

BMC's Application Service Assurance product can be used to provide application recovery. All the components of an application can be recovered to a specific point in time. This product supports many applications, including SAP R/3, PeopleSoft, Baan, and Oracle.

However, even with the kernel's ability to mask certain failure and the high availability software's ability to move applications to redundant servers, ultimately, you still need to repair failed components. For hardware problems, Support Tool Manager (STM) can provide fast diagnosis on HP-UX systems. SyMON can be used for Solaris environments. To fix OS problems, system vendors typically provide support information on their respective Web sites.

Comparison of Application Monitoring Products

To monitor applications properly, being able to display them graphically is best. BMC PATROL can show process information in the PATROL Console. With the use of its specialized KMs, PATROL can also show icons for application instances, but displaying an arbitrary application can be difficult. IT/O provides only a system view in its windows, although ClusterView adds an application view when used with NNM or IT/O in an MC/ServiceGuard environment.

ClusterView can automatically detect an application failure and change the color of the application's icon. However, its diagnostic information is limited. EcoSNAP can detect application failures and send notifications through a variety of mechanisms. EMS supports more notification methods, but can't access all the diagnostic information available from EcoSNAP. MC/ServiceGuard, in addition to detecting failures, can restart applications.

The use of MC/ServiceGuard with EMS enables you to make explicit links between an application and its dependent resources. Those dependent resources are then monitored, and a failure directly results in an MC/ServiceGuard package failure. Although a resource configuration step is required, the effort saves time in troubleshooting the failures later, because the root cause is already provided.

Application performance data is available from a variety of products, including Measure-Ware, BMC PATROL, and SMART Plug-Ins. BMC PATROL provides the most metrics for specialized applications, such as SAP R/3, but SMART Plug-Ins have the best integration with IT/O and PerfView, enabling event correlation and detailed performance graphs.

## CHAPTER 8

Monitoring the Database

Databases are often key applications in a company's environment. Companies are more stringent in their demands on databases, requiring high availability Online Transaction Processing (OLTP) and quick response to decision support queries. Databases and database servers are built on sophisticated architectures with an array of configuration options, making them a tough management challenge.

Tools are needed to reduce the time spent detecting and isolating database problems. A database is dependent on the underlying system, disks, and networks. Each of these components is discussed in other chapters of this book. This chapter provides information on monitoring tools that are specific to databases.

Identifying Important Database Monitoring Categories

Depending on a company's organization, various people may be controlling different aspects of the databases. Database administrators, database and system operators, application managers, system administrators, and network managers each may have roles in either monitoring or configuring the company databases. In smaller companies, multiple roles are filled by a single person. Database operators keep the database up and available, solve performance problems, and back up the data. Database administrators manage security issues, handle load balancing and capacity planning issues, and deploy new database applications. Each may also have different needs for database monitoring tools.

These different monitoring activities can be grouped into the following categories:

- Configuration management
- Fault management
- Performance and resource management
- Security
- Backup

These groups are described in more detail next. The appropriate level of monitoring in each of these areas depends on your specific database responsibilities.

Configuring the Database

Before you can effectively monitor a database, you should verify the proper database configuration. Both system and database configuration files should be checked for correctness. An invalid database configuration can prevent database access. Each database relies on several configuration files. For example, Oracle depends on the following configuration files:

- tnsnames.ora
- init.ora
- listener.ora
- sqlnet.ora

These files can be corrupted if configured manually or not distributed consistently to all systems in the computing environment using the database. The database administrator should ensure that the initial configuration and subsequent configurations are correct. Appropriate event notification should be put in place so that the operator can be aware of any configuration changes. The events can serve as an audit history when later trying to track down the cause of a problem.

Network General's Database Module for Oracle7 is one example of a tool that can monitor configuration information. This module is used as an add-on to a network analyzer to study database traffic. SQL packets are decoded, enabling the analyzer to scan configuration information contained in connection packets to see whether or not a configuration problem exists. Other approaches are to check periodically the modification dates of the system and database configuration files to see whether it has made changes. An older copy of the configuration should be kept for comparison purposes.

Note that the correct database configuration depends on how the database will be used. Online transaction processing applications have different workload characterizations than decision support applications, for example.

Watching for Database Faults

The database operator must continually watch for failures in the database environment. This includes system and networking components, in addition to the database. System failures can prevent access to the database, and the loss of system components could severely degrade performance. Monitoring the database server system is not sufficient, because the network connecting the clients to the server can also fail. Techniques for monitoring the system, disks, and networks are discussed in other chapters.

Various database software or hardware components can fail that, in turn, cause the database to fail. The operator may simply want to log on to the database application periodically to ensure that it is still running. For example, critical Oracle components to check include the Oracle Names servers, Oracle servers, SQL*NET Listeners, and the Oracle MultiProtocol Interchange (MPI), which is used to translate between different network transport stacks, such as TCP/IP and IPX/SPX.

Managing Database Resources and Performance

Monitoring database resources and performance can ensure that the database is being used effectively. The most common database problems are related to resource management. Some common errors are:

- Out of disk space
- Log file full
- Performance overload

System and database resources should be studied periodically to detect trends. The operator should check the free space for tables, tablespaces, and indexes. Continual modifications and updates to a database can lead to database fragmentation, which means that the available storage for the database is scattered. Each available storage area is too small to be used and thus is wasted. Eventually, increased database fragmentation can lead to performance problems or even database failure. Some database monitoring tools help detect database fragmentation so that corrective action can be taken, such as restructuring the database objects.

Performance problems can be difficult to diagnose. Many database performance problems are caused by a poorly designed database, or programs that are not coded efficiently. For these cases, a simple solution is unlikely. Therefore, the database operator needs monitoring tools that can predict performance problems and provide corrective actions when appropriate.

Keeping the Database Server Secure

You should also be able to detect security intrusions or access violations related to the database server. Monitoring tools can track unsuccessful logins, privileged statement executions, and other events that are important for maintaining database security.

You may also want to use the network monitoring tools discussed in Chapter 6 to help keep your systems secure. Network firewalls can stop intruders before they are able to access a computer system.

Ensuring Successful Database Backups

You also need to back up the systems and ensure that the backups run successfully. Depending on how the database is being used, different types of backup tools may be needed. A system operator responsible for the backup and restore procedures for hundreds of systems may not have the expertise to handle the procedures associated with a database vendor's backup tool. Automated tools for managing and monitoring database backup can be helpful in lowering the skill level needed for the job.

As mentioned earlier, the database administrator is responsible for trending analysis and capacity planning. Ideally, the administrator is focused on these strategic and planning activities, but often they spend time helping operators troubleshoot database problems. Automated tools for database operations help free the administrator to focus on these longer-range planning tasks. The administrator is likely to use some of the same tools as the operator for performance and resource management. For example, PerfView can be used to forecast future performance bottlenecks, and can also help to analyze existing resource problems.

The remainder of this chapter describes a variety of tools and products that can be used to provide monitoring capabilities for databases. The emphasis is on the fault and performance and resource management categories; not many tools are available in the other important areas. Generic system and application tools, as well as database-specific tools, are covered in this chapter.

Oracle is, by far, the dominant vendor for UNIX database servers and thus gets the most attention in this chapter. Informix is another important UNIX database vendor and is used for comparison purposes.

Using Standard Database Commands and Tools

This section describes the commands and tools that are either included with a database product or are part of the operating system.

UNIX Commands

UNIX commands and tools, such as ps and pstat, can be used to check on some of the important database processes. The database listeners and names servers are examples of some of these critical database processes. Listing 8-1 shows an example of using ps to find the Oracle processes on the system. Note that Oracle appends the database instance name to the end of the process names associated with each instance.

The who command can be used to list the UNIX users logged in to the system. This gives you an idea of who is using the system, but doesn't necessarily help you to determine who is using the database. Other tools, also described in this section, can be used to display information about current database users.

SQL Commands

SQL commands can be used to check database status or the available space. Sometimes, the best way to know whether a database is working is to try to use it. This is a manual process, unless the commands are put into scripts.

If a database problem exists, determining who is currently using the database may be useful. Listing 8-2 shows how you can make an SQL query to obtain this information in an Oracle environment.

Listing 8-3 shows an example of using this SQL query on an Oracle 7.3 system with multiple active database users.

Listing 8-1   Output showing Oracle database processes.

```
# ps -efa |grep oracle
  oracle 21488    1  0   Dec 13   ?       7:36 ora_lgwr_CINDY
  oracle 23446    1  0   Dec 13   ?      62:44 dbsnmp
  oracle 21492    1  0   Dec 13   ?       0:32 ora_smon_CINDY
  oracle 23165    1  0   Dec 13   ?       0:50 ora_smon_ora2
  oracle 23154    1  0   Dec 13   ?       6:56 ora_pmon_ora2
  oracle 21494    1  0   Dec 13   ?       0:04 ora_reco_CINDY
  oracle 23459    1  0   Dec 13   ?       0:43 oracleora2 (LOCAL=NO)
  oracle 21912    1  0 09:50:42   ?       0:00 oracleora2 (LOCAL=NO)
  oracle 21483    1  0   Dec 13   ?      10:34 ora_dbwr_CINDY
  oracle 23438    1  0   Dec 13   ?       0:00 /rdbms/oracle/8.0.3/bin/tnslsnr
  oracle 23156    1  0   Dec 13   ?      14:17 ora_dbwr_ora2
  oracle 21490    1  0   Dec 13   ?       6:42 ora_ckpt_CINDY
  oracle 28717 28614 0   Dec 15   pts/2   0:00 ksh
  oracle 21481    1  0   Dec 13   ?       6:27 ora_pmon_CINDY
  oracle 23161    1  0   Dec 13   ?       7:30 ora_lgwr_ora2
  oracle 23163    1  0   Dec 13   ?       6:04 ora_ckpt_ora2
  oracle 21908 23446 0 09:50:41   ?       0:04 dbsnmp
  oracle 23167    1  0   Dec 13   ?       0:04 ora_reco_ora2
    root 21974 21936 2 10:21:42   pts/4   0:00 grep oracle
#
```

Explaining SQL statements is beyond the scope of this book. For more information, you may want to read *SQL For Dummies, Third Edition*, by Allen G. Taylor (IDG Books Worldwide, 1998).

SNMP MIB Monitoring

If you're using the HP OpenView Network Node Manager, then the OpenView MIB Browser can be used to get additional information about the database and database server. Because your database server is dependent on the underlying system and network, you may want to access the MIB-II and the HP-UNIX MIB, which contain generic system information, such as filesystem

Listing 8-2   Using SQL SELECT to find the current database users.

```
SELECT nvl(S.OSUSER,S.type) OS_Usercode,
    S.USERNAME              Oracle_Usercode,
    S.sid                   Oracle_SID,
    S.process               F_Ground,
    P.spid                  B_Ground
FROM sys.V_$SESSION S,
    sys.V_$PROCESS p
WHERE s.paddr = p.addr
ORDER BY s.sid
```

Listing 8-3   Output showing active Oracle database users.

```
SQL> SELECT nvl(S.OSUSER,S.type) OS_Usercode,
2 S.USERNAME Oracle_Usercode,
3 S.sid Oracle_SID,
4 S.process F_Ground,
5 P.spid B_Ground
6 FROM sys.V_$SESSION S,
7 sys.V_$PROCESS p
8 WHERE s.paddr = p.addr
9 ORDER BY s.sid
10 ;


OS_USERCODE  ORACLE_USERCODE  ORACLE_SID  F_GROUND  B_GROUND
-----------  ---------------  ----------  --------  ----------
oradba                                 1  1322      1322
oradba                                 2  1324      1324
oradba                                 3  1331      1331
oradba                                 4  1334      1334
oradb                                  5  1338      1338
oradba                                 6  1342      1342
george       JUNGLE                    7  277:412   3056
sam          SAMS                     10  181:245   28975
sam          SAM                      12  187:282   1686
lily         LILY                     13  29902     21430
sam          SAM                      16  292:197   28959
sam          SAM                      19  187:282   28989

12 rows selected.
SQL>
```

information and network interface status. HP OpenView IT/O enables you to set up ongoing monitoring of MIB variables. Management frameworks, such as Unicenter TNG, also provide a MIB Browser. Public-domain MIB Browsers are available, too.

Database vendors, such as Oracle, Sybase, and Informix, each support the Relational Database Management System (RDBMS) MIB, which provides information such as the database status. (The entire contents of this MIB is provided in Appendix A.) Because the database vendors have standardized their representation of some key information, an operator can access this information in the same way regardless of which database is being used. This information can then be combined with information learned from MIB-II and the HP-UNIX MIB, to get a broader understanding of the condition of the databases. The Gartner Group estimates that every Fortune 1000 organization has an average of five database sources, so the use of a standard MIB for monitoring can provide some much needed consistency and reduce the amount of database operator training.

Although the RDBMS MIB defines nine tables, only five are truly vendor-independent. These tables are shown in Table 8-1. The rdbmsSrvParamTable is also served by the major database vendors, but the server configuration information contained in this table is database-specific and may contain customized parameters. Informix and Oracle do not support the other three tables defined in the MIB: rdbmsDbParamTable, rdbmsDbLimitedResourceTable, and rdbmsSrvLimitedResourceTable.

Two SNMP traps, rdbmsStateChange and rdbmsOutOfSpace, are defined in the RDBMS MIB, but only rdbmsStateChange is consistently implemented. The trap is sent when the database or database server's state changes to restricted or unavailable. You may need to modify trap configuration files on your management station to receive new traps.

The RDBMS MIB is primarily used for monitoring, not administration. However, much of the information is static configuration information, which is not useful for continual monitoring. The major database vendors also support the Network Services MIB, defined in RFC 2248, as a repository for database process information. The Network Services MIB is casually referred to as the "Application MIB," although the Internet Engineering Task Force (IETF) has now defined a different MIB with that name. Table 8-2 contains a list of useful fields from the RDBMS MIB, as well as the application table (applTable) in the Network Services MIB. Only MIB variables available for both Oracle and Informix are included in this table.

Many of the variables listed in Table 8-2 are used to monitor the status of the database or database server. The applOperStatus field can be used to indicate the operational status of the database server: up, down, congested, or restarting. The applInBoundAssociations variable can be used to determine the number of active connections to the database. rdbmsRelState indicates the status of the database: active, available, restricted, unavailable, or other.

Some of the database monitoring variables can also be used for resource control. The rdbmsDbInfoSizeAllocated and rdbmsDbInfoSizeUsed variables can be used to determine the amount of free disk space available for the database, indicating whether more space should be allocated. applInboundAssociations can be compared to the maximum allowed inbound associations from the server info table.

You can use these variables in conjunction with Hewlett-Packard's Process Resource Manager (PRM) to increase or restrict system resource entitlements when too many users are active. The server info table includes several interesting statistics about the number of transactions handled, and the number of reads and writes made by the server. The ratio of logical to

Table 8-1   Vendor-Independent RDBMS MIB Tables

Table Name	Description
rdbmsDbTable	Information about databases installed on system
rdbmsDbInfoTable	More (dynamic) information about databases on system
rdbmsSrvTable	Table of database servers running or installed on system
rdbmsSrvInfoTable	Table of database server statistics
rdbmsRelTable	Table showing the relation (or mapping) of databases to servers

Table 8-2   Database Monitoring Variables

Variable	MIB Table	Description
applUptime	applTable	Length of time database has been running
applOperStatus	applTable	Status of database server
applInboundAssociations	applTable	Number of currently active local and remote conversations
rdbmsSrvInfoStartupTime	rdbmsSrvInfoTable	Timestamp of last server restart
rdbmsSrvInfoFinished- Transactions	rdbmsSrvInfoTable	Number of transactions committed or aborted
rdbmsSrvInfoDiskReads	rdbmsSrvInfoTable	Number of physical reads by server
rdbmsSrvInfoLogicalReads	rdbmsSrvInfoTable	Number of logical reads by server
rdbmsSrvInfoDiskWrites	rdbmsSrvInfoTable	Number of physical writes by server
rdbmsSrvInfoLogicalWrites	rdbmsSrvInfoTable	Number of logical writes by server
rdbmsSrvInfoHighwater- InboundAssociations	rdbmsSrvInfoTable	Greatest number of simultaneous inbound associations handled by server
rdbmsSrvInfoMaxInbound- Associations	rdbmsSrvInfoTable	Maximum number of simultaneous inbound associations allowed
rdbmsDbInfoSizeAllocated	rdbmsDbInfoTable	Disk space allocated for this database
rdbmsDbInfoSizeUsed	rdbmsDbInfoTable	Disk space actually used by this database
rdbmsRelState	rdbmsRelTable	Status of database

physical reads can be used to determine the appropriate cache size, for example. However, the information in the server info table is aggregated for the database server, so database-specific statistics are not available here (unless the database server is handling only one database). The database relation table is used to match a database to its server.

If you want to monitor Informix, the rdbmsSrvLimitedResource table is useful, because it contains current resource limits and thresholds reached. This table is not supported for Oracle. Other interesting variables in the RDBMS MIB not generally available for Oracle, but available for Informix, include:

- rdbmsDbInfoLastBackup: Indicates the timestamp of the last database backup.
- rdbmsSrvInfoDiskOutOfSpaces: Indicates the number of times the database server has been unable to obtain the disk space that it wanted.
- rdbmsRelActiveTime: Indicates the time this database was made active by the database server.

Because MIB definitions rarely change, after you configure some MIB variables to be monitored, the configuration is likely to work with multiple database versions. This can help to reduce the burden of recertification for a new database software release.

These MIBs provide information that can help with configuration management, resource management, and fault management. For performance management, I/O rates can be calculated by monitoring performance metrics in the RDBMS MIB. Collecting I/O rates over time can provide you with a simple way to track I/O performance.

Although access to MIB data is readily available, MIB browsing is a manual process, usually requiring you to poll for the information you need. The manual query captures only a snapshot. Like many metrics, you really need to collect the information over a period of time, so that you can make comparisons.

Database Vendor Tools

This section describes some monitoring capabilities provided by the database vendors. Later sections discuss the sophisticated database monitoring tools provided by third parties.

Oracle Enterprise Manager

Oracle has developed a database management platform called the Oracle Enterprise Manager (OEM) for database administration. OEM includes utilities for monitoring network and database objects, scheduling jobs on multiple systems, and distributing software. Oracle Diagnostics Pack, Oracle Tuning Pack, and Oracle Change Management Pack are optional software packages that provide additional capabilities, such as database tuning and capacity planning. OEM has many different components, including the following:

- **Console:** Includes functions for mapping and event management. Navigator windows show hierarchies of objects, such as listeners, names servers, and databases, which you can select and show on maps. You can use filtering to reduce the number of objects shown. You can create Map windows to show only the important objects that you need to monitor, by dragging objects from the Navigator hierarchy into the Map window. After you create and customize maps, you can save and recall them at any time via menu options. The console can also be used to monitor active jobs and job history. An Event window shows events occurring on databases, listeners, and nodes. You can acknowledge events or see a history of events, which includes the name administrator that acknowledged the event.

- **Repository:** A set of database tables that is used to store information about the tasks associated with a given administrator and any customized views that have been defined. The repository database can be on any node accessible to the OEM console. To use OEM, you connect or log in to the console, which then finds the repository associated with your user name.

- **Intelligent agents:** Processes running on remote nodes in the network. To monitor events on a remote server or to schedule and run remote jobs, an intelligent agent must be running on that server. The intelligent agents can detect when a configured event has occurred. When an agent detects an event, it can automatically launch recovery actions and send notification to administrators.

• **Communication daemon:** Used be the console to communicate with the intelligent agents. Events are sent by the agents to the console. When received at the console, the events appear in the Event window. If you are not currently logged in, events are queued until the next time you log in to the console.

The database objects need to be registered at the console to maintain their status. Status is shown graphically, with color indicating severity. Objects can be grouped together with a special container icon. The worst status of any of the members is propagated to the group icon. Hierarchies of groups can be created, and you can take actions on a group.

Objects also have *property sheets*. The database property sheet can show status, or it can be used to start or stop a database. Database administration tools shown in the Tools Application menu can be launched on an object by first selecting the object and then selecting the tool. The OEM database administration tools can be used to manage schema objects, back up, recover, and restore a database, and distribute software.

The events shown in the Event window contain a variety of information, including the name of the event, event severity, source node, type of event, and timestamp. Event severities are shown with different colors. Events also affect the color of the object in the Map window. Threshold parameters determine whether the event should be displayed as a serious alert or merely as a warning. Events can be acknowledged and then annotations can be associated with an event.

OEM contains a predefined set of events that can report the status of nodes, databases, and listeners. You choose the events and then set the polling interval and threshold conditions that determine when the events should be generated. You do this from the Event menu at the OEM console. After you create an event set, you need to register it, to be able to monitor events on a specific system. During registration, you specify who to notify and how notification should be sent. To allow for different administrators to receive different events based on their responsibilities, each administrator's mail address or pager number, system responsibility, and availability need to be configured. E-mail and paging are two notification options. Notification can also be sent directly to the console or forwarded to SNMP-based management stations.

OEM is also extensible. You can write your own applications that can be launched from the console. A scripting capability can be used to create customized events.

Jobs are run by intelligent agents on the local system, so connectivity with the OEM console is needed only when a job is initially scheduled. If the agent is unavailable, the job request is queued until the agent becomes available. Jobs can be scheduled to run on a set of databases or nodes, or on a user-defined group of objects.

Recovery actions can be configured to run as jobs when an event occurs. These are referred to as "fixit" jobs. The Job Scheduler can be used to create these jobs. This type of job runs as a recovery action in response to an event, instead of being scheduled for execution, which is the Job Scheduler's usual task. The job is submitted to an agent at the remote node where the event is being monitored. The job, for example, may execute a predefined SQL*Plus script file or a UNIX command or custom script that you created.

The previously mentioned predefined fault management events that come with OEM provide status information on the database, listener, and computer system. Predefined resource and performance management events require the additional purchase of the Oracle Diagnostics Pack, which includes the following Oracle components:

- **Performance Manager:** Used to collect system and database performance information and display the data in charts or graphs on the OEM console. The user can control the sampling interval. The available data includes CPU utilization, library and dictionary cache performance, and memory sort performance.
- **Capacity Planner:** Used to analyze system and database capacity information. You can use this information to plan for future growth.
- **Trace Manager:** Used to start and stop data collection for applications that use the Oracle Trace API (described later in this chapter). Using the Trace API, the Trace Manager can discover all the applications that are on systems managed by the console.
- **Trace Data Viewer:** Enables you to examine the information from the data collections from the Trace Manager.
- **TopSessions:** Used to identify the database sessions that are using the most system or database resources. The list can be based on resource usage, open cursors, user transactions, or block changes. Runaway sessions can be identified and then terminated.
- **Advanced Events:** Provides additional sets of predefined events to be used with the OEM, such as additional fault management events, and resource and performance-management events.
- **Lock Manager:** Used to graphically monitor the use of database locks. You can also see who is waiting for or using individual locks.

All events discovered by the OEM agent can also be sent as SNMP traps (defined in Oracle's OEM MIB). The following is a list of the events that can be sent as SNMP traps from the OEM agent:

- Unknown event
- Database has gone down
- Database has new message in its alert log
- OEM unable to establish a new connection to database
- Process blocked on lock held by a user session
- Database archive log full
- Database dump device full
- Tablespace segment approaching maximum extent
- Tablespace segment unable to allocate additional extents
- Number of database data files approaching maximum allowed
- Current database locks approaching maximum allowed
- Current database processes approaching maximum allowed

- Current database sessions approaching maximum allowed
- Current database users approaching maximum allowed
- Buffer cache hit ratio below configured threshold
- Tables or clusters in database have chained rows
- Data dictionary cache miss ratio above configured threshold
- Physical disk I/O rate above configured threshold
- Library cache miss ratio above configured threshold
- Network I/O rate above configured threshold
- Database response time above configured threshold
- Value of V$SYSSTAT exceeded configured threshold
- Change in value of V$SYSSTAT exceeded configured threshold
- Listener has gone down
- CPU load for system exceeded configured threshold
- CPU utilization for system exceeded configured threshold
- Paging rate for system exceeded configured threshold
- Available swap for system below configured threshold
- Disk space on one or more disks below configured threshold

The Oracle Tuning Pack includes Oracle Expert, which is used for performance analysis and tuning and workload analysis, and Oracle Tablespace Manager, which can monitor and manage tablespace usage.

In OEM 2, the product has been tightly integrated with HP IT/O. Each product can send events to the other. OEM can launch IT/O, and IT/O can launch OEM in the context of a reported problem from its Application Bank.

Oracle Private MIBs

Oracle also provides several non-standard database MIBs for managing its RDBMS. Oracle supports a Private Database MIB for Oracle7 and later servers, an OEM MIB, and MIBs for the Oracle Network Listener, Oracle Multiprotocol Interchange, and Oracle Names components. The OEM intelligent agent can provide direct access to these database MIB variables.

Oracle's Private Database MIB includes several useful metrics for performance monitoring. Here are some of the more important variables in this MIB:

- Number of sort requests to disk
- Number of sort requests to memory
- Number of user calls
- Number of consistent gets
- Number of block gets
- Number of physical reads
- Number of user commits
- Number of redo log space requests

- Number of redo log entries
- Number of library cache pin requests
- Number of library cache reloads

These metrics are useful when measured over time, to calculate a rate, or in comparison with other metrics as a ratio. Information on how to use these metrics can be found in the section "Using Database Performance Data," later in this chapter, or in Oracle's Oracle Server Tuning Guide.

Informix Private Database MIB

Informix provides a Private Database MIB for its Informix-Online Dynamic Server product. It is meant to supplement the RDBMS MIB. Several of the following fields are useful for resource or performance management:

- Number of sort requests to disk
- Number of sort requests to memory
- Last SQL statement executed by each session
- Number of buffer waits
- Table pages allocated
- Tables pages used
- Lock requests
- Waits or timeouts on lock requests
- State of each session
- Pages allocated to fragments
- Fragment pages in use

This MIB also has some fault management information, such as the mode (state) of the server, recovery and backup status for the tablespaces, and status of each chunk.

Using Fault Detection and Recovery Tools

This section provides a sampling of tools for database fault management. By knowing the processes that are critical to the database, you can do some basic fault monitoring. You can set up scripts to do ps and parse the output, to ensure that the processes you care about are still active. More sophisticated application monitoring can be done with Compuware's EcoSNAP, which can detect application failures and report problems, with diagnostic information included. The rest of this section describes tools that are specifically for databases.

MC/ServiceGuard

MC/ServiceGuard is a high availability product from Hewlett-Packard that is used to protect your critical applications and servers. MC/ServiceGuard is most commonly used in a multisystem or clustered environment. The MC/ServiceGuard software on each system monitors the other systems in the cluster. MC/ServiceGuard can detect the failure of systems, networks, and applications. For example, if a LAN card fails, MC/ServiceGuard transparently recovers from the failure by activating a standby LAN card.

After deciding which applications need to be protected, you configure them as packages, using MC/ServiceGuard commands or the GUI accessible from SAM. Several attributes of the application need to be defined, such as the following:

- Name of application
- Scripts used to start or stop application
- Processes or services that make up application
- Subnetworks used by application
- Alternate systems on which application can run
- Additional resource dependencies

MC/ServiceGuard monitors these services and dependencies. If a failure occurs, the package is either restarted locally or moved and restarted on another system. Similarly, when a system failure occurs, MC/ServiceGuard software can detect the problem and automatically restart critical applications on an alternate node.

MC/ServiceGuard software detects a variety of error conditions, but does not have a sophisticated notification mechanism for customers to learn what happened. Errors often are written to the system log file (/var/adm/syslog/syslog.log) or to application-specific logs, which helps to retrace what happened.

Because MC/ServiceGuard can automatically move applications to other systems, it may be difficult for you to know the current status of an application. MC/ServiceGuard commands, such as cmviewcl, can tell you the current state of a cluster and its packages. This information is also contained in the MC/ServiceGuard MIB. To learn why a package has failed, check the system log file on each system in the cluster for specific MC/ServiceGuard messages.

MC/ServiceGuard can provide some level of protection for database availability by encapsulating the database application into a package. Redundant hardware components can help to ensure that the database survives some failure scenarios. Some failures may require the database to be restarted, but this can be handled automatically by MC/ServiceGuard. In response to a catastrophic system failure, MC/ServiceGuard can restart the database on another system.

MC/ServiceGuard is a general-purpose tool, and its only database-specific knowledge comes from the user-configured package definition. MC/ServiceGuard provides database templates to make this configuration easier, but this enables it to monitor only that database processes are alive. You may also want to monitor the status of database tables and check for potential deadlock situations. This requires the use of other tools, which are not integrated with the MC/ServiceGuard product.

No changes to the database application need to be made for MC/ServiceGuard to monitor the application.

The MC/LockManager product is modeled after MC/ServiceGuard and provides support for concurrent database access to Oracle databases by using Oracle Parallel Server. This cluster solution can provide continuous access to the database despite the loss of a server. MC/Lock-Manager relies on the generic monitoring capabilities of MC/ServiceGuard, and also monitors the Distributed Lock Manager.

MC/ServiceGuard provides help for database fault management only. It does not help you to manage database resources and performance, and provides no help for monitoring service response time to detect performance issues or uncover trends that could lead to problems.

Note that MC/ServiceGuard is supported only on HP 9000 Series 800 systems running HP-UX 10.x or later operating systems. Similar high availability cluster products are available for other platforms, such as Solstice HA for Sun Solaris environments.

ClusterView

ClusterView is an HP OpenView application that can be used to monitor MC/ServiceGuard or MC/LockManager clusters. ClusterView presents windows for each high availability cluster in a company's environment. In each window, you can see the status of packages and the systems on which applications are running. ClusterView can show database servers and their status, if they are configured as MC/ServiceGuard packages.

EMS HA Monitors

The Event Monitoring Service (EMS) is a free set of monitoring functions for HP-UX systems. In addition to free library routines for creating your own monitors, EMS provides a set of free monitors when you purchase a system. These include hardware diagnostic monitors. More sophisticated monitors are provided with the EMS HA Monitors product, which includes a disk monitor and a database monitor, as well as other monitors.

The database monitor included in the EMS HA Monitors product currently supports only Oracle environments. Both database and database server information is provided. One set of database resources is provided for each configured database (see Table 8-3), and one set of database server resources is provided for each active database server (see Table 8-4).

The EMS Database Monitor can detect changes in the state of a database, and can send events before the database runs out of critical database resources. With this monitor, MC/ServiceGuard can detect a database problem before failure and start recovery actions sooner, such as restarting a package on an alternate node.

The status field can be used to determine whether the database is functioning properly. The other fields in the table provide information on the amount of disk space available for the database.

As mentioned earlier, process information obtained from ps or other commands can indicate whether a database instance is running or has failed. Status information obtained from EMS can give more detailed information, such as whether the server is congested or whether the transaction rate is below an acceptable value. The EMS database monitor is focused on fault management,

Table 8-3 EMS Database Resources

Resource Instance	Description
status	Status of database
allocated	Disk space allocated for database
used	Disk space actually used by database
usage	Percentage of disk space actually used by database

Table 8-4 EMS Database Server Resources

Resource Instance	Description
status	Status of database server
connects	Number of currently active local and remote connections
allowed_max_connects	Maximum number of simultaneous connections allowed
usage	Percentage of maximum connections currently active
started	Time database server started execution
uptime	Length of time server has been running
disk_reads	Number of physical reads
disk_reads_per_sec	Rate of physical reads per second
logical_reads	Number of logical reads
logical_reads_per_sec	Logical reads per second
read_cache_hit_rate	Percentage of reads in cache
disk_writes	Number of physical writes
disk_writes_per_sec	Number of physical writes per second
logical_writes	Number of logical writes
logical_writes_per_sec	Number of logical writes per second
write_cache_hit_rate	Percentage of writes in cache
commits	Number of transactions committed or aborted
commits_per_sec	Number of committed or aborted transactions per second

although it does provide some performance information, such as the transaction rate for each database server.

All EMS monitors support a variety of notification methods, including SNMP, e-mail, TCP or UDP messages, or writing to an arbitrary log file. EMS monitors can also notify MC/ServiceGuard directly of an event, so that appropriate recovery actions can be initiated immediately.

EMS also allows for different operators to receive different events or use different notification criteria. This information is configured using the EMS configuration GUI, which is part of SAM. Thus, a system operator can get basic status information, while a database administrator receives more detailed performance alarms.

Figure 8-1 shows the EMS GUI screen for adding monitoring of database status for the bak1 database instance. The status of bak1 is ACTIVE. The resource name for this resource is /rdbms/database/status/bak1.

Figure 8-1   Using the EMS GUI to configure database status monitoring.

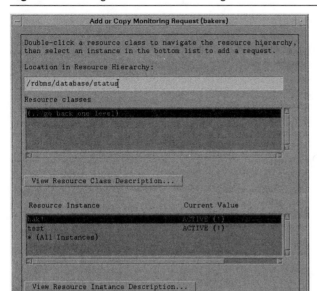

Resource and Performance Monitoring Tools

As mentioned earlier, the majority of database performance problems are the result of a poor database design or poorly coded database queries. Other reasons for performance problems are data access contention ("hot spots"), inadequate hardware resources, or a poorly configured database server. This section describes a variety of tools and techniques for locating database performance problems.

Application Resource Measurement

Because measuring the performance of an application is difficult, Hewlett-Packard and Tivoli Systems jointly developed an open set of APIs for measuring application response times. This standard set of APIs is called Application Resource Measurement (ARM). If an application has been modified to use the new APIs at key points, then you can measure and control the application's end-to-end performance. API calls are made in the application to mark the beginning and end of transactions. A Software Developer's Kit (SDK) is freely available for ARM from either Tivoli or Hewlett-Packard to make this process easier. Table 8-5 lists and describes the few available ARM APIs.

Baan has announced that the next release of its ERP application will be instrumented using the ARM API, which will make collecting application performance data for Baan more straightforward.

Table 8-5 ARM APIs

Name	Function
arm_init	Initializes ARM environment for application
arm_getid	Names each transaction class used in application
arm_start	Marks the start of execution of transaction instance
arm_update	Updates information about transaction instance
arm_stop	Marks the end of transaction
arm_end	Cleans up application's memory used by ARM

After the application data is collected, it can be presented through performance management tools such as MeasureWare and HP PerfView.

Oracle Trace

Oracle has an API called Oracle Trace that is similar to the ARM APIs, except that Oracle Trace is available only for Oracle environments. Oracle7 server release 7.3.2 and SQL*NET release 2.3 are already instrumented with Oracle Trace calls. Oracle Trace can be used to instrument an Oracle application to get performance data. This set of APIs can also be used to detect the following two types of events occurring in an application:

• **Duration or transaction events:** Have a start and stop time associated with them.
• **Asynchronous events:** Refer to special conditions, such as errors.

Tables 8-6 and 8-7 show the Oracle Server 7.3 duration and asynchronous events, respectively, that are instrumented for Oracle Trace.

An operator can use the asynchronous events to create an audit trail of database accesses, for example. The duration of various database transactions can be studied over time to look for trends.

An application that has been modified to include calls to Oracle Trace routines is called a *facility*. The user configures the facility definition file to define which metrics, or *items*, to collect when the application is traced. Table 8-8 shows the items available, by default, for every event.

Additional cross-facility items, such as the Oracle7 Server Transaction ID, can be used to correlate data collected from multiple applications.

After an application has been instrumented, performance analysis can be enabled from the OEM console. In fact, the Oracle Trace Manager can automatically discover applications that have been instrumented using Oracle Trace APIs. A trace can be started or stopped, and data can be viewed from past or currently active traces. Applications can also start and stop tracing from within themselves. Multiple facilities can be included in the same trace. When the trace, called a *collection*, is stopped, the data is written to a collection file.

In addition to viewing trace information from the GUI, reports can be run against the collection file. The otrcrep command generates a detailed trace report, displaying statistics for all

Table 8-6 Oracle Trace Duration Events

Event	Description
Parse Start	Start of event containing SQL query information (actual text of query)
Parse End	End of event containing SQL query information
Execute Start	Start of event containing information for execution of SQL query plan
Execute End	End of event containing information for execution of SQL query plan
Fetch Start	Start of event containing actual row retrieval information
Fetch End	End of event containing actual row retrieval information
LogicalTX Start	Start of event marking the first time a database update is performed that may change the database status
LogicalTX End	End of event marking the first time a database update is performed that may change the database status
PhysicalTX Start	Start of event marking a definite change in database status
PhysicalTX End	End of event marking a definite change in database status

Table 8-7 Oracle Trace Asynchronous Events

Event	Description
Connection	Records each connection to a database
Disconnect	Records each disconnection from a database
ErrorStack	Code stack for core dump
Migration	Session migration between shared server processes
ApplReg	Application context information
RowSource	Row information
SQLSegment	Text of SQL statement
Wait	Records a generic WAIT event; context is provided in the event strings

Table 8-8 Oracle Trace Standard Items

Name	Description
UCPU	Amount of CPU time in user mode
SCPU	Amount of CPU time in system mode
INPUT_IO	Number of times filesystem performed input
OUTPUT_IO	Number of times filesystem performed output
PAGEFAULTS	Number of hard and soft page faults
PAGEFAULT_IO	Number of hard page faults
MAX_RSSIZE	Maximum resident set size used

items associated with every occurrence of every event for every facility involved in the collection. Reports can be generated for a specific event or for a specific process, for example. Data can also be exported to an Oracle7 Server database, where data can be queried using SQL scripts. Oracle provides a set of sample scripts to show how this is done.

Oracle provides a function for calculating the elapsed time for duration events. Reports can also be generated on the frequency of different types of events, such as connection events. Statistics available include the minimum, maximum, and average times spent doing different events. The Oracle Trace APIs are listed with a brief description in Table 8-9.

Oracle V$ Tables

Oracle provides a set of virtual tables that can be used to access memory structures within the shared global area. Many of these tables contain database performance information that is continuously updated. Table 8-10 lists and describes the contents of some of the more interesting V$ tables.

Table 8-9   Oracle Trace APIs

Name	Function
epc_init	Initial trace call; used to register facility with Oracle Trace
epc_add_reg_id	Adds a registration ID for a facility
epc_remove_reg_id	Removes a registration ID for a facility
epc_start_event	Records start of duration event
epc_end_event	Records end of duration event
epc_event	Records asynchronous event
epc_collect	Starts a collection from within a facility
epc_cancel	Stops a collection started by epc_collect
epc_bind	Binds a process to a collection that is already active
epc_flush	Writes collection data buffers to disk
epc_context	Stores collection data on per-thread basis
epc_delete_context	Indicates the end of thread
epc_set_cf_items	Sends cross-facility items to another process
epc_cf_value	Assigns values to cross-facility items
epc_get_cf_items	Obtains cross-facility items from another process

Table 8-10   Oracle V$ Tables

V$ Table	Contains
V$DATABASE	Database information from the control file
V$FILESTAT	File read/write statistics
V$INSTANCE	Status information for the current instance
V$LIBRARYCACHE	Library cache performance information
V$LICENSE	Information on license limits
V$PROCESS	Process information
V$ROWCACHE	Data dictionary performance information
V$SESSION	Session information
V$SESSTAT	Information on the memory usage for each current session
V$SGA	Summary information on system global area
V$SGASTAT	Detailed information on system global area
V$SYSSTAT	Current system-wide value for each variable in V$SESSTAT

To get a list of all available Oracle V$ performance monitoring tables, execute the following SQL query: SELECT * FROM X$KQFVI;

For more information on the V$ tables, consult Oracle's Oracle Server Tuning Guide and Oracle Server Reference manuals.

GlancePlus Pak 2000

GlancePlus Pak 2000 is a product from Hewlett-Packard. It includes performance management, fault management, and real-time performance monitoring. It has three components:

- MeasureWare
- GlancePlus
- ITO/Special Edition

MeasureWare is an HP product that collects and logs resource and performance metrics. MeasureWare agents run and collect data on the individual server systems being monitored. Agents exist for many platforms and operating systems, including HP-UX, Solaris, and AIX.

The MeasureWare agents collect data, summarize it, timestamp it, log it, and send alarms when appropriate. The agents collect and report on a wide variety of system resources, performance metrics, and user-defined data. The information can then be exported to spreadsheets or to performance analysis programs, such as PerfView. The data can be used by these programs to generate alarms to warn of potential performance problems. By using historical data, you can discover trends, which can help you address resource issues before they affect system performance.

MeasureWare collects system, application, process, and transaction data. MeasureWare agents collect data at three different levels: global system metrics, application, and process metrics. Global and application data is summarized at five-minute intervals, whereas process data is summarized at one-minute intervals.

GlancePlus is a real-time, graphical, performance monitoring tool from Hewlett-Packard. It is used to monitor the performance and system resource utilization of a single system. You should use GlancePlus to see whether a performance problem can be isolated to the system or the database. Both Motif-based and character-based interfaces are available. The product can be used on HP-UX, Solaris, and many other operating systems.

GlancePlus collects information similar to MeasureWare, but samples data more frequently. GlancePlus can be used to graphically view current CPU, memory, swap, and disk activity, as well as utilization at the system level. It can also show application and process information. Transaction information can be shown if the MeasureWare Agent is installed and active.

ITO/Special Edition is the single-system version of IT/O. From the Java-based GUI, you can view events from a single system in the Event Browser. Diagnostic tools are also provided from the GUI. ITO/Special Edition uses IT/O's intelligent agent technology, which includes the ability to collect data from various sources and execute automated actions.

To monitor an application in GlancePlus or MeasureWare, the application must first be defined. To define important applications, you must first define the processes that comprise the application. This is done in the parm file (located at /var/opt/perf/parm), in which you list the process names that make up the application. Wildcards can be used if the exact names vary. For example, ora* could be used to define an application based on all processes beginning with ora. GlancePlus and MeasureWare summarize process information for processes listed in the application definition.

Customizable rules determine when a system performance problem should be sent as an alarm. In GlancePlus, the rules are managed by the GlancePlus Adviser. Choosing the Edit Adviser Syntax option on the Adviser menu enables you to see and modify all alarm conditions. The GlancePlus Adviser syntax file (/var/opt/perf/adviser.syntax) contains the symptom and alarm configuration. Additional syntax files can also be used. For MeasureWare, alarms are defined in the alarmdef file, located at /var/opt/perf/alarmdef.

In GlancePlus, alarms result in onscreen notifications, with color representing the criticality of an alarm. An alarm can also trigger a command or script to be executed automatically. Instead of sending an alarm, GlancePlus can print messages or notify you by executing a UNIX command, such as mailx, using its EXEC feature.

You can also have alarms sent according to conditions that are based on a combination of metrics. For example, a CPU bottleneck alarm can be based on the CPU use and CPU run queue length. MeasureWare agents provide these alarms to PerfView for analysis, and to the IT/O management console. SNMP traps can also be sent at the time a threshold condition is met. Automated actions can be taken, or the operator can choose to take a suggested action.

Application- and transaction-level information is available. Transactions must be defined by the application using the ARM API. The following are some of the available metrics:

- Transaction average response time
- Distribution of transaction response times
- Number of aborted transactions
- Response time of aborted transactions

More than 600 metrics are accessible from GlancePlus and MeasureWare. The complete list of metrics can be found by using the product's online help facility. On systems with GlancePlus Pak 2000 installed, this information can also be found in the directory /opt/perf/paperdocs/gp/C.

Hewlett-Packard also provides a separate product, the Process Resource Manager (PRM), which can be used to control CPU, memory, and disk utilization between users or applications. PRM has done some special integration with Oracle, as well. If PRM is being used, GlancePlus shows how well PRM application groups are staying within their resource entitlements. From GlancePlus, you can also change PRM process group entitlements.

Although MeasureWare provides extensive performance and resource information, it has limited configuration information and no data about system faults. For further information, visit the HP Resource and Performance Management Web site at http://www.openview.hp.com/solutions/application/.

Oracle Management Pak

The Oracle Management Pak from Hewlett-Packard can be used to monitor Oracle databases and is used in conjunction with GlancePlus Pak 2000. You can also migrate from this single-server-environment solution to an enterprise solution simply by adding the intelligent agent for IT/O.

Numerous database metrics are available. Oracle Management Pak can report the status of the database instance, individual tablespaces and rollback segments, and configured Oracle background processes. The number of snapshot refresh errors can also be reported.

The following is a summary of the resource management metrics that are included for Oracle:

- Maximum number of sessions since server was last started
- Percentage of free tablespace to total available
- Number of free chunks in tablespace
- Number of segments that cannot add extents
- Number of segments approaching maximum extents
- Percentage of open cursors to total cursors configured
- Percentage of DML locks used
- Percentage of maximum processes used
- Percentage of enqueue resources used
- Number of current user logons
- Archive free-space percentage
- Space remaining on dump devices

In addition to resource management, the following Oracle performance metrics are available:

- Ratio of blocks read to physical reads
- Disk sort rate
- Percentage of memory sorts to total
- Average number of rows per sort
- Block buffer hit ratio (current and total)
- Dictionary cache hit ratio
- Library cache reload percentage
- Percentage of free memory to total shared pool memory
- Transaction commit rate
- Transaction rollback rate
- Percentage of rollbacks to commits
- Background checkpoint completion rate
- User call rate

- Ratio of recursive calls to user calls
- Percentage of chained rows fetched to total
- Rate at which full table scans occur
- Buffer busy rate
- Number of waits for redo log buffer space
- Percentage of rollback buffer waits to gets

All of the threshold monitoring and real-time graphs included with GlancePlus Pak 2000 can be applied to these database metrics as well.

PerfView

PerfView is a graphical performance analysis tool from Hewlett-Packard. It is used to graphically display performance and system resource utilization for one system or for multiple systems simultaneously, so comparisons can be made. A variety of performance graphs can be displayed. The graphs are based on data collected over a period of time, unlike the real-time graphs of GlancePlus, which show only recent history. PerfView runs on HP-UX or NT systems and works with data collected by MeasureWare agents.

PerfView has three main components:

- **PerfView Monitor:** Provides the ability to receive alarms. A textual description of an alarm can be displayed. Alarms can be filtered by severity, type, or source system. Also, after an alarm is received, the alarm can be selected, which displays a graph of related metrics. An operator can monitor trends leading to failures, and can then take proactive actions to avoid problems. Graphs can be used for comparison between systems and to show a history of resource consumption. An internal database is maintained that keeps a history of alarm notification messages.
- **PerfView Analyzer:** Provides resource and performance analysis for disks and other resources. System metrics can be shown at three different levels: process, application (configured by the user as a set of processes), and global system information. It relies on data received from MeasureWare agents on the managed nodes. Data can be analyzed from up to eight systems concurrently. All MeasureWare data sources are supported. PerfView Analyzer is required by both PerfView Monitor and PerfView Planner.
- **PerfView Planner:** Provides forecasting capability. Graphs can be extrapolated into the future. A variety of graphs (such as linear, exponential, s-curve, and smoothed) can be shown for forecasted data.

In addition to graphing and analyzing system resources, process and application resources can be graphed and analyzed using PerfView. With PerfView, users can define the set of processes that make up an application. PerfView can then be used to show a history of a specified application's utilization. PerfView's ability to show history and trend information can be helpful in diagnosing system problems. Graphing performance information can help you understand whether a persistent problem exists or an anomaly is simply a momentary spike of activity.

With PerfView, you can analyze, alarm, forecast, and report on the Oracle Management Pak metrics and compare them with system, network, and application metrics. The graph in Figure 8-2 shows commit, or transaction, rates over time.

To diagnose a problem further, PerfView Monitor enables you to change time intervals, to try to find the specific time a problem occurred. The graph is redrawn showing the new time period.

PerfView is integrated with several other monitoring tools. You can launch GlancePlus from within PerfView by accessing the Tools menu. PerfView can be launched from the IT/O Applications Bank. When troubleshooting an event in the IT/O Message Browser window, you can launch PerfView to see a related performance graph.

When using IT/O with PerfView, the PerfView Monitor is disabled. The IT/O Message Browser should be used to view alarms, instead. When an alarm is received in IT/O, you can click the alarm to display a related PerfView graph.

In a single performance graph, PerfView can show information collected from multiple systems. The PerfView and ClusterView products have also been integrated, enabling you to select a cluster symbol on an HP OpenView submap and launch the PerfView application, to quickly show a performance comparison between all systems in the cluster.

Figure 8-2   Graphing transaction rates in PerfView.

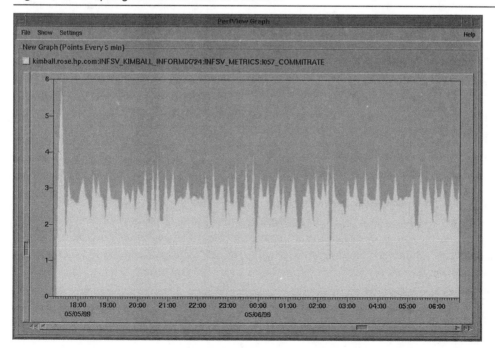

For further information, visit the HP Resource and Performance Management Web site at http://www.openview.hp.com/solutions/application/.

SMART Plug-Ins for Databases

IT/Operations is meant to provide a consistent interface for managing systems and networks. The goal of HP's SMART Plug-Ins (SPIs) is to extend support for applications and databases. SPIs are preconfigured solutions that are intended to be used with IT/O, although IT/O is not required. Today, SPIs exist for SAP R/3, Baan, Oracle, Informix, and Sybase.

SPIs for Databases provide the same set of metrics as provided by the Oracle Management Pak, plus the ability to report information via IT/O's reliable RPC mechanism, not via SNMP traps.

The tight integration between SPIs and IT/O means that other features are available to SPIs, such as event filtering and correlation, and task escalation. Events include built-in instructions and operator text that can aid in diagnosis and recovery. Corrective actions are predefined for many SPI events.

Figure 8-3 shows how the SPI for Informix integrates into IT/O. You can see the new message groups that were added for Informix by the SPI for Informix. The Application Group window shows all the database tools added for SPI for Informix. The Message Browser enables you to see messages about the Informix database.

Unlike EMS, which is focused on fault management, SPIs for Databases focus on database configuration and resource management. IT/O templates can specify different thresholds for different database instances. SPIs can verify that the database processes defined in Oracle's init.ora configuration file are actually running, and their performance can be monitored in GlancePlus and PerfView as a single application.

BMC PATROL Knowledge Modules

BMC Software, Inc. provides monitoring capabilities through its PATROL software suite. With PATROL, you can define thresholds and send events to a console or to other management applications. PATROL consists of a console, intelligent agents, and more than 40 different monitoring programs, or Knowledge Modules (KMs). Each KM is optional, so you can pick the monitors that are best for your environment.

The console provides a centralized graphical display, with icons representing system components or other monitored components. Icons change color to correspond to their status. For example, an icon may change to red to represent a critical event on its node or component. The PATROL console also provides an Event Browser, in which you can filter, correlate, sort, and escalate events. Alarms can be configured so that events are sent to the console and shown in the Event Browser. Events can also be configured to go to HP OpenView IT/O or other SNMP-based management stations.

Intelligent agents provide the ability to discover the system, database, and application components in an enterprise. The agents reside on each server. On an ongoing basis, the agents

Figure 8-3 Using IT/O to see events about Informix databases.

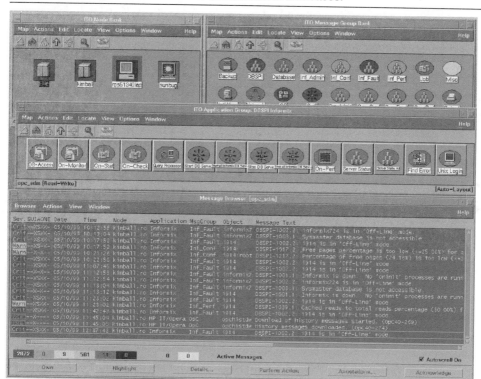

look for problems; when they discover a problem, they either take preconfigured actions or send notification so that recovery can be done manually.

The KMs contain the expertise used by PATROL to know what to monitor and how to react when problems occur. KMs are used to monitor a set of "parameters," which can include a description of the monitored attribute, the polling interval, the method for measuring the attribute, and a threshold for abnormal values. The KMs provide rules to detect events and perform corrective actions. Events are sent to an operator console when an error or warning condition occurs. BMC PATROL includes KMs for UNIX, SAP R/3, Oracle, Informix, and other applications.

BMC's primary business is database and application monitoring. It provides KMs for Oracle, Sybase, and Informix databases. BMC also has KMs for DB2, Red Brick, and Ingres. PATROL arguably provides more database metrics than are available from the other products described in this chapter, although you may need to include multiple KMs.

For Oracle environments, PATROL monitors more than 70 metrics for Oracle servers, tablespaces, and users. Metrics include user connection information, active locks, I/O statistics, dictionary hit ratios, and CPU utilization. Remote servers can be monitored by using SQL*NET, even if the server is not running the PATROL agent software. After the Oracle KM is loaded, PATROL determines all the Oracle database instances on the system. The PATROL administrator manually starts and stops the monitoring of instances.

PATROL provides the following categories of monitoring information for Oracle:

- Overall Database Performance
- Server Instance Information
    - Log Buffer
    - Shared Pool
    - Internal Structures
- Multithreaded Server Information
- Database Information
    - General Statistics
    - Trace & Archive
    - Space Management
- User and Application Information
- Transaction Information
    - General Statistics
    - Block Level
    - Row Level
    - User & Application
    - Rollback
- User Session Information
    - Backup and Recovery
    - Miscellaneous

A variety of database performance graphs are available as icons from the PATROL console. Figure 8-4 shows some of the metrics maintained by the KM for Oracle. You can double-click these icons to see a graph or gauge.

BMC also provides database administration tools. PATROL DB includes database administrative tools such as Pathfinder, DB-Alter, DB-Reorg, DB-Change Manager, DB-Integrity, DB-Voyager, and SQL-Explorer. These tools are integrated into the PATROL framework and can be launched from the PATROL console. By contrast, IT/O provides monitoring only, relying on database vendors to provide these administrative tools.

BMC has bundled its database products into a PATROL Availability Suite for Oracle. The product bundle includes the PATROL KM for Oracle, PATROL DB-Stats for Oracle, PATROL DB-Reorg for Oracle, and PATROL DB-Integrity.

Unlike MC/ServiceGuard, PATROL does not provide any failover capability. However, a limited set of automated recovery actions is available. Recovery actions can be performed by the agents without requiring communication with the console.

Figure 8-4 BMC PATROL icons for performance graphs.

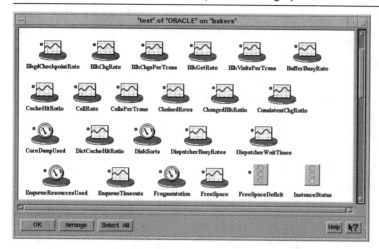

HP used to rely on PATROL to provide database information to its MeasureWare Agent, but the Database KMs were resold through a special licensing agreement, so HP now uses its SPIs for Databases or the Oracle Management Pak to gather database information for MeasureWare.

PLATINUM DBVision

PLATINUM Technology, Inc. provides the ProVision suite of products for monitoring the performance of servers, databases, applications, and networks. ProVision consists of four products:

- **ServerVision:** Provides performance information about the computer system, including the load average, number of current users, disk rates, most active CPU process, and CPU and disk usage per process.
- **DBVision**: PLATINUM's product for database monitoring, it can monitor Oracle, Sybase, Informix, and DB2 databases. A Motif GUI and a Windows NT GUI are supported. The emphasis is on resource and performance monitoring. DBVision can detect problems such as running out of available tablespace, high CPU utilization, low swap space, processes waiting for locks, and runaway processes. The product can also be used to see which user is tying up system resources.
- **TransTracker:** A pre-deployment tool for measuring the system, database, and network usage of a transaction. Instead of requiring an application to be instrumented, TransTracker is able to identify transactions by collecting data from network packets.
- **WireTap:** Also used to measure transaction response time, it provides network monitoring by capturing packet-level data and categorizing data by protocol (such as HTTP and TCP). The user can identify SQL statements to look for, and define alarm thresholds so that notification can be sent when transaction response times are not acceptable. WireTap provides Web performance data for HTML requests, as well as Web server "hit" rates.

When problems are detected, alerts can be sent to a pager, via e-mail, or to a centralized console receiving information from multiple databases. In response to an event, predetermined corrective actions can be taken, which can be defined in customized scripts that are executed automatically.

The database performance data provided by DBVision includes the following statistics:

- Average number of physical writes per second per database instance
- Average total physical reads per second
- Average total physical writes per second
- Average block reads per second
- Average block writes per second
- Average number of logical reads per second
- Total active transactions
- Active transactions per session
- Block change ratio

DBVision also includes database resource information, such as:

- Free tablespace
- Number of current logins
- Tablespace fragmentation
- A table's number of extents
- Free space per chunk

In addition to database monitoring, PLATINUM provides tools for database administration and for identifying database performance bottlenecks. Database administration tools include Enterprise DBA and TSReorg.

Enterprise DBA provides user administration, schema, and content management. Administrative tasks can be done across different databases, with Oracle, Informix, and DB2 databases supported. Remote agents are used to change the database.

TSReorg supports both Oracle and Sybase databases. It can be used to reorganize database tables, indexes, and tablespaces. Using DBVision and TSReorg together, you can configure corrective actions to be performed automatically by TSReorg in response to a DBVision event. Tablespaces can be monitored so that database reorganization is triggered automatically. Tablespaces can be reorganized while a database stays online. TSReorg can also be used to view database structures graphically, showing where database fragmentation exists.

A Database Analyzer tool can be used to graphically display tablespace and database usage information, which can be used for capacity planning. The Oracle Server Manager can also be used to monitor Oracle databases. Log Analyzer can be used as an additional troubleshooting tool for Sybase and DB2 database environments.

Using Database Performance Data

Possible causes of database performance problems include a poor design of the data model or a poorly written database application program. Programs should first be tested heavily in a development environment before going into production. However, resolving design and programming problems are beyond the scope of this book. You may want to consult documentation from the database vendors, such as Oracle's *Oracle Server Concepts*, to get more information on these topics.

Additional causes of performance problems can be an inappropriate system configuration or an ineffective use of database resources. To identify these types of situations, you need to collect performance statistics, using the metrics and tools discussed earlier in this chapter. With the database in production, performance monitoring tools should be used to monitor loads and collect performance data. By collecting performance statistics, you can establish a baseline to compare against when a major performance problem exists. Because application workloads change and usage varies, it is important to collect data over a period of time rather than rely on a single snapshot of data.

Avoiding Performance Issues

Proactive monitoring against established baselines can enable you to identify resource usage trends that could lead to performance problems. In doing this, you can correct a situation before the end-user experiences poor response times.

Other types of performance problems involve the inability to prioritize different workloads and allocate to each a designated amount of system resources. Two products can help to prioritize database workloads: the Process Resource Manager and Oracle Database Resource Manager.

The Process Resource Manager (PRM) can be used to control system resource allocations for users and applications. Both minimum and maximum entitlements can be specified. CPU, real memory, and disk I/O bandwidth can be controlled by PRM. PRM, however, is available only on HP-UX.

You can use PRM on HP-UX to isolate database applications from other applications. The database management system can be given resource entitlements for CPU, memory, and I/O to help reduce interference from other applications. If the system is busy, PRM ensures that the database applications get their configured share of system resources. If an application doesn't need all the resources it is entitled to, PRM can be configured to distribute its resources to other applications. PRM can also be configured to limit an application's maximum resource usage for capacity planning purposes.

In addition to isolating the database management system from other applications on the system, PRM has special Oracle support to allow resources to be allocated to specific databases. Oracle imbeds the database name in the processes that it creates to handle database accesses. By configuring processes for each database instance to be in separate PRM groups, you can manage each database separately. This is especially useful if some database applications have a higher priority than others. For example, if long-running database jobs are of a lower priority, but need access to the same disks accessed by interactive users, then PRM I/O bandwidth controls can be used to ensure that the jobs make continual progress without seriously impacting other users. A less sophisticated approach may be to have policies in place to ensure that long-running jobs are not executed during periods of heavy database or system usage. Another approach is simply to run those jobs at a lower priority than the other applications on the system.

Oracle also provides resource management capabilities with its Oracle8i release. The Oracle Database Resource Manager can be used to prioritize database workloads between different users. For example, users running OLTP applications could be given more of the CPU than decision-support users. Only the CPU usage associated with Oracle is being manipulated; the CPU entitlements for other applications running on the server should not be impacted. However, the Database Resource Manager behaves optimally if Oracle is the only application running on the server.

Checking for System Contention

If users are complaining of a performance problem, you may want to check the user call rate or database transaction rate first to get an idea of how much useful work, if any, is being done. This information is available in the RDBMS MIB for standard databases. In addition, Oracle provides metrics for the number of user calls and the number of user commits in its Private Database MIB. By monitoring this data over a period of time, you can calculate rates for these measures. Transaction rates can be compared to a known baseline to give you some idea of whether a performance problem exists. Transaction rates can be unreliable metrics, however, because low numbers could also indicate less end-user activity. Ideally, you would check the database response time, but no good way exists to track this metric directly.

If a performance problem is reported, you need to determine whether the cause is a system bottleneck, a disk bottleneck, or misconfigured database parameters. Potential causes of system resource bottlenecks are an untuned operating system, a system that is too small to accommodate the database workloads, or other applications running on the system. You may need to increase the capacity of the system by adding more memory or processors. As previously mentioned, PRM can help you prioritize resources among applications.

To check for real memory bottlenecks, you can first check the amount of free memory. It should not drop below 5 percent of the total available. If the system can't keep up with the demands for memory, it will start paging and swapping. Excessive paging and swapping may be a sign of a memory bottleneck. GlancePlus, MeasureWare, and BMC PATROL are some of the tools available to show you paging rates.

CPU resource contention can be identified by high utilization and a long run queue. This should be sustained over a period of time to indicate a serious CPU bottleneck. In a database environment, check for memory contention first, because much of the CPU's time is spent paging and swapping data between disk and main memory. High CPU usage can be an indication of an application problem, such as a missing database index. You should also look for runaway processes dominating the CPU usage.

Networking bottlenecks may be identified by high utilization and many collisions on shared media. They can be addressed by redesigning an application to reduce its network traffic. Other options are to use higher-capacity network links, or to move client and server systems closer together.

Checking for Disk Bottlenecks

Disk-related metrics can be used to identify unbalanced I/O activity. If this is the problem, you may need to restructure the database and relocate data files on different disks to avoid disk and controller bottlenecks. You should not have the database files on the disk used for swapping. Database tables and their indexes should be on different disks, because they are accessed concurrently. If the database is updated frequently, the redo logs should also be put on a different disk, because the logs are frequently updated as well. You should also try to place tables that are commonly used together onto separate disks. Ensure that OS disk striping and Oracle striping are being used appropriately. You should also see whether a system memory bottleneck exists, to determine whether adding more real memory to the system may fix the problem.

Database tables, indexes, and rollback segments are each created with an initial disk allocation. If these allocations are exceeded, then more space must be allocated dynamically, potentially all over the disk. This disk fragmentation slows down I/O operations and can lead to disk bottlenecks. An administrator may need to restructure the database periodically to repair problems, such as a significant amount of database fragmentation. PLATINUM's TSReorg tool can show database fragmentation graphically, so that you can quickly assess the size of the problem. TSReorg can be used together with DBVision so that actions such as a database reorganization can be taken in response to a database problem event.

Checking Database Buffer and Pool Sizes

For Oracle databases, some parameters in the init.ora configuration file can be adjusted to reduce system resource contention and improve memory performance. Another option is for the database administrator to limit or control user logins. The number of concurrent users can be controlled to help ensure adequate response times. Policies can be enforced to disconnect inactive sessions.

Sorting can be a very time-consuming part of a database query. Oracle provides several configurable parameters in the init.ora file, such as SORT_AREA_SIZE, SORT_WRITE_BUFFERS, and SORT_WRITE_BUFFER_SIZE. These parameters determine how much of a sort is done in main memory. Having a large sort area can make database queries faster; but, because the resource parameters are applied to each user session, this impacts contention for system memory. Having a small sort area may require writes to disk during the sort.

If periods during which jobs are run with few users logged in to the system are available, perhaps during evenings, you may want to switch between two sets of configuration parameters. After business hours, you can take advantage of more free memory to increase the sort area size, and then switch to a smaller size during peak usage to account for the larger number of users. Oracle keeps track of the number of sorts that go to disk in its Private Database MIB. Comparing this to the total number of sorts yields a sort overflow ratio, which should be zero for OLTP applications.

As mentioned earlier, a number of resources are allocated on a per-user basis. If a performance problem exists, you may want to check who is currently logged in, to determine if unauthorized users are logged in or if some users have logged in multiple times. You can use who or check the number of inbound associations using the RDBMS MIB to get an idea of system activity. Earlier in the chapter, Listing 8-2 showed how an SQL SELECT statement could be used to display the current database user processes. Monitoring the number of concurrent sessions over time can be useful in identifying any spikes in usage. Oracle7 and Oracle8 have the ability to establish resource limits for a user's CPU time and amount of disk I/O. These parameters are defined in the user's database profile.

Oracle has a single buffer cache and shared pool area that is shared among all database users. The DB_BLOCK_BUFFERS and SHARED_POOL_SIZE parameters in the init.ora file control the size of these resources. Data from database tables, indexes, clusters, and rollback segments may be stored in the buffer cache. The buffer cache hit ratio can be calculated for Oracle by using the number of consistent gets, number of block gets, and number of physical reads metrics stored in Oracle's Private Database MIB. Other tools, such as BMC PATROL's KM for Oracle, also keep track of the buffer cache hit ratio. By checking the buffer cache hit ratio, you can see whether the size of the buffer cache is appropriate. The hit ratio should be 70 to 85 percent. If the hit rate is low and free memory exists, consider increasing the size of the buffer cache, because this is likely to improve performance. You can increase the cache size until the hit ratio stops increasing, as long as free memory is available and no CPU bottleneck exists. In cases where a CPU bottleneck exists and no memory is available, reducing the size of the buffer cache may be appropriate, to transfer some of the work from the CPU to disk. Balancing system resources this way can lead to better overall response times for database users.

The shared pool area is used for dictionary information and shared SQL and PL/SQL code. A lot of SQL statement reloading may indicate that the shared pool area is too small. For Oracle, the metrics needed to calculate the library cache miss ratio are in the library cache table of the Oracle Private Database MIB.

Database checkpointing affects disk performance because it increases the I/O activity to the disk. The LOG_CHECKPOINT_INTERVAL parameter in Oracle's init.ora file determines how often changed data in the buffer cache is written to the database. Make sure the LOG_CHECKPOINT_INTERVAL is equal to or larger than the size of the redo logs.

Oracle's LOG_BUFFER parameter is used to determine the amount of modified data that should be buffered before writes are made to the redo log files. Increasing the amount buffered reduces the number of disk writes needed, by writing data in larger blocks. This may be useful if many changes are being made to the database. If system memory is a bottleneck and not many database updates are taking place, it could indicate that the log buffer is too large. You can observe the log buffer's effectiveness by monitoring the I/O rate of the disk containing the redo log and the number of times a user has waited for space in the redo log buffer, which ideally should be zero. In BMC PATROL, the RedoSpaceRequests metric will tell you this. From Oracle's Private Database MIB, you can use the redo log space requests and redo log entries to calculate a redo log space wait ratio, which should stay below 1/5000.

Contention may occur if multiple users try to access the redo log buffer latches. BMC PATROL monitors this metric as RedoAllocationLatch. If contention is occurring, decrease the LOG_SMALL_ENTRY_MAX_SIZE parameter, which indicates the largest log entry that can be written on a redo allocation latch without obtaining the redo buffer copy latch. This forces the larger copy latch to be used. You should also increase LOG_SIMULTANEOUS_COPIES to twice the number of CPUs on the system.

Database chaining occurs if a row is updated and becomes too large to fit in a single physical database block. Multiple block reads are necessary to read data from a chained row, causing performance to degrade. To determine whether this is a problem, you need to check periodically the percentage of chained row fetches being made. If this number is large, you may need to increase the database block size, which requires re-creating the database.

Avoiding Database Problems

You can take several proactive steps to avoid database problems. System and database server failures can be difficult to predict, but some of the root causes can be monitored. You can monitor how many rows a table gains over time, to monitor database growth. Gradual performance degradation or an available tablespace falling below critical thresholds could be an indication that a failure is imminent. Loss of data can be avoided through the use of data redundancy. Several techniques are available, such as disk mirroring. This is not sufficient, however, unless the failure of a disk mirror, for example, is quickly detected and repaired. The EMS HA Monitors product is one tool for detecting mirror failures.

The database operator should also periodically check system and database log files (such as Oracle's alert file) to look for failure information or unusual events.

Tools for monitoring system performance can be found in Chapter 4. A tool such as PerfView can be used to discover any resource utilization and performance trends. This information can be used by a database administrator to project database growth and plan for increased capacity. Various monitoring tools, such as BMC PATROL or SMART Plug-Ins, can be used to gather resource threshold information. If a database is out of available space, you need to archive or delete unneeded data, or allocate more space.

Some tools are available to help you properly tune your system. Oracle provides an add-on product, Oracle Expert, which is an expert system that uses configuration and tuning rules specific for Oracle databases. BMC PATROL has built-in self-tuning and load-balancing capabilities, such as compressing log files and resizing extents.

Monitoring backups and security are two additional proactive steps that you can take. Database backups should be verified periodically to ensure that data can be restored when needed. By maintaining audit logs of system access, you can more easily detect security intrusions and respond before experiencing database outages.

Recovering from Database Problems

Tools such as BMC PATROL can detect failures of key database processes and restart them automatically. MC/ServiceGuard provides a similar capability, and is also able to restart an application on another system.

Assuming successful backups exist, databases such as Oracle can recover from a disk failure without losing data. This requires a trained database administrator, because the process typically is not automated. The Oracle Recovery Manager product can be used to manage the backup, restore, and recovery processes.

After a system failure, Oracle can automatically recover data to a consistent state by performing full recovery. This is done by ensuring that committed changes are applied to the database and that uncommitted changes are undone. This can be a time-consuming activity. If the system problem is persistent, the workload may need to be moved to another system. For HP-UX systems, MC/ServiceGuard provides the capability of automatically moving a workload. To avoid the downtime associated with a single node failure, Oracle Parallel Server can be used. HP's MC/LockManager provides high availability for HP-UX Oracle Parallel Server environments.

In addition to system failures, human error, such as deleting the wrong rows in a database table, can lead to downtime. Successful database backups are critical, to ensure that the system can be returned to a good, consistent state.

To determine how to recover from Oracle database problems, refer to the following documents from Oracle: *Oracle7 Server Administrator's Guide*, *Oracle7 Server Tuning*, *Oracle7 Server Reference*, and *Oracle7 Server SQL Reference*. Similar manuals exist for later versions of Oracle as well.

Comparison of Database Monitoring Products

Your choice of a database monitoring product is likely to depend on your database responsibilities and the details of your computing environment. For example, EMS is available only for HP-UX environments and has special capabilities if used on servers in an MC/ServiceGuard cluster. The HA cluster products, such as MC/ServiceGuard and Solstice HA, are only available on a single OS platform. Other database monitoring tools, such as MIB Browsers, SPIs, and BMC PATROL, are available for a variety of UNIX platforms.

For configuration management, Network General's Database Module product can help detect when database connectivity problems are caused by misconfigurations. EMS provides a file status change monitor that can be used to ensure that nobody is altering a database configuration file unexpectedly.

For fault management, you can protect your database with either Sun's Solstice HA or Hewlett-Packard's MC/ServiceGuard product, depending on the platform you are using. If MC/ServiceGuard is being used, you can use ClusterView to see graphically any database failures that occur. EMS HA Monitors can provide additional database and server status information. In addition to supporting a variety of notification methods, EMS is the only tool that can send failure information to MC/ServiceGuard. EMS can also send alarms to HP Predictive Support for proactive care of the system, but currently, Predictive monitors only hardware events.

The PATROL KMs from BMC and SPIs from HP provide the most complete solutions for database resource and performance management. Both provide several performance metrics and have solutions for multiple databases. SPIs can be used with MeasureWare and PerfView and are also tightly integrated with IT/O. Because of their tight integration with the IT/O agent, SPIs can provide more sophisticated event correlation and filtering than BMC PATROL. SPIs also have more resource granularity, enabling you to choose the database objects to monitor. For example, you don't need to include read-only tablespaces when monitoring tablespace free space.

For the budget-conscious, EMS HA Monitors can provide some resource monitoring of tablespaces. You can get a lot of useful performance data by browsing the database MIBs, if you have the time. The MIB browsing capability may be useful in small database environments. Operators must bring up the MIB Browser and poll for individual database values, instead of responding to problems on an exception basis. This quickly becomes labor-intensive for even medium-sized installations. However, it can be a useful mechanism for getting additional information after a database problem is reported. MIB data can help diagnose the causes of performance problems. For example, you can go to the Informix Private MIB to see the last SQL query executed by a session.

Thus, a variety of ways to obtain database performance information are available. GlancePlus and MeasureWare add the ability to look at transaction-level performance data. The HA cluster products provide the ability to detect and recover from database problems without user intervention. For example, MC/ServiceGuard can restart a database server on another system in the event of a system failure. BMC PATROL and PLATINUM ProVision provide database administration tools in addition to detection capabilities. SMART Plug-Ins provide textual guidance on how to recover from problems, but rely on their integration with database vendor tools, such as OEM, for administrative tasks.

For database security and backup management, the tools are pretty weak. Network General's Database Module can detect attempts to breach security because it monitors all database network traffic. IT/O can detect failed superuser logins at the system level. Informix stores some information about past backups in its Private MIB.

Combinations of these tools may be used. For example, BMC PATROL, SPIs, and EMS can each send events to IT/O. Thus, a BMC PATROL database KM can detect a problem and send a message to IT/O's Message Browser, on which an IT/O administrator can already have enabled an automatic action to be taken.

EMS, BMC PATROL, and SPIs each provide additional solutions for system, disk, and network monitoring. Your choice for database monitoring may depend on the products that are already being used in your environment.

Enterprise Management

Much of this book is focused on tools for monitoring a single UNIX system. You may, however, be responsible for monitoring tens or hundreds of systems. Also, it is likely that you are managing a heterogeneous environment in which it is important to monitor heterogeneous systems consistently. For example, a company may have decided to migrate from UNIX to NT, but does not want to replace their UNIX applications, such as SAP. The company may choose to keep a portion of the application (e.g., the database server) on UNIX, while moving the application servers to NT. Using consistent tools for monitoring different platforms can make your job easier. Standards such as SNMP are especially important for this type of environment.

This chapter focuses on some of the issues that arise if you are managing multiple systems. This includes issues with monitoring systems across an enterprise. A section on using event correlation tools discusses how you can reduce the volume of messages that can be generated in an enterprise environment. We'll look at some issues with monitoring multiple systems, including clusters. There may also be cross-platform monitoring issues for systems in a heterogeneous environment. And finally, since no single tool will solve all of your monitoring needs, we'll look at some of the tools that can be used together for this purpose.

Monitoring Across an Enterprise

There are problems with trying to manage a large number of systems. Typically, an IT department will be responsible for managing multiple systems, most likely on multiple platforms. Big companies have a large number of systems that need to be managed.

Keeping track of multiple systems on multiple platforms can be a complex task. Some companies want to implement a lights-out environment, in which operators are not required at every computing location in the enterprise. Other companies require the availability of systems 24 hours a day, 7 days a week. Most companies also have a disaster recovery plan to protect their critical data and application resources. These are some of the issues you must deal with when managing an enterprise of computer systems and applications.

Several solutions are available to aid in enterprise management. For example, HP Open-View IT/Operations (IT/O) is one product designed to help with enterprise management. It provides an Event Browser and a topology map with different icons to represent all of the various systems in an environment. IT/O uses different icons on the map to represent different platforms. For example, there are distinctive icons used to identify NT systems and HP-UX systems.

Using a standard like SNMP from IT/O, you can receive events and poll heterogeneous systems in the enterprise using a common interface. IT/O allows you to distribute monitoring and message templates to multiple systems. It is scalable, so you can easily add additional systems to be managed. To aid in event management, you can integrate one of several event correlation tools to coordinate and reduce the number of messages coming in from systems in the enterprise. IT/O also supports a sophisticated architecture in which events can be forwarded, with annotations, to another IT/O management station.

For disaster recovery, many companies have sophisticated procedures in place and practice disaster recovery annually. One thing to consider is a backup plan for the enterprise management platform itself. Many of the enterprise management frameworks discussed in this book have been certified to run in an MC/ServiceGuard environment, meaning the whole enterprise management framework can start up on an alternate node in the event of a system failure.

When managing multiple systems in an enterprise, using common tools and standards can greatly reduce the number of tools you need to learn. Using a centralized console reduces the number of places you need to look to check for problems. Enterprise monitoring frameworks are important for reducing the complexity of monitoring systems in the enterprise.

Identifying Events

If you have configured your enterprise so that all of the events are sent to a centralized event browser, you may need a way to distinguish events from each other. Event browsers typically include the event source in the message of an event. Many enterprise management frameworks provide some kind of grouping mechanism to group events together.

In IT/O, for example, has message groups. When events are received into IT/O by an agent or at a management station, message groups are assigned based on matching conditions defined in the templates. Message group names are shown along with the event in the Message Browser. Additionally, you can view the Message Group window, which shows the status of each message group. The color of the message group icon represents the status of the worst severity event in that category.

IT/O uses five different colors to represent event severity. Here is a list of the colors and their meaning.

- **Green:** Normal/Up
- **Cyan (Light Blue):** Warning/Marginal
- **Yellow:** Minor warning
- **Orange:** Major warning
- **Red:** Critical/Down

Figure 9-1 shows message groups configured into IT/O. In this example, OpenView SMART Plug-Ins have added a whole set of database message groups, including groups for configuration events, faults, and performance.

Using Event Correlation Tools

As a company's enterprise grows to include more systems and devices, the company probably also wants to reduce the number of staff people needed to manage the enterprise. The sheer volume of events can be overwhelming.

To avoid floods of information in an environment with multiple managed nodes, some type of event correlation is needed. For example, in a clustered environment, each node may notice the failure of a shared disk device. Without intelligent event filtering, the management station may receive a critical event from each cluster node. Event correlation tools provide event reduction and consolidation, exclude unnecessary and meaningless information, and identify root causes.

In addition to the notification flexibility provided by IT/O, EMS, and other tools, you need additional control over the messages received. A network printer failure provides a good example. Although you may like to know when a network printer fails, if the event is detected and reported by all users of the printer it could inundate the Message Browser. Similarly, if the same event is reported multiple times, you may miss a more critical event. Filtering could make man-

Figure 9-1   Using IT/O Message Groups to categorize events.

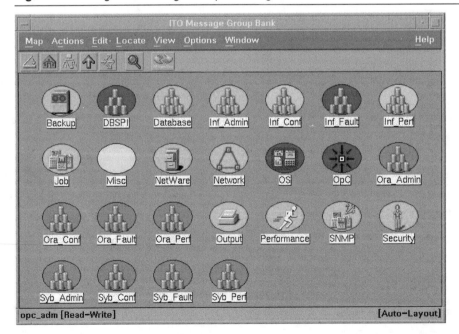

agement of these types of scenarios much easier. Correlation tools can also be used to help resolve problems. For example, a network printer may be down to some of the users, but not all. The tools can be used to pinpoint the problem.

We have selected a few event correlation tools to discuss in this section. Many other event correlation products are available. Here is a list of some that are not discussed:

- NetCool/OMNIbus from Micromuse provides event correlation capabilities. The Netcool/Reporter can generate reports based on events interesting to a particular user.
- Tivoli Enterprise Console, part of Tivoli TME, can be configured to do simple event correlation.
- COMMAND/POST, from Boole & Babbage Inc., does event correlation. It works with Tivoli TME, BMC PATROL, and OpenView.
- InCharge, from System Management Arts (SMARTS), does event correlation. It is pre-configured with information about common network problems. InCharge is integrated with Tivoli TME.

OpenView Event Correlation Services

HP OpenView provides the Event Correlation Services (ECS) tool that integrates with Open-View NNM and IT/O. ECS can be used to reduce and consolidate events. It can also be used to suppress and reduce event storms. This tool can be configured to filter out unnecessary information and help you identify the root cause of a problem. Using ECS, you only need to be notified of critical events. ECS is capable of receiving events as SNMP traps, CMIP notifications, opcmsg messages, and ASCII events. It can be used to manage networks, systems, databases, and applications and is extensible, so new events/sources are easy to add.

The OpenView ECS product has two major components: the ECS Designer and the ECS Engine. The ECS Engine is a runtime correlation engine. It is the real-time component that acts against defined correlation rules. The ECS Designer is a graphical utility used to simplify developing and designing correlation rules. It also provides simulation capabilities to test rules before deploying them.

A *correlation circuit* in ECS is a collection of nodes that are configured to perform correlation and filtering. ECS can correlate events independent of the order in which they were received. You can also configure ECS to suppress repeated events using a time-based filter.

With the ECS integration in IT/O, correlation of events can be done from multiple devices locally by the agent or centrally at the management server. This not only reduces network traffic, but also allows for the root cause to be determined faster and closer to the source, providing more efficient problem resolution.

Correlation templates are easy to distribute to managed nodes. They are distributed the same way as other IT/O templates. Automatic and operator-initiated actions can also be configured and executed locally, even when the management server is down.

ECS also integrates with NNM. ECS can discover the network topology from NNM and can use it for correlation. It also comes with some out-of-the-box correlation circuits for network event correlation.

Seagate NerveCenter

Seagate NerveCenter provides network event correlation and behavior management for UNIX and NT systems. It uses rules-based filtering and advanced correlation to pinpoint root causes and help you manage the volume of critical network issues and events in the enterprise. Nerve-Center can also be configured to perform automated corrective actions.

NerveCenter has three main components: NCServer, AdminTool, and NC Client. The NCServer maintains a database of events. It detects events, distributes information to clients, and communicates with the network management platform. The AdminTool is used for maintaining and configuring NerveCenter domains.

NerveCenter comes with a graphical alarm interface. It provides a display to show the health of the environment at a glance. There is an Alarm and Traffic Summary window that shows existing alarms and their severity.

Rules are also user-configurable via a drag-and-drop GUI. The user can specify particular events and define corrective actions.

Behavior models are used to define the relationships between critical conditions and specific corrective actions. NerveCenter comes with several predefined models for monitoring network traffic, performance, status, security, and error conditions.

There are many different types of automatic actions available to configure for specific events. The following is a list of automatic actions available from NerveCenter:

- Send a notification to a management station or another NCServer.
- Execute a UNIX or NT command or Perl script.
- Log data to a file or database.
- Send a page or e-mail.
- Send an SNMP trap.
- Perform an SNMP set.

NerveCenter correlates across network devices, UNIX systems, and NT systems. Correlation can be done at a central management station or using a distributed management model. In the distributed model, each NCServer is responsible for managing different domains.

NerveCenter correlates events through SNMP polling and listening for SNMP traps. It can be configured to monitor specific MIB variables. New MIBs can easily be added, so NerveCenter can be configured to poll additional MIB objects.

NerveCenter integrates in most network management platforms, including OpenView NNM and ITO, IBM NetView for AIX, Tivoli TME, and Unicenter TNG. It can also be run standalone. With IT/O integration, NerveCenter can forward messages to IT/O, and IT/O can forward messages to NerveCenter.

IT Masters MasterCell

IT Masters provides an event correlation tool called MasterCell. It provides event management capabilities for mission-critical applications in a distributed environment.

MasterCell uses a distributed architecture, which employs agents and a central server. The agents perform limited filtering and can perform actions as well as forward events to the server. Using intelligent agents, MasterCell can eliminate bottlenecks by adding more cells to distribute the load. Also, using this multi-tiered structure puts intelligence as close to the source as possible. Events can be analyzed through intermediate queries and then selectively propagated. This architecture also eliminates an SPOF of the event management environment.

MasterCell has four main components: the event processors/cells, an event browser, the Knowledge Base Editor, and adapters. Adapters, which run on the managed nodes, feed events into the cells. The cells collect and analyze the events. The event browser and Knowledge Base Editor, which connect to one or more cells, are written in Java, so you can run them from anywhere.

Cells are the event processors in the MasterCell environment. These lightweight correlation engines are distributed across the enterprise. They collect and analyze events, then respond, store, propagate, or group events according to defined rules and actions. You can have networks of cells called domains. Cells can be grouped by geographical, functional, or organizational boundaries. Operators can be assigned to specific cell domains. Local actions can be performed on the workstation where a cell is installed.

The MasterCell event browser can be used to browse events from one or more cells. Cells group events into collectors. Grouped events are shown as icons in the browser with color-coded indicators. You can drill down to view the events for each collector. Figure 9-2 shows an example of the collectors and their status indicators defined under demo1. You can also interactively trigger corrective actions from the browser.

The Knowledge Base Editor, or KB Editor, is used to define classes and event instances. It is also used to define configuration rules. A wizard is available to walk you through the steps. You can

Figure 9-2   Using the MasterCell event browser to view the status of collectors.

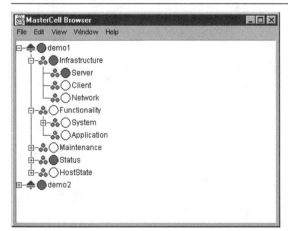

edit the knowledge base(s) offline, then distribute them to the cells. Figure 9-3 shows some instances of application events, such as APP_DOWN, which have been defined using the KB Editor.

Several new features have been added in the 2.0 release of MasterCell to dynamically maintain up-to-date configurations across cells and browsers in the enterprise. Configuration changes in the knowledge bases are maintained on a configuration server and are automatically distributed to the cells. When invoking the browser, configuration data from the server is retrieved automatically.

The *adapters* feed events into cells. Adapters, which run on monitored systems, are background processes responsible for detecting events, translating the events into BAROC, and notifying MasterCell. MasterCell understands events using the BAROC language. This language is also understood at the Tivoli Enterprise Console. The adapters convert events into BAROC and send the events to the cell. MasterCell comes with adapters for SNMP, the NT event log, and generic text logs such as syslog. Events will be buffered if the adapter is unable to propagate them to the cell.

The MasterCell rules engine goes through nine distinct processing steps for each event collected by a cell. It refines an event by gathering more information about the event or executing a command to qualify the event before the event is processed. It filters events, deciding whether an event should be dropped or passed on based on knowledge base rules. It regulates events by holding repetitive occurrences of events until a threshold based on time is met. It updates existing events in response to new events. It does abstraction, which creates higher-level events by combining low-level events. It also correlates an event with others to establish cause-and-

Figure 9-3   Using the MasterCell KB Editor to define events and rules.

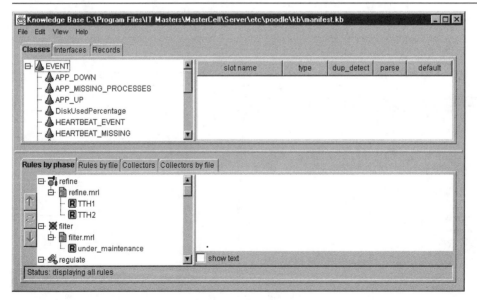

effect relationships. The execute phase is where operators are notified and corrective actions based on rules are performed. The timer phase schedules actions based on time factors in the rules. It also propagates, forwarding events to other cells.

MasterCell also has a performance throttling feature to control the rate at which events are processed. This feature can be used to control the impact of event storms on server resources.

MasterCell runs on Solaris, AIX, HP-UX, and Windows NT. In addition, it integrates with Tivoli's TME Enterprise Console, BMC PATROL, and Remedy AR System.

Monitoring Multiple Systems

If you have a set of systems that needs to be managed in similar ways, being able to perform operations on groups of systems, rather than individual systems, can cut down on your having to do repeated tasks. Several tools allow you to cluster or group systems together, which can help you to apply management policies or monitor configurations in a single operation.

IT/O

IT/O managed nodes can be grouped into *node groups*. When configuring monitoring for IT/O managed nodes, you can assign templates to an entire node group. Then, when you update the managed nodes, templates are distributed to all of the systems that are defined in the node group. This makes it easier to configure multiple systems in a consistent way and there is less room for error. If you assign templates to node groups, however, it becomes difficult to customize monitoring for each system. Customization requires separate templates that get applied individually to each node as needed.

ClusterView

Some companies group critical systems together into a high availability configuration referred to as a *cluster*. ClusterView has special monitoring capabilities for HP-UX and Windows NT high availability clusters. It can report on the overall status of a cluster. In some cases, a cluster is considered to be available when at least one system in the cluster is up.

ClusterView also allows you to define management clusters as a group of HP-UX systems. Then, from IT/O, you can apply management operations, such as applying templates or graphing metrics in PerfView, on a group of systems in a single step.

In a single-system environment, you know where your application is running. When running applications in an MC/ServiceGuard environment, you may not always know where your applications are running. ClusterView shows where your applications are running or where they last attempted to run and their status.

Enterprise Management Frameworks

The enterprise management frameworks are designed for centralized operations with monitoring of multiple systems. Agents are typically deployed on multiple systems. Most frameworks provide a developer's kit, which allows you to extend the agent's monitoring capabilities so that you can provide monitoring in a consistent interface provided by the framework.

Many of the enterprise management frameworks provide platform-specific agents to monitor systems across a heterogeneous environment. They provide a centralized event browser at the management station. This way, operations can be run in a consistent fashion.

IT/O can monitor HP-UX, IBM AIX, Sun Solaris, Windows NT, as well as other platforms. CA Unicenter TNG and Tivoli TME also provide agents that can be managed from a centralized console for many different platforms.

ClusterView

ClusterView can monitor HA clusters on HP-UX and NT systems. It provides a consistent interface for receiving events and getting information about HA clusters regardless of whether they are on NT or HP-UX systems. This is useful for administrators, because they do not have to learn a separate tool for each platform.

Monitoring Agents

BMC PATROL agents and MeasureWare agents can run on many platforms. Data collected by these agents can then be analyzed using common tools in a common and consistent way. Each provides agents on most UNIX platforms, as well as on NT. Both products provide developer's kits to extend the functionality and metrics that can be monitored and tracked.

Using Multiple Tools

Vendors realize that no single product can provide a total solution that fits every need of an enterprise. And because you probably won't find one tool or enterprise management platform that fits all of your fault management needs, several vendors provide integration tools. This features provides you with more flexibility in selecting the tools that best fit your monitoring needs. This means that you can select best-in-class monitoring tools and manage them from your enterprise management framework platform of choice.

Many of the monitoring tools integrate with enterprise management frameworks, such as IT/O, Unicenter TNG, and Tivoli TME. This section covers a few of the integration tools, but not all of them.

There are many other combinations of integration tools. For example, Oracle's OEM product is integrated with IT/O such that each tool can be launched from the other. IT/O can launch OEM in context. Also, OpenView SMART Plug-Ins work with MeasureWare, PerfView, and IT/O.

IT/Operations and the Network Node Manager

OpenView IT/O includes the Network Node Manager (NNM). NNM can be used separately, however, integration provides all of the NNM capabilities from within the IT/O environment, and also includes more system and problem management capabilities.

IT/O provides more managed node capabilities, while NNM provides mostly monitoring capabilities through standards such as SNMP. With IT/O agents, you can do more than just monitor managed nodes. You can manage them, too. With IT/O, you can set up more sophisticated message conditions and configure automatic or operator-initiated actions to run on the managed nodes. IT/O also provides more flexibility to add additional monitoring to your managed nodes.

In both NNM and IT/O, colored icons on the graphical map are used to reflect node status. In NNM, node status is usually determined by the network status of the system, including the status of the network interface cards. In IT/O, node status is determined not only by the network status of the system, but also by the IT/O alarm status for that node.

IT/O and PerfView

PerfView can be integrated into the IT/O Application Bank. With this integration, you can easily select a managed node, then use PerfView to graph metrics collected on the selected node. Additionally, templates can be configured so that if you receive a PerfView alarm condition in the IT/O Message Browser, you can run an operator-initiated action that will invoke PerfView to create a graph showing metrics related to the alarm condition.

If you have the MeasureWare Agent installed on an IT/O managed node, it will detect the IT/O agent running and automatically start sending alarms to it.

BMC PATROL and IT/O

PATROL does not require a special management console. Instead, its server-based PATROL agents can send monitoring information via SNMP traps to management platforms such as HP OpenView NNM and IT/O, CA UniCenter TNG, and Tivoli TME. This level of integration requires an additional product called PATROLVIEW, and there are special versions for OpenView, Cabletron SPECTRUM, Remedy AR, Sun's Solstice Domain Manager, and Tivoli TME. The PATROL product can be integrated with Unicenter TNG through a special product called PatroLink.

You need to install PATROLVIEW on the IT/O management station. This process installs and sets up message groups, message templates, node groups, threshold monitors, and application icons.

One of the unique things about PATROL's integration with IT/O is that PATROL agents from many systems, not just IT/O managed nodes, can send events to IT/O. PATROLVIEW includes a PATROL Event Translator server, the PET server, which translates PATROL events in IT/O events. The PATROL agents send events to the PET server on the IT/O managed node. The PET server processes and forwards the events to the IT/O agent.

The PET server runs on one or more IT/O managed nodes. It receives and processes events from one or more PATROL agents, then forwards the data to the IT/O agent that processes the events and forwards them, if necessary, to the IT/O console. You can also install the PET server on more than one managed node. This is useful if one of your PET servers goes down. If you have only one PET server configured and it goes down, you will lose the connection to all of the PATROL agents that send events to the PET server and on to IT/O.

If you want access to the PATROL console or agent configuration utilities from your IT/O management station, these tools must be installed there as well.

PLATINUM ProVision and IT/O

PLATINUM provides the ProVision Adapter for HP OpenView. This provides you with a single point of integration to ProVision. The adapter automatically enables all ProVision tools from within the IT/O environment. The adapter comes with IT/O templates and monitors that get configured into IT/O at installation time.

Using the PLATINUM IT/O Event Adapter, ProVision tools send events through the POEMS event manager to the IT/O agent at the IT/O managed node.

PLATINUM also provides an MIB that can be used by any SNMP-ready management framework to receive events as SNMP traps from ProVision tools. The MIB can be loaded into NNM, IT/O, or AIX NetView, for example.

PLATINUM ProVision is also tightly integrated with Tivoli TME. PLATINUM has integrated their products into TME to provide a common interface to the PLATINUM products from the TME environment.

EMS and OpenView NNM or IT/O

EMS provides templates for receiving events into OpenView NNM and IT/O. With EMS, you can configure events to be sent as SNMP traps. If the system where you are configuring EMS monitors is an IT/O managed node, you can configure an event to be sent as an opcmsg. In addition to configuring EMS notification targets, you also need to configure your management station to receive, recognize, and display events.

For NNM, you need to load the EMS-specific trap configuration file. You also need to make sure the management station is listed as a trap destination on the monitored system.

For IT/O, you need to configure the templates into IT/O. Templates include message conditions, automatic actions to gather additional event data, and instructions about each event. Once configured at the management station, EMS templates need to be assigned and distributed to managed nodes.

Also available for IT/O is an Application Bank utility called monvols. With monvols, you can configure monitoring of all logical or physical disk volumes on an HP-UX managed node in a single operation. Event notifications are sent to the IT/O Message Browser.

OpenView NNM and IT/O templates for receiving EMS events are freely available, along with the EMS Developer's Kit and other tools at the Hewlett-Packard software Web site at http://www.software.hp.com, under High Availability. monvols is also available at this Web site.

UNIX Futures

System vendors will be making various fault management improvements over the next few years. Systems themselves are becoming more resilient. More monitors are being written to detect events, and system vendors are providing facilities to make troubleshooting and recovering from problems easier. This chapter describes some of the capabilities being added by the two key UNIX server providers, Sun and Hewlett-Packard.

Future Trends in Fault Management

More recovery and repair capabilities are being built into servers. Server providers are making efforts to reduce the failure rates of individual hardware components. Currently, on many servers, the loss of a processor causes the system to fail. In the future, the capability to detect a problem, de-allocate the processor, and continue operations with reduced performance will be standard on multiprocessor systems. The problem will still be reported, so that a repair can be made at a later time. You will also be able to add and remove all the key server components, such as CPU, memory, and I/O, without bringing down the system.

Because systems will no longer fail in these situations, your ability to obtain individual component failure events will become more important than ever. Otherwise, you may have difficulty realizing that something has gone wrong—until it's too late.

Sun and Hewlett-Packard both have high availability cluster products that are continuing to be enhanced. High availability products provide automatic recovery from some problems and give you more time to repair the original faults. Today, with its Mission Critical Server Suites, HP provides a 99.95-percent uptime guarantee. This equates to less than five hours of downtime each year. By the end of 2000, HP intends to provide a 99.999-percent uptime guarantee, as part of its 5 nines: 5 minutes High Availability (HA) program. HP plans to accomplish this goal by partnering with key application providers and by improving the detection and recovery of the HP-UX operating system. The application, database, and network will also be included in the HA guarantee.

You can find more information on HP's intentions for HA on its Web site at http://www.hp .com/go/ha.

Both Sun and HP realize the importance of having complete system fault instrumentation. Sun is adding new monitoring agents to send events to SyMON, and HP is adding more EMS monitors. Both Sun and HP provide developer's kits to make it easier for third parties to add monitoring components. As system instrumentation becomes more extensive, vendors will extend their monitoring capabilities into application software, such as databases and Enterprise Resource Planning (ERP) applications.

System vendors are realizing that they need to provide monitors for more than just failure events. For a complete fault management solution, system operators need improved monitors to detect the following:

• Configuration changes
• Additional security intrusion conditions
• Thresholds being exceeded for system resource usage

Using thresholds is important, to detect trends and to provide more time to react before real problems occur. Both Sun and HP are planning more predictive capabilities.

Today, a variety of notification methods are available to report events to a management station. New methods will need to be added to support emerging standards, such as the Desktop Management Interface (DMI).

Troubleshooting will become easier, because the increased granularity of events will make locating the root cause of problems easier. However, without corresponding improvements in event filtering and correlation capabilities, the increasing number of events is still likely to overwhelm system operators. Correlation will become more common, so operators will have to see only those events for which they must take some action.

More extensive help information will be included with events in the future. Currently, operators are given event messages without many suggestions on how to react. HP is looking to provide additional ways to correct problems.

Both Sun and HP want to provide more autonomous recovery capabilities on managed systems. Sun refers to these capabilities as "intelligent, autonomous agents"; HP refers to them as "self-healing systems." Regardless of the name, the concept is essentially the same: The local agents will try to take the appropriate recovery action without involving the system operator. Actions may be based on policies that are predefined by the system administrator.

Online capabilities (mentioned earlier in the chapter) will lead to faster recovery times. A system operator will not have to wait for the next planned downtime period to make repairs to the server. The operator will also be able to increase capacity more frequently.

Resource management and fault management will become more tightly integrated over the next few years. Both Sun and HP are reviewing ways to integrate their resource management tools with their event management facilities. Sun plans to integrate its Resource Manager with the

SyMON product. Sun can already dynamically reconfigure a protection domain and reallocate system resources in response to performance-related events. HP has announced plans to integrate its Process Resource Manager with event management, enabling the Process Resource Manager to meet service-level objectives by reallocating resources in response to system bottlenecks.

These are just some of the new capabilities that will be coming in the next few years. Fault management is considered strategic by many vendors, and is viewed as one important way to differentiate product offerings.

Standards

Using SNMP and MIBs

Simple Network Management Protocol (SNMP) is a standard protocol used for communication between a system being managed and a management application. SNMP, introduced in the 1980s, is now the de facto standard for the communication of management information. Although initially SNMP was used only to manage network components, such as routers, bridges, and hubs, it is now used for systems, software applications, and middleware products as well.

SNMP *subagents* are the processes responsible for the management of different system components. SNMP communication from a management station is forwarded to the appropriate subagent by a *master agent* process on the system being managed. SNMP communication is sent over the User Datagram Protocol (UDP). The master agent listens for requests on a well-known UDP port (161), decodes the requests, and forwards them to the appropriate subagent. Each subagent registers with the master agent at startup and indicates the requests that should be forwarded to it. The master agent also sends traps on behalf of a subagent. Figure A-1 shows all SNMP traffic going through the master agent, to or from the subagents on the system. On HP-UX, the master agent is provided through EMANATE technology, licensed from SNMP Research International, Inc. More information about EMANATE can be found at http://www.snmp.com.

SNMP subagents represent the management information that they supply in the form of a hierarchical structure called a *Management Information Base (MIB)*. Figure A-2 shows how the individual MIBs, MIB-II and RDBMS MIB, fit into the overall MIB hierarchy. MIB Browsers are often included with enterprise management frameworks, such as HP OpenView Network Node Manager. These graphical tools can allow operators to navigate the MIB tree structure, to look for specific management information. In addition to showing the MIB Object Identifier (OID), the MIB Browser typically also shows the value of the MIB object. The MIB Browser uses SNMP requests to query the subagent for the MIB values on the managed system.

Names, as well as numeric values, are assigned with each component of the MIB OIDs. For example, the MIB-II is a standard MIB for system information with a root OID of

Figure A-1 SNMP architecture.

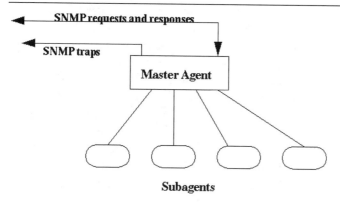

1.3.6.1.2.1. This corresponds to the mnemonic OID iso.org.dod.internet.mgmt.mib_2. Note that although some SNMP tools expect an OID to be preceded by a dot ("."), it is omitted from this appendix, for readability.

SNMP Research International provides an EMANATE Subagent Development Kit (SADK) to allow additional subagents to be written. Another way to configure new SNMP objects to be monitored is through the HP OpenView Extensible SNMP Agent product. The

Figure A-2 MIB hierarchy.

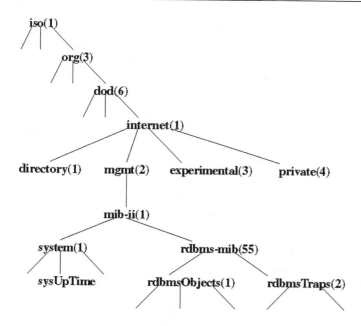

agent can be extended through configuration files that describe new managed objects and actions to be taken. The MIB value can be the output from a command, or the contents of a user-specified file. The Extensible SNMP Agent can generate user-defined SNMP traps based on configured conditions. When it is used with HP OpenView Network Node Manager (NNM) or IT/Operations (IT/O), automated actions can also be taken when the trap is received.

MIBs often originate as Internet draft documents. These draft specifications can be created by anyone, but before becoming standards, they are reviewed by the Internet Engineering Task Force (IETF). After review, these documents are published as Requests For Comments (RFCs). RFC specifications can be found on the Web at http://www.ietf.org, along with other IETF documents.

In addition to the standard MIBs, many vendors provide unique MIBs for their own hardware or software products. Hewlett-Packard, for example, provides an MIB for its MC/Service-Guard product. Oracle provides its own proprietary MIB specifications under the private branch. These private documents are subject only to the reviews appropriate to the issuing organization.

A management application can receive the MIB information by making an SNMP Get request, which can be a blocking or nonblocking call. The reply from the subagent includes the OID, variable type, and value. SNMP also supports SNMP Set requests, but this capability often isn't implemented by the subagents.

In addition to responding to SNMP requests for information, a subagent can initiate notification of an event through the SNMP trap mechanism. SNMP *traps* are an important tool for integrating with other management frameworks, because a process is typically provided on the management station that listens for these traps. Subagents can forward key event information to different management applications by using this one mechanism.

SNMP trap configuration information is stored in the configuration file /etc/SnmpAgent.d /snmpd.conf, which is where you specify SNMP community names. If configured, the SNMP agent allows only those requests with the specified community name. You can specify a different community name configuration for SNMP Set and Get requests. The destination addresses where traps should be sent are also specified in this configuration file. You should be sure to list the IP address of your management station.

The Event Monitoring Service (EMS) uses SNMP traps as one method of forwarding resource events to target applications. EMS has a MIB defined, which includes the various traps that can be sent. The enterprise OID for EMS traps is 1.3.6.1.4.1.11.2.3.1.7. Using the SNMP trap notification provided by EMS, monitors can generate events via SNMP traps to multiple applications and platforms without having to make SNMP function calls directly

Like most enterprise management platforms, Hewlett-Packard's OpenView IT/O and NNM provide event handlers that listen for SNMP traps and can display events, log events, and generate automatic actions when they are received. Templates are provided to define the handling of specific SNMP traps. The templates define the event message to be displayed, the severity of the event, the name of the system sending the event, the message group or category for the event, and the automatic or operator-initiated action for the event. New trap definitions can easily be added to a template so that the event will be recognized and properly formatted.

Each trap is identified by its OID as well as generic and specific trap numbers. The trap includes the address of the agent sending the event and a list of variables. Using the template, the event handler assigns the event to a category and then assigns the severity configured in the template. The message is formatted based on the format string in the template. The variables contained in the trap message can be used in the formatted event message that is displayed in the Message Browser.

Management platforms, such as OpenView NNM, provide several tools for accessing the MIB information. An MIB Browser is useful for exploring MIBs and querying for the MIB values. Figure A-3 shows the result of querying for the operational status of the LAN interface cards from the MIB-II.

NNM not only provides a simple MIB Browser, it also provides a Data Collector tool that collects the MIB data for historical trending and problem monitoring. You can define thresholds to generate an event when specified thresholds are exceeded. The NNM Application Builder MIB tool enables you to quickly develop an application to monitor the MIB variables. The

Figure A-3   The NNM MIB Browser.

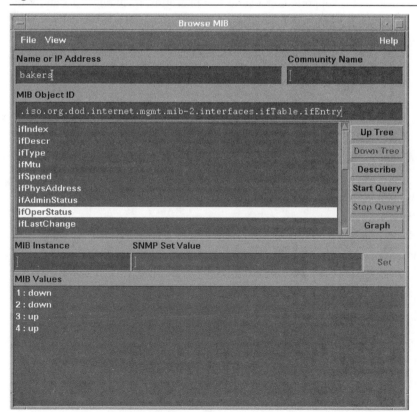

Application Builder enables you to report the MIB data in the form of a table, form, or graph. IT/O also includes the MIB *monitor templates*, which enable you to set up monitoring for any MIB variable. Monitor templates provide tight integration with the IT/O Message Browser and provide the ability to specify automatic actions based on events.

A summary of SNMP and the latest revisions to SNMP version 2 can be found in Marshall T. Rose's *The Simple Book: An Introduction to Internet Management* (Prentice Hall, 1994). More information about SNMP can also be found in RFCs 1441 and 1442, available on the Web at http://www.ietf.org.

The following sections describe some important MIB specifications that take advantage of the SNMP standard. These documents include information about your system, peripherals, and database, as well as other software applications. This information can be invaluable in providing the appropriate level of monitoring for your Unix system. Note that in the following the MIB specifications, an asterisk (*) suffix indicates that the variable serves as an index for a table entry.

MIB-II

The MIB-II is often referred to as the *System MIB*. It is a standard repository for information about a computer system that is supported on a variety of platforms, including Unix and Windows NT. The MIB-II contains information about a computer system, such as its name, system contact, and the length of time it has been running. It also contains statistics from the key networking protocols, such as TCP, UDP, and IP. Statistics include packet transmission counts and error counts.

MIB Definition

Listing A-1 shows the complete definition for the MIB-II, as defined in RFCs 1213 and 1214.

Listing A-1   MIB-II specification.

```
mgmt
|   [1 ] mib_2
|   |   [1 ] system
|   |   |   [1 ] sysDescr
|   |   |   [2 ] sysObjectID
|   |   |   [3 ] sysUpTime
|   |   |   [4 ] sysContact
|   |   |   [5 ] sysName
|   |   |   [6 ] sysLocation
|   |   |   [7 ] sysServices
|   |   [2 ] interfaces
|   |   |   [1 ] ifNumber
|   |   |   [2 ] ifTable
|   |   |   |   [1 ] ifEntry
|   |   |   |   |   [1 ] ifIndex*
|   |   |   |   |   [2 ] ifDescr
```

```
|   |   |   |   |   | [3 ] ifType
|   |   |   |   |   | [4 ] ifMtu
|   |   |   |   |   | [5 ] ifSpeed
|   |   |   |   |   | [6 ] ifPhysAddress
|   |   |   |   |   | [7 ] ifAdminStatus
|   |   |   |   |   | [8 ] ifOperStatus
|   |   |   |   |   | [9 ] ifLastChange
|   |   |   |   |   | [10] ifInOctets
|   |   |   |   |   | [11] ifInUcastPkts
|   |   |   |   |   | [12] ifInNUcastPkts
|   |   |   |   |   | [13] ifInDiscards
|   |   |   |   |   | [14] ifInErrors
|   |   |   |   |   | [15] ifInUnknownProtos
|   |   |   |   |   | [16] ifOutOctets
|   |   |   |   |   | [17] ifOutUcastPkts
|   |   |   |   |   | [18] ifOutNUcastPkts
|   |   |   |   |   | [19] ifOutDiscards
|   |   |   |   |   | [20] ifOutErrors
|   |   |   |   |   | [21] ifOutQLen
|   |   |   |   |   | [22] ifSpecific
|   |   [3 ] at
|   |   |   [1 ] atTable
|   |   |   |   [1 ] atEntry
|   |   |   |   |   [1 ] atIfIndex*
|   |   |   |   |   [2 ] atPhysAddress
|   |   |   |   |   [3 ] atNetAddress*
|   |   [4 ] ip
|   |   |   [1 ] ipForwarding
|   |   |   [2 ] ipDefaultTTL
|   |   |   [3 ] ipInReceives
|   |   |   [4 ] ipInHdrErrors
|   |   |   [5 ] ipInAddrErrors
|   |   |   [6 ] ipForwDatagrams
|   |   |   [7 ] ipInUnknownProtos
|   |   |   [8 ] ipInDiscards
|   |   |   [9 ] ipInDelivers
|   |   |   [10] ipOutRequests
|   |   |   [11] ipOutDiscards
|   |   |   [12] ipOutNoRoutes
|   |   |   [13] ipReasmTimeout
|   |   |   [14] ipReasmReqds
|   |   |   [15] ipReasmOKs
|   |   |   [16] ipReasmFails
|   |   |   [17] ipFragOKs
|   |   |   [18] ipFragFails
|   |   |   [19] ipFragCreates
```

Continued

Listing A-1   Continued

```
|   |   |   [20] ipAddrTable
|   |   |   |   [1 ] ipAddrEntry
|   |   |   |   |   [1 ] ipAdEntAddr*
|   |   |   |   |   [2 ] ipAdEntIfIndex
|   |   |   |   |   [3 ] ipAdEntNetMask
|   |   |   |   |   [4 ] ipAdEntBcastAddr
|   |   |   |   |   [5 ] ipAdEntReasmMaxSize
|   |   |   [21] ipRouteTable
|   |   |   |   [1 ] ipRouteEntry
|   |   |   |   |   [1 ] ipRouteDest*
|   |   |   |   |   [2 ] ipRouteIfIndex
|   |   |   |   |   [3 ] ipRouteMetric1
|   |   |   |   |   [4 ] ipRouteMetric2
|   |   |   |   |   [5 ] ipRouteMetric3
|   |   |   |   |   [6 ] ipRouteMetric4
|   |   |   |   |   [7 ] ipRouteNextHop
|   |   |   |   |   [8 ] ipRouteType
|   |   |   |   |   [9 ] ipRouteProto
|   |   |   |   |   [10] ipRouteAge
|   |   |   |   |   [11] ipRouteMask
|   |   |   |   |   [12] ipRouteMetric5
|   |   |   |   |   [13] ipRouteInfo
|   |   |   [22] ipNetToMediaTable
|   |   |   |   [1 ] ipNetToMediaEntry
|   |   |   |   |   [1 ] ipNetToMediaIfIndex*
|   |   |   |   |   [2 ] ipNetToMediaPhysAddress
|   |   |   |   |   [3 ] ipNetToMediaNetAddress*
|   |   |   |   |   [4 ] ipNetToMediaType
|   |   |   [23] ipRoutingDiscards
|   |   [5 ] icmp
|   |   |   [1 ] icmpInMsgs
|   |   |   [2 ] icmpInErrors
|   |   |   [3 ] icmpInDestUnreachs
|   |   |   [4 ] icmpInTimeExcds
|   |   |   [5 ] icmpInParmProbs
|   |   |   [6 ] icmpInSrcQuenchs
|   |   |   [7 ] icmpInRedirects
|   |   |   [8 ] icmpInEchos
|   |   |   [9 ] icmpInEchoReps
|   |   |   [10] icmpInTimestamps
|   |   |   [11] icmpInTimestampReps
|   |   |   [12] icmpInAddrMasks
|   |   |   [13] icmpInAddrMaskReps
|   |   |   [14] icmpOutMsgs
|   |   |   [15] icmpOutErrors
```

```
|   |   |   [16]  icmpOutDestUnreachs
|   |   |   [17]  icmpOutTimeExcds
|   |   |   [18]  icmpOutParmProbs
|   |   |   [19]  icmpOutSrcQuenchs
|   |   |   [20]  icmpOutRedirects
|   |   |   [21]  icmpOutEchos
|   |   |   [22]  icmpOutEchoReps
|   |   |   [23]  icmpOutTimestamps
|   |   |   [24]  icmpOutTimestampReps
|   |   |   [25]  icmpOutAddrMasks
|   |   |   [26]  icmpOutAddrMaskReps
|   |   [6 ] tcp
|   |   |   [1 ] tcpRtoAlgorithm
|   |   |   [2 ] tcpRtoMin
|   |   |   [3 ] tcpRtoMax
|   |   |   [4 ] tcpMaxConn
|   |   |   [5 ] tcpActiveOpens
|   |   |   [6 ] tcpPassiveOpens
|   |   |   [7 ] tcpAttemptFails
|   |   |   [8 ] tcpEstabResets
|   |   |   [9 ] tcpCurrEstab
|   |   |   [10] tcpInSegs
|   |   |   [11] tcpOutSegs
|   |   |   [12] tcpRetransSegs
|   |   |   [13] tcpConnTable
|   |   |   |   [1 ] tcpConnEntry
|   |   |   |   |   [1 ] tcpConnState
|   |   |   |   |   [2 ] tcpConnLocalAddress*
|   |   |   |   |   [3 ] tcpConnLocalPort*
|   |   |   |   |   [4 ] tcpConnRemAddress
|   |   |   |   |   [5 ] tcpConnRemPort
|   |   |   [14] tcpInErrs
|   |   |   [15] tcpOutRsts
|   |   [7 ] udp
|   |   |   [1 ] udpInDatagrams
|   |   |   [2 ] udpNoPorts
|   |   |   [3 ] udpInErrors
|   |   |   [4 ] udpOutDatagrams
|   |   |   [5 ] udpTable
|   |   |   |   [1 ] udpEntry
|   |   |   |   |   [1 ] udpLocalAddress*
|   |   |   |   |   [2 ] udpLocalPort*
|   |   [8 ] egp
|   |   |   [1 ] egpInMsgs
|   |   |   [2 ] egpInErrors
|   |   |   [3 ] egpOutMsgs
```

Continued

Listing A-1   Continued

```
|   |   |   [4 ] egpOutErrors
|   |   |   [5 ] egpNeighTable
|   |   |   |   [1 ] egpNeighEntry
|   |   |   |   |   [1 ] egpNeighState
|   |   |   |   |   [2 ] egpNeighAddr*
|   |   |   |   |   [3 ] egpNeighAs
|   |   |   |   |   [4 ] egpNeighInMsgs
|   |   |   |   |   [5 ] egpNeighInErrs
|   |   |   |   |   [6 ] egpNeighOutMsgs
|   |   |   |   |   [7 ] egpNeighOutErrs
|   |   |   |   |   [8 ] egpNeighInErrMsgs
|   |   |   |   |   [9 ] egpNeighOutErrMsgs
|   |   |   |   |   [10] egpNeighStateUps
|   |   |   |   |   [11] egpNeighStateDowns
|   |   |   |   |   [12] egpNeighIntervalHello
|   |   |   |   |   [13] egpNeighIntervalPoll
|   |   |   |   |   [14] egpNeighMode
|   |   |   |   |   [15] egpNeighEventTrigger
|   |   |   [6 ] egpAs
|   |   [10] transmission
|   |   [11] snmp
|   |   |   [1 ] snmpInPkts
|   |   |   [2 ] snmpOutPkts
|   |   |   [3 ] snmpInBadVersions
|   |   |   [4 ] snmpInBadCommunityNames
|   |   |   [5 ] snmpInBadCommunityUses
|   |   |   [6 ] snmpInASNParseErrs
|   |   |   [8 ] snmpInTooBigs
|   |   |   [9 ] snmpInNoSuchNames
|   |   |   [10] snmpInBadValues
|   |   |   [11] snmpInReadOnlys
|   |   |   [12] snmpInGenErrs
|   |   |   [13] snmpInTotalReqVars
|   |   |   [14] snmpInTotalSetVars
|   |   |   [15] snmpInGetRequests
|   |   |   [16] snmpInGetNexts
|   |   |   [17] snmpInSetRequests
|   |   |   [18] snmpInGetResponses
|   |   |   [19] snmpInTraps
|   |   |   [20] snmpOutTooBigs
|   |   |   [21] snmpOutNoSuchNames
|   |   |   [22] snmpOutBadValues
|   |   |   [24] snmpOutGenErrs
|   |   |   [25] snmpOutGetRequests
|   |   |   [26] snmpOutGetNexts
```

```
|   |   |   [27]  snmpOutSetRequests
|   |   |   [28]  snmpOutGetResponses
|   |   |   [29]  snmpOutTraps
|   |   |   [30]  snmpEnableAuthenTraps
```

Monitoring Notes

When navigating the MIB hierarchy using a tool such as the HP OpenView MIB Browser, you see the mnemonic names for the MIB variables. The mnemonic for the MIB-II is iso.org.dod.internet.mgmt.mib-2. However, if you intend to write your own SNMP application, you need to know the numeric root OID of the MIB-II, which is 1.3.6.1.2.1. An operator can query this information and correlate it to track error rates.

This MIB contains some fault information. For example, Hewlett-Packard's EMS HA Monitors product uses this MIB to monitor the status of each network interface.

The MIB-II also contains network performance information, including the amount of data sent and received per protocol. However, data is not correlated or converted to rates. Consequently, to get an accurate picture of your network performance, you must collect this data over a period of time and then note the changes yourself.

RMON MIB

The RMON MIB is meant to provide a standard method for collecting network performance data. Monitors, or *probes*, are placed on specific LAN segments and then collect data on those segments. Network packet statistics and a history of network performance can be stored in the MIB. RMON also provides lists of the top network users, such as the systems that are sending the most packets with errors.

MIB Definition

Listing A-2 shows the complete RMON specification, as defined in RFC 1757.

Listing A-2 RMON MIB specification.

```
mib_2
|   [16]  rmon
|   |   [1 ]  statistics
|   |   |   [1 ]  etherStatsTable
|   |   |   |   [1 ]  etherStatsEntry
|   |   |   |   |   [1 ]  etherStatsIndex*
|   |   |   |   |   [2 ]  etherStatsDataSource
|   |   |   |   |   [3 ]  etherStatsDropEvents
|   |   |   |   |   [4 ]  etherStatsOctets
|   |   |   |   |   [5 ]  etherStatsPkts
```

Continued

Listing A-2 Continued

```
|  |  |  |  |  [6 ] etherStatsBroadcastPkts
|  |  |  |  |  [7 ] etherStatsMulticastPkts
|  |  |  |  |  [8 ] etherStatsCRCAlignErrors
|  |  |  |  |  [9 ] etherStatsUndersizePkts
|  |  |  |  |  [10] etherStatsOversizePkts
|  |  |  |  |  [11] etherStatsFragments
|  |  |  |  |  [12] etherStatsJabbers
|  |  |  |  |  [13] etherStatsCollisions
|  |  |  |  |  [14] etherStatsPkts64Octets
|  |  |  |  |  [15] etherStatsPkts65to127Octets
|  |  |  |  |  [16] etherStatsPkts128to255Octets
|  |  |  |  |  [17] etherStatsPkts256to511Octets
|  |  |  |  |  [18] etherStatsPkts512to1023Octets
|  |  |  |  |  [19] etherStatsPkts1024to1518Octets
|  |  |  |  |  [20] etherStatsOwner
|  |  |  |  |  [21] etherStatsStatus
|  |  [2 ] history
|  |  |  [1 ] historyControlTable
|  |  |  |  [1 ] historyControlEntry
|  |  |  |  |  [1 ] historyControlIndex*
|  |  |  |  |  [2 ] historyControlDataSource
|  |  |  |  |  [3 ] historyControlBucketsRequested
|  |  |  |  |  [4 ] historyControlBucketsGranted
|  |  |  |  |  [5 ] historyControlInterval
|  |  |  |  |  [6 ] historyControlOwner
|  |  |  |  |  [7 ] historyControlStatus
|  |  |  [2 ] etherHistoryTable
|  |  |  |  [1 ] etherHistoryEntry
|  |  |  |  |  [1 ] etherHistoryIndex*
|  |  |  |  |  [2 ] etherHistorySampleIndex*
|  |  |  |  |  [3 ] etherHistoryIntervalStart
|  |  |  |  |  [4 ] etherHistoryDropEvents
|  |  |  |  |  [5 ] etherHistoryOctets
|  |  |  |  |  [6 ] etherHistoryPkts
|  |  |  |  |  [7 ] etherHistoryBroadcastPkts
|  |  |  |  |  [8 ] etherHistoryMulticastPkts
|  |  |  |  |  [9 ] etherHistoryCRCAlignErrors
|  |  |  |  |  [10] etherHistoryUndersizePkts
|  |  |  |  |  [11] etherHistoryOversizePkts
|  |  |  |  |  [12] etherHistoryFragments
|  |  |  |  |  [13] etherHistoryJabbers
|  |  |  |  |  [14] etherHistoryCollisions
|  |  |  |  |  [15] etherHistoryUtilization
|  |  [3 ] alarm
|  |  |  [1 ] alarmTable
```

```
| | | | [1 ] alarmEntry
| | | | | [1 ] alarmIndex*
| | | | | [2 ] alarmInterval
| | | | | [3 ] alarmVariable
| | | | | [4 ] alarmSampleType
| | | | | [5 ] alarmValue
| | | | | [6 ] alarmStartupAlarm
| | | | | [7 ] alarmRisingThreshold
| | | | | [8 ] alarmFallingThreshold
| | | | | [9 ] alarmRisingEventIndex
| | | | | [10] alarmFallingEventIndex
| | | | | [11] alarmOwner
| | | | | [12] alarmStatus
| | [4 ] hosts
| | | [1 ] hostControlTable
| | | | [1 ] hostControlEntry
| | | | | [1 ] hostControlIndex*
| | | | | [2 ] hostControlDataSource
| | | | | [3 ] hostControlTableSize
| | | | | [4 ] hostControlLastDeleteTime
| | | | | [5 ] hostControlOwner
| | | | | [6 ] hostControlStatus
| | | [2 ] hostTable
| | | | [1 ] hostEntry
| | | | | [1 ] hostAddress*
| | | | | [2 ] hostCreationOrder
| | | | | [3 ] hostIndex*
| | | | | [4 ] hostInPkts
| | | | | [5 ] hostOutPkts
| | | | | [6 ] hostInOctets
| | | | | [7 ] hostOutOctets
| | | | | [8 ] hostOutErrors
| | | | | [9 ] hostOutBroadcastPkts
| | | | | [10] hostOutMulticastPkts
| | | [3 ] hostTimeTable
| | | | [1 ] hostTimeEntry
| | | | | [1 ] hostTimeAddress
| | | | | [2 ] hostTimeCreationOrder*
| | | | | [3 ] hostTimeIndex*
| | | | | [4 ] hostTimeInPkts
| | | | | [5 ] hostTimeOutPkts
| | | | | [6 ] hostTimeInOctets
| | | | | [7 ] hostTimeOutOctets
| | | | | [8 ] hostTimeOutErrors
| | | | | [9 ] hostTimeOutBroadcastPkts
| | | | | [10] hostTimeOutMulticastPkts
```

Continued

Listing A-2   Continued

```
|   |   [5 ] hostTopN
|   |   |   [1 ] hostTopNControlTable
|   |   |   |   [1 ] hostTopNControlEntry
|   |   |   |   |   [1 ] hostTopNControlIndex*
|   |   |   |   |   [2 ] hostTopNHostIndex
|   |   |   |   |   [3 ] hostTopNRateBase
|   |   |   |   |   [4 ] hostTopNTimeRemaining
|   |   |   |   |   [5 ] hostTopNDuration
|   |   |   |   |   [6 ] hostTopNRequestedSize
|   |   |   |   |   [7 ] hostTopNGrantedSize
|   |   |   |   |   [8 ] hostTopNStartTime
|   |   |   |   |   [9 ] hostTopNOwner
|   |   |   |   |   [10] hostTopNStatus
|   |   |   [2 ] hostTopNTable
|   |   |   |   [1 ] hostTopNEntry
|   |   |   |   |   [1 ] hostTopNReport*
|   |   |   |   |   [2 ] hostTopNIndex*
|   |   |   |   |   [3 ] hostTopNAddress
|   |   |   |   |   [4 ] hostTopNRate
|   |   [6 ] matrix
|   |   |   [1 ] matrixControlTable
|   |   |   |   [1 ] matrixControlEntry
|   |   |   |   |   [1 ] matrixControlIndex*
|   |   |   |   |   [2 ] matrixControlDataSource
|   |   |   |   |   [3 ] matrixControlTableSize
|   |   |   |   |   [4 ] matrixControlLastDeleteTime
|   |   |   |   |   [5 ] matrixControlOwner
|   |   |   |   |   [6 ] matrixControlStatus
|   |   |   [2 ] matrixSDTable
|   |   |   |   [1 ] matrixSDEntry
|   |   |   |   |   [1 ] matrixSDSourceAddress*
|   |   |   |   |   [2 ] matrixSDDestAddress
|   |   |   |   |   [3 ] matrixSDIndex*
|   |   |   |   |   [4 ] matrixSDPkts
|   |   |   |   |   [5 ] matrixSDOctets
|   |   |   |   |   [6 ] matrixSDErrors
|   |   |   [3 ] matrixDSTable
|   |   |   |   [1 ] matrixDSEntry
|   |   |   |   |   [1 ] matrixDSSourceAddress
|   |   |   |   |   [2 ] matrixDSDestAddress*
|   |   |   |   |   [3 ] matrixDSIndex*
|   |   |   |   |   [4 ] matrixDSPkts
|   |   |   |   |   [5 ] matrixDSOctets
|   |   |   |   |   [6 ] matrixDSErrors
|   |   [7 ] filter
```

```
|   |   |   [1 ] filterTable
|   |   |   |   [1 ] filterEntry
|   |   |   |   |   [1 ] filterIndex*
|   |   |   |   |   [2 ] filterChannelIndex
|   |   |   |   |   [3 ] filterPktDataOffset
|   |   |   |   |   [4 ] filterPktData
|   |   |   |   |   [5 ] filterPktDataMask
|   |   |   |   |   [6 ] filterPktDataNotMask
|   |   |   |   |   [7 ] filterPktStatus
|   |   |   |   |   [8 ] filterPktStatusMask
|   |   |   |   |   [9 ] filterPktStatusNotMask
|   |   |   |   |   [10] filterOwner
|   |   |   |   |   [11] filterStatus
|   |   |   [2 ] channelTable
|   |   |   |   [1 ] channelEntry
|   |   |   |   |   [1 ] channelIndex*
|   |   |   |   |   [2 ] channelIfIndex
|   |   |   |   |   [3 ] channelAcceptType
|   |   |   |   |   [4 ] channelDataControl
|   |   |   |   |   [5 ] channelTurnOnEventIndex
|   |   |   |   |   [6 ] channelTurnOffEventIndex
|   |   |   |   |   [7 ] channelEventIndex
|   |   |   |   |   [8 ] channelEventStatus
|   |   |   |   |   [9 ] channelMatches
|   |   |   |   |   [10] channelDescription
|   |   |   |   |   [11] channelOwner
|   |   |   |   |   [12] channelStatus
|   |   [8 ] capture
|   |   |   [1 ] bufferControlTable
|   |   |   |   [1 ] bufferControlEntry
|   |   |   |   |   [1 ] bufferControlIndex*
|   |   |   |   |   [2 ] bufferControlChannelIndex
|   |   |   |   |   [3 ] bufferControlFullStatus
|   |   |   |   |   [4 ] bufferControlFullAction
|   |   |   |   |   [5 ] bufferControlCaptureSliceSize
|   |   |   |   |   [6 ] bufferControlDownloadSliceSize
|   |   |   |   |   [7 ] bufferControlDownloadOffset
|   |   |   |   |   [8 ] bufferControlMaxOctetsRequested
|   |   |   |   |   [9 ] bufferControlMaxOctetsGranted
|   |   |   |   |   [10] bufferControlCapturedPackets
|   |   |   |   |   [11] bufferControlTurnOnTime
|   |   |   |   |   [12] bufferControlOwner
|   |   |   |   |   [13] bufferControlStatus
|   |   |   [2 ] captureBufferTable
|   |   |   |   [1 ] captureBufferEntry
|   |   |   |   |   [1 ] captureBufferControlIndex*
```

Continued

Listing A-2   Continued

```
|   |   |   |   |   | [2 ] captureBufferIndex*
|   |   |   |   |   | [3 ] captureBufferPacketID
|   |   |   |   |   | [4 ] captureBufferPacketData
|   |   |   |   |   | [5 ] captureBufferPacketLength
|   |   |   |   |   | [6 ] captureBufferPacketTime
|   |   |   |   |   | [7 ] captureBufferPacketStatus
|   | [9 ] event
|   |   | [1 ] eventTable
|   |   |   | [1 ] eventEntry
|   |   |   |   | [1 ] eventIndex*
|   |   |   |   | [2 ] eventDescription
|   |   |   |   | [3 ] eventType
|   |   |   |   | [4 ] eventCommunity
|   |   |   |   | [5 ] eventLastTimeSent
|   |   |   |   | [6 ] eventOwner
|   |   |   |   | [7 ] eventStatus
|   |   | [2 ] logTable
|   |   |   | [1 ] logEntry
|   |   |   |   | [1 ] logEventIndex*
|   |   |   |   | [2 ] logIndex*
|   |   |   |   | [3 ] logTime
|   |   |   |   | [4 ] logDescription
```

Monitoring Notes

If you intend to write your own SNMP application, the numeric root OID of the RMON MIB is 1.3.6.1.2.1.16.

The RMON MIB is divided into the following sections: statistics, history, alarm, hosts, hostsTopN, matrix, filter, capture, and event.

The statistics section provides information regarding the amount of data being sent on a particular Ethernet interface, including the number of broadcasts, errors, and collisions. You can also see the distribution of packets of different sizes.

The history group enables you to sample statistics at a specified polling interval and sum them over time.

The alarm and event groups are used to report when configured thresholds are crossed. Statistics are periodically checked to see whether a threshold has been crossed. After an event is sent, no additional events are sent until the opposite threshold has been crossed.

RMON probes can discover new systems, or *hosts*, by watching the source and destination station addresses in packets passing on a LAN segment. The hosts group stores each address seen on the interface. A variety of important statistics are kept about each system, such as the number of packets sent and received, error packets sent, and broadcasts sent. This can be invaluable information for catching a misbehaving system that is dominating the network bandwidth on a LAN segment.

The hostsTopN group keeps track of the top systems on a segment for a specific statistic, such as the number of packets received, error packets sent, or broadcast packets sent. The number of systems in the list is configurable.

The matrix group can be used to determine traffic problems. Statistics are kept on the network conversations between two addresses. Information collected includes the number of packets sent in either direction and the number of error packets.

The filter and capture groups work together to capture packets sent on a segment. A management station can then download the packets.

Note that this MIB also supports two traps that can be sent when an alarm entry either rises above or falls below a threshold.

RMON II MIB

RMON II extends the RMON specification to include additional network performance information for the transport-, session-, presentation-, and application-layer protocols. These network layers are defined in Chapter 6.

MIB Definition

Listing A-3 shows the complete specification for RMON II, as defined in RFC 2021.

Listing A-3 RMON II MIB specification.

```
mib_2
|  [16] rmon
|  |  [11] protocolDir
|  |  |  [1 ] protocolDirLastChange
|  |  |  [2 ] protocolDirTable
|  |  |  |  [1 ] protocolDirEntry
|  |  |  |  |  [1 ] protocolDirID*
|  |  |  |  |  [2 ] protocolDirParameters*
|  |  |  |  |  [3 ] protocolDirLocalIndex*
|  |  |  |  |  [4 ] protocolDirDescr
|  |  |  |  |  [5 ] protocolDirType
|  |  |  |  |  [6 ] protocolDirAddressMapConfig
|  |  |  |  |  [7 ] protocolDirHostConfig
|  |  |  |  |  [8 ] protocolDirMatrixConfig
|  |  |  |  |  [9 ] protocolDirOwner
|  |  |  |  |  [10] protocolDirStatus
|  |  [12] protocolDist
|  |  |  [1 ] protocolDistControlTable
|  |  |  |  [1 ] protocolDistControlEntry
|  |  |  |  |  [1 ] protocolDistControlIndex*
|  |  |  |  |  [2 ] protocolDistControlDataSource
|  |  |  |  |  [3 ] protocolDistControlDroppedFrames
```

Continued

Listing A-3   Continued

```
|   |   |   |   | [4 ] protocolDistControlCreateTime
|   |   |   |   | [5 ] protocolDistControlOwner
|   |   |   |   | [6 ] protocolDistControlStatus
|   |   | [2 ] protocolDistStatsTable
|   |   |   | [1 ] protocolDistStatsEntry
|   |   |   |   | [1 ] protocolDistStatsPkts
|   |   |   |   | [2 ] protocolDistStatsOctets
|   | [13] addressMap
|   |   | [1 ] addressMapInserts
|   |   | [2 ] addressMapDeletes
|   |   | [3 ] addressMapMaxDesiredEntries
|   |   | [4 ] addressMapControlTable
|   |   |   | [1 ] addressMapControlEntry
|   |   |   |   | [1 ] addressMapControlIndex*
|   |   |   |   | [2 ] addressMapControlDataSource
|   |   |   |   | [3 ] addressMapControlDroppedFrames
|   |   |   |   | [4 ] addressMapControlOwner
|   |   |   |   | [5 ] addressMapControlStatus
|   |   | [5 ] addressMapTable
|   |   |   | [1 ] addressMapEntry
|   |   |   |   | [1 ] addressMapTimeMark*
|   |   |   |   | [2 ] addressMapNetworkAddress
|   |   |   |   | [3 ] addressMapSource
|   |   |   |   | [4 ] addressMapPhysicalAddress
|   |   |   |   | [5 ] addressMapLastChange
|   | [14] nlHost
|   |   | [1 ] hlHostControlTable
|   |   |   | [1 ] hlHostControlEntry
|   |   |   |   | [1 ] hlHostControlIndex*
|   |   |   |   | [2 ] hlHostControlDataSource
|   |   |   |   | [3 ] hlHostControlNlDroppedFrames
|   |   |   |   | [4 ] hlHostControlNlInserts
|   |   |   |   | [5 ] hlHostControlNlDeletes
|   |   |   |   | [6 ] hlHostControlNlMaxDesiredEntries
|   |   |   |   | [7 ] hlHostControlAlDroppedFrames
|   |   |   |   | [8 ] hlHostControlAlInserts
|   |   |   |   | [9 ] hlHostControlAlDeletes
|   |   |   |   | [10] hlHostControlAlMaxDesiredEntries
|   |   |   |   | [11] hlHostControlOwner
|   |   |   |   | [12] hlHostControlStatus
|   |   | [2 ] nlHostTable
|   |   |   | [1 ] nlHostEntry
|   |   |   |   | [1 ] nlHostTimeMark*
|   |   |   |   | [2 ] nlHostAddress
|   |   |   |   | [3 ] nlHostInPkts
```

```
|   |   |   |   |   | [4 ]  nlHostOutPkts
|   |   |   |   |   | [5 ]  nlHostInOctets
|   |   |   |   |   | [6 ]  nlHostOutOctets
|   |   |   |   |   | [7 ]  nlHostOutMacNonUnicastPkts
|   |   |   |   |   | [8 ]  nlHostCreateTime
|   |   [15] nlMatrix
|   |   |   [1 ]  hlMatrixControlTable
|   |   |   |   [1 ]  hlMatrixControlEntry
|   |   |   |   |   [1 ]  hlMatrixControlIndex*
|   |   |   |   |   [2 ]  hlMatrixControlDataSource
|   |   |   |   |   [3 ]  hlMatrixControlNlDroppedFrames
|   |   |   |   |   [4 ]  hlMatrixControlNlInserts
|   |   |   |   |   [5 ]  hlMatrixControlNlDeletes
|   |   |   |   |   [6 ]  hlMatrixControlNlMaxDesiredEntries
|   |   |   |   |   [7 ]  hlMatrixControlAlDroppedFrames
|   |   |   |   |   [8 ]  hlMatrixControlAlInserts
|   |   |   |   |   [9 ]  hlMatrixControlAlDeletes
|   |   |   |   |   [10] hlMatrixControlAlMaxDesiredEntries
|   |   |   |   |   [11] hlMatrixControlOwner
|   |   |   |   |   [12] hlMatrixControlStatus
|   |   |   [2 ]  nlMatrixSDTable
|   |   |   |   [1 ]  nlMatrixSDEntry
|   |   |   |   |   [1 ]  nlMatrixSDTimeMark*
|   |   |   |   |   [2 ]  nlMatrixSDSourceAddress
|   |   |   |   |   [3 ]  nlMatrixSDDestAddress
|   |   |   |   |   [4 ]  nlMatrixSDPkts
|   |   |   |   |   [5 ]  nlMatrixSDOctets
|   |   |   |   |   [6 ]  nlMatrixSDCreateTime
|   |   |   [3 ]  nlMatrixDSTable
|   |   |   |   [1 ]  nlMatrixDSEntry
|   |   |   |   |   [1 ]  nlMatrixDSTimeMark*
|   |   |   |   |   [2 ]  nlMatrixDSSourceAddress
|   |   |   |   |   [3 ]  nlMatrixDSDestAddress
|   |   |   |   |   [4 ]  nlMatrixDSPkts
|   |   |   |   |   [5 ]  nlMatrixDSOctets
|   |   |   |   |   [6 ]  nlMatrixDSCreateTime
|   |   |   [4 ]  nlMatrixTopNControlTable
|   |   |   |   [1 ]  nlMatrixTopNControlEntry
|   |   |   |   |   [1 ]  nlMatrixTopNControlIndex*
|   |   |   |   |   [2 ]  nlMatrixTopNControlMatrixIndex
|   |   |   |   |   [3 ]  nlMatrixTopNControlRateBase
|   |   |   |   |   [4 ]  nlMatrixTopNControlTimeRemaining
|   |   |   |   |   [5 ]  nlMatrixTopNControlGeneratedReports
|   |   |   |   |   [6 ]  nlMatrixTopNControlDuration
|   |   |   |   |   [7 ]  nlMatrixTopNControlRequestedSize
|   |   |   |   |   [8 ]  nlMatrixTopNControlGrantedSize
```

Continued

Listing A-3   Continued

```
|  |  |  |  |  | [9 ] nlMatrixTopNControlStartTime
|  |  |  |  |  | [10] nlMatrixTopNControlOwner
|  |  |  |  |  | [11] nlMatrixTopNControlStatus
|  |  |  | [5 ] nlMatrixTopNTable
|  |  |  |  | [1 ] nlMatrixTopNEntry
|  |  |  |  |  | [1 ] nlMatrixTopNIndex*
|  |  |  |  |  | [2 ] nlMatrixTopNProtocolDirLocalIndex
|  |  |  |  |  | [3 ] nlMatrixTopNSourceAddress
|  |  |  |  |  | [4 ] nlMatrixTopNDestAddress
|  |  |  |  |  | [5 ] nlMatrixTopNPktRate
|  |  |  |  |  | [6 ] nlMatrixTopNReversePktRate
|  |  |  |  |  | [7 ] nlMatrixTopNOctetRate
|  |  |  |  |  | [8 ] nlMatrixTopNReverseOctetRate
|  | [16] alHost
|  |  | [1 ] alHostTable
|  |  |  | [1 ] alHostEntry
|  |  |  |  | [1 ] alHostTimeMark*
|  |  |  |  | [2 ] alHostInPkts
|  |  |  |  | [3 ] alHostOutPkts
|  |  |  |  | [4 ] alHostInOctets
|  |  |  |  | [5 ] alHostOutOctets
|  |  |  |  | [6 ] alHostCreateTime
|  | [17] alMatrix
|  |  | [1 ] alMatrixSDTable
|  |  |  | [1 ] alMatrixSDEntry
|  |  |  |  | [1 ] alMatrixSDTimeMark*
|  |  |  |  | [2 ] alMatrixSDPkts
|  |  |  |  | [3 ] alMatrixSDOctets
|  |  |  |  | [4 ] alMatrixSDCreateTime
|  |  | [2 ] alMatrixDSTable
|  |  |  | [1 ] alMatrixDSEntry
|  |  |  |  | [1 ] alMatrixDSTimeMark*
|  |  |  |  | [2 ] alMatrixDSPkts
|  |  |  |  | [3 ] alMatrixDSOctets
|  |  |  |  | [4 ] alMatrixDSCreateTime
|  |  | [3 ] alMatrixTopNControlTable
|  |  |  | [1 ] alMatrixTopNControlEntry
|  |  |  |  | [1 ] alMatrixTopNControlIndex*
|  |  |  |  | [2 ] alMatrixTopNControlMatrixIndex
|  |  |  |  | [3 ] alMatrixTopNControlRateBase
|  |  |  |  | [4 ] alMatrixTopNControlTimeRemaining
|  |  |  |  | [5 ] alMatrixTopNControlGeneratedReports
|  |  |  |  | [6 ] alMatrixTopNControlDuration
|  |  |  |  | [7 ] alMatrixTopNControlRequestedSize
|  |  |  |  | [8 ] alMatrixTopNControlGrantedSize
```

```
|   |   |   |   |   [9 ] alMatrixTopNControlStartTime
|   |   |   |   |   [10] alMatrixTopNControlOwner
|   |   |   |   |   [11] alMatrixTopNControlStatus
|   |   |   [4 ] alMatrixTopNTable
|   |   |   |   [1 ] alMatrixTopNEntry
|   |   |   |   |   [1 ] alMatrixTopNIndex*
|   |   |   |   |   [2 ] alMatrixTopNProtocolDirLocalIndex
|   |   |   |   |   [3 ] alMatrixTopNSourceAddress
|   |   |   |   |   [4 ] alMatrixTopNDestAddress
|   |   |   |   |   [5 ] alMatrixTopNAppProtocolDirLocalIndex
|   |   |   |   |   [6 ] alMatrixTopNPktRate
|   |   |   |   |   [7 ] alMatrixTopNReversePktRate
|   |   |   |   |   [8 ] alMatrixTopNOctetRate
|   |   |   |   |   [9 ] alMatrixTopNReverseOctetRate
|   |   [18] usrHistory
|   |   |   [1 ] usrHistoryControlTable
|   |   |   |   [1 ] usrHistoryControlEntry
|   |   |   |   |   [1 ] usrHistoryControlIndex*
|   |   |   |   |   [2 ] usrHistoryControlObjects
|   |   |   |   |   [3 ] usrHistoryControlBucketsRequested
|   |   |   |   |   [4 ] usrHistoryControlBucketsGranted
|   |   |   |   |   [5 ] usrHistoryControlInterval
|   |   |   |   |   [6 ] usrHistoryControlOwner
|   |   |   |   |   [7 ] usrHistoryControlStatus
|   |   |   [2 ] usrHistoryObjectTable
|   |   |   |   [1 ] usrHistoryObjectEntry
|   |   |   |   |   [1 ] usrHistoryObjectIndex*
|   |   |   |   |   [2 ] usrHistoryObjectVariable
|   |   |   |   |   [3 ] usrHistoryObjectSampleType
|   |   |   [3 ] usrHistoryTable
|   |   |   |   [1 ] usrHistoryEntry
|   |   |   |   |   [1 ] usrHistorySampleIndex*
|   |   |   |   |   [2 ] usrHistoryIntervalStart
|   |   |   |   |   [3 ] usrHistoryIntervalEnd
|   |   |   |   |   [4 ] usrHistoryAbsValue
|   |   |   |   |   [5 ] usrHistoryValStatus
|   |   [19] probeConfig
|   |   |   [1 ] probeCapabilities
|   |   |   [2 ] probeSoftwareRev
|   |   |   [3 ] probeHardwareRev
|   |   |   [4 ] probeDateTime
|   |   |   [5 ] probeResetControl
|   |   |   [6 ] probeDownloadFile
|   |   |   [7 ] probeDownloadTFTPServer
|   |   |   [8 ] probeDownloadAction
|   |   |   [9 ] probeDownloadStatus
```

Continued

Listing A-3   Continued

```
|   |   |   [10] serialConfigTable
|   |   |     [1 ] serialConfigEntry
|   |   |   |   |   [1 ] serialMode
|   |   |   |   |   [2 ] serialProtocol
|   |   |   |   |   [3 ] serialTimeout
|   |   |   |   |   [4 ] serialModemInitString
|   |   |   |   |   [5 ] serialModemHangUpString
|   |   |   |   |   [6 ] serialModemConnectResp
|   |   |   |   |   [7 ] serialModemNoConnectResp
|   |   |   |   |   [8 ] serialDialoutTimeout
|   |   |   |   |   [9 ] serialStatus
|   |   |   [11] netConfigTable
|   |   |   |   [1 ] netConfigEntry
|   |   |   |   |   [1 ] netConfigIPAddress
|   |   |   |   |   [2 ] netConfigSubnetMask
|   |   |   |   |   [3 ] netConfigStatus
|   |   |   [12] netDefaultGateway
|   |   |   [13] trapDestTable
|   |   |   |   [1 ] trapDestEntry
|   |   |   |   |   [1 ] trapDestIndex*
|   |   |   |   |   [2 ] trapDestCommunity
|   |   |   |   |   [3 ] trapDestProtocol
|   |   |   |   |   [4 ] trapDestAddress
|   |   |   |   |   [5 ] trapDestOwner
|   |   |   |   |   [6 ] trapDestStatus
|   |   |   [14] serialConnectionTable
|   |   |   |   [1 ] serialConnectionEntry
|   |   |   |   |   [1 ] serialConnectIndex*
|   |   |   |   |   [2 ] serialConnectDestIpAddress
|   |   |   |   |   [3 ] serialConnectType
|   |   |   |   |   [4 ] serialConnectDialString
|   |   |   |   |   [5 ] serialConnectSwitchConnectSeq
|   |   |   |   |   [6 ] serialConnectSwitchDisconnectSeq
|   |   |   |   |   [7 ] serialConnectSwitchResetSeq
|   |   |   |   |   [8 ] serialConnectOwner
|   |   |   |   |   [9 ] serialConnectStatus
|   |   [20] rmonConformance
|   |   |   [1 ] rmon2MIBCompliances
|   |   |   |   [1 ] rmon2MIBCompliance
|   |   |   |   [2 ] rmon2MIBApplicationLayerCompliance
|   |   |   [2 ] rmon2MIBGroups
|   |   |   |   [1 ] protocolDirectoryGroup
|   |   |   |   [2 ] protocolDistributionGroup
|   |   |   |   [3 ] addressMapGroup
|   |   |   |   [4 ] nlHostGroup
|   |   |   |   [5 ] nlMatrixGroup
```

```
|   |   |   |   [6 ]  alHostGroup
|   |   |   |   [7 ]  alMatrixGroup
|   |   |   |   [8 ]  usrHistoryGroup
|   |   |   |   [9 ]  probeInformationGroup
|   |   |   |   [10]  probeConfigurationGroup
|   |   |   |   [11]  rmon1EnhancementGroup
|   |   |   |   [12]  rmon1EthernetEnhancementGroup
|   |   |   |   [13]  rmon1TokenRingEnhancementGroup
```

Monitoring Notes

If you intend to write your own SNMP application, the numeric root OID of the RMON MIB is 1.3.6.1.2.1.16. RMON II is an extension of this MIB.

The protocol directory lists all the protocols that the monitor supports. A monitor can add more protocols, but the extensibility is limited.

The protocol distribution group shows per-protocol statistics for the amount of data and packets being sent on a LAN segment. From this information, you can calculate the bandwidth utilization per protocol and, hopefully, isolate a troublesome application.

The address mappings group is used to map a network address to the station address to which it is bound. The network layer host group then shows the amount of traffic for each network address. The network layer matrix group shows network traffic statistics between pairs of network addresses. You can also see the top traffic producers.

The application layer host shows network traffic statistics for a particular network address, broken down by protocol. Similarly, the application layer matrix shows this information for traffic between a pair of network addresses.

Host Resources MIB

The Host Resources MIB is a proposed IETF standard for representing host information. This MIB requires the implementation of portions of the MIB-II. The Host Resources MIB includes information such as the current and maximum number of processes on a system and the system uptime. This MIB may be used to represent information about a computer system or about a device, such as a network printer.

MIB Definition

Listing A-4 shows the complete specification for the Host Resources MIB, as defined in RFC 1514.

Listing A-4   Host Resources MIB specification.

```
mib_2
|   [25] host
|   |   [1 ] hrSystem
```

Continued

Listing A-4   Continued

```
|   |   |   [1 ] hrSystemUptime
|   |   |   [2 ] hrSystemDate
|   |   |   [3 ] hrSystemInitialLoadDevice
|   |   |   [4 ] hrSystemInitialLoadParameters
|   |   |   [5 ] hrSystemNumUsers
|   |   |   [6 ] hrSystemProcesses
|   |   |   [7 ] hrSystemMaxProcesses
|   |   [2 ] hrStorage
|   |   |   [1 ] hrStorageTypes
|   |   |   |   [1 ] hrStorageOther
|   |   |   |   [2 ] hrStorageRam
|   |   |   |   [3 ] hrStorageVirtualMemory
|   |   |   |   [4 ] hrStorageFixedDisk
|   |   |   |   [5 ] hrStorageRemovableDisk
|   |   |   |   [6 ] hrStorageFloppyDisk
|   |   |   |   [7 ] hrStorageCompactDisc
|   |   |   |   [8 ] hrStorageRamDisk
|   |   |   [2 ] hrMemorySize
|   |   |   [3 ] hrStorageTable
|   |   |   |   [1 ] hrStorageEntry
|   |   |   |   |   [1 ] hrStorageIndex*
|   |   |   |   |   [2 ] hrStorageType
|   |   |   |   |   [3 ] hrStorageDescr
|   |   |   |   |   [4 ] hrStorageAllocationUnits
|   |   |   |   |   [5 ] hrStorageSize
|   |   |   |   |   [6 ] hrStorageUsed
|   |   |   |   |   [7 ] hrStorageAllocationFailures
|   |   [3 ] hrDevice
|   |   |   [1 ] hrDeviceTypes
|   |   |   |   [1 ] hrDeviceOther
|   |   |   |   [2 ] hrDeviceUnknown
|   |   |   |   [3 ] hrDeviceProcessor
|   |   |   |   [4 ] hrDeviceNetwork
|   |   |   |   [5 ] hrDevicePrinter
|   |   |   |   [6 ] hrDeviceDiskStorage
|   |   |   |   [10] hrDeviceVideo
|   |   |   |   [11] hrDeviceAudio
|   |   |   |   [12] hrDeviceCoprocessor
|   |   |   |   [13] hrDeviceKeyboard
|   |   |   |   [14] hrDeviceModem
|   |   |   |   [15] hrDeviceParallelPort
|   |   |   |   [16] hrDevicePointing
|   |   |   |   [17] hrDeviceSerialPort
|   |   |   |   [18] hrDeviceTape
|   |   |   |   [19] hrDeviceClock
```

```
|   |   |   |   [20] hrDeviceVolatileMemory
|   |   |   |   [21] hrDeviceNonVolatileMemory
|   |   |   [9 ] hrFSTypes
|   |   |   |   [1 ] hrFSOther
|   |   |   |   [2 ] hrFSUnknown
|   |   |   |   [3 ] hrFSBerkeleyFFS
|   |   |   |   [4 ] hrFSSys5FS
|   |   |   |   [5 ] hrFSFat
|   |   |   |   [6 ] hrFSHPFS
|   |   |   |   [7 ] hrFSHFS
|   |   |   |   [8 ] hrFSMFS
|   |   |   |   [9 ] hrFSNTFS
|   |   |   |   [10] hrFSVNode
|   |   |   |   [11] hrFSJournaled
|   |   |   |   [12] hrFSiso9660
|   |   |   |   [13] hrFSRockRidge
|   |   |   |   [14] hrFSNFS
|   |   |   |   [15] hrFSNetware
|   |   |   |   [16] hrFSAFS
|   |   |   |   [17] hrFSDFS
|   |   |   |   [18] hrFSAppleshare
|   |   |   |   [19] hrFSRFS
|   |   |   |   [20] hrFSDGCFS
|   |   |   |   [21] hrFSBFS
|   |   |   [2 ] hrDeviceTable
|   |   |   |   [1 ] hrDeviceEntry
|   |   |   |   |   [1 ] hrDeviceIndex*
|   |   |   |   |   [2 ] hrDeviceType
|   |   |   |   |   [3 ] hrDeviceDescr
|   |   |   |   |   [4 ] hrDeviceID
|   |   |   |   |   [5 ] hrDeviceStatus
|   |   |   |   |   [6 ] hrDeviceErrors
|   |   |   [3 ] hrProcessorTable
|   |   |   |   [1 ] hrProcessorEntry
|   |   |   |   |   [1 ] hrProcessorFrwID
|   |   |   |   |   [2 ] hrProcessorLoad
|   |   |   [4 ] hrNetworkTable
|   |   |   |   [1 ] hrNetworkEntry
|   |   |   |   |   [1 ] hrNetworkIfIndex
|   |   |   [5 ] hrPrinterTable
|   |   |   |   [1 ] hrPrinterEntry
|   |   |   |   |   [1 ] hrPrinterStatus
|   |   |   |   |   [2 ] hrPrinterDetectedErrorState
|   |   |   [6 ] hrDiskStorageTable
|   |   |   |   [1 ] hrDiskStorageEntry
|   |   |   |   |   [1 ] hrDiskStorageAccess
```

Continued

Listing A-4 Continued

```
|   |   |   |   |   [2 ] hrDiskStorageMedia
|   |   |   |   |   [3 ] hrDiskStorageRemoveble
|   |   |   |   |   [4 ] hrDiskStorageCapacity
|   |   |   [7 ] hrPartitionTable
|   |   |   |   [1 ] hrPartitionEntry
|   |   |   |   |   [1 ] hrPartitionIndex*
|   |   |   |   |   [2 ] hrPartitionLabel
|   |   |   |   |   [3 ] hrPartitionID
|   |   |   |   |   [4 ] hrPartitionSize
|   |   |   |   |   [5 ] hrPartitionFSIndex
|   |   |   [8 ] hrFSTable
|   |   |   |   [1 ] hrFSEntry
|   |   |   |   |   [1 ] hrFSIndex*
|   |   |   |   |   [2 ] hrFSMountPoint
|   |   |   |   |   [3 ] hrFSRemoteMountPoint
|   |   |   |   |   [4 ] hrFSType
|   |   |   |   |   [5 ] hrFSAccess
|   |   |   |   |   [6 ] hrFSBootable
|   |   |   |   |   [7 ] hrFSStorageIndex
|   |   |   |   |   [8 ] hrFSLastFullBackupDate
|   |   |   |   |   [9 ] hrFSLastPartialBackupDate
|   |   [4 ] hrSWRun
|   |   |   [1 ] hrSWOSIndex
|   |   |   [2 ] hrSWRunTable
|   |   |   |   [1 ] hrSWRunEntry
|   |   |   |   |   [1 ] hrSWRunIndex*
|   |   |   |   |   [2 ] hrSWRunName
|   |   |   |   |   [3 ] hrSWRunID
|   |   |   |   |   [4 ] hrSWRunPath
|   |   |   |   |   [5 ] hrSWRunParameters
|   |   |   |   |   [6 ] hrSWRunType
|   |   |   |   |   [7 ] hrSWRunStatus
|   |   [5 ] hrSWRunPerf
|   |   |   [1 ] hrSWRunPerfTable
|   |   |   |   [1 ] hrSWRunPerfEntry
|   |   |   |   |   [1 ] hrSWRunPerfCPU
|   |   |   |   |   [2 ] hrSWRunPerfMem
|   |   [6 ] hrSWInstalled
|   |   |   [1 ] hrSWInstalledLastChange
|   |   |   [2 ] hrSWInstalledLastUpdateTime
|   |   |   [3 ] hrSWInstalledTable
|   |   |   |   [1 ] hrSWInstalledEntry
|   |   |   |   |   [1 ] hrSWInstalledIndex*
|   |   |   |   |   [2 ] hrSWInstalledName
|   |   |   |   |   [3 ] hrSWInstalledID
|   |   |   |   |   [4 ] hrSWInstalledType
|   |   |   |   |   [5 ] hrSWInstalledDate
```

Monitoring Notes

If you intend to write your own SNMP application, the numeric root OID of the Host Resources MIB is 1.3.6.1.2.1.25.

The valid states for the hrDeviceStatus field in the hrDeviceTable are unknown, running, warning, testing, and down. When used for printers, this status can be combined with printer status fields to determine a more specific status of a printer device, such as active, busy, or unavailable.

Printer MIB

The Printer MIB is the proposed IETF standard for defining a printer's attributes and current status. The MIB focuses on management of the printer itself, not the queuing or scheduling of print jobs. The Printer MIB can report critical alerts such as "Out of Paper". Several printer vendors have already adopted this MIB. For example, Hewlett-Packard uses this MIB to record information about its LaserJet 5Si and many other printer models.

MIB Definition

Listing A-5 shows the complete specification for the Printer MIB, as defined in RFC 1759.

Listing A-5   Printer MIB specification.

```
mib_2
|  [43] printmib
|  |  [5 ] prtGeneral
|  |  |  [1 ] prtGeneralTable
|  |  |  |  [1 ] prtGeneralEntry
|  |  |  |  |  [1 ] prtGeneralConfigChanges
|  |  |  |  |  [2 ] prtGeneralCurrentLocalization
|  |  |  |  |  [3 ] prtGeneralReset
|  |  |  |  |  [4 ] prtGeneralCurrentOperator
|  |  |  |  |  [5 ] prtGeneralServicePerson
|  |  |  |  |  [6 ] prtInputDefaultIndex
|  |  |  |  |  [7 ] prtOutputDefaultIndex
|  |  |  |  |  [8 ] prtMarkerDefaultIndex
|  |  |  |  |  [9 ] prtMediaPathDefaultIndex
|  |  |  |  |  [10] prtConsoleLocalization
|  |  |  |  |  [11] prtConsoleNumberOfDisplayLines
|  |  |  |  |  [12] prtConsoleNumberOfDisplayChars
|  |  |  |  |  [13] prtConsoleDisable
|  |  |  [2 ] prtStorageRefTable
|  |  |  |  [1 ] prtStorageRefEntry
|  |  |  |  |  [1 ] prtStorageRefSeqNumber*
|  |  |  |  |  [2 ] prtStorageRefIndex
|  |  |  [3 ] prtDeviceRefTable
|  |  |  |  [1 ] prtDeviceRefEntry
|  |  |  |  |  [1 ] prtDeviceRefSeqNumber*
```

Continued

Listing A-5   Continued

```
|   |   |   |   |   [2 ] prtDeviceRefIndex
|   |   [6 ] prtCover
|   |   |   [1 ] prtCoverTable
|   |   |   |   [1 ] prtCoverEntry
|   |   |   |   |   [1 ] prtCoverIndex*
|   |   |   |   |   [2 ] prtCoverDescription
|   |   |   |   |   [3 ] prtCoverStatus
|   |   [7 ] prtLocalization
|   |   |   [1 ] prtLocalizationTable
|   |   |   |   [1 ] prtLocalizationEntry
|   |   |   |   |   [1 ] prtLocalizationIndex*
|   |   |   |   |   [2 ] prtLocalizationLanguage
|   |   |   |   |   [3 ] prtLocalizationCountry
|   |   |   |   |   [4 ] prtLocalizationCharacterSet
|   |   [8 ] prtInput
|   |   |   [2 ] prtInputTable
|   |   |   |   [1 ] prtInputEntry
|   |   |   |   |   [1 ] prtInputIndex*
|   |   |   |   |   [2 ] prtInputType
|   |   |   |   |   [3 ] prtInputDimUnit
|   |   |   |   |   [4 ] prtInputMediaDimFeedDirDeclared
|   |   |   |   |   [5 ] prtInputMediaDimXFeedDirDeclared
|   |   |   |   |   [6 ] prtInputMediaDimFeedDirChosen
|   |   |   |   |   [7 ] prtInputMediaDimXFeedDirChosen
|   |   |   |   |   [8 ] prtInputCapacityUnit
|   |   |   |   |   [9 ] prtInputMaxCapacity
|   |   |   |   |   [10] prtInputCurrentLevel
|   |   |   |   |   [11] prtInputStatus
|   |   |   |   |   [12] prtInputMediaName
|   |   |   |   |   [13] prtInputName
|   |   |   |   |   [14] prtInputVendorName
|   |   |   |   |   [15] prtInputModel
|   |   |   |   |   [16] prtInputVersion
|   |   |   |   |   [17] prtInputSerialNumber
|   |   |   |   |   [18] prtInputDescription
|   |   |   |   |   [19] prtInputSecurity
|   |   |   |   |   [20] prtInputMediaWeight
|   |   |   |   |   [21] prtInputMediaType
|   |   |   |   |   [22] prtInputMediaColor
|   |   |   |   |   [23] prtInputMediaFormParts
|   |   [9 ] prtOutput
|   |   |   [2 ] prtOutputTable
|   |   |   |   [1 ] prtOutputEntry
|   |   |   |   |   [1 ] prtOutputIndex*
|   |   |   |   |   [2 ] prtOutputType
```

```
|   |   |   |   |   | [3 ] prtOutputCapacityUnit
|   |   |   |   |   | [4 ] prtOutputMaxCapacity
|   |   |   |   |   | [5 ] prtOutputRemainingCapacity
|   |   |   |   |   | [6 ] prtOutputStatus
|   |   |   |   |   | [7 ] prtOutputName
|   |   |   |   |   | [8 ] prtOutputVendorName
|   |   |   |   |   | [9 ] prtOutputModel
|   |   |   |   |   | [10] prtOutputVersion
|   |   |   |   |   | [11] prtOutputSerialNumber
|   |   |   |   |   | [12] prtOutputDescription
|   |   |   |   |   | [13] prtOutputSecurity
|   |   |   |   |   | [14] prtOutputDimUnit
|   |   |   |   |   | [15] prtOutputMaxDimFeedDir
|   |   |   |   |   | [16] prtOutputMaxDimXFeedDir
|   |   |   |   |   | [17] prtOutputMinDimFeedDir
|   |   |   |   |   | [18] prtOutputMinDimXFeedDir
|   |   |   |   |   | [19] prtOutputStackingOrder
|   |   |   |   |   | [20] prtOutputPageDeliveryOrientation
|   |   |   |   |   | [21] prtOutputBursting
|   |   |   |   |   | [22] prtOutputDecollating
|   |   |   |   |   | [23] prtOutputPageCollated
|   |   |   |   |   | [24] prtOutputOffsetStacking
|   |   [10] prtMarker
|   |   |   [2 ] prtMarkerTable
|   |   |   |   [1 ] prtMarkerEntry
|   |   |   |   |   [1 ] prtMarkerIndex*
|   |   |   |   |   [2 ] prtMarkerMarkTech
|   |   |   |   |   [3 ] prtMarkerCounterUnit
|   |   |   |   |   [4 ] prtMarkerLifeCount
|   |   |   |   |   [5 ] prtMarkerPowerOnCount
|   |   |   |   |   [6 ] prtMarkerProcessColorants
|   |   |   |   |   [7 ] prtMarkerSpotColorants
|   |   |   |   |   [8 ] prtMarkerAddressabilityUnit
|   |   |   |   |   [9 ] prtMarkerAddressabilityFeedDir
|   |   |   |   |   [10] prtMarkerAddressabilityXFeedDir
|   |   |   |   |   [11] prtMarkerNorthMargin
|   |   |   |   |   [12] prtMarkerSouthMargin
|   |   |   |   |   [13] prtMarkerWestMargin
|   |   |   |   |   [14] prtMarkerEastMargin
|   |   |   |   |   [15] prtMarkerStatus
|   |   [11] prtMarkerSupplies
|   |   |   [1 ] prtMarkerSuppliesTable
|   |   |   |   [1 ] prtMarkerSuppliesEntry
|   |   |   |   |   [1 ] prtMarkerSuppliesIndex*
|   |   |   |   |   [2 ] prtMarkerSuppliesMarkerIndex
|   |   |   |   |   [3 ] prtMarkerSuppliesColorantIndex
```

Continued

Listing A-5   Continued

```
|   |   |   |   |   | [4  ] prtMarkerSuppliesClass
|   |   |   |   |   | [5  ] prtMarkerSuppliesType
|   |   |   |   |   | [6  ] prtMarkerSuppliesDescription
|   |   |   |   |   | [7  ] prtMarkerSuppliesSupplyUnit
|   |   |   |   |   | [8  ] prtMarkerSuppliesMaxCapacity
|   |   |   |   |   | [9  ] prtMarkerSuppliesLevel
|   |   [12] prtMarkerColorant
|   |   |   [1  ] prtMarkerColorantTable
|   |   |   |   [1  ] prtMarkerColorantEntry
|   |   |   |   |   | [1  ] prtMarkerColorantIndex*
|   |   |   |   |   | [2  ] prtMarkerColorantMarkerIndex
|   |   |   |   |   | [3  ] prtMarkerColorantRole
|   |   |   |   |   | [4  ] prtMarkerColorantValue
|   |   |   |   |   | [5  ] prtMarkerColorantTonality
|   |   [13] prtMediaPath
|   |   |   [4  ] prtMediaPathTable
|   |   |   |   [1  ] prtMediaPathEntry
|   |   |   |   |   | [1  ] prtMediaPathIndex*
|   |   |   |   |   | [2  ] prtMediaPathMaxSpeedPrintUnit
|   |   |   |   |   | [3  ] prtMediaPathMediaSizeUnit
|   |   |   |   |   | [4  ] prtMediaPathMaxSpeed
|   |   |   |   |   | [5  ] prtMediaPathMaxMediaFeedDir
|   |   |   |   |   | [6  ] prtMediaPathMaxMediaXFeedDir
|   |   |   |   |   | [7  ] prtMediaPathMinMediaFeedDir
|   |   |   |   |   | [8  ] prtMediaPathMinMediaXFeedDir
|   |   |   |   |   | [9  ] prtMediaPathType
|   |   |   |   |   | [10] prtMediaPathDescription
|   |   |   |   |   | [11] prtMediaPathStatus
|   |   [14] prtChannel
|   |   |   [1  ] prtChannelTable
|   |   |   |   [1  ] prtChannelEntry
|   |   |   |   |   | [1  ] prtChannelIndex*
|   |   |   |   |   | [2  ] prtChannelType
|   |   |   |   |   | [3  ] prtChannelProtocolVersion
|   |   |   |   |   | [4  ] prtChannelCurrentJobCntlLangIndex
|   |   |   |   |   | [5  ] prtChannelDefaultPageDescLangIndex
|   |   |   |   |   | [6  ] prtChannelState
|   |   |   |   |   | [7  ] prtChannelIfIndex
|   |   |   |   |   | [8  ] prtChannelStatus
|   |   [15] prtInterpreter
|   |   |   [1  ] prtInterpreterTable
|   |   |   |   [1  ] prtInterpreterEntry
|   |   |   |   |   | [1  ] prtInterpreterIndex*
|   |   |   |   |   | [2  ] prtInterpreterLangFamily
|   |   |   |   |   | [3  ] prtInterpreterLangLevel
```

```
|   |   |   |   |   | [4 ] prtInterpreterLangVersion
|   |   |   |   |   | [5 ] prtInterpreterDescription
|   |   |   |   |   | [6 ] prtInterpreterVersion
|   |   |   |   |   | [7 ] prtInterpreterDefaultOrientation
|   |   |   |   |   | [8 ] prtInterpreterFeedAddressability
|   |   |   |   |   | [9 ] prtInterpreterXFeedAddressability
|   |   |   |   |   | [10] prtInterpreterDefaultCharSetIn
|   |   |   |   |   | [11] prtInterpreterDefaultCharSetOut
|   |   |   |   |   | [12] prtInterpreterTwoWay
|   | [16] prtConsoleDisplayBuffer
|   |   | [5 ] prtConsoleDisplayBufferTable
|   |   |   | [1 ] prtConsoleDisplayBufferEntry
|   |   |   |   | [1 ] prtConsoleDisplayBufferIndex*
|   |   |   |   | [2 ] prtConsoleDisplayBufferText
|   | [17] prtConsoleLights
|   |   | [6 ] prtConsoleLightTable
|   |   |   | [1 ] prtConsoleLightEntry
|   |   |   |   | [1 ] prtConsoleLightIndex*
|   |   |   |   | [2 ] prtConsoleOnTime
|   |   |   |   | [3 ] prtConsoleOffTime
|   |   |   |   | [4 ] prtConsoleColor
|   |   |   |   | [5 ] prtConsoleDescription
|   | [18] prtAlert
|   |   | [2 ] printerV1Alert
|   |   |   | [0 ] printerV2AlertPrefix
|   |   |   |   | [1 ] printerV2Alert
|   |   | [1 ] prtAlertTable
|   |   |   | [1 ] prtAlertEntry
|   |   |   |   | [1 ] prtAlertIndex*
|   |   |   |   | [2 ] prtAlertSeverityLevel
|   |   |   |   | [3 ] prtAlertTrainingLevel
|   |   |   |   | [4 ] prtAlertGroup
|   |   |   |   | [5 ] prtAlertGroupIndex
|   |   |   |   | [6 ] prtAlertLocation
|   |   |   |   | [7 ] prtAlertCode
|   |   |   |   | [8 ] prtAlertDescription
|   |   |   |   | [9 ] prtAlertTime
|   | [2 ] prtMIBConformance
|   |   | [2 ] prtMIBGroups
|   |   |   | [1 ] prtGeneralGroup
|   |   |   | [2 ] prtResponsiblePartyGroup
|   |   |   | [3 ] prtInputGroup
|   |   |   | [4 ] prtExtendedInputGroup
|   |   |   | [5 ] prtInputMediaGroup
|   |   |   | [6 ] prtOutputGroup
|   |   |   | [7 ] prtExtendedOutputGroup
```

Continued

Listing A-5   Continued

```
|   |   |   |   [8 ]  prtOutputDimensionsGroup
|   |   |   |   [9 ]  prtOutputFeaturesGroup
|   |   |   |   [10]  prtMarkerGroup
|   |   |   |   [11]  prtMarkerSuppliesGroup
|   |   |   |   [12]  prtMarkerColorantGroup
|   |   |   |   [13]  prtMediaPathGroup
|   |   |   |   [14]  prtChannelGroup
|   |   |   |   [15]  prtInterpreterGroup
|   |   |   |   [16]  prtConsoleGroup
|   |   |   |   [17]  prtAlertTableGroup
|   |   |   |   [18]  prtAlertTimeGroup
|   |   |   [1 ]  prtMIBCompliance
```

Monitoring Notes

If you intend to write your own SNMP application, the numeric root OID of the Printer MIB is 1.3.6.1.2.1.43.

The Printer MIB requires portions of the MIB-II and the Host Resources MIB to be implemented. Many of the tables in the Printer MIB are indexed by hrDeviceIndex, from the Host Resources MIB.

The hrDeviceStatus field in the hrDeviceTable is combined with the hrPrinterStatus and hrPrinterDetectedErrorState fields in the hrPrinterTable to determine the specific status of a printer device. For example, if the hrPrinterStatus indicates an idle status and the hrDeviceStatus indicates a running status, then the corresponding printer is functioning normally. However, if the hrPrinterStatus is idle and the hrDeviceStatus indicates a warning status, then the printer has a status of noncritical alert active.

The prtAlertTable can record the list of alerts occurring for a printer device. The prtAlertCode indicates the specific printer problem, such as a paper jam, a paper tray missing, or low toner.

The HP-UNIX MIB

The HP-UNIX MIB is a private MIB provided by Hewlett-Packard. It is meant to be an extension to the MIB-II. The HP-UNIX MIB contains important information about the users, jobs, filesystems, memory, and processes of a system. The number of users logged in to the system and the number of jobs running are both indications of how busy the system is. The amount of free swap space or filesystem space can be a warning of potential problems. The process status can be checked to see whether a particular application is still running normally on the target system.

MIB Definition

Listing A-6 shows the complete specification for the HP-UNIX MIB, as defined by Hewlett-Packard.

Listing A-6   HP-UNIX MIB specification.

```
enterprises
|   [11] hp
|   |   [2 ] nm
|   |   |   [3 ] system
|   |   |   |   [1 ] general
|   |   |   |   |   [1 ] computerSystem
|   |   |   |   |   |   [1 ] computerSystemUpTime
|   |   |   |   |   |   [2 ] computerSystemUsers
|   |   |   |   |   |   [3 ] computerSystemAvgJobs1
|   |   |   |   |   |   [4 ] computerSystemAvgJobs5
|   |   |   |   |   |   [5 ] computerSystemAvgJobs15
|   |   |   |   |   |   [6 ] computerSystemMaxProc
|   |   |   |   |   |   [7 ] computerSystemFreeMemory
|   |   |   |   |   |   [8 ] computerSystemPhysMemory
|   |   |   |   |   |   [9 ] computerSystemMaxUserMem
|   |   |   |   |   |   [10] computerSystemSwapConfig
|   |   |   |   |   |   [11] computerSystemEnabledSwap
|   |   |   |   |   |   [12] computerSystemFreeSwap
|   |   |   |   |   |   [13] computerSystemUserCPU
|   |   |   |   |   |   [14] computerSystemSysCPU
|   |   |   |   |   |   [15] computerSystemIdleCPU
|   |   |   |   |   |   [16] computerSystemNiceCPU
|   |   |   |   |   [2 ] fileSystem
|   |   |   |   |   |   [1 ] fileSystemMounted
|   |   |   |   |   |   [2 ] fileSystemTable
|   |   |   |   |   |   |   [1 ] fileSystemEntry
|   |   |   |   |   |   |   |   [1 ] fileSystemID1*
|   |   |   |   |   |   |   |   [2 ] fileSystemID2*
|   |   |   |   |   |   |   |   [3 ] fileSystemName
|   |   |   |   |   |   |   |   [4 ] fileSystemBlock
|   |   |   |   |   |   |   |   [5 ] fileSystemBfree
|   |   |   |   |   |   |   |   [6 ] fileSystemBavail
|   |   |   |   |   |   |   |   [7 ] fileSystemBsize
|   |   |   |   |   |   |   |   [8 ] fileSystemFiles
|   |   |   |   |   |   |   |   [9 ] fileSystemFfree
|   |   |   |   |   |   |   |   [10] fileSystemDir
|   |   |   |   |   [4 ] processes
|   |   |   |   |   |   [1 ] processNum
|   |   |   |   |   |   [2 ] processTable
|   |   |   |   |   |   |   [1 ] processEntry
|   |   |   |   |   |   |   |   [1 ] processPID*
|   |   |   |   |   |   |   |   [2 ] processIdx
|   |   |   |   |   |   |   |   [3 ] processUID
|   |   |   |   |   |   |   |   [4 ] processPPID
```

Continued

Listing A-6 Continued

```
|   |   |   |   |   |   |   |   |   [5 ]  processDsize
|   |   |   |   |   |   |   |   |   [6 ]  processTsize
|   |   |   |   |   |   |   |   |   [7 ]  processSsize
|   |   |   |   |   |   |   |   |   [8 ]  processNice
|   |   |   |   |   |   |   |   |   [9 ]  processMajor
|   |   |   |   |   |   |   |   |   [10]  processMinor
|   |   |   |   |   |   |   |   |   [11]  processPgrp
|   |   |   |   |   |   |   |   |   [12]  processPrio
|   |   |   |   |   |   |   |   |   [13]  processAddr
|   |   |   |   |   |   |   |   |   [14]  processCPU
|   |   |   |   |   |   |   |   |   [15]  processUtime
|   |   |   |   |   |   |   |   |   [16]  processStime
|   |   |   |   |   |   |   |   |   [17]  processStart
|   |   |   |   |   |   |   |   |   [18]  processFlags
|   |   |   |   |   |   |   |   |   [19]  processStatus
|   |   |   |   |   |   |   |   |   [20]  processWchan
|   |   |   |   |   |   |   |   |   [21]  processProcNum
|   |   |   |   |   |   |   |   |   [22]  processCmd
|   |   |   |   |   |   |   |   |   [23]  processTime
|   |   |   |   |   |   |   |   |   [24]  processCPUticks
|   |   |   |   |   |   |   |   |   [25]  processCPUticksTotal
|   |   |   |   |   |   |   |   |   [26]  processFss
|   |   |   |   |   |   |   |   |   [27]  processPctCPU
|   |   |   |   |   |   |   |   |   [28]  processRssize
|   |   |   |   |   |   |   |   |   [29]  processSUID
|   |   |   |   |   |   |   |   |   [30]  processUname
|   |   |   |   |   |   |   |   |   [31]  processTTY
|   |   |   |   |   [5 ]  cluster
|   |   |   |   |   |   [1 ]  isClustered
|   |   |   |   |   |   [2 ]  clusterTable
|   |   |   |   |   |   |   [1 ]  clusterEntry
|   |   |   |   |   |   |   |   [1 ]  clusterID*
|   |   |   |   |   |   |   |   [2 ]  clusterMachineID
|   |   |   |   |   |   |   |   [3 ]  clusterType
|   |   |   |   |   |   |   |   [4 ]  clusterCnodeName
|   |   |   |   |   |   |   |   [5 ]  clusterSwapServingCnode
|   |   |   |   |   |   |   |   [6 ]  clusterKcsp
|   |   |   |   |   |   |   |   [7 ]  clusterCnodeAddress
|   |   |   |   |   |   [3 ]  clusterCnodeID
|   |   |   |   [2 ]  hpux
|   |   |   |   |   [2 ]  hp9000s300
|   |   |   |   |   [3 ]  hp9000s800
|   |   |   |   |   [5 ]  hp9000s700
|   |   |   |   [10]  hpsun
|   |   |   |   |   [1 ]  sparc
```

```
|   |   |   |   |   |   [1 ] sun4
|   |   |   |   |   |   [2 ] sun5
|   |   |   |   [8 ] hp386
|   |   |   [4 ] interface
|   |   |   [1 ] ieee8023Mac
|   |   |   |   [1 ] ieee8023MacTable
|   |   |   |   |   [1 ] ieee8023MacEntry
|   |   |   |   |   |   [1 ] ieee8023MacIndex*
|   |   |   |   |   |   [2 ] ieee8023MacTransmitted
|   |   |   |   |   |   [3 ] ieee8023MacNotTransmitted
|   |   |   |   |   |   [4 ] ieee8023MacDeferred
|   |   |   |   |   |   [5 ] ieee8023MacCollisions
|   |   |   |   |   |   [6 ] ieee8023MacSingleCollisions
|   |   |   |   |   |   [7 ] ieee8023MacMultipleCollisions
|   |   |   |   |   |   [8 ] ieee8023MacExcessCollisions
|   |   |   |   |   |   [9 ] ieee8023MacLateCollisions
|   |   |   |   |   |   [10] ieee8023MacCarrierLostErrors
|   |   |   |   |   |   [11] ieee8023MacNoHeartBeatErrors
|   |   |   |   |   |   [12] ieee8023MacFramesReceived
|   |   |   |   |   |   [13] ieee8023MacUndeliverableFramesReceived
|   |   |   |   |   |   [14] ieee8023MacCRCErrors
|   |   |   |   |   |   [15] ieee8023MacAlignmentErrors
|   |   |   |   |   |   [16] ieee8023MacResourceErrors
|   |   |   |   |   |   [17] ieee8023MacControlFieldErrors
|   |   |   |   |   |   [18] ieee8023MacUnknownProtocolErrors
|   |   |   |   |   |   [19] ieee8023MacMulticastsAccepted
|   |   [7 ] icmp
|   |   |   [1 ] icmpEchoReq
|   |   [13] snmp
|   |   |   [1 ] trap
|   |   |   |   [1 ] trapDestinationNum
|   |   |   |   [2 ] trapDestinationTable
|   |   |   |   |   [1 ] trapDestinationEntry
|   |   |   |   |   |   [1 ] trapDestination*
|   |   |   [2 ] snmpdConf
|   |   |   |   [1 ] snmpdConfRespond
|   |   |   |   [2 ] snmpdReConfigure
|   |   |   |   [3 ] snmpdFlag
|   |   |   |   [4 ] snmpdLogMask
|   |   |   |   [5 ] snmpdVersion
|   |   |   |   [6 ] snmpdStatus
|   |   |   |   [7 ] snmpdSize
|   |   |   |   [9 ] snmpdWhatString
|   |   |   [4 ] authfail
|   |   |   |   [1 ] authFailTable
|   |   |   |   |   [1 ] authFailEntry
```

Continued

Listing A-6 Continued

```
|   |   |   |   |   |   |   | [1 ] authIpAddress*
|   |   |   |   |   |   |   | [2 ] authTime
|   |   |   |   |   |   |   | [3 ] authCommunityName
|   |   |   [17] openView
|   |   |   | [2 ] openViewTrapVars
|   |   |   |   | [1 ] openViewSourceId
|   |   |   |   | [2 ] openViewSourceName
|   |   |   |   | [3 ] openViewObjectId
|   |   |   |   | [4 ] openViewData
|   |   |   |   | [5 ] openViewSeverity
|   |   |   |   | [6 ] openViewCategory
|   |   |   |   | [7 ] openViewFilter
|   |   |   |   | [8 ] openViewEntity
|   |   |   |   | [9 ] openViewAddress
|   |   |   |   | [10] openViewPid
|   |   |   | [1 ] hpOpenView
```

Monitoring Notes

The mnemonic root OID for the HP-UNIX MIB is iso.org.dod.internet.private.enterprises.hp.nm. If you intend to write your own SNMP application, you need to know the numeric root OID of the HP-UNIX MIB is 1.3.6.1.4.1.11.2.

HP's EMS HA Monitors product uses this MIB to monitor the current number of users and jobs on a system and the amount of free filesystem space.

This MIB can be a useful place to find information about the specific processes running on a system, such as their CPU utilization, priority, and resident set size. However, you may have a difficult time using a MIB Browser to wade through the numerous process table entries; this information is best queried from a customized SNMP application.

Note that this MIB contains information on NFS diskless clusters, but not on HP's high availability or EPS clusters. Information on these clusters is provided in the following sections.

HP Cluster MIB

The HP Cluster MIB is a private MIB provided by Hewlett-Packard. It defines cluster membership information for the high availability and EPS clusters.

MIB Definition

Listing A-7 shows the complete specification for the HP Cluster MIB, as defined by Hewlett-Packard.

Listing A-7 HP Cluster specification.

```
enterprises
|   [11] hp
|   |   [2 ] nm
|   |   |   [3 ] system
|   |   |   |   [1 ] general
|   |   |   |   |   [6 ] hpmcCluster
|   |   |   |   |   |   [1 ] hpmcClusterObjects
|   |   |   |   |   |   |   [1 ] hpmcGenInfo
|   |   |   |   |   |   |   |   [1 ] hpmcNumClusters
|   |   |   |   |   |   |   |   [2 ] hpmcClusterTable
|   |   |   |   |   |   |   |   |   [1 ] hpmcClusterEntry
|   |   |   |   |   |   |   |   |   |   [1 ] hpmcClusterIndex*
|   |   |   |   |   |   |   |   |   |   [2 ] hpmcClusterName
|   |   |   |   |   |   |   |   |   |   [3 ] hpmcClusterType
|   |   |   |   |   |   |   |   |   |   [4 ] hpmcClusterDescr
|   |   |   |   |   |   |   |   |   |   [5 ] hpmcClusterSWVersion
|   |   |   |   |   |   |   |   |   |   [6 ] hpmcClusterState
|   |   |   |   |   |   |   |   |   |   [7 ] hpmcClusterLastStateChange
|   |   |   |   |   |   |   |   |   |   [8 ] hpmcClusterLastReconfig
|   |   |   |   |   |   |   |   |   |   [9 ] hpmcClusterPrimaryNode
|   |   |   |   |   |   |   |   |   |   [10] hpmcNodeStatus
|   |   |   |   |   |   |   |   |   |   [11] hpmcNodeLastEvent
|   |   |   |   |   |   |   |   |   |   [12] hpmcNodeLastEventTime
|   |   |   |   |   |   |   |   |   |   [13] hpmcClusterUpTime
|   |   |   |   |   |   |   [2 ] hpmcMemberInfo
|   |   |   |   |   |   |   |   [1 ] hpmcCNodeTable
|   |   |   |   |   |   |   |   |   [1 ] hpmcCNodeEntry
|   |   |   |   |   |   |   |   |   |   [1 ] hpmcNodeID*
|   |   |   |   |   |   |   |   |   |   [2 ] hpmcNodeName
|   |   |   |   |   |   |   |   |   |   [3 ] hpmcNodeRole
|   |   |   |   |   |   [2 ] hpmcClusterTypes
|   |   |   |   |   |   |   [1 ] hpmcServiceGuard
|   |   |   |   |   |   |   [2 ] hpmcNFSDiskless
|   |   |   |   |   |   |   [3 ] hpmcMCSE
|   |   |   |   |   |   |   [4 ] hpmcLockManager
|   |   |   |   |   |   [3 ] hpmcTypeSpecific
```

Monitoring Notes

If you intend to write your own SNMP application, the root OID of the HP Cluster MIB is
1.3.6.1.4.1.11.2.3.1.6.

You can use this MIB to find out which systems are part of a cluster and how long the cluster software has been running.

Additional fields specific to MC/ServiceGuard and MC/LockManager clusters are described in the following section. EPS clusters don't have any unique MIB variables. Note that this MIB does not include information on NFS or "diskless" clusters.

HP MC/ServiceGuard MIB

The HP MC/ServiceGuard MIB is an extension of the HP Cluster MIB, providing additional MIB variables specific to the MC/ServiceGuard high availability product. A better name might have been the HP HA MIB, because it also supports the HP MC/LockManager high availability product.

MIB Definition

Listing A-8 shows the complete specification for the HP MC/ServiceGuard MIB, as defined by Hewlett-Packard.

Listing A-8 HP MC/ServiceGuard specification.

```
enterprises
 |   [11] hp
 |    |   [2 ] nm
 |    |    |   [3 ] system
 |    |    |    |   [1 ] general
 |    |    |    |    |   [6 ] hpmcCluster
 |    |    |    |    |    |   [3 ] hpmcTypeSpecific
 |    |    |    |    |    |    |   [1 ] hpmcSGCluster
 |    |    |    |    |    |    |    |   [0 ] hpmcSGTraps
 |    |    |    |    |    |    |    |    |   [1 ] hpmcSGSubagentUp
 |    |    |    |    |    |    |    |    |   [2 ] hpmcSGReconfig
 |    |    |    |    |    |    |    |    |   [3 ] hpmcSGClusterUp
 |    |    |    |    |    |    |    |    |   [4 ] hpmcSGClusterDown
 |    |    |    |    |    |    |    |    |   [5 ] hpmcSGConfigChange
 |    |    |    |    |    |    |    |    |   [6 ] hpmcSGPkgStart
 |    |    |    |    |    |    |    |    |   [7 ] hpmcSGPkgUp
 |    |    |    |    |    |    |    |    |   [8 ] hpmcSGPkgHalt
 |    |    |    |    |    |    |    |    |   [9 ] hpmcSGPkgDown
 |    |    |    |    |    |    |    |    |   [10] hpmcSGSvcDown
 |    |    |    |    |    |    |    |    |   [11] hpmcSGPkgFlags
 |    |    |    |    |    |    |    |    |   [12] hpmcSGIPAddrUp
 |    |    |    |    |    |    |    |    |   [13] hpmcSGIPAddrDown
 |    |    |    |    |    |    |    |    |   [14] hpmcSGLocalSwitch
 |    |    |    |    |    |    |    |    |   [15] hpmcSGSubnetUp
 |    |    |    |    |    |    |    |    |   [16] hpmcSGSubnetDown
 |    |    |    |    |    |    |    |    |   [17] hpmcSGNodeUp
 |    |    |    |    |    |    |    |    |   [18] hpmcSGNodeHalted
 |    |    |    |    |    |    |    |    |   [19] hpmcSGNodeFailed
 |    |    |    |    |    |    |    |   [1 ] hpmcSGObjects
```

```
| | | | | | | | | | [1 ] hpmcSGGenInfo
| | | | | | | | | | | [1 ] hpmcSGClusterIndex
| | | | | | | | | | | [2 ] hpmcSGClusterID
| | | | | | | | | | | [3 ] hpmcSGHeartbeatInterval
| | | | | | | | | | | [4 ] hpmcSGNodeTimeout
| | | | | | | | | | | [5 ] hpmcSGAutoStartTimeout
| | | | | | | | | | | [6 ] hpmcSGNetworkPollingInterval
| | | | | | | | | | [2 ] hpmcSGLockInfo
| | | | | | | | | | | [1 ] hpmcSGLockTable
| | | | | | | | | | | | [1 ] hpmcSGLockEntry
| | | | | | | | | | | | | [1 ] hpmcSGVolumeIndex*
| | | | | | | | | | | | | [2 ] hpmcSGPhysicalVolume
| | | | | | | | | | [3 ] hpmcSGIfInfo
| | | | | | | | | | | [1 ] hpmcSGNetTable
| | | | | | | | | | | | [1 ] hpmcSGNetEntry
| | | | | | | | | | | | | [1 ] hpmcSGNetIfIndex*
| | | | | | | | | | | | | [2 ] hpmcSGNetIfName
| | | | | | | | | | | | | [3 ] hpmcSGNetBridgedNet
| | | | | | | | | | | | | [4 ] hpmcSGNetIfFlags
| | | | | | | | | | | | | [5 ] hpmcSGNetLastEvent
| | | | | | | | | | | | | [6 ] hpmcSGNetLastEventTime
| | | | | | | | | | | | | [7 ] hpmcSGNetIfHwPath
| | | | | | | | | | [4 ] hpmcSGPkgInfo
| | | | | | | | | | | [1 ] hpmcSGPkgTable
| | | | | | | | | | | | [1 ] hpmcSGPkgEntry
| | | | | | | | | | | | | [1 ] hpmcSGPkgIndex*
| | | | | | | | | | | | | [2 ] hpmcSGPkgName
| | | | | | | | | | | | | [3 ] hpmcSGPkgDescr
| | | | | | | | | | | | | [4 ] hpmcSGPkgStatus
| | | | | | | | | | | | | [5 ] hpmcSGPkgCurrNode
| | | | | | | | | | | | | [6 ] hpmcSGPkgLastEvent
| | | | | | | | | | | | | [7 ] hpmcSGPkgLastEventTime
| | | | | | | | | | | | | [8 ] hpmcSGPkgRunScriptPath
| | | | | | | | | | | | | [9 ] hpmcSGPkgHaltScriptPath
| | | | | | | | | | | | | [10] hpmcSGPkgRunScriptTimeout
| | | | | | | | | | | | | [11] hpmcSGPkgHaltScriptTimeout
| | | | | | | | | | | [2 ] hpmcSGPkgSubnetTable
| | | | | | | | | | | | [1 ] hpmcSGPkgSubnetEntry
| | | | | | | | | | | | | [1 ] hpmcSGPkgSubnet*
| | | | | | | | | | | | | [2 ] hpmcSGPkgSubnetStatus
| | | | | | | | | | | | | [3 ] hpmcSGPkgOverrideMACAddr
| | | | | | | | | | | [3 ] hpmcSGPkgAddrTable
| | | | | | | | | | | | [1 ] hpmcSGPkgAddrEntry
| | | | | | | | | | | | | [1 ] hpmcSGPkgAddr*
| | | | | | | | | | | | | [2 ] hpmcSGPkgID
| | | | | | | | | | | [4 ] hpmcSGPkgSvcTable
```

Continued

Listing A-8 Continued

```
| | | | | | | | | | | | [1 ] hpmcSGPkgSvcEntry
| | | | | | | | | | | |   [1 ] hpmcSGPkgSvcIndex*
| | | | | | | | | | | |   [2 ] hpmcSGPkgSvcName
| | | | | | | | | | | |   [3 ] hpmcSGPkgSvcStatus
| | | | | | | | | | | |   [4 ] hpmcSGPkgSvcFlags
| | | | | | | | | | | |   [5 ] hpmcSGPkgSvcHaltTimeout
| | | | | | | | | | | |   [6 ] hpmcSGPkgSvcMaxRestarts
| | | | | | | | | | | |   [7 ] hpmcSGPkgSvcRestartCount
| | | | | | | | | | [5 ] hpmcSGPkgNodeTable
| | | | | | | | | | [1 ] hpmcSGPkgNodeEntry
| | | | | | | | | | | [1 ] hpmcSGPkgNodeRank*
| | | | | | | | | | | [2 ] hpmcSGPkgNode
| | | | | | | | | | | [3 ] hpmcSGPkgLocalSwitchEnable
```

Monitoring Notes

If you intend to write your own SNMP application, the root OID of the HP Cluster MIB is 1.3.6.1.4.1.11.2.3.1.6. The cluster type, hpmcClusterTypes, should indicate MC/ServiceGuard or MC/LockManager, with the additional MIB variables referring to a high availability cluster.

You can check this MIB to ensure that high availability configuration parameters are set correctly, such as the heartbeat interval. You can also use this MIB to determine the critical applications running in the cluster and their status. Note, however, that the package status is accurate only on the cluster's coordinator node.

HP's EMS HA Monitors product uses this MIB to monitor MC/ServiceGuard and MC/LockManager cluster, node, package, and service status.

Network Services MIB

The Network Services MIB contains information that is meant to be generic for all network server applications. Database vendors use this MIB to store database server data. For example, Oracle takes advantage of this MIB to store information for the Oracle7 Server, the Oracle MultiProtocol Interchange, and the Oracle Names products.

MIB Definition

Listing A-9 shows the complete specification for the Network Services MIB, as defined in RFC 2248.

Listing A-9 Network Services MIB specification.

```
mib_2
| [27] application
| | [3 ] applConformance
| | | [1 ] applGroups
```

```
|   |   |   |   |   [1 ] applGroup
|   |   |   |   |   [2 ] assocGroup
|   |   |   |   [2 ] applCompliances
|   |   |   |   |   [1 ] applCompliance
|   |   |   |   |   [2 ] assocCompliance
|   |   [4 ] applTCPProtoID
|   |   [5 ] applUDPProtoID
|   |   [1 ] applTable
|   |   |   [1 ] applEntry
|   |   |   |   [1 ] applIndex*
|   |   |   |   [2 ] applName
|   |   |   |   [3 ] applDirectoryName
|   |   |   |   [4 ] applVersion
|   |   |   |   [5 ] applUptime
|   |   |   |   [6 ] applOperStatus
|   |   |   |   [7 ] applLastChange
|   |   |   |   [8 ] applInboundAssociations
|   |   |   |   [9 ] applOutboundAssociations
|   |   |   |   [10] applAccumulatedInboundAssociations
|   |   |   |   [11] applAccumulatedOutboundAssociations
|   |   |   |   [12] applLastInboundActivity
|   |   |   |   [13] applLastOutboundActivity
|   |   |   |   [14] applRejectedInboundAssociations
|   |   |   |   [15] applFailedOutboundAssociations
|   |   |   |   [16] applDescription
|   |   |   |   [17] applURL
|   |   [2 ] assocTable
|   |   |   [1 ] assocEntry
|   |   |   |   [1 ] assocIndex*
|   |   |   |   [2 ] assocRemoteApplication
|   |   |   |   [3 ] assocApplicationProtocol
|   |   |   |   [4 ] assocApplicationType
|   |   |   |   [5 ] assocDuration
```

Monitoring Notes

If you intend to write your own SNMP application, the root OID of the Network Services MIB is 1.3.6.1.2.1.27.

Important fields in this MIB include the application's name, uptime, version, and current status. You can also use this MIB to determine the current number of connections to an application.

Both Informix and Oracle support this MIB, but don't support all the MIB variables. The following fields in the applTable are supported by both vendors:

- applName
- applVersion

- `applUptime`
- `applOperStatus`
- `applLastChange`
- `applInboundAssociations`

Note that although Oracle and other database vendors use this MIB, it is not being used for more traditional network services, such as telnet.

RDBMS MIB

The Relational Database Management System (RDBMS) MIB contains information that is meant to be generic for all RDBMS systems. This MIB is supported by all the major database vendors. It provides availability information, such as database status and server uptime, and performance information, such as the number of logical database reads.

MIB Definition

Listing A-10 shows the complete specification for the RDBMS MIB, as defined in RFC 1697.

Listing A-10   RDBMS MIB specification.

```
mib_2
|   [39] rdbmsMIB
|   |   [1 ] rdbmsObjects
|   |   |   [10] rdbmsWellKnownLimitedResources
|   |   |   |   [1 ] rdbmsLogSpace
|   |   |   [1 ] rdbmsDbTable
|   |   |   |   [1 ] rdbmsDbEntry
|   |   |   |   |   [1 ] rdbmsDbIndex*
|   |   |   |   |   [2 ] rdbmsDbPrivateMibOID
|   |   |   |   |   [3 ] rdbmsDbVendorName
|   |   |   |   |   [4 ] rdbmsDbName
|   |   |   |   |   [5 ] rdbmsDbContact
|   |   |   [2 ] rdbmsDbInfoTable
|   |   |   |   [1 ] rdbmsDbInfoEntry
|   |   |   |   |   [1 ] rdbmsDbInfoProductName
|   |   |   |   |   [2 ] rdbmsDbInfoVersion
|   |   |   |   |   [3 ] rdbmsDbInfoSizeUnits
|   |   |   |   |   [4 ] rdbmsDbInfoSizeAllocated
|   |   |   |   |   [5 ] rdbmsDbInfoSizeUsed
|   |   |   |   |   [6 ] rdbmsDbInfoLastBackup
|   |   |   [3 ] rdbmsDbParamTable
|   |   |   |   [1 ] rdbmsDbParamEntry
|   |   |   |   |   [1 ] rdbmsDbParamName*
|   |   |   |   |   [2 ] rdbmsDbParamSubIndex
|   |   |   |   |   [3 ] rdbmsDbParamID
```

```
|   |   |   |   | [4 ] rdbmsDbParamCurrValue
|   |   |   |   | [5 ] rdbmsDbParamComment
|   |   | [4 ] rdbmsDbLimitedResourceTable
|   |   |   | [1 ] rdbmsDbLimitedResourceEntry
|   |   |   |   | [1 ] rdbmsDbLimitedResourceName*
|   |   |   |   | [2 ] rdbmsDbLimitedResourceID
|   |   |   |   | [3 ] rdbmsDbLimitedResourceLimit
|   |   |   |   | [4 ] rdbmsDbLimitedResourceCurrent
|   |   |   |   | [5 ] rdbmsDbLimitedResourceHighwater
|   |   |   |   | [6 ] rdbmsDbLimitedResourceFailures
|   |   |   |   | [7 ] rdbmsDbLimitedResourceDescription
|   |   | [5 ] rdbmsSrvTable
|   |   |   | [1 ] rdbmsSrvEntry
|   |   |   |   | [1 ] rdbmsSrvPrivateMibOID
|   |   |   |   | [2 ] rdbmsSrvVendorName
|   |   |   |   | [3 ] rdbmsSrvProductName
|   |   |   |   | [4 ] rdbmsSrvContact
|   |   | [6 ] rdbmsSrvInfoTable
|   |   |   | [1 ] rdbmsSrvInfoEntry
|   |   |   |   | [1 ] rdbmsSrvInfoStartupTime
|   |   |   |   | [2 ] rdbmsSrvInfoFinishedTransactions
|   |   |   |   | [3 ] rdbmsSrvInfoDiskReads
|   |   |   |   | [4 ] rdbmsSrvInfoLogicalReads
|   |   |   |   | [5 ] rdbmsSrvInfoDiskWrites
|   |   |   |   | [6 ] rdbmsSrvInfoLogicalWrites
|   |   |   |   | [7 ] rdbmsSrvInfoPageReads
|   |   |   |   | [8 ] rdbmsSrvInfoPageWrites
|   |   |   |   | [9 ] rdbmsSrvInfoDiskOutOfSpaces
|   |   |   |   | [10] rdbmsSrvInfoHandledRequests
|   |   |   |   | [11] rdbmsSrvInfoRequestRecvs
|   |   |   |   | [12] rdbmsSrvInfoRequestSends
|   |   |   |   | [13] rdbmsSrvInfoHighwaterInboundAssociations
|   |   |   |   | [14] rdbmsSrvInfoMaxInboundAssociations
|   |   | [7 ] rdbmsSrvParamTable
|   |   |   | [1 ] rdbmsSrvParamEntry
|   |   |   |   | [1 ] rdbmsSrvParamName*
|   |   |   |   | [2 ] rdbmsSrvParamSubIndex
|   |   |   |   | [3 ] rdbmsSrvParamID
|   |   |   |   | [4 ] rdbmsSrvParamCurrValue
|   |   |   |   | [5 ] rdbmsSrvParamComment
|   |   | [8 ] rdbmsSrvLimitedResourceTable
|   |   |   | [1 ] rdbmsSrvLimitedResourceEntry
|   |   |   |   | [1 ] rdbmsSrvLimitedResourceName*
|   |   |   |   | [2 ] rdbmsSrvLimitedResourceID
|   |   |   |   | [3 ] rdbmsSrvLimitedResourceLimit
|   |   |   |   | [4 ] rdbmsSrvLimitedResourceCurrent
```

Continued

Listing A-10 Continued

```
|   |   |   |   |   [5 ] rdbmsSrvLimitedResourceHighwater
|   |   |   |   |   [6 ] rdbmsSrvLimitedResourceFailures
|   |   |   |   |   [7 ] rdbmsSrvLimitedResourceDescription
|   |   |   [9 ] rdbmsRelTable
|   |   |   |   [1 ] rdbmsRelEntry
|   |   |   |   |   [1 ] rdbmsRelState
|   |   |   |   |   [2 ] rdbmsRelActiveTime
|   |   [2 ] rdbmsTraps
|   |   |   [1 ] rdbmsStateChange
|   |   |   [2 ] rdbmsOutOfSpace
|   |   [3 ] rdbmsConformance
|   |   |   [1 ] rdbmsCompliances
|   |   |   |   [1 ] rdbmsCompliance
|   |   |   [2 ] rdbmsGroups
|   |   |   |   [1 ] rdbmsGroup
```

Monitoring Notes

If you intend to write your own SNMP application, the root OID of the RDBMS MIB is
1.3.6.1.2.1.39.

The RDBMS MIB contains both fault and performance information. The MIB contains
the state of each database. The status of a database instance is obtained by cross-referencing the
server tables with the application entries in the Network Services MIB. In this way, you can see
the process status (applOperStatus). To verify that the server is responding, you can check
applAccumulatedInboundAssociations to see whether the number of connections is still increasing. This field is supported by Informix, but not Oracle.

Performance information includes the number of committed database transactions and
database I/O and cache hit rates.

You can also use this MIB to determine whether database tables are reaching their configured limits.

Database vendors don't implement all components of this MIB. Oracle and Informix, for
example, don't implement the following tables of the RDBMS MIB:

- rdbmsDbParamTable
- rdbmsDbLimitedResourceTable

In addition, Oracle doesn't implement the rdbmsSrvLimitedResourceTable in the RDBMS
MIB.

Oracle Private Database MIB

Oracle's Private Database MIB contains additional RDBMS statistics specific to the Oracle7 architecture. It is meant to be used as a supplement to the RDBMS MIB. The majority of the information in this MIB is performance-related.

MIB Definition

Listing A-11 shows the complete specification for Oracle's Private Database MIB, as defined by Oracle.

Listing A-11   Oracle Private Database MIB specification.

```
enterprises
 |   [111] oracle
 |   |   [4 ] oraDbMIB
 |   |   |   [1 ] oraDbObjects
 |   |   |   |   [1 ] oraDbSysTable
 |   |   |   |   |   [1 ] oraDbSysEntry
 |   |   |   |   |   |   [1 ] oraDbSysConsistentChanges
 |   |   |   |   |   |   [2 ] oraDbSysConsistentGets
 |   |   |   |   |   |   [3 ] oraDbSysDbBlockChanges
 |   |   |   |   |   |   [4 ] oraDbSysDbBlockGets
 |   |   |   |   |   |   [5 ] oraDbSysFreeBufferInspected
 |   |   |   |   |   |   [6 ] oraDbSysFreeBufferRequested
 |   |   |   |   |   |   [7 ] oraDbSysParseCount
 |   |   |   |   |   |   [8 ] oraDbSysPhysReads
 |   |   |   |   |   |   [9 ] oraDbSysPhysWrites
 |   |   |   |   |   |   [10] oraDbSysRedoEntries
 |   |   |   |   |   |   [11] oraDbSysRedoLogSpaceRequests
 |   |   |   |   |   |   [12] oraDbSysRedoSyncWrites
 |   |   |   |   |   |   [13] oraDbSysSortsDisk
 |   |   |   |   |   |   [14] oraDbSysSortsMemory
 |   |   |   |   |   |   [15] oraDbSysSortsRows
 |   |   |   |   |   |   [16] oraDbSysTableFetchRowid
 |   |   |   |   |   |   [17] oraDbSysTableFetchContinuedRow
 |   |   |   |   |   |   [18] oraDbSysTableScanBlocks
 |   |   |   |   |   |   [19] oraDbSysTableScanRows
 |   |   |   |   |   |   [20] oraDbSysTableScansLong
 |   |   |   |   |   |   [21] oraDbSysTableScansShort
 |   |   |   |   |   |   [22] oraDbSysUserCalls
 |   |   |   |   |   |   [23] oraDbSysUserCommits
 |   |   |   |   |   |   [24] oraDbSysUserRollbacks
 |   |   |   |   |   |   [25] oraDbSysWriteRequests
 |   |   |   |   [2 ] oraDbTablespaceTable
 |   |   |   |   |   [1 ] oraDbTablespaceEntry
 |   |   |   |   |   |   [1 ] oraDbTablespaceIndex*
```

Continued

Listing A-11   Continued

```
|   |   |   |   |   |   [2  ] oraDbTablespaceName
|   |   |   |   |   |   [3  ] oraDbTablespaceSizeAllocated
|   |   |   |   |   |   [4  ] oraDbTablespaceSizeUsed
|   |   |   |   |   |   [5  ] oraDbTablespaceState
|   |   |   |   |   |   [6  ] oraDbTablespaceLargestAvailableChunk
|   |   |   |   [3  ] oraDbDataFileTable
|   |   |   |   |   [1  ] oraDbDataFileEntry
|   |   |   |   |   |   [1  ] oraDbDataFileIndex*
|   |   |   |   |   |   [2  ] oraDbDataFileName
|   |   |   |   |   |   [3  ] oraDbDataFileSizeAllocated
|   |   |   |   |   |   [4  ] oraDbDataFileDiskReads
|   |   |   |   |   |   [5  ] oraDbDataFileDiskWrites
|   |   |   |   |   |   [6  ] oraDbDataFileDiskReadBlocks
|   |   |   |   |   |   [7  ] oraDbDataFileDiskWrittenBlocks
|   |   |   |   |   |   [8  ] oraDbDataFileDiskReadTimeTicks
|   |   |   |   |   |   [9  ] oraDbDataFileDiskWriteTimeTicks
|   |   |   |   [4  ] oraDbLibraryCacheTable
|   |   |   |   |   [1  ] oraDbLibraryCacheEntry
|   |   |   |   |   |   [1  ] oraDbLibraryCacheIndex*
|   |   |   |   |   |   [2  ] oraDbLibraryCacheNameSpace
|   |   |   |   |   |   [3  ] oraDbLibraryCacheGets
|   |   |   |   |   |   [4  ] oraDbLibraryCacheGetHits
|   |   |   |   |   |   [5  ] oraDbLibraryCachePins
|   |   |   |   |   |   [6  ] oraDbLibraryCachePinHits
|   |   |   |   |   |   [7  ] oraDbLibraryCacheReloads
|   |   |   |   |   |   [8  ] oraDbLibraryCacheInvalidations
|   |   |   |   [5  ] oraDbLibraryCacheSumTable
|   |   |   |   |   [1  ] oraDbLibraryCacheSumEntry
|   |   |   |   |   |   [1  ] oraDbLibraryCacheSumGets
|   |   |   |   |   |   [2  ] oraDbLibraryCacheSumGetHits
|   |   |   |   |   |   [3  ] oraDbLibraryCacheSumPins
|   |   |   |   |   |   [4  ] oraDbLibraryCacheSumPinHits
|   |   |   |   |   |   [5  ] oraDbLibraryCacheSumReloads
|   |   |   |   |   |   [6  ] oraDbLibraryCacheSumInvalidations
|   |   |   |   [6  ] oraDbSGATable
|   |   |   |   |   [1  ] oraDbSGAEntry
|   |   |   |   |   |   [1  ] oraDbSGAFixedSize
|   |   |   |   |   |   [2  ] oraDbSGAVariableSize
|   |   |   |   |   |   [3  ] oraDbSGADatabaseBuffers
|   |   |   |   |   |   [4  ] oraDbSGARedoBuffers
|   |   |   |   [7  ] oraDbConfigTable
|   |   |   |   |   [1  ] oraDbConfigEntry
|   |   |   |   |   |   [1  ] oraDbConfigDbBlockBuffers
|   |   |   |   |   |   [2  ] oraDbConfigDbBlockCkptBatch
|   |   |   |   |   |   [3  ] oraDbConfigDbBlockSize
```

```
| | | | | | [4 ] oraDbConfigDbFileSimWrites
| | | | | | [5 ] oraDbConfigDbMultiBlockReadCount
| | | | | | [6 ] oraDbConfigDistLockTimeout
| | | | | | [7 ] oraDbConfigDistRecoveryConnectHold
| | | | | | [8 ] oraDbConfigDistTransactions
| | | | | | [9 ] oraDbConfigLogArchiveBufferSize
| | | | | | [10] oraDbConfigLogArchiveBuffers
| | | | | | [11] oraDbConfigLogBuffer
| | | | | | [12] oraDbConfigLogCheckpointInterval
| | | | | | [13] oraDbConfigLogCheckpointTimeout
| | | | | | [14] oraDbConfigLogFiles
| | | | | | [15] oraDbConfigMaxRollbackSegments
| | | | | | [16] oraDbConfigMTSMaxDispatchers
| | | | | | [17] oraDbConfigMTSMaxServers
| | | | | | [18] oraDbConfigMTSServers
| | | | | | [19] oraDbConfigOpenCursors
| | | | | | [20] oraDbConfigOpenLinks
| | | | | | [21] oraDbConfigOptimizerMode
| | | | | | [22] oraDbConfigProcesses
| | | | | | [23] oraDbConfigSerializable
| | | | | | [24] oraDbConfigSessions
| | | | | | [25] oraDbConfigSharedPool
| | | | | | [26] oraDbConfigSortAreaSize
| | | | | | [27] oraDbConfigSortAreaRetainedSize
| | | | | | [28] oraDbConfigTransactions
| | | | | | [29] oraDbConfigTransactionsPerRollback
```

Monitoring Notes

The mnemonic root OID for Oracle's Private Database MIB is iso.org.dod.internet.private.enterprises.oracle.oraDbMIB. If you intend to write your own SNMP application, the numeric root OID of Oracle's Private Database MIB is 1.3.6.1.4.1.111.4.

Many of the table entries in this MIB are indexed by using applIndex from the Network Services MIB.

This MIB contains several fields that are useful for performance monitoring. They supply statistics such as the number of block changes, user calls, consistent Gets, block Gets, physical reads, recursive calls, user commits, and consistent changes. This data needs to be queried at regular intervals to establish baselines and to be able to determine whether a persistent performance problem exists.

Each entry in the oraDbSysTable corresponds to a current database instance on the system. The table is indexed by rdbmsDbIndex, from the RDBMS MIB.

Each entry in the oraDbTablespaceTable represents a given tablespace within a current database instance. The table is indexed by rdbmsDbIndex, from the RDBMS MIB, and by oraDbTablespaceIndex.

One rdbmsDbTable entry is likely to correspond to multiple tablespace table entries. For example, addition to indicating the amount of space allocated and in use, the state variable oraDbTablespaceState indicates whether the tablespace is offline or accessible.

The oraDbDataFileTable keeps track of the number of disk reads and writes being made to a data file. The oraDbConfigTable stores important database configuration parameters, such as DB_BLOCK_BUFFERS, which is used to determine the buffer cache size.

The oraDbLibraryCacheTable keeps track of performance data about the library cache. Variables in this table, such as oraDbLibraryCachePins and oraDbLibraryCacheReloads, can be used to calculate the library cache miss rate. Each table entry represents a given library cache within a current database instance on the system. The oraDbLibraryCacheSumTable provides summary information for all the library caches in a database instance.

Oracle Network Listener MIB

The Oracle Network Listener MIB is a protocol-independent application that receives connection requests from remote database users. Oracle provides a private Network Listener MIB that includes additional information about the current status of the listener process.

MIB Definition

Listing A-12 shows the complete specification for Oracle's private Network Listener MIB, as defined by Oracle.

Listing A-12   Oracle Network Listener MIB specification.

```
enterprises
|   [111] oracle
|   |   [5 ] oraListenerMIB
|   |   |   [1 ] oraListenerObjects
|   |   |   |   [1 ] oraListenerTable
|   |   |   |   |   [1 ] oraListenerEntry
|   |   |   |   |   |   [1 ] oraListenerIndex*
|   |   |   |   |   |   [2 ] oraListenerName
|   |   |   |   |   |   [3 ] oraListenerVersion
|   |   |   |   |   |   [4 ] oraListenerStartDate
|   |   |   |   |   |   [5 ] oraListenerUptime
|   |   |   |   |   |   [6 ] oraListenerTraceLevel
|   |   |   |   |   |   [7 ] oraListenerSecurityLevel
|   |   |   |   |   |   [8 ] oraListenerParameterFile
|   |   |   |   |   |   [9 ] oraListenerLogFile
|   |   |   |   |   |   [10] oraListenerTraceFile
|   |   |   |   |   |   [11] oraListenerState
|   |   |   |   |   |   [12] oraListenerNumberOfServices
|   |   |   |   |   |   [13] oraListenerContact
|   |   |   |   [5 ] oraSIDTable
```

```
|   |   |   |   |   [1 ] oraSIDEntry
|   |   |   |   |   |   [1 ] oraSIDListenerIndex*
|   |   |   |   |   |   [2 ] oraSIDName*
|   |   |   |   |   |   [3 ] oraSIDCurrentConnectedClients
|   |   |   |   |   |   [4 ] oraSIDReservedConnections
|   |   |   |   [2 ] oraDedicatedSrvTable
|   |   |   |   |   [1 ] oraDedicatedSrvEntry
|   |   |   |   |   |   [1 ] oraDedicatedSrvIndex*
|   |   |   |   |   |   [2 ] oraDedicatedSrvEstablishedConnections
|   |   |   |   |   |   [3 ] oraDedicatedSrvRejectedConnections
|   |   |   |   [3 ] oraDispatcherTable
|   |   |   |   |   [1 ] oraDispatcherEntry
|   |   |   |   |   |   [1 ] oraDispatcherIndex*
|   |   |   |   |   |   [2 ] oraDispatcherEstablishedConnections
|   |   |   |   |   |   [3 ] oraDispatcherRejectedConnections
|   |   |   |   |   |   [4 ] oraDispatcherCurrentConnections
|   |   |   |   |   |   [5 ] oraDispatcherMaximumConnections
|   |   |   |   |   |   [6 ] oraDispatcherState
|   |   |   |   |   |   [7 ] oraDispatcherProtocolInfo
|   |   |   |   [4 ] oraPrespawnedSrvTable
|   |   |   |   |   [1 ] oraPrespawnedSrvEntry
|   |   |   |   |   |   [1 ] oraPrespawnedSrvIndex*
|   |   |   |   |   |   [2 ] oraPrespawnedSrvEstablishedConnections
|   |   |   |   |   |   [3 ] oraPrespawnedSrvRejectedConnections
|   |   |   |   |   |   [4 ] oraPrespawnedSrvCurrentConnections
|   |   |   |   |   |   [5 ] oraPrespawnedSrvMaximumConnections
|   |   |   |   |   |   [6 ] oraPrespawnedSrvState
|   |   |   |   |   |   [7 ] oraPrespawnedSrvProtocolInfo
|   |   |   |   |   |   [8 ] oraPrespawnedSrvProcessorID
|   |   |   |   [6 ] oraListenAddressTable
|   |   |   |   |   [1 ] oraListenAddressEntry
|   |   |   |   |   |   [1 ] oraListenAddressIndex*
|   |   |   |   |   |   [2 ] oraListenAddress
|   |   |   [2 ] oraListenerTraps
|   |   |   |   [1 ] oraListenerStateChange
```

Monitoring Notes

If you intend to write your own SNMP application, the root OID of Oracle's Network Listener MIB is 1.3.6.1.4.1.111.5.

Each entry in the oraListenerTable represents the network listener for a current database instance on the system. You should monitor the state of the listener, oraListenerState, to ensure that the process is still running. If the listener isn't running, then no new client connection requests can be processed. You can monitor this by having your management station listen for an oraListenerStateChange trap, indicating that the listener has changed state. This is the only trap currently provided by the MIB. Note that Oracle's OEM MIB also includes a trap that is sent when the OEM agent detects that the listener has gone down.

One oraSIDEntry exists for each database instance for which the listener listens. You should compare the current number of connected clients with the maximum reserved, to see whether you are nearing the limit. When the limit is reached, new requests are redirected to dedicated servers, which require more system resources.

Dispatchers and prespawned servers are optional processes to help clients connect to the database. Again, to check whether a problem is imminent, check whether the current number of connections is approaching the maximum number of connections allowed.

Oracle Names MIB

The Oracle Names product provides an enterprise directory service for database information. More information about Oracle Names can be found in *Oracle Names Administrator's Guide* from Oracle. This private Oracle MIB provides additional information about the current status of the Oracle Names product.

MIB Definition

Listing A-13 shows the complete specification for Oracle's Names MIB, as defined by Oracle.

Listing A-13   Oracle Names MIB specification.

```
enterprises
|  [111] oracle
|  |  [6 ] oraNamesMIB
|  |  |  [1 ] oraNamesObjects
|  |  |  |  [1 ] oraNamesTNSTable
|  |  |  |  |  [1 ] oraNamesTNSEntry
|  |  |  |  |  |  [1 ] oraNamesTNSstartDate
|  |  |  |  |  |  [2 ] oraNamesTNStraceLevel
|  |  |  |  |  |  [3 ] oraNamesTNSsecurityLevel
|  |  |  |  |  |  [4 ] oraNamesTNSparameterFile
|  |  |  |  |  |  [5 ] oraNamesTNSlogFile
|  |  |  |  |  |  [6 ] oraNamesTNStraceFile
|  |  |  |  |  |  [7 ] oraNamesTNSstate
|  |  |  |  |  |  [8 ] oraNamesTNScontact
|  |  |  |  |  |  [9 ] oraNamesTNSlistenAddresses
|  |  |  |  |  |  [10] oraNamesTNSfailedListenAddresses
|  |  |  |  |  |  [11] oraNamesTNSreload
|  |  |  |  |  |  [12] oraNamesTNSrunningTime
|  |  |  |  [2 ] oraNamesConfigTable
|  |  |  |  |  [1 ] oraNamesConfigEntry
|  |  |  |  |  |  [1 ] oraNamesConfigAdminRegion
|  |  |  |  |  |  [2 ] oraNamesConfigAuthorityRequired
|  |  |  |  |  |  [3 ] oraNamesConfigAutoRefreshExpire
```

```
|  |  |  |  |  |  |     [4 ]  oraNamesConfigAutoRefreshRetry
|  |  |  |  |  |  |     [5 ]  oraNamesConfigCacheCheckpointFile
|  |  |  |  |  |  |     [6 ]  oraNamesConfigCacheCheckpointInterval
|  |  |  |  |  |  |     [7 ]  oraNamesConfigConfigCheckpointFile
|  |  |  |  |  |  |     [8 ]  oraNamesConfigDefaultForwarders
|  |  |  |  |  |  |     [9 ]  oraNamesConfigDefaultForwardersOnly
|  |  |  |  |  |  |     [10]  oraNamesConfigDomainCheckpointFile
|  |  |  |  |  |  |     [11]  oraNamesConfigDomainHints
|  |  |  |  |  |  |     [12]  oraNamesConfigDomains
|  |  |  |  |  |  |     [13]  oraNamesConfigForwardingAvailable
|  |  |  |  |  |  |     [14]  oraNamesConfigForwardingDesired
|  |  |  |  |  |  |     [15]  oraNamesConfigLogDirectory
|  |  |  |  |  |  |     [16]  oraNamesConfigLogStatsInterval
|  |  |  |  |  |  |     [17]  oraNamesConfigLogUnique
|  |  |  |  |  |  |     [18]  oraNamesConfigMaxOpenConnections
|  |  |  |  |  |  |     [19]  oraNamesConfigMaxReforwards
|  |  |  |  |  |  |     [20]  oraNamesConfigMessagePoolStartSize
|  |  |  |  |  |  |     [21]  oraNamesConfigNoModifyRequests
|  |  |  |  |  |  |     [22]  oraNamesConfigNoRegionDatabase
|  |  |  |  |  |  |     [23]  oraNamesConfigResetStatsInterval
|  |  |  |  |  |  |     [24]  oraNamesConfigServerName
|  |  |  |  |  |  |     [25]  oraNamesConfigTopologyCheckpointFile
|  |  |  |  |  |  |     [26]  oraNamesConfigTraceDirectory
|  |  |  |  |  |  |     [27]  oraNamesConfigTraceFunc
|  |  |  |  |  |  |     [28]  oraNamesConfigTraceMask
|  |  |  |  |  |  |     [29]  oraNamesConfigTraceUnique
|  |  |  |  |  [3 ] oraNamesServerTable
|  |  |  |  |  |  [1 ] oraNamesServerEntry
|  |  |  |  |  |  |     [1 ]  oraNamesServerQueriesReceived
|  |  |  |  |  |  |     [2 ]  oraNamesServerLastNnamesNotFound
|  |  |  |  |  |  |     [3 ]  oraNamesServerQueriesTotalTime
|  |  |  |  |  |  |     [4 ]  oraNamesServerDeletesReceived
|  |  |  |  |  |  |     [5 ]  oraNamesServerDeletesRefused
|  |  |  |  |  |  |     [6 ]  oraNamesServerDeletesTotalTime
|  |  |  |  |  |  |     [7 ]  oraNamesServerRenamesReceived
|  |  |  |  |  |  |     [8 ]  oraNamesServerRenamesRefused
|  |  |  |  |  |  |     [9 ]  oraNamesServerRenamesTotalTime
|  |  |  |  |  |  |     [10]  oraNamesServerUpdatesReceived
|  |  |  |  |  |  |     [11]  oraNamesServerUpdatesRefused
|  |  |  |  |  |  |     [12]  oraNamesServerUpdatesTotalTime
|  |  |  |  |  |  |     [13]  oraNamesServerCorruptMessagesReceived
|  |  |  |  |  |  |     [14]  oraNamesServerResponsesSent
|  |  |  |  |  |  |     [15]  oraNamesServerErrorResponsesSent
|  |  |  |  |  |  |     [16]  oraNamesServerAliasLoopsDetected
|  |  |  |  |  |  |     [17]  oraNamesServerLookupsAttempted
|  |  |  |  |  |  |     [18]  oraNamesServerCreatedOnLookup
```

Continued

Listing A-13   Continued

```
|  |  |  |  |  |   [19]  oraNamesServerLookupFailures
|  |  |  |  |  |   [20]  oraNamesServerExactMatches
|  |  |  |  |  |   [21]  oraNamesServerForwardFailures
|  |  |  |  |  |   [22]  oraNamesServerForwardTimeouts
|  |  |  |  |  |   [23]  oraNamesServerResponsesReceived
|  |  |  |  |  |   [24]  oraNamesServerErrorResponsesReceived
|  |  |  |  |  |   [25]  oraNamesServerRequestsForwarded
|  |  |  |  |  |   [26]  oraNamesServerLastReload
|  |  |  |  |  |   [27]  oraNamesServerReloadCheckFailures
|  |  |  |  |  |   [28]  oraNamesServerLastCheckpoint
|  |  |  |  |  |   [29]  oraNamesServerName
|  |  |  |  |  |   [30]  oraNamesServerAdminRegion
```

Monitoring Notes

If you intend to write your own SNMP application, the root OID of the Oracle Names MIB is 1.3.6.1.4.1.111.6.

The table entries in this MIB are indexed using appIndex from the Network Services MIB.

Running time in the oraNamesTNSTable table can be used to get an idea of how long the server has been running. Several fields in this table are not supported for Oracle Names, including the start date, security level, state, listen addresses, and failed listen addresses.

The oraNamesConfigTable includes important configuration information, such as the server name and administrative region name. Several fields in the table aren't supported for Oracle Names, including the configuration's checkpoint file, the default forwarders, fields related to domains, the configuration log file directory, the configuration unique log flag, the maximum number of open connections, the message pool start size, the region database flag, the topology checkpoint file, and the fields related to tracing.

The oraNamesServerTable includes important performance information, such as the number of queries received and responses sent, and the time spent processing the queries. Several fields aren't supported: last few names not found; information on deletes, renames, and updates; statistics on error responses; the last reload time; and the last checkpoint time.

Oracle Enterprise Manager MIB

Oracle Enterprise Manager (OEM) provides database management and monitoring. OEM supports the private Oracle Enterprise Manager MIB, which includes information about database events discovered by the OEM agent.

MIB Definition

Listing A-14 shows the complete specification for the Oracle Enterprise Manager MIB, as defined by Oracle.

Listing A-14   Oracle Enterprise Manager MIB specification.

```
enterprises
|   [111] oracle
|   |   [12] oraAgent
|   |   |   [1 ] oraAgentObjects
|   |   |   |   [1 ] oraAgentEventTable
|   |   |   |   |   [1 ] oraAgentEventEntry
|   |   |   |   |   |   [1 ] oraAgentEventIndex*
|   |   |   |   |   |   [2 ] oraAgentEventName
|   |   |   |   |   |   [3 ] oraAgentEventID
|   |   |   |   |   |   [4 ] oraAgentEventService
|   |   |   |   |   |   [5 ] oraAgentEventTime
|   |   |   |   |   |   [6 ] oraAgentEventSeverity
|   |   |   |   |   |   [7 ] oraAgentEventUser
|   |   |   |   |   |   [8 ] oraAgentEventAppID
|   |   |   |   |   |   [9 ] oraAgentEventMessage
|   |   |   |   |   |   [10] oraAgentEventArguments
|   |   |   |   |   |   [11] oraAgentEventResults
|   |   |   [2 ] oraAgentTraps
|   |   |   |   [1 ] oraAgentEventOcc
|   |   |   |   [2 ] oraAgentEventDbUpdown
|   |   |   |   [3 ] oraAgentEventDbAlert
|   |   |   |   [4 ] oraAgentEventDbProbe
|   |   |   |   [5 ] oraAgentEventDbUserBlock
|   |   |   |   [6 ] oraAgentEventDbArchFull
|   |   |   |   [7 ] oraAgentEventDbDumpFull
|   |   |   |   [8 ] oraAgentEventDbMaxExtent
|   |   |   |   [9 ] oraAgentEventDbChunkSmall
|   |   |   |   [10] oraAgentEventDbDatafileLimit
|   |   |   |   [11] oraAgentEventDbLockLimit
|   |   |   |   [12] oraAgentEventDbProcessLimit
|   |   |   |   [13] oraAgentEventDbSessionLimit
|   |   |   |   [14] oraAgentEventDbUserLimit
|   |   |   |   [15] oraAgentEventDbBufferCache
|   |   |   |   [16] oraAgentEventDbChainRow
|   |   |   |   [17] oraAgentEventDbDataDictionaryCache
|   |   |   |   [18] oraAgentEventDbDiskIORate
|   |   |   |   [19] oraAgentEventDbLibraryCache
|   |   |   |   [20] oraAgentEventDbNetIORate
|   |   |   |   [21] oraAgentEventDbResponseTime
|   |   |   |   [22] oraAgentEventDbSysStat
|   |   |   |   [23] oraAgentEventDbSysStatDelta
|   |   |   |   [24] oraAgentEventSQLNetUpDown
|   |   |   |   [25] oraAgentEventHostCPULoad
|   |   |   |   [26] oraAgentEventHostCPUUtil
|   |   |   |   [27] oraAgentEventHostPaging
|   |   |   |   [28] oraAgentEventHostSwapFull
|   |   |   |   [29] oraAgentEventHostDiskFull
```

Monitoring Notes

If you intend to write your own SNMP application, the root OID of the Oracle Enterprise Manager MIB is 1.3.6.1.4.1.111.12.

All events discovered by the OEM agent can also be sent as SNMP traps. Possible traps include reaching the limits on available file space or concurrent locks and sessions, falling below configured limits for cache hit ratios, and reaching system performance thresholds, such as CPU utilization.

Oracle MultiProtocol Interchange MIB

Oracle MultiProtocol Interchange is a product that is used to provide application connectivity by translating between different network transport stacks. It supports the private Oracle MultiProtocol Interchange MIB, which includes information about the current status of the MultiProtocol Interchange (MPI) and its components.

MIB Definition

Listing A-15 shows the complete specification for Oracle's private MultiProtocol Interchange MIB, as defined by Oracle.

Listing A-15   Oracle MultiProtocol Interchange MIB specification.

```
enterprises
|   [111] oracle
|   |   [7 ] oraInterchangeMIB
|   |   |   [1 ] oraInterchangeObjects
|   |   |   |   [1 ] oraInterchgTable
|   |   |   |   |   [1 ] oraInterchgEntry
|   |   |   |   |   |   [1 ] oraInterchgConfigDirectory
|   |   |   |   |   |   [2 ] oraInterchgContactInfo
|   |   |   |   |   [2 ] oraNavigatorTable
|   |   |   |   |   |   [1 ] oraNavigatorEntry
|   |   |   |   |   |   |   [1 ] oraNavigatorRunningTime
|   |   |   |   |   |   |   [2 ] oraNavigatorLogging
|   |   |   |   |   |   |   [3 ] oraNavigatorLoggingLevel
|   |   |   |   |   |   |   [4 ] oraNavigatorLogFile
|   |   |   |   |   |   |   [5 ] oraNavigatorTraceLevel
|   |   |   |   |   |   |   [6 ] oraNavigatorTraceFile
|   |   |   |   |   |   |   [7 ] oraNavigatorStoppable
|   |   |   |   |   |   |   [8 ] oraNavigatorAccumulatedSuccessfulRequests
|   |   |   |   |   |   |   [9 ] oraNavigatorAccumulatedFailedRequests
|   |   |   |   |   |   |   [10] oraNavigatorState
|   |   |   |   |   |   |   [11] oraNavigatorErrors
|   |   |   |   |   |   |   [12] oraNavigatorErrorMessage
|   |   |   |   [3 ] oraNavigatorListenAddressTable
```

```
|   |   |   |   |   | [1 ] oraNavigatorListenAddressEntry
|   |   |   |   |   |   | [1 ] oraNavigatorListenAddressIndex*
|   |   |   |   |   |   | [2 ] oraNavigatorListenAddress
|   |   |   |   | [4 ] oraNavigatorFailedAddressTable
|   |   |   |   |   | [1 ] oraNavigatorFailedAddressEntry
|   |   |   |   |   |   | [1 ] oraNavigatorFailedAddressIndex*
|   |   |   |   |   |   | [2 ] oraNavigatorFailedAddress
|   |   |   |   | [5 ] oraNavigatorRouteAddressTable
|   |   |   |   |   | [1 ] oraNavigatorRouteAddressEntry
|   |   |   |   |   |   | [1 ] oraNavigatorRouteAddressIndex*
|   |   |   |   |   |   | [2 ] oraNavigatorRouteAddress
|   |   |   |   | [6 ] oraCmanagerTable
|   |   |   |   |   | [1 ] oraCmanagerEntry
|   |   |   |   |   |   | [1 ] oraCmanagerStartTime
|   |   |   |   |   |   | [2 ] oraCmanagerRunningTime
|   |   |   |   |   |   | [3 ] oraCmanagerLogging
|   |   |   |   |   |   | [4 ] oraCmanagerLogFile
|   |   |   |   |   |   | [5 ] oraCmanagerTraceLevel
|   |   |   |   |   |   | [6 ] oraCmanagerTraceFile
|   |   |   |   |   |   | [7 ] oraCmanagerStoppable
|   |   |   |   |   |   | [8 ] oraCmanagerMaximumPumps
|   |   |   |   |   |   | [9 ] oraCmanagerMaximumConnectionsPerPump
|   |   |   |   |   |   | [10] oraCmanagerPumpStrategy
|   |   |   |   |   |   | [11] oraCmanagerActivePumps
|   |   |   |   |   |   | [12] oraCmanagerMaximumConnections
|   |   |   |   |   |   | [13] oraCmanagerCurrentConnectionsInUse
|   |   |   |   |   |   | [14] oraCmanagerAccumulatedSuccessfulConnections
|   |   |   |   |   |   | [15] oraCmanagerAccumulatedFailedConnections
|   |   |   |   |   |   | [16] oraCmanagerImmediateAverageBytes
|   |   |   |   |   |   | [17] oraCmanagerMaximumConnectTime
|   |   |   |   |   |   | [18] oraCmanagerMinimumConnectTime
|   |   |   |   |   |   | [19] oraCmanagerAverageConnectTime
|   |   |   |   |   |   | [20] oraCmanagerMaximumConnectDuration
|   |   |   |   |   |   | [21] oraCmanagerState
|   |   |   |   |   |   | [22] oraCmanagerErrors
|   |   |   |   |   |   | [23] oraCmanagerErrorMessage
|   |   |   |   | [7 ] oraCmanagerListenAddressTable
|   |   |   |   |   | [1 ] oraCmanagerListenAddressEntry
|   |   |   |   |   |   | [1 ] oraCmanagerListenAddressIndex*
|   |   |   |   |   |   | [2 ] oraCmanagerListenAddress
|   |   |   |   | [8 ] oraCmanagerFailedAddressTable
|   |   |   |   |   | [1 ] oraCmanagerFailedAddressEntry
|   |   |   |   |   |   | [1 ] oraCmanagerFailedAddressIndex*
|   |   |   |   |   |   | [2 ] oraCmanagerFailedAddress
|   |   |   |   | [9 ] oraPumpTable
|   |   |   |   |   | [1 ] oraPumpEntry
```

Continued

Listing A-15 Continued

```
| | | | | | | [1 ] oraPumpIndex*
| | | | | | | [2 ] oraPumpActiveTime
| | | | | | | [3 ] oraPumpTraceLevel
| | | | | | | [4 ] oraPumpTraceFile
| | | | | | | [5 ] oraPumpActiveConnections
| | | | | | | [6 ] oraPumpSuccessfulConnections
| | | | | | | [7 ] oraPumpFailedConnections
| | | | | | | [8 ] oraPumpAccumulatedBytesSent
| | | | | | | [9 ] oraPumpCurrentBytesPerSecond
| | | | | | | [10] oraPumpMaximumAverageBytes
| | | | | | | [11] oraPumpImmediateAverageBytes
| | | | | | | [12] oraPumpMaximumConnectTime
| | | | | | | [13] oraPumpMinimumConnectTime
| | | | | | | [14] oraPumpAverageConnectTime
| | | | | | | [15] oraPumpMaximumConnectDuration
| | | | | | | [16] oraPumpMaximumBuffers
| | | | | | | [17] oraPumpBufferUtilization
| | | | | | | [18] oraPumpErrors
| | | | | | | [19] oraPumpErrorMessage
| | | | | [10] oraPumpListenAddressTable
| | | | | | [1 ] oraPumpListenAddressEntry
| | | | | | | [1 ] oraPumpListenAddressIndex
| | | | | | | [2 ] oraPumpListenAddress
| | | | | [11] oraPumpFailedAddressTable
| | | | | | [1 ] oraPumpFailedAddressEntry
| | | | | | | [1 ] oraPumpFailedAddressIndex
| | | | | | | [2 ] oraPumpFailedAddress
| | | | | [12] oraConnectionTable
| | | | | | [1 ] oraConnectionEntry
| | | | | | | [1 ] oraConnectionIndex
| | | | | | | [2 ] oraConnectionPumpID
| | | | | | | [3 ] oraConnectionIdleTime
| | | | | | | [4 ] oraConnectionDuration
| | | | | | | [5 ] oraConnectionSourceAddress
| | | | | | | [6 ] oraConnectionDestinationAddress
| | | | [2 ] oraInterchgTraps
```

Monitoring Notes

If you intend to write your own SNMP application, the root OID of Oracle's MultiProtocol Interchange MIB is 1.3.6.1.4.1.111.7.

Many of the table entries in this MIB are indexed by using applIndex from the Network Services MIB.

This MIB includes information about several components of MPI, such as the Navigator and Connection Manager. The duration and idle time of each connection are also provided.

Informix Private Database MIB

The Informix-Online Dynamic Server has a private database MIB in addition to its support of the RDBMS MIB. Information available includes lock requests, checkpoint status, and the number of deadlocks.

MIB Definition

Listing A-16 shows the complete specification for the Informix-Online Private Database MIB, as defined by Informix.

Listing A-16   Informix-Online Private Database MIB specification.

```
enterprises
|   [893] informix
|   |   [1 ] servers
|   |   |   [1 ] onlineMIB
|   |   |   |   [1 ] onlineObjects
|   |   |   |   |   [1 ] onServerTable
|   |   |   |   |   |   [1 ] onServerEntry
|   |   |   |   |   |   |   [1 ] onServerMode
|   |   |   |   |   |   |   [2 ] onServerCheckpointInProgress
|   |   |   |   |   |   |   [3 ] onServerPageSize
|   |   |   |   |   |   |   [4 ] onServerThreads
|   |   |   |   |   |   |   [5 ] onServerVPs
|   |   |   |   |   |   |   [6 ] onServerVirtualMemory
|   |   |   |   |   |   |   [7 ] onServerResidentMemory
|   |   |   |   |   |   |   [8 ] onServerMessageMemory
|   |   |   |   |   |   |   [9 ] onServerIsamCalls
|   |   |   |   |   |   |   [10] onServerLatchWaits
|   |   |   |   |   |   |   [11] onServerLockRequests
|   |   |   |   |   |   |   [12] onServerLockWaits
|   |   |   |   |   |   |   [13] onServerBufferWaits
|   |   |   |   |   |   |   [14] onServerCheckpoints
|   |   |   |   |   |   |   [15] onServerCheckpointWaits
|   |   |   |   |   |   |   [16] onServerDeadLocks
|   |   |   |   |   |   |   [17] onServerLockTimeouts
|   |   |   |   |   |   |   [18] onServerLogicalLogRecords
|   |   |   |   |   |   |   [19] onServerLogicalLogPageWrites
|   |   |   |   |   |   |   [20] onServerLogicalLogWrites
|   |   |   |   |   |   |   [21] onServerBufferFlushes
|   |   |   |   |   |   |   [22] onServerForegroundWrites
|   |   |   |   |   |   |   [23] onServerLRUWrites
|   |   |   |   |   |   |   [24] onServerChunkWrites
|   |   |   |   |   |   |   [25] onServerReadAheadPages
|   |   |   |   |   |   |   [26] onServerReadAheadPagesUsed
|   |   |   |   |   |   |   [27] onServerSequentialScans
|   |   |   |   |   |   |   [28] onServerMemorySorts
```

Continued

Listing A-16   Continued

```
|   |   |   |   |   |   |   |   [29] onServerDiskSorts
|   |   |   |   |   |   |   |   [30] onServerMaxSortSpace
|   |   |   |   |   |   |   |   [31] onServerNetworkReads
|   |   |   |   |   |   |   |   [32] onServerNetworkWrites
|   |   |   |   |   |   |   |   [33] onServerPDQCalls
|   |   |   |   |   |   [2 ] onDatabaseTable
|   |   |   |   |   |   |   [1 ] onDatabaseEntry
|   |   |   |   |   |   |   |   [1 ] onDatabaseDbspace
|   |   |   |   |   |   |   |   [2 ] onDatabaseCreated
|   |   |   |   |   |   |   |   [3 ] onDatabaseLogging
|   |   |   |   |   |   |   |   [4 ] onDatabaseOpenStatus
|   |   |   |   |   |   |   |   [5 ] onDatabaseUsers
|   |   |   |   |   |   [3 ] onTableTable
|   |   |   |   |   |   |   [1 ] onTableEntry
|   |   |   |   |   |   |   |   [1 ] onTableIndex
|   |   |   |   |   |   |   |   [2 ] onTableName
|   |   |   |   |   |   |   |   [3 ] onTableOwner
|   |   |   |   |   |   |   |   [4 ] onTableType
|   |   |   |   |   |   |   |   [5 ] onTableLockLevel
|   |   |   |   |   |   |   |   [6 ] onTableCreated
|   |   |   |   |   |   |   |   [7 ] onTableFirstDbspace
|   |   |   |   |   |   |   |   [8 ] onTableRowSize
|   |   |   |   |   |   |   |   [9 ] onTableRows
|   |   |   |   |   |   |   |   [10] onTableColumns
|   |   |   |   |   |   |   |   [11] onTableIndices
|   |   |   |   |   |   |   |   [12] onTableExtents
|   |   |   |   |   |   |   |   [13] onTablePagesAllocated
|   |   |   |   |   |   |   |   [14] onTablePagesUsed
|   |   |   |   |   |   |   |   [15] onTableFragments
|   |   |   |   |   |   |   |   [16] onTableFragmentStrategy
|   |   |   |   |   |   |   |   [17] onTableActiveFragments
|   |   |   |   |   |   [4 ] onActiveTableTable
|   |   |   |   |   |   |   [1 ] onActiveTableEntry
|   |   |   |   |   |   |   |   [1 ] onActiveTableStatus
|   |   |   |   |   |   |   |   [2 ] onActiveTableIsBeingAltered
|   |   |   |   |   |   |   |   [3 ] onActiveTableUsers
|   |   |   |   |   |   |   |   [4 ] onActiveTableLockRequests
|   |   |   |   |   |   |   |   [5 ] onActiveTableLockWaits
|   |   |   |   |   |   |   |   [6 ] onActiveTableLockTimeouts
|   |   |   |   |   |   |   |   [7 ] onActiveTableIsamReads
|   |   |   |   |   |   |   |   [8 ] onActiveTableIsamWrites
|   |   |   |   |   |   |   |   [9 ] onActiveTableBufferReads
|   |   |   |   |   |   |   |   [10] onActiveTableBufferWrites
|   |   |   |   |   |   [5 ] onFragmentTable
|   |   |   |   |   |   |   [1 ] onFragmentEntry
```

```
|  |  |  |  |  |  |  |  [1 ]  onFragmentIndex
|  |  |  |  |  |  |  |  [2 ]  onFragmentType
|  |  |  |  |  |  |  |  [3 ]  onFragmentDbspace
|  |  |  |  |  |  |  |  [4 ]  onFragmentExpression
|  |  |  |  |  |  |  |  [5 ]  onFragmentIndexName
|  |  |  |  |  |  |  |  [6 ]  onFragmentExtents
|  |  |  |  |  |  |  |  [7 ]  onFragmentPagesAllocated
|  |  |  |  |  |  |  |  [8 ]  onFragmentPagesUsed
|  |  |  |  |  |  |  |  [9 ]  onFragmentIsamReads
|  |  |  |  |  |  |  |  [10]  onFragmentIsamWrites
|  |  |  |  |  [6 ]  onDbspaceTable
|  |  |  |  |  |  [1 ]  onDbspaceEntry
|  |  |  |  |  |  |  [1 ]  onDbspaceIndex*
|  |  |  |  |  |  |  [2 ]  onDbspaceName
|  |  |  |  |  |  |  [3 ]  onDbspaceOwner
|  |  |  |  |  |  |  [4 ]  onDbspaceCreated
|  |  |  |  |  |  |  [5 ]  onDbspaceChunks
|  |  |  |  |  |  |  [6 ]  onDbspaceType
|  |  |  |  |  |  |  [7 ]  onDbspaceMirrorStatus
|  |  |  |  |  |  |  [8 ]  onDbspaceRecoveryStatus
|  |  |  |  |  |  |  [9 ]  onDbspaceBackupStatus
|  |  |  |  |  |  |  [10]  onDbspaceMiscStatus
|  |  |  |  |  |  |  [11]  onDbspacePagesAllocated
|  |  |  |  |  |  |  [12]  onDbspacePagesUsed
|  |  |  |  |  |  |  [13]  onDbspaceBackupDate
|  |  |  |  |  [7 ]  onChunkTable
|  |  |  |  |  |  [1 ]  onChunkEntry
|  |  |  |  |  |  |  [1 ]  onChunkIndex
|  |  |  |  |  |  |  [2 ]  onChunkFileName
|  |  |  |  |  |  |  [3 ]  onChunkFileOffset
|  |  |  |  |  |  |  [4 ]  onChunkPagesAllocated
|  |  |  |  |  |  |  [5 ]  onChunkPagesUsed
|  |  |  |  |  |  |  [6 ]  onChunkType
|  |  |  |  |  |  |  [7 ]  onChunkStatus
|  |  |  |  |  |  |  [8 ]  onChunkMirroring
|  |  |  |  |  |  |  [9 ]  onChunkReads
|  |  |  |  |  |  |  [10]  onChunkPageReads
|  |  |  |  |  |  |  [11]  onChunkWrites
|  |  |  |  |  |  |  [12]  onChunkPageWrites
|  |  |  |  |  |  |  [13]  onChunkMirrorFileName
|  |  |  |  |  |  |  [14]  onChunkMirrorFileOffset
|  |  |  |  |  |  |  [15]  onChunkMirrorStatus
|  |  |  |  |  [8 ]  onLogicalLogTable
|  |  |  |  |  |  [1 ]  onLogicalLogEntry
|  |  |  |  |  |  |  [1 ]  onLogicalLogIndex*
|  |  |  |  |  |  |  [2 ]  onLogicalLogID
```

Continued

Listing A-16 Continued

```
| | | | | | | |     [3 ] onLogicalLogDbspace
| | | | | | | |     [4 ] onLogicalLogStatus
| | | | | | | |     [5 ] onLogicalLogContainsLastCheckpoint
| | | | | | | |     [6 ] onLogicalLogIsTemporary
| | | | | | | |     [7 ] onLogicalLogPagesAllocated
| | | | | | | |     [8 ] onLogicalLogPagesUsed
| | | | | | | |     [9 ] onLogicalLogFillTime
| | | | | |   [9 ] onPhysicalLogTable
| | | | | |     [1 ] onPhysicalLogEntry
| | | | | |       [1 ] onPhysicalLogDbspace
| | | | | |       [2 ] onPhysicalLogBufferSize
| | | | | |       [3 ] onPhysicalLogBufferUsed
| | | | | |       [4 ] onPhysicalLogPageWrites
| | | | | |       [5 ] onPhysicalLogWrites
| | | | | |       [6 ] onPhysicalLogPagesAllocated
| | | | | |       [7 ] onPhysicalLogPagesUsed
| | | | | |   [10] onSessionTable
| | | | | |     [1 ] onSessionEntry
| | | | | | | |     [1 ] onSessionIndex*
| | | | | | | |     [2 ] onSessionUserName
| | | | | | | |     [3 ] onSessionUserProgramVersion
| | | | | | | |     [4 ] onSessionUserProcessId
| | | | | | | |     [5 ] onSessionUserTime
| | | | | | | |     [6 ] onSessionState
| | | | | | | |     [7 ] onSessionDatabase
| | | | | | | |     [8 ] onSessionCurrentMemory
| | | | | | | |     [9 ] onSessionThreads
| | | | | | | |     [10] onSessionLockRequests
| | | | | | | |     [11] onSessionLocksHeld
| | | | | | | |     [12] onSessionLockWaits
| | | | | | | |     [13] onSessionLockTimeouts
| | | | | | | |     [14] onSessionLogRecords
| | | | | | | |     [15] onSessionIsamReads
| | | | | | | |     [16] onSessionIsamWrites
| | | | | | | |     [17] onSessionPageReads
| | | | | | | |     [18] onSessionPageWrites
| | | | | | | |     [19] onSessionLongTxs
| | | | | | | |     [20] onSessionLogSpace
| | | | | | | |     [21] onSessionHighwaterLogSpace
| | | | | | | |     [22] onSessionSqlStatement
| | | | | | | |     [23] onSessionSqlIsolation
| | | | | | | |     [24] onSessionSqlLockWaitMode
| | | | | | | |     [25] onSessionSqlEstimatedCost
| | | | | | | |     [26] onSessionSqlEstimatedRows
```

```
|   |   |   |   |   |   |   |   [27]  onSessionSqlError
|   |   |   |   |   |   |   |   [28]  onSessionSqlIsamError
|   |   |   |   |   |   |   |   [29]  onSessionTransactionStatus
|   |   |   |   |   |   |   |   [30]  onSessionTransactionBeginLog
|   |   |   |   |   |   |   |   [31]  onSessionTransactionLastLog
|   |   |   |   |   |   [11]  onLockTable
|   |   |   |   |   |   |   [1 ]  onLockEntry
|   |   |   |   |   |   |   |   [1 ]  onLockIndex
|   |   |   |   |   |   |   |   [2 ]  onLockDatabaseName
|   |   |   |   |   |   |   |   [3 ]  onLockTableName
|   |   |   |   |   |   |   |   [4 ]  onLockType
|   |   |   |   |   |   |   |   [5 ]  onLockGranularity
|   |   |   |   |   |   |   |   [6 ]  onLockRowId
|   |   |   |   |   |   |   |   [7 ]  onLockWaiters
|   |   |   |   |   |   |   |   [8 ]  onLockGrantTime
|   |   |   |   |   |   [12]  onBarTable
|   |   |   |   |   |   |   [1 ]  onBarEntry
|   |   |   |   |   |   |   |   [1 ]  onBarActivityIndex*
|   |   |   |   |   |   |   |   [2 ]  onBarObjectIndex
|   |   |   |   |   |   |   |   [3 ]  onBarObjectName
|   |   |   |   |   |   |   |   [4 ]  onBarObjectType
|   |   |   |   |   |   |   |   [5 ]  onBarBackupLevel
|   |   |   |   |   |   |   |   [6 ]  onBarActionStatus
|   |   |   |   |   |   |   |   [7 ]  onBarTimeStamp
|   |   |   |   |   |   [13]  onSqlHostTable
|   |   |   |   |   |   |   [1 ]  onSqlHostEntry
|   |   |   |   |   |   |   |   [1 ]  onSqlHostIndex*
|   |   |   |   |   |   |   |   [2 ]  onSqlHostName
|   |   |   |   |   |   |   |   [3 ]  onSqlHostNetType
|   |   |   |   |   |   |   |   [4 ]  onSqlHostServerName
|   |   |   |   |   |   |   |   [5 ]  onSqlHostServiceName
|   |   |   |   |   |   [14]  onSnmpTable
|   |   |   |   |   |   |   [1 ]  onSnmpEntry
|   |   |   |   |   |   |   |   [1 ]  onSnmpIndex*
|   |   |   |   |   |   |   |   [2 ]  onSnmpName
|   |   |   |   |   |   |   |   [3 ]  onSnmpOID
|   |   |   |   |   |   |   |   [4 ]  onSnmpRefreshType
|   |   |   |   |   |   |   |   [5 ]  onSnmpRefreshInterval
|   |   |   |   |   |   |   |   [6 ]  onSnmpNextRefresh
|   |   |   |   |   |   |   |   [7 ]  onSnmpRefreshes
|   |   |   |   |   |   |   |   [8 ]  onSnmpHoldInterval
|   |   |   |   |   |   |   |   [9 ]  onSnmpRows
|   |   |   |   |   |   |   |   [10]  onSnmpColumns
|   |   |   |   |   |   |   |   [11]  onSnmpRetries
|   |   |   |   |   |   |   |   [12]  onSnmpFailures
```

Monitoring Notes

If you intend to write your own SNMP application, the root OID of the Informix-Online Private Database MIB is 1.3.6.1.4.1.893.1.1.

Many of the table entries in this MIB are indexed by using applIndex from the Network Services MIB and rdbmsDbIndex from the RDBMS MIB.

You can use the server mode, onServerMode, to determine whether the server is online, shutting down, or backing up. The MIB variable onServerCheckpointInProgress can give additional information about the server's activities. The Informix MIB also provides status information on all open tables, the database recovery process, and log files.

A variety of performance and resource management information is included in this MIB. For example, to determine whether your sort area is too small, you can check onServerDiskSorts to see how many sorts are requiring disk space.

Using DMI and MIFs

The Desktop Management Interface (DMI) is a standard for storing and accessing management information. DMI was created by the Desktop Management Task Force (DMTF), an industry consortium focused on improving the manageability of personal computers and related products.

Management information is represented in a text file in the Management Information Format (MIF). Management information is divided by component. Each component's information consists of one or more groups, and each group has one or more attributes. If a group has multiple instantiations, then it is called a table. Each managed component must provide a separate MIF file describing its manageable attributes.

Each component has an interface to provide information to the DMI service layer. A DMI Service Provider (SP) is responsible for giving component information to the management applications that request it. Management applications communicate with the SP via DMI functions, collectively referred to as the *Procedural Management Interface*, to obtain information about a component. The interaction between these modules is shown in Figure A-4. Similar to SNMP, DMI has Get and Set commands to read and write component information.

After being queried, the SP uses additional APIs to get its information and send replies to the requesting management application. A management application can also use a list command to get information about the MIF definition itself.

The SP enables applications to register for events associated with a component. An *indication* refers to any notification by the DMI SP to an event consumer, including event notifications and notifications of changes in the SP's database, such as the addition or modification of a group in the database. The SP delivers the indication to all applications that have registered for it. The event is included in an indication data structure that is meant to look identical to a reply message to a DMI Get request.

The following list shows the required attributes associated with an indication:

Figure A-4 DMI architecture.

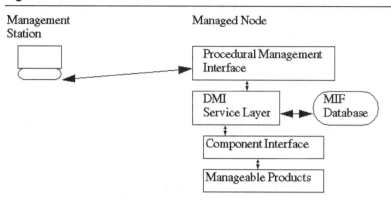

- **Event type**: Provides the reason for the event.
- **Event severity**: Describes the type of event. Severities of OK, Non-Critical, Critical, and Non-Recoverable are used for state-based events. A severity of Monitor is used for an expected periodic event; a severity of Information is used for a nonperiodic event.
- **Whether event is state-based**: State-based event generators are expected to generate no more than one event of any given event type for each relevant state transition. Events with an OK severity are expected to clear each of these events. An event generator that is not state-based sends an event for each condition that occurs, and doesn't send corresponding OK events.
- **Event state key**: Refers to the number of the row in the event state group that is associated with the component. This is used only for state-based events.
- **Associated group:** Identifies the group generating the event.
- **Event system:** Refers to the specific part of the component causing the event.
- **Event subsystem:** Also refers to the specific part of the component causing the event.

Optional fields that can be part of an event include a recommended corrective action and vendor-specific data.

The event data received by an application is a DmiMultiRowData structure. The first DmiRowData structure contains the foregoing event attributes. A second DmiRowData structure is used when the group generating the event has multiple instances. A *key* refers to the specific instance generating the event. The third DmiRowData structure is used when an event is forwarded to its eventual destination, and it contains the address of the source system. Additional rows contain any proprietary information that might be associated with the event.

Additional information about DMI data structures and current MIF specifications can be found in the DMTF's *Desktop Management Interface Specification* on the Web at http://www.dmtf.org.

The following sections describe two important Unix MIFs: the System MIF and Software MIF. Note that in the following MIF specifications, an asterisk (*) suffix indicates that the variable serves as an index for a table entry.

System MIF

The DMI System MIF contains general information about the server, as well as specifics about disks and filesystems. Some information, such as the system name, uptime, and operating system version, is also provided in the MIB-II. The System MIF provides for events to be sent for disk device and storage allocation errors.

MIF Definition

Listing A-17 shows the complete System MIF specification, as defined by the DMTF.

Listing A-17   System MIF specification.

```
DMTF
|   [1 ] ComponentID
|   |   [1 ] Manufacturer
|   |   [2 ] Product
|   |   [3 ] Version
|   |   [4 ] Serial Number
|   |   [5 ] Installation
|   |   [6 ] Verify
|   [  ] General Information
|   |   [1 ] System Name
|   |   [2 ] System Location
|   |   [3 ] System Primary User Name
|   |   [4 ] System Primary User Phone
|   |   [5 ] System Boot Up Time
|   |   [6 ] System Date Time
|   |   [7 ] System Secondary User Name
|   |   [8 ] System Secondary User Phone
|   |   [9 ] System Primary Pager
|   |   [10] System Secondary Pager
|   [  ] Operating System
|   |   [1 ] Operating System Index*
|   |   [2 ] Operating System Name
|   |   [3 ] Operating System Version
|   |   [4 ] Primary Operating System
|   |   [5 ] Operating System Description
|   [  ] Host System Group
|   |   [1 ] SystemUpTime
|   |   [2 ] SystemInitialLoadDevice
|   |   [3 ] SystemInitialLoadParameters
|   |   [4 ] SystemNumUsers
```

```
|   |   [5 ] SystemProcesses
|   |   [6 ] SystemMaxProcesses
|   [   ] Host Storage Group
|   |   [1 ] Physical Main Memory Size
|   [   ] Host Storage Table
|   |   [1 ] Table Index*
|   |   [2 ] Type of Storage
|   |   [3 ] Description
|   |   [4 ] Allocation Units
|   |   [5 ] Size
|   |   [6 ] Used
|   |   [7 ] Storage Allocation Failures
|   [   ] Host Device Table
|   |   [1 ] Device Table Index*
|   |   [2 ] Device Type
|   |   [3 ] Device Description
|   |   [4 ] ID
|   |   [5 ] Device Status
|   |   [6 ] Device Errors
|   |   [**] Event Generation
|   [   ] Host Processor Table
|   |   [1 ] Processor Table Index*
|   |   [2 ] ProcessorFrwID
|   |   [3 ] ProcessorLoad
|   |   [**] Event Generation
|   [   ] Host Disk Storage Table
|   |   [1 ] Table Index*
|   |   [2 ] Disk Storage Access
|   |   [3 ] Disk Storage Media
|   |   [4 ] Disk Storage Removable
|   |   [5 ] Disk Storage Capacity
|   |   [**] Event Generation
|   [   ] Host FSTable
|   |   [1 ] FSIndex*
|   |   [2 ] FSMountPoint
|   |   [3 ] RemoteFSMountPoint
|   |   [4 ] FSType
|   |   [5 ] FSAccess
|   |   [6 ] FSBootable
|   |   [7 ] FSStorageIndex
|   |   [8 ] FSLastFullBackupDate
|   |   [9 ] FSLastPartialBackupDate
|   [   ] System Contact Information
|   |   [1 ] Contact Index*
|   |   [2 ] Contact Name
|   |   [3 ] Contact Type
|   |   [4 ] Contact Information
```

Monitoring Notes

Like MIB-II, the System MIF can be used to get generic system information, such as how long the system has been running and system contact information. It can also be useful for checking for any disk-related errors.

Software MIF

The DMI Software MIF supplies information about the software products and product bundles installed on the system. Fileset and vendor information are also included. The swlist command provides most of the instrumentation.

MIF Definition

Listing A-18 shows the complete Software MIF specification, as defined by the DMTF.

Listing A-18   Software MIF specification.

```
DMTF
|   [1 ] ComponentID
|   |   [1 ] Manufacturer
|   |   [2 ] Product
|   |   [3 ] Version
|   |   [4 ] Serial Number
|   |   [5 ] Installation
|   |   [6 ] Verify
|   [2 ] Software Location
|   |   [1 ] Path
|   |   [2 ] Catalog
|   |   [3 ] Dfiles
|   |   [4 ] Layout Version
|   |   [5 ] Pfiles
|   [3 ] Vendors
|   |   [1 ] Tag*
|   |   [2 ] Index*
|   |   [3 ] Title
|   |   [4 ] Description
|   [4 ] Bundles
|   |   [1 ] Bundle Software Specification*
|   |   [2 ] Tag
|   |   [3 ] Architecture
|   |   [4 ] Location
|   |   [5 ] Qualifier
|   |   [6 ] Revision
|   |   [7 ] Vendor Tag
|   |   [8 ] Create Time
|   |   [9 ] Description
```

```
|   |   [10] Modification Time
|   |   [11] Size
|   |   [12] Title
|   |   [13] Copyright
|   |   [14] Directory
|   |   [15] Instance Identifier
|   |   [16] Is Locatable
|   |   [17] Layout Version
|   |   [18] Machine Type
|   |   [19] Number
|   |   [20] Operating System Name
|   |   [21] Operating System Release
|   |   [22] Operating System Version
|   [5 ] Bundle Contents
|   |   [1 ] Bundle Software Specification*
|   |   [2 ] Index*
|   |   [3 ] Content
|   [6 ] Products
|   |   [1 ] Product Software Specification*
|   |   [2 ] Tag
|   |   [3 ] Architecture
|   |   [4 ] Location
|   |   [5 ] Qualifier
|   |   [6 ] Revision
|   |   [7 ] Vendor Tag
|   |   [8 ] Create Time
|   |   [9 ] Description
|   |   [10] Modification Time
|   |   [11] Size
|   |   [12] Title
|   |   [13] All Filesets
|   |   [14] Control Directory
|   |   [15] Copyright
|   |   [16] Directory
|   |   [17] Instance Identifier
|   |   [18] Is Locatable
|   |   [19] Post Kernel Path
|   |   [20] Layout Version
|   |   [21] Machine Type
|   |   [22] Number
|   |   [23] Operating System Name
|   |   [24] Operating System Release
|   |   [25] Operating System Version
|   [7 ] Product  Contents
|   |   [1 ] Product Software Specification*
|   |   [2 ] Index*
```

Continued

Listing A-18   Continued

```
|   |   [3 ] Content
|   |   [4 ] Content Type
|   [8 ] Product Control Files
|   |   [1 ] Product Software Specification*
|   |   [2 ] Tag*
|   |   [3 ] Cksum
|   |   [4 ] Compressed Cksum
|   |   [5 ] Compressed Size
|   |   [6 ] Compression State
|   |   [7 ] Compression Type
|   |   [8 ] Revision
|   |   [9 ] Size
|   |   [10] Source
|   |   [11] Interpreter
|   |   [12] Path
|   |   [13] Result
|   [9 ] Subproducts
|   |   [1 ] Subproduct Software Specification*
|   |   [2 ] Tag
|   |   [3 ] Create Time
|   |   [4 ] Description
|   |   [5 ] Modification Time
|   |   [6 ] Size
|   |   [7 ] Title
|   |   [8 ] Contents
|   [10] Filesets
|   |   [1 ] Fileset Software Specification*
|   |   [2 ] Tag
|   |   [3 ] Create Time
|   |   [4 ] Description
|   |   [5 ] Modification Time
|   |   [6 ] Size
|   |   [7 ] Title
|   |   [8 ] Control Directory
|   |   [9 ] Is Kernel
|   |   [10] Is Locatable
|   |   [11] Is Reboot
|   |   [12] Location
|   |   [13] Media Sequence List
|   |   [14] Revision
|   |   [15] State
|   [11] Fileset Contents
|   |   [1 ] Fileset Software Specification*
|   |   [2 ] Index*
```

```
|   |   [3 ] Content
|   |   [4 ] Content Type
|   [12] Fileset Dependencies
|   |   [1 ] Fileset Software Specification*
|   |   [2 ] Index*
|   |   [3 ] Dependency
|   |   [4 ] Dependency Type
|   [13] Fileset Control Files
|   |   [1 ] Fileset Software Specification*
|   |   [2 ] Tag*
|   |   [3 ] Cksum
|   |   [4 ] Compressed Cksum
|   |   [5 ] Compressed Size
|   |   [6 ] Compression State
|   |   [7 ] Compression Type
|   |   [8 ] Revision
|   |   [9 ] Size
|   |   [10] Source
|   |   [11] Interpreter
|   |   [12] Path
|   |   [13] Result
|   [14] Fileset Files
|   |   [1 ] Fileset Software Specification*
|   |   [2 ] Path*
|   |   [3 ] Cksum
|   |   [4 ] Compressed Cksum
|   |   [5 ] Compressed Size
|   |   [6 ] Compression State
|   |   [7 ] Compression Type
|   |   [8 ] Revision
|   |   [9 ] Size
|   |   [10] Source
|   |   [11] Gid
|   |   [12] Group
|   |   [13] Is Volatile
|   |   [14] Link Source
|   |   [15] Major
|   |   [16] Minor
|   |   [17] Mode
|   |   [18] Mtime
|   |   [19] Owner
|   |   [20] File Type
|   |   [21] Uid
```

Monitoring Notes

The Software MIF can be a useful tool after discovering a problem with a product. Using a MIF Browser, you can examine the Software MIF to see whether the problem might be caused by a bad patch installation or a modified file. The MIF contains revision information for each product, and its creation and modification times. Version information can be checked to see whether a compatibility problem exists. Finally, the product's vendor information is provided, in case you need to contact product support personnel.

AAL ATM Adaptation Layer. The AAL translates digital voice, image, video, and data signals into the ATM cell format, and vice versa. There are four AALs defined (AAL1, AAL2, AAL3/4, and AAL5) that provide different services and have been recommended by the CCITT. The services have three distinguishing attributes: whether or not they require the transfer of timing information between source and destination, whether a constant or variable bit rate is supported, and whether the service is connectionless or connection-oriented. For example, AAL5 supports connection-oriented variable bit rate data services.

ABAP A programming language used with SAP R/3.

ARM Application Resource Measurement. ARM is a standardized set of APIs for measuring application transactions.

ARP Address Resolution Protocol. This protocol is used to find the station address associated with a given higher-level protocol address such as an IP address. The mappings between IP address and station address are then stored on the local system in an ARP cache.

ATM Asynchronous Transfer Mode. A form of digital transmission based on the transfer of units of information known as cells. It is suitable for the transmission of image, voice, video, and data. Asynchronous operations are allowed between the sender clock and receiver clock, with empty packets in the stream used to resolve clock differences.

CCITT International Consultative Committee for Telecommunications and Telegraphy. CCITT defines international standards for telephony and telegraphy. CCITT standards include ATM, but in general their standards are identified by a letter, followed by a period, followed by a number. X.400 is an example.

CCMS Computing Center Management System. CCMS is a management tool for the SAP R/3 application.

cell A transmission unit of a fixed length used in cell relay transmission techniques, such as ATM. An ATM cell is made up of 53 bytes (octets), including a 5-byte header and a 48-byte data payload. The 48-byte standard was a compromise between the 32-byte size recommended by Europe, and the 64-byte size promoted by the U.S. and Japan.

CiscoWorks A network management product from Cisco Corporation.

cluster A generic term used to refer to a set of computer systems sharing a common attribute. For HP-UX 10.*x* and 11.*x* operating systems, a cluster is often associated with the set of HP series 800 computer systems running MC/ServiceGuard high availability software and being commonly administered.

ClusterView A Hewlett-Packard product used to manage groups of systems, or clusters. It is an HP OpenView application designed primarily to monitor high availability clusters such as MC/ServiceGuard and MC/LockManager. ClusterView can also monitor Windows NT high availability clusters, and other groups of systems, such as an EPS cluster.

CMIP Common Management Information Protocol. CMIP is a protocol standardized by Open Systems Interconnection for accessing management information and receiving status events.

collision A network transmission error caused by two network devices trying to send data on a shared medium at the same time.

COPS Computer Oracle and Password System. A network monitoring product for Unix systems. COPS checks for security weaknesses and provides warnings.

CPU Central Processing Unit. The computer component responsible for executing the machine instructions on behalf of user and system processes.

CRC Cyclic Redundancy Check. LAN technologies such as Ethernet and Token Ring use a CRC field in the network packet to ensure that the data is exchanged with the target without error.

DBA Database Administrator.

DHCP Dynamic Host Configuration Protocol. A protocol to help with the administration of IP addresses and other configuration information. A client requests its configuration information from a DHCP server automatically, instead of requiring manual configuration by a system administrator.

DML Data Manipulation Language. DML is the set of SQL commands that affect the contents of database objects (e.g., SELECT, insert, update).

DNS Domain Name System. A name service for translating between computer system names and IP addresses.

DSI Data Source Integration. A MeasureWare API that allows the MeasureWare Agent to collect data from different data sources.

ELAN Emulated LAN. An ELAN interface is an ATM card running LAN emulation.

EPS Enterprise Parallel Server. Enterprise Parallel Server is Hewlett-Packard's high-end clustered server product.

ERP Enterprise Resource Planning. ERP applications such as Baan and SAP R/3 are used by corporations for supply-chain management.

extent An amount of disk space allocated to a file with the intent of keeping future records physically close together.

FCS Frame Check Sequence. A checksum used to indicate whether a packet has been corrupted on the network medium.

FDDI Fiber Distributed Data Interface. FDDI is a LAN technology that uses fiber optics and is capable of data rates of 100Mbps.

firewall A system separating multiple networks to limit access by enforcing a security policy.

GlancePlus A real-time, graphical, performance monitoring product from Hewlett-Packard.

ICMP Internet Control Message Protocol. This networking protocol is part of the TCP/IP protocol suite and is used for passing error and control information between gateways and other systems. The ping command uses the ICMP protocol. The ICMP protocol uses IP datagrams for transmitting its information.

inode A kernel data structure associated with a file or directory in the filesystem.

IP Internet Protocol. IP is a network protocol and is part of the TCP/IP protocol suite. IP provides the packet routing and delivery functions for TCP, UDP, and ICMP.

IP address Internet Protocol address. An IP address is currently a 32-bit address consisting of a network identifier and a system identifier. A name resolution service can convert a system name to an IP address. Network applications usually use a name or IP address for communication. The networking kernel software then converts the IP address to a station address using ARP.

ISO International Standards Organization. An international organization that creates standards to facilitate the exchange of goods and services among nations.

IT/O IT/Operations. A network management product from Hewlett-Packard. IT/O includes the Network Node Manager and also provides an Application Desktop for launching administrative tools.

JFS Journalled File System. A journalled filesystem can track updates to a file so that if the file is damaged, it can be recovered.

kernel The operating system controlling system services such as memory management, CPU scheduling, and device I/O.

LAN Emulation Local Area Network Emulation. A protocol to make an ATM network look and behave like an Ethernet or Token Ring LAN. The LANE protocol defines a service interface for higher-layer (the network layer) protocols that is identical to that of existing LANs. Data sent across the ATM network is encapsulated in the appropriate LAN packet format. LAN Emulation allows interoperability between ATM and existing LAN technology.

LVM Logical Volume Manager. A set of commands for managing your disks. In addition to setting up logical volumes, LVM can be used to stripe data across disks and to mirror data.

MAC Media Access Control. Station addresses are also referred to as MAC addresses.

managed node The computer system being monitored or managed.

management station The computer system from which you monitor other systems in the enterprise.

Mbps Million bits per second.

MC/LockManager A high availability product from Hewlett-Packard. It is used to protect applications running in the Oracle Parallel Server environment on HP-UX systems.

MCSE Multi-Computer System Environment. MCSE refers to the Hewlett-Packard management software used to support the Enterprise Parallel Server. This software has been rendered obsolete by the ClusterView product.

MC/ServiceGuard A high availability product from Hewlett-Packard that protects HP-UX systems and restarts applications when they fail.

MeasureWare A performance management product from Hewlett-Packard.

MERIT Maximizing Efficiency of Resources in Information Technology. A project sponsored by Computer Associates, Inc.

MIB Management Information Base. A MIB is an SNMP format for representing information about managed components.

MIB-II A standard defining how to store management information pertaining to a computer system.

MIF Management Information Format. A MIF is a Desktop Management Interface format for representing information about managed components.

MPI MultiProtocol Interchange. An Oracle product used to provide application connectivity by translating between different network transport stacks such as TCP/IP and IPX/SPX. MPI uses SQL*NET.

MTU Maximum Transmission Unit. The MTU is the maximum size of a packet that can be sent on a network link. For example, the data portion of an Ethernet frame cannot exceed 1500 bytes. Transfer of data across links with different MTU sizes can lead to fragmentation by the IP layer.

NetManager A network management product from Sun Microsystems.

NetMetrix A network performance management product from Hewlett-Packard.

NetView A network management product from IBM Corporation.

NFS Network File System. NFS provides transparent access to remote, networked filesystems. The physical location of files is hidden from the user.

NIS Network Information Service. NIS can be used to store and distribute information such as configuration data from a central location.

NNM Network Node Manager. NNM is a network management product from Hewlett-Packard. It provides status and discovery of network devices.

OID Object Identifier. An OID refers to the unique identifier for a MIB variable.

Oracle Names A product providing a directory service by making database address and database link information available to all systems throughout the network.

Oracle Network Listener An Oracle process that is part of SQL*NET. It is used to receive remote database connection requests.

OSI Open Systems Interconnection. The ISO model for computer networks that is a standard way to describe network behavior. Networks are divided into seven layers: physical, data link, network, transport, session, presentation, and application.

package An MC/ServiceGuard package is an application that has been specifically configured with high availability protection. The package configuration includes the control scripts needed to start and stop the application, and the list of processes and resources needed to run the application.

packet A block of data sent over the network.

PerfView A graphical performance monitoring product from Hewlett-Packard.

PID Process Identification. A unique identifier for a process running on a computer system.

ping Packet Internet Groper. The ping command uses the ICMP protocol to test the connectivity to a remote system.

promiscuous mode A LAN interface in promiscuous mode will read all packets given to the system, not just those addressed to it.

PVC Permanent Virtual Circuit. A PVC is a channel through a network provided by a carrier between two end points for dedicated, long-term information transfer between two locations.

RAM Random Access Memory. All or a portion of a program's pages are loaded into RAM to be executed.

RARP Reverse Address Resolution Protocol. RARP is a protocol that maps a station address to an IP address. It can be used by a diskless workstation to get its IP address.

RDBMS Relational Database Management System. For example, Oracle, Sybase, and Informix are relational database management systems.

RFC Request For Comments. RFCs are publicly available specifications for Internet protocols.

RMON A remote monitoring standard for collecting network performance data.

RPC Remote Procedure Call. With RPC, a procedure call on a local system results in a procedure being executed on a remote system.

SAM System Administration Manager. SAM is an administration tool for HP-UX computer systems.

SATAN Security Administrator Tool for Analyzing Networks. SATAN is a public-domain tool for analyzing system security and identifying weaknesses.

SGA Shared Global Area, or System Global Area. The shared database segment containing temporary data caches used by the Oracle7 and Oracle8 server's while the server is running.

SNMP Simple Network Management Protocol. SNMP is a standard for getting and setting management information, and for reporting management events.

SONET Synchronous Optical Network. SONET is a set of standards for the digital transmission of information over fibre optics.

SP Service Provider. An SP is an intermediary between management applications and the information about a managed component.

SPOF (or SPoF) Single Point Of Failure. A single hardware or software component that is unprotected such that its failure will make your application or service unavailable. Configuring redundancy into your environment can avoid these single points of failure.

SQL Structured Query Language. SQL is a language that allows you to specify database queries as relational expressions.

SQL*NET Oracle software that provides remote connectivity for clients to the database server. It is the SQL database module at the session layer in the OSI protocol stack.

station address The unique address of a network interface card. It is also referred to as a MAC address, or physical address. The station addresses on an Ethernet are 48 bits. The first 24 bits are assigned to a hardware vendor, and the vendor is then responsible for keeping the remaining bits unique.

subnet A portion of a network sharing a network address with other portions of the network. The host portion of the address is further subdivided into a subnet number and a host number, with a subnet mask specifying how many bits are used by each.

SVC Switched Virtual Circuit. A channel established on demand that is used for transferring information between two locations. The connection is established by network signalling, and lasts only for the duration of the transfer.

swapping A technique used by the memory management service during periods of heavy memory use on the computer system. The pages in memory of a process that is not executing are swapped out to disk to make room for the code and data needed by the currently executing process.

SyMON A management software product for Sun Solaris systems.

TCP Transmission Control Protocol. A transport protocol providing a reliable, connection-oriented service for transferring network data.

TME Tivoli Management Environment. TME is an enterprise management framework from Tivoli, a subsidiary of IBM Corporation.

TNS Transparent Network Substrate. The lower layer of SQL*NET that establishes, maintains, and tears down connections for Oracle7 servers.

Token Ring A LAN technology providing data transfer rates of 4Mbps and 16Mbps.

Transcend A suite of network performance management and troubleshooting products from 3Com Corporation. The available products include Traffix Manager, Network Control Services, and Enterprise Monitor.

UDP User Datagram Protocol. A transport protocol providing an unreliable, connectionless service for transferring network data. Its network service is provided by the Internet Protocol.

Unicenter A product from Computer Associates, Inc. for network and system management.

V$ table An Oracle term for a virtual database table that allows a user to access memory structures within the shared global area. V$ tables can be used to monitor the performance of processes of an Oracle instance. These tables are also called dynamic performance tables.

X.25 A CCITT standard for packet-switched networks.

X.400 A CCITT standard for electronic mail.

zombie process A process that exited without cleaning up its system resources properly. The process terminated and the parent was not waiting for it.

Index

Hewlett-Packard Computer Education and Training

Hewlett-Packard's world-class education and training offers hands on education solutions including:

- Linux
- HP-UX System and Network Administration
- Y2K HP-UX Transition
- Advanced HP-UX System Administration
- IT Service Management using advanced Internet technologies
- Microsoft Windows NT
- Internet/Intranet
- MPE/iX
- Database Administration
- Software Development

HP's new IT Professional Certification program provides rigorous technical qualification for specific IT job roles including HP-UX System Administration, Network Management, Unix/NT Servers and Applications Management, and IT Service Management. For more information, go to http://education.hp.com/hpcert.htm.

In addition, HP's IT Resource Center is the perfect knowledge source for IT professionals. Through a vibrant and rich Web environment, IT professionals working in the areas of UNIX, Microsoft, networking, or MPE/iX gain access to continually updated knowledge pools.

http://education.hp.com

In the U.S. phone 1-800-HPCLASS (472-5277)